T0329997

Rural Poverty, Risk and Development

To Phedon

Rural Poverty, Risk and Development

Marcel Fafchamps

Department of Economics and Mansfield College, University of Oxford, UK

Edward Elgar

Cheltenham, UK • Northampton, MA, USA

Published by
Edward Elgar Publishing Limited
Glensanda House
Montpellier Parade
Cheltenham
Glos GL50 1UA
UK

Edward Elgar Publishing, Inc.
136 West Street
Suite 202
Northampton
Massachusetts 01060
USA

A catalogue record for this book
is available from the British Library

Library of Congress Cataloguing in Publication Data
Fafchamps, Marcel,
    Rural poverty, risk and development / by Marcel Fafchamps.
        p. cm.
    1. Rural poor–Developing countries. 2. Rural development–Developing
countries. 3. Risk assessment. I. Title.

HC59.72.P6F34 2004
339.4'6'091734–dc22   2003057279

ISBN 1 84376 436 9

Printed and bound in Great Britain by MPG Books Ltd, Bodmin, Cornwall

Contents

List of figures vii
Preface ix

1 Introduction 1

2 Risk and poverty 5
 2.1 Life and risk 5
 2.2 Risk in poor rural economies 8

3 The risk coping strategies of the rural poor 12
 3.1 Reducing exposure to shocks 13
 3.2 Saving and liquidating assets 21
 3.3 Risk sharing 32
 3.4 Allocation of scarce resources within the household 55

4 The limits to risk coping 58
 4.1 The limits to self-protection 58
 4.2 Risk sharing, self-interest, and commitment failure 65
 4.3 Sharing and power 80
 4.4 Risk sharing and credit 90
 4.5 Information asymmetries 96
 4.6 Risk sharing networks 103
 4.7 The breakdown of the solidarity system 106
 4.8 Conclusion 108

5 Risk and inequality 109
 5.1 A stylized economy 111
 5.2 No marketable assets 113
 5.3 Accumulation with no risk sharing 116
 5.4 Accumulation and risk sharing 129
 5.5 Imperfect commitment 133
 5.6 Risk and poverty trap 136
 5.7 Conclusion 143

6 Risk and development 146

	6.1	Nutrition and human capital	146
	6.2	Risk and technological innovation	151
	6.3	Commercial crops vs. subsistence farming	162
	6.4	Precautionary saving and investment constraints	176
	6.5	Risk sharing and risk taking	188
7	Conclusion		196
	7.1	What we have learned	196
	7.2	What we do not know	202
	7.3	What local governments can do	206
	7.4	What the international community can do	210
	Notes		213
	Appendix		221
	Bibliography		227
	Index		257

Figures

4.1   Risk sharing and impatience   76
4.2   Renegotiation-proof equilibria   79
4.3   Coalition-proof equilibria   87
4.4   Coalitions and asymmetry   88

5.1   Inequality over time for three realizations of labour income   118
5.2   Inequality over time with precautionary saving only   122
5.3   Consumption inequality and return on savings   123
5.4   Law of motion of inequality with fixed total asset   126
5.5   Polarization   127

6.1   Effect of the variance of the food price   170
6.2   Effect of the market price elasticity of the cash crop   172
6.3   Effect of the market price elasticity of the food crop   173
6.4   Effect of the correlation between crop revenues   174
6.5   Value of investment option   181

Preface

The purpose of this book is to discuss the relationships between rural poverty, risk and development. The focus is primarily conceptual, although numerous references to econometric evidence are provided throughout the book. The reason is that a proper understanding of risk and its relationship with poverty and growth are difficult to achieve given the complexity of the topic when much insurance is provided by informal channels. A special emphasis is put on informal risk coping institutions.

This book is the outcome of more than ten years of personal research on these issues, both on the theory and empirical side. The book is organized as much as possible as a coherent and articulated coverage of the current literature. Although the material presented here aims to be a fair reflection of current thinking, the treatment of the material and the choice of emphasis largely reflect my personal views.

The primary audience for this book is academic researchers and policy makers interested in development issues, principally those interested in social insurance, banking, and credit. The book can also be used as a teaching tool for advanced undergraduates or graduate students in economic development.

There exist other volumes dedicated to risk and development, most notably the early volume by Roumasset (1976), the edited volume by Roumasset et al. (1979), the well documented book by Dasgupta (1993) devoted to destitution and the 2000 World Bank Development Report devoted to poverty (The World Bank 2000). There are also a number of literature reviews published in academic journals (such as Morduch 1995, Townsend 1995a, Dercon 2002). Risk and poverty have also often been discussed in the context of agrarian institutions (e.g. Bardhan 1984, Hoff et al. 1993). This volume differs from previous efforts in that it provides a comprehensive coverage of a wide range of issues and provides modern conceptual tools that help sharpen our understanding of the underlying processes.

As with any research project of this magnitude, I am indebted to many collaborators for their help and input. Working with them over the years has helped shape and refine my views, something that is largely reflected here. Those I am most indebted to are a group of former Stanford students whom I initially advised and subsequently collaborated with – notably Takashi Kurosaki, Susan Lund, John Pender and Yasuyuki Sawada. I have also enjoyed working with Flore Gubert with whom I began collaborating while she was visiting Oxford University.

Much of the research presented here has been written on my own time. But I must acknowledge receiving financial support from the Food and Agricultural Organization to put together an early draft of this book. I also received some funding from WIDER when writing on inequality and risk. I am very grateful to Kostas Stamoulis and Stefan Dercon for their support.

1. Introduction

This book investigates the relationships between rural poverty, risk, and development. Building upon the author's work in the area, it summarizes the contributions of recent theoretical and empirical work to our understanding of rural poverty and risk in developing countries. Over their lifetime, all men and women are subject to risk. Some external shocks affect their well being in the most direct manner: illness, accident, death. Other shocks affect their ability to support and feed themselves, either temporarily – unemployment, crop failure, loss of property – or permanently – disability, skill obsolescence. The purpose of this book is to summarize what we know and do not know about the sources of risk faced by the rural poor and the coping strategies they have developed to deal with shocks. We also examine how risk and risk coping strategies impact the rural poor's capacity to develop. So doing, a better handle can be gained on how governments and international organizations can assist the rural poor to better deal with risk and overcome their poverty.

The book starts in Chapter Two with a brief overview of the issues surrounding poverty and risk in underdeveloped rural areas. Not only is risk higher in poor rural economies, but poor people are also less able to deal with risk. Apart from localized efforts, they are largely left to their own devices as far as socialized care is concerned. Low assets also make it difficult to absorb shocks. Poverty is thus not only associated with higher ambient risk; it also reduces people's capacity to absorb shocks.

In response, the rural poor have developed a variety of strategies for coping with risk which are discussed in Chapter Three. These multi-faceted strategies include: settling relatively safe areas; breeding plants and species that survive in difficult environments; diversifying sources of income; preserving flexibility and keeping options open; accumulating precautionary savings; forming strong and large households; seeking the protection of the rich and powerful; and sharing risk with a large network of friends and relatives.

These strategies are subject to serious technological, environmental, and economic constraints that limit their effectiveness. These constraints are reviewed in Chapter Four. Commitment failure, in particular, seriously limits society's capacity to share risk. This may explain the formation of long-term solidarity relationships with networks of friends and relatives.

Moral norms and village ideologies can similarly be seen as attempts to mitigate the perverse effects that self-interest and information asymmetries have on mutual insurance.

Chapter Five examines how wealth accumulation and risk sharing affect the evolution of inequality over time. We first assume risk sharing away and examine how inequality evolves over time when agents accumulate an asset. If asset accumulation is unbounded and the asset yields a positive return, inequality converges to a single value over time. If the asset yields a zero or negative return (for example, grain storage), there is no persistent inequality but inequality is nevertheless correlated over time. If wealth yields a positive return but is in finite supply (for example, land), persistent inequality arises if one agent is more thrifty than the other. Multiple equilibria may obtain. Societies might prevent polarization by closing down markets in such assets.

We then introduce risk sharing. With perfect risk sharing, welfare inequality is constant across time. For continued participation in mutual insurance to be voluntary, asset inequality must remain 'close' to welfare inequality. With imperfect commitment, the end result is a hybrid situation half-way between the risk sharing model and the pure accumulation model. If risk aversion is high for poor agents but low for rich ones, patronage arises whereby the rich on average take away from the poor. There is therefore a trade-off between risk sharing and social mobility. We also discuss the possibility of poverty traps and their effect on dynamic inequality. Heavy indebtedness is discussed in this context. We find that access to alternative sources of finance and insurance is key to prevent informal risk sharing from degenerating into exploitative patronage and debt trap.

Chapter Six is devoted to development and growth issues. The relationship between risk, poverty, and economic development is complex but our understanding has progressed dramatically with recent theoretical and empirical advances. Chronic rural poverty, by itself, is unlikely to raise net fertility. It also seldom leads to starvation – except in cases of extreme destitution. Rather, it negatively impacts welfare by raising vulnerability to adverse shocks. The effects of these shocks manifest themselves not only in terms of short-term reduction in consumption but also in terms of reduced ability to deal with subsequent shocks. In this sense, risk is fundamental to the reproduction of poverty over time.

Next, we examine the relationship between rural poverty, risk, and technological innovation. We revisit the traditional risk aversion explanation and discuss many of its shortcomings. We also discuss the relationship between poverty, risk, and experimentation with new technologies and we identify the non-divisibility of technology and its learning process as a major stumbling block on the road to adoption by poor farmers. We argue that the variance of output is, by itself, unimportant, except inasmuch as it raises fears of bankruptcy. The main factors that hinder technology adoption by poor risk averse farmers are likely to be: large cash outlays, loss of diversification after adoption, and large risk during experimentation and learning.

We then turn toward credit constraints and saving and show that poor individuals with a precautionary motive for saving find it very hard to save enough to finance a large lumpy investment. The link between poverty and low investment apparent in these results is reminiscent of 'vicious circle' and 'big push' theories of development propounded decades ago.

In the final part of Chapter Six, we discuss the relationship between risk sharing and risk taking. Communities subject to lots of external shocks might fear the concentration of wealth that would naturally arise, were asset and credit markets allowed to freely develop. In order to ensure long-term social cohesion, these communities might institute egalitarian norms that prohibit certain transactions and require the redistribution of material wealth. We then investigate whether egalitarian norms of redistribution dilute incentives to invest. Social stratification based on patronage is likely to be inimical to large scale industrialization but to favour the accumulation of social capital, an essential ingredient in trade.

Lessons are drawn in Chapter Seven. Although we have learned a lot about risk and rural poverty, there remains a lot to be learned. Little is known, for instance, about geographical patterns of rural settlement and resettlement. Yet many areas where the rural poor currently live are unsustainable. In the long run we need to know what will motivate them to move out of these areas. More research needs to be done on financial saving by the poor and the retailing of safe savings instruments to rural areas. The household formation process plays a key role in how individuals cope with risk; unfortunately, we know precious little about what brings individuals together to form household units and how resources are allocated within these units. The formation and maintenance of social networks also deserves further study, as well as the relationship between risk and power. The effect of poverty on development is also not fully understood, with many ideas being proposed but few scrutinized rigorously.

In conclusion, we make a series of specific suggestions regarding policy action by governments and international organizations. These recommendations focus on settlement patterns, disease prevention, savings instruments, divisible technology, and support to existing informal institutions. International organizations must continue to serve in their role of insurer of last resort in times of crisis, with as little of a political agenda as possible. They should also support efforts where cross-country externalities are large and returns to scale important, such as in the eradication of diseases and pests, the development of vaccines, and agricultural research. They can also assist poor countries gain access to European and US markets for the agricultural products and crafts that the rural poor can produce, such as sugar, vegetable oils, livestock, and feed crops.

2 Risk and poverty

2.1 LIFE AND RISK

Life is subject to all kinds of fluctuations. Some of these fluctuations are predictable: the absence of rain in the dry season, the utter helplessness of the newborn, the declining strength of the old. Others occur in a haphazard fashion that cannot be predicted, at least not precisely. These fluctuations constitute the rhythm of life. They must be dealt with, in one way or another, otherwise life can become highly unpleasant. Taking care of these fluctuations constitutes risk coping strategies. The main concern is with the strategies people use to minimize the impact of these fluctuations on their welfare. Thus, the definition of risk factors encompasses both predictable and unpredictable variations in income and health.

In a recent review of informal insurance mechanisms, Morduch (1999) proposes three conceptual distinctions that are useful to characterize risk factors in general: high and low frequency risks; autocorrelated and non-autocorrelated risks; and covariate and idiosyncratic risks (see also Morduch (1995) and Fafchamps (2003a)).

High and low frequency risk: Risk is, by definition, a process that unfolds over time. Certain risk factors such as minor illnesses occur frequently; others such as locust attacks are fortunately quite rare. As a first approximation, individual risk factors can be thought of as being realizations of a Poisson process in which the number of occurrences $Z_j(t)$ of a particular shock j over a time interval t follow:

$$\Pr[Z_j(t) = z] = \frac{e^{v_j t} v_j^z t^z}{z!} \qquad (2.1)$$

where parameter v_j denotes the mean rate of occurrence of shock j (for example, Mood et al. (1974), p.95). High frequency risk factors are those with high v_j, low frequency risk factors with a low v_j. Other things being equal, high frequency risks are more dangerous than low frequency risks.

Low intensity and high intensity risks: To judge how serious a risk factor j is, however, one must also know its intensity s_j: obviously, high frequency risk factors that only have a minor incidence on someone's welfare – such as an insect bite – are less serious than low frequency risks that have dramatic consequences – such as cancer. If we aggregate risks factors of different frequencies and intensities together, we can represent the risk faced by individual i at time t by a single risk vector $\pi_{it} = -\Sigma_j z_{jit} s_{jit}$, with an associated probability distribution derived from those of the z_j's and s_j's. By convention, we shall think of low values of π_{it} as representing unfavourable events – bad health, low income – and high values as representing good events.

Autocorrelated and non-stationary risk: The Poisson process discussed above assumes that shock realizations are independently distributed over time. This need not be the case. Like the seven plagues of Egypt, bad times can follow bad times. In this case, the distribution of shocks π_{it} is autocorrelated over time. Shocks at one point in time may also affect an individual's capacity to withstand another, similar shock in the future. Malnutrition, for instance, reduces the body's resistance to common diseases. Exposure to one type of risk – such as crop failure – may lead to malnutrition which, in turn, raises vulnerability to other risk factors. In these examples, risk itself need not be serially correlated but one shock today has permanent or long-lasting effects on welfare through its effect on vulnerability. Risk may also be non-stationary. Certain shocks indeed have a permanent effect on people's health or capacity to generate income. Perhaps the most dramatic example of non-stationarity is simply death: this shock is quite permanent. Catching an incurable disease, becoming permanently disabled, or losing productive assets are other examples of sources of non-stationarity.

Collective and idiosyncratic risk: Shocks not only vary over time; they also vary across individuals. The literature on risk customarily distinguishes between covariate or collective risk factors that affect a group, such as droughts, epidemics, and warfare, and idiosyncratic risk factors that affect isolated individuals, such as illness, unemployment, or accident. This definition, however, is not sufficiently precise to be workable. For instance, what percentage of farmers must be affected by crop failure or disease before one calls it a drought or an epidemic? To obtain a more precise definition, let the risk faced by the collection of individuals $i \in N$ be defined as:

$$\Pi_t \equiv \frac{1}{N} \sum_{i \in N} \pi_{it} \qquad (2.2)$$

Idiosyncratic risk θ_{it} then is:

$$\theta_{it} \equiv \pi_{it} - \Pi_t \qquad (2.3)$$

The central limit theorem implies that, if individual risks π_{it} are independent among individuals and if the group is large, then collective risk Π_t is approximately 0 for all *t*. The extent of collective risk therefore depends on the size of the group and the extent to which risks π_{it} are correlated across individuals: the smaller the group and the higher the correlation between the π_{it}'s, the higher collective risk is.

While these three distinctions are useful in characterizing the nature of risk, they say little about the object of risk, i.e., what is at risk. In this respect, it is useful to distinguish between utility risk, income risk, and what I call ritual risk. The distinction between utility and income risk is well known and has important implications regarding strategies to reduce exposure to risk. Ritual risk, in contrast, is a little studied type of risk that is conceptually distinct from the other two.

Utility and income risk: So far, we have treated risk as if it were an undifferentiated quantity. There is, however, a drastic difference between those risk factors that affect individual welfare or utility directly, and those that affect income and wealth only. We shall call the former utility risk and the latter income risk. In practice, however, the boundary between the two might be blurred. Disease and disability, for instance, affect welfare directly and in this sense are a form of utility risk. But they may also have an effect on income if they strike workers. In contrast, unemployment and crop failure affect income directly and in this sense are a form of income risk. But they may also have an indirect effect on self-esteem and quality of life, which would be a form of utility risk. The classification of particular sources of risk as utility or income risk is thus a matter of degree. The distinction is nevertheless useful because analyses of risk coping strategies often ignore utility risk and focus exclusively on income risk, such as when they evaluate the economic impact of diseases in terms of income loss, not in terms of pain and suffering.

If not adequately dealt with, income risk creates unwanted fluctuations in consumption. In this context, agents' ability to deal with risk can be measured by their capacity to smooth consumption expenditures over time and across states of nature. In contrast, utility risk induces voluntary fluctuations in consumption because, in their effort to mitigate the effect of utility risk on their welfare, individuals typically incur additional consumption expenditures, such as purchasing drugs and medical services. This distinction is important and has not received enough attention in the literature.[1] We shall get back to it later in this book.

Ritual risk: There is yet another type of risk that does not fit easily in either the utility or the income risk category. In many societies, social customs dictate that customary expenditures be incurred to mark particular events. Some of these events are fairly predictable; others are not. These customary expenditures serve many purposes, one of which is to create a rhythm in the life of a group and demonstrate its cohesiveness. For

instance, the party that parents feel obliged to organize to celebrate the
birth of a new son or the death of a close parent fall into this category.
Other ritual expenditures include the consumption of sheep at Tabaski,[2]
ritual payments to the paramount chief, family reunions at seasonal holi-
days, and the like. The risk that is induced by ritual obligations is different
from other sources of risk in that it results from social pressure more than
physical need. It is people's desire to live up to social expectations and to
ascertain their continued membership to a group that induces them to abide
by its social norms. To capture these differences, this category is called ritual
risk.[3] Given the lack of economic work in this area (see, however,
Fafchamps and Lund (2003)), ritual risk will not receive further attention
here. Evidence nevertheless suggests that efforts to meet excessive social
obligations – wedding ceremony, dowry payment – are an important engine
of poverty as households enter into debt to meet them. This issue deserves
further inquiry.

2.2   RISK IN POOR RURAL ECONOMIES

The general categories of risk discussed so far apply to all societies. The
precise sources of risk to which rural inhabitants of poor countries are
exposed are quite different from those observed elsewhere, however (see for
instance Binswanger and Rosenzweig (1986), Binswanger and McIntire
(1987), and Bromley and Chavas (1989) for a discussion). Certain types of
risk affect developed economics but are essentially non-existent in poor
rural economies, such as trade cycle fluctuations, stock market plunges,
technological obsolescence, and product cycles. But in general, risk is more
prevalent in rural areas of the Third World than in developed economies.
Kamanou and Morduch (2002) for instance develop a methodology to
measure the vulnerability of households to poverty and apply it to Cote
d'Ivoire. Ligon (2002) proposes an original methodology for identifying
particularly vulnerable households and applies the idea to Indian data. He
then discusses practical implications regarding targeting.

First of all, poor rural economies are characterized by a much higher
incidence of diseases and environmental hazards (Sauerborn et al. 1995).
Infectious diseases such as measles, tetanus, and tuberculosis, to name but
a few, are much more prevalent than in the developed world. Parasitic infections carried by water or insects are commonplace and they take a tremen-
dous toll on people and animals alike. Malaria alone – an endemic disease
in many parts of the Third World – kills millions of people every year. Pests
and weeds abound that affect trees and crops. The combined damages
caused to crops in the field and in storage by insects, birds, monkeys, rats,

and other wildlife are enormous. People also suffer from proximity to wild animals. It is, for instance, not uncommon for children living in the Third World today to be gobbled up by crocodiles or trampled by elephants. In fact, the range of health hazards one is exposed to by living in rural poor areas is so daunting that people fortunate enough to live elsewhere often simply refuse to go there at all. It is therefore not surprising that every year millions of Third World inhabitants leave the countryside for the relative safety of the city.

Business risk is a second important risk factor. This follows from the fact that the large majority of households living in poor rural economies have at least one – and possibly several – businesses: a farm, an artisanal workshop, a trading activity, or a service operation. This stands in sharp contrast with the employment structure of developed economies where most people work for a wage and are thereby relatively immune to business risk, except through unemployment. The rudimentary technology of production activities, especially farming, offers little protection against natural events. Lybbert et al. (2000), for instance, describe the risk faced by pastoralists – specialized livestock producers – and show that livestock mortality is high but primarily idiosyncratic. In addition, most of the businesses found in poor rural areas are small, undercapitalized, and underequipped, and thus very vulnerable to shocks (Daniels 1994). Rural wage employment, when it exists, is typically casual, not permanent.[4] Unemployment risk is thus quite high as well. The frequency with which rural dwellers move in and out of a job or business is thus very high, and so is the potential for income instability.

The extent of business risk is magnified by the high dependence of poor economies on the export of a few primary products (see for example World Bank 1989, Deaton and Miller 1996, Collier 2002). Fluctuations in the price or output of these primary products represent massive macroeconomic shocks that ripple through the entire economy and affect rural dwellers in various ways, such as through the prices of agricultural outputs and inputs, the value of rural assets, access to off-farm job opportunities, and remittances from migrants (Fafchamps and Gavian 1997). Large collective shocks such as droughts and warfare also have deleterious effects on the demand for farm and non-farm products, and thus on business and wage incomes. Sen (1981), for instance, in his account of the Ethiopian famine of 1973 points out that the categories of households worst hit by the famine were not farmers but artisans and domestic workers: the collapse in the demand for their goods and services resulted in an entitlement failure.

The vulnerability of rural businesses to idiosyncratic and sectoral technology shocks also leads to poor levels of contractual compliance. Business risk thus tends to ripple through the rural economy. Moreover, shocks are so frequent that it is easy for opportunists to falsely claim being unable to comply with their contractual obligations due to circumstances beyond their control. True business risk is thus compounded by opportunistic risk. The anthropology and rural sociology literatures abound with horror stories about unfulfilled orders, labour absenteeism, broken contracts, and low quality of service (Poewe 1989). In some instances, the fear of breach of contract is so severe that markets are totally non-existent. For example, the absence of an active rental market for bullocks and oxen in India or Ethiopia has been blamed on owners' fear that renters will mistreat the animals. The literature on sharecropping and agrarian structure in developing countries similarly emphasizes moral hazard and the high cost of supervising workers (for example Eswaran and Kotwal 1985, Feder 1985). Although contractual risk has been little studied empirically,[5] there is sufficient circumstantial evidence to suspect that it constitutes a non-negligible addition to the risk faced by rural dwellers.

Risk factors inherent to the presence of environmental and health hazards, the importance of self-employment and casual labour contracts, and the fragility of the macro-economy are further compounded by the relative isolation of many poor rural communities. Imperfect spatial integration of markets for agricultural outputs, labour, assets, and the like implies that the geographical pooling of market risk is not fully achieved (for example Ravallion 1986, Baulch 1997b, Fafchamps and Gavian 1996). At first glance, it might seem that market integration, even if imperfect, is preferable to complete isolation (Fafchamps 1992b). This need not be the case, however, as suggested by two papers devoted to Sahelian livestock markets by Fafchamps and Gavian (1996) and Fafchamps and Gavian (1997). The authors show that livestock markets in Niger are sufficiently integrated to make prices respond to large aggregate shocks, but not enough to smooth out local price variations. This outcome can be understood as a consequence of transactions costs: erratic fluctuations in local livestock supply and demand do not necessarily trigger arbitrage because of transport costs; but large aggregate demand or supply shocks affect prices whenever animals are traded over space. Although limited market integration has enabled Nigerien livestock producers to partake in the fruits of commodity booms in Niger and Nigeria, in terms of risk the result appears worse than complete isolation or perfect market integration. A similar situation is likely to prevail for labour and rural commodities.

In addition to having poor transport infrastructure, poor economies also have fragile or non-existent social programmes. Although governments vary in their willingness to provide a minimum level of social services to their population (World Bank 1989), low provision is largely a consequence of the fact that poor economies cannot afford such programmes. With the exception of a handful of well documented exceptions (such as Kerala, Cuba until the late 1980s), the delivery of health services, for instance, is problematic in most rural areas of the Third World. Hospitals and clinics are seldom available and, when they are, drugs and staff are often lacking (World Bank 1989). Insufficient health services naturally thwart efforts of individuals to mitigate the effect of utility risk on their welfare (for example Gertler et al. 1987, Gertler and Strum 1997, Gertler and Gruber 2002, Leonard 1998). Socialized care for orphan children, the old, the disabled, or the mentally handicapped is similarly absent or insufficient. Whether public or private, retirement insurance is usually limited to formal employment in cities and the public sector. Finally, the funding of social programmes, when they exist, is dependent on macro-economic conditions: come a commodity price or structural adjustment crunch, funding disappears and existing programmes become empty shells. Apart from localized efforts by churches, NGOs, and occasional government programmes, poor rural areas are largely left to their own devices as far as socialized care is concerned. Sauerborn et al. (1996b) and Sauerborn et al. (1995) for instance document the out-of-pocket costs of illness for rural Burkinabe households and show them to be quite high.

Not only is risk higher in poor rural economies, but poor people are also less able to deal with risk. For instance, it is highly likely that malnutrition increases the body's susceptibility to debilitating diseases. Hence it contributes to both the incidence, the morbidity, and the mortality from common diseases such as diarrhoea and bronchitis. People with low incomes and wealth find it harder to buy food and shelter or to pay for health and veterinary care, when it is available. Low financial assets also make it difficult to absorb business and employment shocks at both the individual and the collective level. Poverty thus not only raises ambient risk; it also reduces people's capacity to absorb shocks.

These circumstances lead us to suspect that poor rural societies have developed various ways of mitigating the effect of risk on their livelihoods. Anyone interested in assisting the poor better deal with risk must first understand what these strategies are, how they work, and when they fail. This is the purpose of the next chapter.

3. The risk coping strategies of the rural poor

This chapter presents a conceptual summary of risk coping strategies, together with a review of the existing evidence regarding the respective roles they play in various circumstances. Before delving into the various strategies themselves, it is worthwhile discussing some of the terms and phrases that have been used in the literature and compare them with those used in this volume. Words are not important by themselves. What matters is that one be understood. To avoid confusion, a short glossary of terms used in the literature is provided below, together with my personal semantic preferences.

First of all, many authors draw the distinction between *ex ante* and *ex post* strategies. The former are strategies that take place before a shock has occurred, while the latter take place after a shock has occurred. This chronological distinction is useful and we will use it throughout this volume with this specific meaning. But the distinction can be misleading. Many so-called ex post strategies, to be effective, require ex ante planning. For instance, sending firemen to extinguish a fire is an ex post strategy since it takes place after a fire has started. But it only works because a fire service is set up in the first place. A more useful distinction is between strategies that seek to reduce risk itself and strategies that seek to insulate welfare from risk – one could say, preventive and curative measures.

Some authors use the terms 'risk coping' and 'risk reduction' strategies as synonymous of ex post and ex ante strategies, respectively, while the term 'risk management' is used as all-encompassing term. I do not like the term 'risk management' when referring to the rural poor because so much risk is unmanageable that people cannot, in fact 'manage'. For this reason I find that, somehow, the term belittles the experience of the poor. The rationale for equating risk coping with ex post strategies is that people cope with shocks after they have occurred. By this logic, the term 'risk coping' should be confined to strategies used only after shocks have occurred. In my view, this distinction confuses the concept of shock and that of risk. A shock coping strategy would, by definition, be ex post. But risk is the prospect of a shock. A strategy to cope with the prospect of a shock can be planned in advance. In this volume, we shall use the phrase risk coping strategies to encompass all the possible strategies by which individuals reduce the negative influence that risk has on their welfare.

The term 'smoothing' is also often used as synonymous of risk reduction (Townsend 1995a). Although intuitive, I do not find this term fully adequate for our purpose because smoothing is not just about risk but also refers to variations due to factors such as seasonality, life-cycle, religious calendar, and the like. In this volume, our focus is on risk only. When we use the word smoothing, it will be with risk in mind.

Morduch (1995) takes the term further and draws a distinction beween income and consumption smoothing, and uses the terms essentially as synonymous of ex ante and ex post reduction in risk, respectively. As we shall see, there are many ex ante strategies that do not focus on income, such as strategies to reduce health risk. Moreover, whenever prices are uncertain, reducing variation in income need not reduce risk, as we will discuss in detail. Income smoothing is thus unnecessarily restrictive for our purpose. Consumption smoothing also fails to capture the full range of ex post strategies. There are many circumstances in which reducing variation in individual welfare requires consumption to increase in response to a shock, as when expenditures on health care, home care, food preparation, and child care have to be incurred because a mother is sick. There are also situations in which households choose to reduce consumption today or delay the purchase of a durable in order to protect consumption tomorrow. There is more to ex post strategies than consumption smoothing alone.

With these semantic distinctions in mind, we are now ready to discuss risk coping strategies themselves. We divide these strategies into three categories: those that operate before shocks occur by reducing the magnitude of the shocks themselves and hence exposure to risk; those that rely on the accumulation of assets as buffer stock; and those that explicitly share risk with others. We also examine ways in which households allocate scarce resources among their members and how this allocation affects the intra-household distribution of welfare.

3.1   REDUCING EXPOSURE TO SHOCKS

One way to deal with risk is simply to reduce risk itself. What Morduch (1995) calls 'income smoothing' belongs to this category. Reducing risk can be achieved in a variety of ways, all of which imply altering production choices.

3.1.1 Selecting and Modifying the Environment

One way poor societies can reduce risk is by locating themselves in areas where parasite infestation is low. Patterns of settlement in Sub-Saharan Africa and Latin America, for instance, reflect these concerns. It is probably not an accident that the East African highlands are more densely populated than other parts of Africa: malaria risk is lower at high altitudes. This is so much true that Ethiopian populations severely affected by the 1984 famine vigorously resisted their relocation from the drought prone Northern highlands to wet Southern lowlands. Personal accounts from students and NGOs who assisted the Ethiopian resettlement effort indicate that many resettled people fled – at the risk of their life – to escape exposure to malaria and other diseases. Morbidity and mortality among those who stayed were high.[6]

By contrast with highland areas, population density in the dense tropical forest is typically very low; they are also the areas where parasitic diseases are most prevalent. Whenever people move into a tropical forest area, it is customary for them to remove much of the forest cover, at least in the immediate surroundings of their settlement, and often in the entire settled area. One of the reasons for doing so is undoubtedly to reduce exposure to disease carrying insects and to depredation from wildlife. Concerns with disease may also help explain why irrigated schemes fail to raise much popular support in Sub-Saharan Africa.[7]

Patterns of settlement also reflect the incidence of particular human and livestock illnesses. Trypanosomiasis, a livestock disease carried by the tse-tse fly, makes it difficult if not impossible to keep domestic animals in much of the humid and semi-humid lowlands of Africa. This undoubtedly contributed to the higher concentration of African livestock in semi-arid areas where livestock could only be raised – at least until the end of the 19th century. Increased population density in the former forest zone of Nigeria has led to a reduction in forest cover and to a simultaneous decrease of tse-tse infestation, hence shifting the livestock raising boundary hundreds of kilometres southward. Onchocercosis – also called river blindness – is another case in point. Repeated exposure to the disease, carried by a small fly living along river beds, leads to blindness. Eradication of the fly from most of West Africa has generated dramatic movements of population to settle previously unoccupied river valleys. As a by-product, these movements have resulted in the loss of much of the remaining wildlife habitat in West Africa.

The threat imposed by proximity to wildlife can also be tackled directly. Hunting is undertaken not only to collect bush meat but also to get rid of pests. Poaching – and the protection granted to poachers by villagers – can be understood in the same light. Certain traditional practices, such as burning field vegetation and pastures, can similarly be understood as ways of controlling rodents and snakes. Even when they do not actively campaign to get rid of wildlife, people protect themselves, their crops, and their animals from it. Most East African pastoralists, for instance, carry guns as protection against lions and other predators. Farmers often keep their livestock inside the house at night for fear of hyenas, and they camp on their fields to chase away birds and monkeys.

Having illustrated various methods by which poor societies seek to select and modify their environment, it should be emphasized that the end result is still characterized by high risk. In spite of their best efforts, the rural poor face a high degree of risk from their environment, such as climatic variability, pests, and diseases. This is because the capacity of poor, non-technological societies to effectively choose and affect their environment is quite limited. Other risk coping strategies must therefore be found. To these we now turn.

3.1.2 Specialization

Another way to reduce exposure to risk is for individuals to adopt production techniques that are resistant to pests, droughts, and other environmental risk factors. Growing pearl millet, an extremely sturdy cereal grown in West Africa, is perhaps the best example of such a strategy. Millet is so perfectly adapted to the peculiar conditions of the Sahel – extreme evapotranspiration, poor sandy soils, short rainy season, erratic torrential rains – that it has enabled human settlement in areas previously reserved to livestock raising.[8] In those areas, millet is the only cultivated plant apart from small garden crops. In areas too dry to support millet, itinerant livestock herding becomes the only production activity. In these two examples, specialization in a single, robust production technique is the main income smoothing technique.

3.1.3 Diversification

In other situations, risk coping is achieved via portfolio diversification instead of specialization. Rural inhabitants often seek to minimize their exposure to risk by diversifying their portfolio of income generating activities. Drawing from multiple data sources, Barrett et al. (2001) provide some descriptive evidence of the extent of diversification among African households. Using data from Pakistan, Kurosaki (2001b) shows that less diversified households are more vulnerable to risk.

Diversification takes many different forms. In areas with less extreme climatic conditions, for instance, farmers often plant different crops, or several varieties of the same crop to obtain a more stable output. Intercropping, that is, planting several crops in the same field is often partially justified by risk considerations as well. Similarly, livestock producers typically combine different species of animals into a single herd to take advantage of differences in their resistance to diseases and drought. Herders also split their livestock holdings into spatially distinct herds to hedge against spatial differences in rainfall.

Diversification is also achieved by combining farm and non-farm activities within a single household. Reardon (1997), for instance, notes that 45% of Sub-Saharan incomes come from non-farm work. Percentages are even higher in Asia (for example Fafchamps and Lund 2003, Fafchamps and Quisumbing 1999). Combining crop and livestock production can also reduce risk whenever crop output serves as input to livestock production. Kurosaki (1997) gives the example of the Pakistan Punjab where fodder self-sufficiency insulates milk producers from fluctuations in green fodder price, and computes the reduction in income variability that results from combining fodder with milk production. Migration to nearby cities, mines, and plantations can also be seen as part of a diversification strategy (Giles 1999). Not all diversification follows a risk motive, however. Using data from Ethiopia and Tanzania, Dercon and Krishnan (1996) examine the portfolios of income earning activities of rural households in these two countries. They conclude that diversification cannot be explained by household behaviour towards risk as is usually suggested. It is better explained by differences in ability, location, and in access to credit.

The conditions under which specialization or diversification are the appropriate response to risk can easily be illustrated using the concept of stochastic dominance. Consider a set of risky production activities j with net return q_j and risk factor π_j. Production of j is an increasing function of the total amount of inputs – such as land, labour, capital, intermediate inputs – allocated to it. Risk affects returns multiplicatively with $E[\pi_j] = 1$. Assume that inputs are chosen prior to observing π_j at prices w.[9] The cost function corresponding to a particular level of expected output for household i can be written l_i where the dependence on w is ignored for notational simplicity. Net returns can thus be written:

$$q_j = l_j \pi_j \qquad (3.1)$$

Let $F_j(\pi)$ denote the cumulative distribution function of activity j. Activity k is said to stochastically dominate activity j if:

$$F_k(\pi) \leq F_j(\pi) \ \forall \pi \qquad (3.2)$$

with strict inequality for some π's. This definition means that the probability that the unit return is at least π is larger with activity k than with activity j for any π; in other words, j yields uniformly lower returns than k. If this is the case, any agent should choose k over j. This, however, ignores the fact that portfolios of activities may be found that stochastically dominate activity k undertaken in isolation.[10] Let l_{ij} be the part of total cost l_i devoted to activity j by household i. We have $\sum_j l_{ij} = l_i$. The unit return to a portfolio is the weighted sum of individual unit returns, that is:

$$\pi^p = \frac{\sum_j l_{ij}\pi_j}{\sum_j l_{ij}}$$

with corresponding cumulative distribution function $F^p(\pi)$. If activity k stochastically dominate all possible portfolios, i.e., if $F^p(\pi) \geq F_k(\pi)$ for all π and all $F^p(.)$, then full specialization is optimal for all agents. If one portfolio exists that stochastically dominates k, then diversification is optimal for all agents.

The same reasoning can be extended to situations in which no activity stochastically dominates all the others provided that we assume that agents are expected utility maximizers. Let the utility that agent i derives from consuming c be denoted $U_i(c)$ and focus on the optimal allocation of a fixed total production expenditure l_i. Individual i will optimally choose activity k over activity j if:

$$EU_i(l_i\pi_k) > EU_i(l_i\pi_j) \tag{3.3}$$

By analogy with the previous example, if there exists a portfolio of activities such that:

$$EU_i(l_i\pi_k) < EU_i\left(\frac{\Sigma l_{ij}\pi_j}{l_i}\right) \tag{3.4}$$

then diversification is preferred to complete specialization by individual i. If no such portfolio exists, then complete specialization is optimal for individual i. From the above we see that if no activity or portfolio stochastically dominates all the others, then specialization and diversification will vary among agents, depending on their resources l_i and on the shape of their utility function $U_i(.)$, that is, on their degree of risk aversion. The complete specialization of an entire region in the production of a single activity or portfolio – such as growing millet – is thus an indication that this activity or portfolio stochastically dominates all others.

One should not assume that risk averse people always act in a cautious manner. Whenever their survival is at stake, they may opt for very risky strategies as the ones that maximize their chance of survival. Perhaps the most striking example of such a strategy is that of Sahelian villagers who responded to the 1984 drought by switching to gold digging – hardly a riskless activity, but certainly better than doing nothing.[11] A more commonly observed situation is the mass exodus of adult males in search of jobs and of women and children in search of food that accompanies famines and warfare (Sen 1981): throwing oneself at the mercy of rogue soldiers, bandits, pirates, and other calamities is hardly a safe choice, but it may be the only one left.[12]

Desperate strategies can easily be integrated into the expected utility framework by assuming that utility falls to a minimum constant level $-K$ whenever consumption is below a given level $\underline{c}$:

$$U(c) = -K \; \forall c \leq \underline{c} \tag{3.5}$$

$\underline{c}$ can be interpreted as the starvation level of consumption. It is easy to see that someone offered two strategies with equal expected consumption $\widehat{c} < \underline{c}$ but different variance will opt for the high variance alternative: so doing takes advantage of the longer tail of the high variance distribution and thus maximizes the probability of survival. A formally similar phenomenon affects firms on the verge of bankruptcy.[13] Whether people 'choose' desperate measures or are forced into them by circumstances is, to a large extent, a semantic issue. The important fact to recognize is that, when pushed into a corner, the rural poor will often take actions that increase their chance of surviving while on average making their situation worse. Running away from home when a famine strikes is a good, though dire, example (Sen 1981).

3.1.4 Self-sufficiency

Another important dimension of risk is food security. Like anyone, rural households worry about being able to feed themselves. When markets are absent or not reliable, it becomes optimal for them to grow their own food (Singh et al. 1986). Self-sufficiency then becomes the natural route toward food security. It has been shown elsewhere (Fafchamps 1992a) that even when food markets exist, imperfect market integration may nevertheless generate enough food price volatility so as to incite households to produce their own food. This can be shown with the following example. Consider an agent who can produce either food q_f or cash q_c but consumes only food. Suppose for simplicity that output is non-stochastic but the price of food p_f is. Production of food is preferable to production of cash whenever:

$$EU_i(q_f) > EU_i\left(\frac{q_c}{p_f}\right) \tag{3.6}$$

Provided that q_c is not too much higher than q_f, risk averse agents will opt for food production as a mean of increasing food security. There is plenty of descriptive evidence that poor households produce much of their food but rigorous tests are rare. Kurosaki and Fafchamps (2002) estimate a structural model of joint production and consumption choices using data from five Pakistani villages. They uniformly reject the hypothesis that consumption preferences do not affect production choices, thus providing rigorous empirical support for the food security model.

The self-sufficiency motive need not be limited to food. Kurosaki and Fafchamps (2002), for instance, show that, in addition to food security considerations, concerns about fodder price volatility incited Punjabi farmers in Pakistan to grow their own fodder. In the absence of perfect labour markets, concerns for self-sufficiency in labour during peak periods of the year (for example Delgado 1979, Fafchamps 1993) may similarly induce households to hoard manpower in the form of numerous children, visitors, and dependent adults.

One should not, however, regard food self-sufficiency as the unique or even most important strategy through which poor rural households ensure their food security. There are many rural households for whom food self-sufficiency is an unattainable objective, either because they live in areas that are inherently unsuitable for agriculture, or because they do not have sufficient productive assets to produce food themselves. Barrett (1997), for instance, shows that most rural inhabitants of Madagascar are, in fact, deficit producers. A similar observation is made in Matlon (1977) for Northern Nigeria. For these people, food security is sought through alternative strategies, many of which are discussed here.

3.1.5   Flexibility

Another way of reducing exposure to risk is to remain flexible and deal with shocks as they unfold. To show this formally, let the return to activity j be a function of two successive exogenous shocks π_{1j} and π_{2j} and one action a with opportunity cost w. If action a must be decided before observing either of the shocks, the decision problem can be written:

$$\max_a \int_{-\infty}^{\infty} U[l_j(a)\pi_{1j}\pi_{2j}]dF(\pi_{1j}, \pi_{2j}) - aw \qquad (3.7)$$

The solution to the above, denoted a^a, is not a function of π_{1j} or π_{2j}. If, in contrast, a is decided after observing π_{1j}, the decision problem is:

$$\max_a \int_{-\infty}^{\infty} U[l_j(a)\pi_{1j}\pi_{2j}]dF(\pi_{2j}|\pi_{1j}) - aw \qquad (3.8)$$

and the optimal a, denoted a^p, is a function of π_{1j}. By comparing the two optimization problems, we see that, by application of the Le Chatelier principle, the expected utility of the decision maker is higher with a^p than with a^a.[14] optimization problem (3.7) is but a constrained version of optimization problem (3.8) where all values of α are required to be the same, no matter what value π_{1j} takes. Flexibility thus has an option value. An immediate corollary is that individuals are likely to resist changes that reduce their choices, and to spend resources expanding the alternatives open to them.

Replanting is a good example of the role of flexibility in coping with risk. In semi-arid tropics, rainfall at the onset of the rainy season is particularly erratic. It is not uncommon for rains to begin only to stop abruptly and restart several weeks later. In such circumstances, seeds planted after the early rains fail to grow. Farmers have to replant. To do so, they must have varieties that can be planted over an extended period of time and are not highly sensitive to the length of day.[15] Another example of how concerns for flexibility affect production choices can also be found in semi-arid areas with purely rainfed agriculture. There, weeding is the most time consuming agricultural task and crop performance is largely a function of the care and timeliness with which weeding was conducted.[16] Weeding, however, is performed half-way through the rainy season, after farmers have gained valuable information about annual rainfall. Elsewhere (Fafchamps 1993) constructed a model has been constructed of the weeding decision of Burkinabe farmers and the model parameters were estimated using structural estimation. It is shown that it is optimal for farmers to plant more than they can perfectly weed because, if rains are bad, they can compensate for low expected output by weeding more carefully. Since less rain also means fewer weeds, farmers can smooth part of the fluctuation in output by adjusting their weeding effort. A consequence of this strategy is that, in a wet year, fields are not weeded properly, a feature that has long puzzled agronomists working in Africa.

Concerns for flexibility similarly explain why rural artisans are reluctant to use sophisticated equipment (it cannot be fixed easily); why many rural households keep their cash savings at home instead of in the bank (it is instantly available if needed); why they resist technological innovations that demand a strict respect of planting and harvesting dates (it reduces their capacity to adjust to external events with limited manpower); and so on. The desire for flexibility also adds another motive for diversification: if one activity does not perform well, more emphasis can be put on another one. For instance, farmers who are also migrant labourers may have the necessary contacts to rapidly find a wage job and feed their family in spite of crop failure. Similarly, if a high yielding but more demanding crop fails due to lack of rain, more attention can be diverted to a drought resistant one. Anticipating this, farmers may find it optimal to plant both. Dekker and Hoogeveen (2002) present another example of how flexibility can be used to reduce risk. They show that, among Zimbabwean households, the obligation to pay bride wealth serves as informal insurance because bride wealth liabilities are contingent claims: payment of bride wealth is made contingent upon shocks affecting the groom's family.

3.2   SAVING AND LIQUIDATING ASSETS

So far we have discussed ways by which individuals can deal with risk by reducing risk itself. Clearly, these strategies cannot eliminate risk altogether: populations may settle in less dangerous areas, they are still subject to disease; they may diversify risk or opt for activities with a stable income stream, they cannot eliminate all risk; they may remain as flexible as possible, they cannot compensate for all the shocks – or doing so would be prohibitively expensive. Some risk, therefore, remains that must be dealt with *ex post*, that is, after shocks have been realized.

3.2.1   Seeking Wage Income

One obvious way to cope with a shortfall in income from agriculture or other self-employment activities is to search for wage employment. Sen (1981), for instance, describes how male heads of households hit by the Ethiopian 1973 drought abandoned their village and family in search of wage employment. While such a strategy might have worked to deal with an idiosyncratic shock, it proved largely ineffective given the large number of rural males searching for a job at the same time. When wives and children left in the village did not receive any wage income, they themselves left the village, this time in search of food relief. According to Sen, this unfortunate sequence of events resulted in a famine of dramatic proportions. It also led many remaining families to become separated as some, too weak to walk, waited for others to seek and bring back help. Similar findings are reported in Greenough (1982).

Kochar (1999) examines the labour supply response of Indian households to idiosyncratic agricultural shocks. She finds that labour markets play an important role in mitigating the effect of unanticipated weather shocks. Imai (2000d) revisits the issue and distinguishes between market work and public employment schemes. He finds that the latter assist poor households deal with negative shocks (see also Imai (2000c)). Giles (1999) examines how Chinese households deal with risk and finds that the opening of a large and active labour market as a result of rapid growth has enabled households to better deal with risk.

3.2.2   Liquidating Productive Assets

For an individual hit by an insurmountable shock, one obvious way to handle the situation is to liquidate productive assets in order to buy food, pay the rent, or take a child to the doctor. Asset liquidation, however, is likely to have a negative impact on future earnings. Households forced to sell their land, for instance, are likely to experience a permanent fall in income. Distress sales of productive assets are but a way to buy time in the hope that things will improve: with luck, future shocks will be better and the household will be able to purchase its assets back. This is, however, largely wishful thinking: on average, there is no reason for things to improve. Households who sell productive assets are more likely to face difficulties meeting their consumption needs in the future, and thus more likely to sell assets again.

The deleterious effects of land distress sales on long term income distribution have been studied by Zimmerman (1993) and Carter and Zimmerman (2000). Using simulation analysis, the authors show that, independently from the initial distribution of land, the process of distress sales naturally leads to an unequal distribution of land and income. The driving force behind their result is that individuals desperate enough to sell their land receive a lower price for it than what they must pay to buy it back. One common way of thinking about this problem is to assume that productive assets attract a lower price because they are less liquid. Zimmerman (1993)'s contribution is to show that, even if productive assets were perfectly liquid, general equilibrium effects induce a negative correlation between asset prices and shocks. This correlation explains why the price of distressed assets is, in general, lower than average.

Many societies recognize this problem and discourage land sales, either directly by declaring all land transactions illegal, or indirectly by defining agricultural land as publicly or communally owned (for example Atwood 1990, Platteau 1995c, Platteau 2000a). To the extent that it is individually rational for the poor to sell land in very bad times – and for the rich to buy it – land sales take place anyway (Pinckney and Kimuyu 1994). The unequalizing process of distress sales and land accumulation by a few often frustrates well-meant efforts to redistribute land more equally. It has indeed been noted that, after a land reform, land inequality often goes back to its pre-reform level within a decade or two, thus frustrating the efforts of government to permanently reduce rural inequality (for example Bardhan 1984, Melmed-Sanjak and Carter 1991). For this reason, many land reform programmes stipulate that redistributed land is inalienable (de Janvry 1981), a provision that, for reasons mentioned above, is hard to enforce. In practice, land redistribution is sustainable only if the income level of poor farmers can be stabilized to remain permanently above the level at which distress land sales become optimal. Ironically, this may require imposing a minimum farm size, thereby de facto excluding a large proportion of the population from land ownership. Stability in land distribution is then achieved by keeping part of the population landless – an outcome that defeats the initial redistributive purpose of the reform.

Land is not the only productive asset that desperate households may wish to liquidate. Other potential candidates for liquidation include livestock, oxen, bullocks, farm tools, artisanal equipment, vehicles, and farm buildings (Rosenzweig and Wolpin 1993). Desperate enough households may also consider liquidating their own manpower or that of their dependants. Although such practices may be relatively infrequent, they have attracted renewed attention with the public attention recently devoted to child labour. The most outrageous cases of child and immigrant labour documented in the press indeed revolve around labour bonding and debt peonage. A good example is the recent case of young Chinese immigrants brought to Guam to work in sweat shops. Other forms of labour bonding and debt peonage persist the world over, even if in less obvious forms. For these reasons, and because labour bonding epitomizes the distress sale of productive assets, we devote some more discussion to it.

3.2.3   Labour Bonding and Debt Peonage

Historically, voluntary enslavement or labour bonding has taken a variety of forms: indentured labour, debt peonage, serfdom, and so on. Of course, to the extent that it is imposed upon dependants, such as children, it can hardly be called voluntary, but the process is the same. Although governments typically refuse to admit it, labour bonding remains a reality in many poor countries, despite being illegal virtually everywhere. Think of child carpet makers, prostitutes, migrant workers in sweat shops, and the like.

The logic of labour bonding is the same as that of distress land sales: faced with the choice between immediate starvation or slavery, it is rational to choose slavery (for example Srinivasan 1989, Genicot 2002).[17] The puzzle is elsewhere, namely, on the demand side. Labour bonding is based on the fundamental assumption that the bonded labourer will be fed by his or her master. Short of that, there is no difference between immediate starvation and labour bonding. Thus for labour bonding to become reality, the marginal value of labour must be above the marginal cost of food. If not, bonded labourers will not find any takers. The only option left to them may be destitution.

To show this formally, let $\underline{c}$ be the survival level of food intake:[18] if workers consume less than $\underline{c}$, they cannot produce and they die. Clearly, the wage rate cannot fall below the efficiency wage $\underline{c}$. Let output of individual i be a function of harvest labour l, i.e., $f(l)\pi_{it}$ with $f'(.) \geq 0$ and $f(0) = 0$. The marginal return to harvest labour on farm i is $f_i'(l)\pi_{it}$ where π_{it} is determined by past rainfall, and so forth. At the minimum possible wage c, the labour demanded by household i is the level of l_i that satisfies:

$$f_i'(l_i)\pi_{it} = \underline{c} \tag{3.9}$$

In case no such l_i can be found, set $l_i = 0$. For a low enough shock, there is nothing to harvest and $l_i = 0$: l_i is thus an increasing function of π_{it}. We can think of l_i as the number of workers whose survival can be supported by farmer i. Let the total number of workers in the community be N. Clearly, if

$$\sum_{i=1}^{N} l_i < N \tag{3.10}$$

some workers will not find employment at the efficiency wage.

Now suppose that workers can credibly commit to deliver their labour power forever at wage $\underline{c}$.[19] Define i's expected discounted utility from refusing the offer as $V_i^r(F_t)$ where $V_i^r(.)$ solves the following Belman equation:

$$V_i^r(F_t, \pi_{it}, w_t) = \max_{l_t \geq 0, F_{t+1} \geq 0} U(\gamma F_t + f(l_t)\pi_{it} - l_t w_t - F_{t+1}) +$$

$$\beta \int_{\underline{c}}^{\infty} \int_{-\infty}^{\infty} V_i^r(F_{t+1}, \pi_{it+1}, w_{t+1},) \, d\Phi(\pi_{it+1}) \, dG(w_{t+1}) \tag{3.11}$$

where $\Phi(.)$ and $G(.)$ denote the cumulative distribution of shocks π_i and wages w respectively.[20] Similarly, define i's expected discounted utility from accepting the offer as $V_i^a(.)$ with:

$$V_i^a(F_t, \pi_{it}, w_t) = \max_{l_t \geq 0, F_{t+1} \geq 0} U(\gamma F_t + f(\underline{s} + l_t)\pi_{it} - \underline{s}\underline{c} - l_t w_t - F_{t+1}) +$$

$$\beta \int_{\underline{c}}^{\infty} \int_{-\infty}^{\infty} V_i^a(F_{t+1}, \pi_{it+1}, w_{t+1}) \, d\Phi(\pi_{it+1}) \, dG(w_{t+1}) \tag{3.12}$$

where $\underline{s}$ stands for bonded labour, assumed constant and inalienable.[21] An employer with food stock F_t finds a bonded labour contract appealing if:

$$V_i^a(F_t, \pi_{it}, w_t) > V_i^r(F_t, \pi_{it}, w_t) \tag{3.13}$$

It is easy to see that $V_i^a - V_i^r$ is an increasing function of F_t and π_{it}: farmers with no stock and little to harvest find it more costly to support workers today in exchange for future labour. Condition (3.13) will thus be satisfied if future wages and shocks are expected to be much higher than current ones and if F_t is sufficiently high so that supporting $\underline{s}$ workers today does not drastically reduce i's current consumption. Famines can thus be thought of as episodes during which the society as a whole cannot support its entire population: there is not enough food to go around so that the more fortunate do not find it profitable to support the less fortunate in exchange for their future labour.

Once this is understood, it is easy to see how bonded labour can last: as long as bonded labourers cannot survive on their own, it is optimal for them to remain bonded. This may explain why labour bonding survives in certain countries in spite of being illegal.[22] The same logic applies to other forms of self-imposed long-term dependency, such as debt peonage and indentures. To the extent that these forms of dependency could easily qualify as 'exploitative', we see that there is a close relationship between exploitative social structures, risk, and poverty. To put it differently, the fact that certain people may voluntarily put themselves entirely at the mercy of others in exchange for survival – or, in the case of migrant workers, in exchange for the promise of a better future for themselves or their progeny – calls for serious concern. We shall get back to these issues when we discuss patron-client relationships.

Using data from the rural Philippines, Fafchamps and Gubert (2002) investigate loan repayment practices for evidence of labour bonding or debt trap. They find no compelling evidence that, in the area studied, debt peonage is a concern. Debt payments in labour are somewhat common but, contrary to the labour bonding idea, they are a form of early payment when the borrower is short of cash and are not subsequently repeated. The authors also find that interest charges, which are waived altogether on the overwhelming majority of loans, are seldom collected in full on interest bearing loans. They also find little evidence that lenders force borrowers into default in order to seize their land or force them into slavery. It is unclear, however, how relevant these findings are for other parts of the world. More research is needed.

3.2.4 Reducing Consumption to Keep Productive Assets

As is clear from the above discussion, liquidating manpower and productive assets to deal with shocks can be extremely damaging to one's long run welfare. Consequently, it is perhaps not too surprising to find that poor rural dwellers often prefer to reduce their consumption rather than liquidating productive assets. Fafchamps et al. (1998), for instance, show that Burkinabe households held onto their livestock even at the height of the 1984 Sahelian drought. In contrast to Rosenzweig and Wolpin (1993) who argue that Indian households smooth consumption through purchases and sales of bullocks, Lim and Townsend (1998) use the same Indian data to show that livestock transactions raise income volatility instead of reducing it. Kang and Sawada (2002) similarly find that Korean households responded to the 1997 crisis by reducing consumption of luxury items while maintaining food, education and health related expenditures.

Using results from livestock price analysis conducted by Fafchamps and Gavian (1996) and Fafchamps and Gavian (1997), Fafchamps et al. (1998) speculate that the reason why farmers are reluctant to liquidate their livestock is because livestock prices are much lower during a drought than they normally are. Similar observations can be found in the anthropological and sociological literatures on pastoralists (for example Monod 1975, Sandford 1983, Oba and Lusigi 1987). In their study of pastoralists in Southern Ethiopia, for instance, Lybbert et al. (2000) argue that the marketing of animals is negligible in response to shocks, suggesting that herders seek to protect their herd from wealth and income shocks. The price drop during a drought implies that the returns from holding livestock are higher than normal immediately after a drought. Fafchamps (1998) shows that the variation in prices is further magnified by externalities in pasture management and by institutional failure. Another reason why results from Burkina Faso are in contrast with results from India is that in the former, land sales are not feasible while in the latter they are. This leads to a more unequal distribution of land ownership in India than in Burkina Faso and, hence, to a more egalitarian distribution of wealth in the latter. As a result, the sale of productive assets might be less of a necessity in Burkina Faso. Differences in land markets may also account for the fact that, based on casual observation and social science literature, cases of labour bonding and debt peonage are less frequent in Africa than in Asia. This issue requires additional research.

Households' desire to protect their assets is not, however, always possible if households do not have access to other ways of sharing risk. As the work of Zimmerman (1993) demonstrates, distress sales will occur even if households correctly anticipate that they will not be able to buy their assets back because of the negative correlation between shocks and asset prices. This is because survival, even at a lower level of utility, is always better than starvation.

3.2.5 Precautionary Saving

Saving is one way by which households can protect themselves against the damaging consequences of the distress sales of productive assets without having to reduce consumption: in anticipation of future shocks, households may build up liquid reserves that can be sold or consumed in times of need. In the literature this practice is commonly referred to as precautionary saving. The liquid assets that are accumulated in this manner by poor rural dwellers include food stocks, gold and jewellery, cash, and, provided a bank is close by, deposits on savings and checking accounts (for example Behrman et al. 1997, Lim and Townsend 1998).

Hall (1978) was among the first to formalize the idea that savings can be used by households to smooth consumption. Hall considers a household with a random wage income π_t who can save in a riskless asset A_t with constant return r. The household's intertemporal optimization problem can be written:

$$\max_{\{c_t\}} E \sum_{t=1}^{T} (1+\delta)^{-t} U(c_t) \tag{3.14}$$

subject to the following budget constraint:

$$A_{t+1} = (A_t - c_t)(1+r) + \pi_t \tag{3.15}$$

and debt repayment constraint:

$$A_T - c_T \geq 0 \tag{3.16}$$

Variable A_t denotes the household's stock of liquid assets at time t, while π_t represents wage income. Parameter T is the household's horizon, possibly infinite. Constraint (3.16) guarantees that the household pays all its debts. If utility is quadratic and T is ∞, it can be shown (Zeldes 1989b) that:

$$c_{CEQ,t} = \frac{r}{1+r}(A_t + H_t) \tag{3.17}$$

where:

$$H_t \equiv E_t \left[\sum_{\tau=1}^{\infty} (1+r)^{\tau} \pi_{t+\tau} \right] \tag{3.18}$$

Variable H_t can thus be interpreted as the agent's human capital from which a wage return of $\pi_{t+\tau}$ is obtained in every period.[23] Equation (3.17) implies that households consume the annuity value of their combined liquid wealth and human capital. The sensitivity of consumption to current income then is:

$$\frac{dc_{CEQ,t}}{d\pi_t} = \frac{r}{1+r} \left[\sum_{\tau=0}^{\infty} (1+r)^{-\tau} \frac{\partial E_t \pi_{t+\tau}}{\partial \pi_{t+\tau}} \right] \qquad (3.19)$$

If wage income π_t *is* uncorrelated over time, equation (3.19) boils down to:

$$\frac{dc_{CEQ,t}}{d\pi_t} = \frac{r}{1+r} \qquad (3.20)$$

Equation (3.20) shows that, with quadratic preferences, the sensitivity of consumption to temporary variations in income is quite small – of the order of $r/1+r$. The propensity to save out of temporary variations in income is predicted to be very high, i.e., of the order of $1/1+r \simeq 1$.

Paxson (1992) tests the certainty equivalent model using savings and consumption data from Thailand. Her estimate of the propensity to save out of temporary income reverts around 0.73/0.83; she cannot reject the hypothesis that the true value is 1 (see, also Paxson (1993) and Chaudhuri and Paxson (2001)). She nevertheless finds that households save a portion of their permanent income as well, a finding that she interprets as circumstantial evidence in favour of credit constraints. It can also be interpreted as evidence of life cycle and bequest motives for saving (Horioka and Watanabe 1997). Fafchamps et al. (1998) use a similar approach to test whether the pattern of sales and purchases of livestock by West African farmers is consistent with the use of livestock as a buffer against risk. Their results indicate that livestock is used less as a hedge against crop income risk than is commonly believed. Their finding is in line with households' willingness to incur fluctuations in consumption in order to protect productive investments (see supra). Other researchers find that livestock is used as a buffer stock but is insufficient to smooth consumption (for example Carraro 1999, Imai 2000a, Imai 2000b). Lim and Townsend (1998) reconstruct the cash balances of poor Indian households and conclude that cash holdings play a major role in smoothing consumption. They also compute the variance of income and the variance of income plus livestock sales and purchases. If households liquidate livestock to absorb income shocks, then the second should be smaller than the former; they find the opposite, again suggesting that livestock is a productive asset that households seek to protect, not a buffer stock. Fafchamps and Lund (2003) similarly find that Filipino rural households make little use of pigs and chickens as hedges against unemployment and 'ritual' shocks (that is, the need to finance funerals and sickness ceremonies). All these results go against the conventional wisdom that livestock, particularly small stock, plays an important role in dealing with risk. More research is needed to ascertain the exact role that livestock plays as a precautionary form of saving.

In the certainty equivalence model, the variance of income has no influence on how much households save – hence the 'certainty equivalence' phrase to describe the model. Intuitively, however, one would expect households facing a more risky environment to save more as a precaution against risk. Kimball (1990) provides a rigorous treatment of the precautionary motive for saving. By analogy with the Arrow-Pratt measures of risk aversion, Kimball defines a coefficient of absolute prudence η as:

$$\eta \equiv -\frac{V'''}{V''} \tag{3.21}$$

where $V(x)$ is the household's value function defined over cash in hand x. Absolute prudence measures the strength of the precautionary saving motive in the sense that a household faced with a mean preserving increase in income risk increases saving proportionally to η.[24] Kimball also shows that, if absolute risk aversion is decreasing, a household which purchases full insurance at a price equal to its maximum willingness to pay increases consumption and reduces savings. An immediate corollary is that any voluntary purchase of full insurance reduces savings, another way of saying that precautionary saving is an insurance substitute.

By defining precautionary savings on the basis of the local curvature of the utility function, Kimball's approach obscures the fact that a precautionary motive for saving can arise from global properties of the utility function. To see why, let us delve for an instant into the literature on inventory stockout risk (for example Tsiang 1969, Kahn 1987, Krane 1994). A simple model of stockout risk can be found, for instance, in Fafchamps et al. (2000). The authors construct a model in which firms' profits are linear in stocks, except for a sharp penalty when the firm runs out of inventories. They show that an increase in the variance of risk raises the probability that the firm runs out of stock for any given level of stock, and hence raises the inventories that the firm holds ex ante. The same logic can easily be applied to rural households: if running out of food stocks means starvation, agents will minimize the probability of starvation by holding stocks.[25] More risk will lead them to hold more stocks.

There is little empirical work on the relationship between the variance of income shocks and saving among the rural poor.[26] Fafchamps et al. (2000) show that contractual risk and to a lesser extent market risk help explain the accumulation of inventories and liquidity reserves among African manufacturers. Rosenzweig and Binswanger (1993) show that the composition of asset portfolios among Indian farmers is significantly affected by farmers' exposure to rainfall variability and risk aversion. Heaton and Lucas (2000) review the literature on portfolio effects with a specific emphasis on developed countries.

3.2.6   Borrowing

We have seen that asset accumulation can serve to smooth consumption. Faced with a sufficiently long series of bad income and utility shocks, individuals will nevertheless run out of assets and will no longer be able to absorb shocks by liquidating assets. One conceivable way out of this quandary is to let households' asset position become negative, that is, to let households borrow.[27] As Carroll (1992) has shown, however, credit constraints are unavoidable if credit contracts are strict, that is, if creditors insist on repayment under any circumstance. To see why, suppose that the lowest value taken by income π_t is π_0 and consider an individual reaching the end of his life at time T. We assume that consumption cannot be negative and that the interest rate r is constant over time. Since debt contracts must be repaid no matter what, the maximum amount the individual can borrow at time $T-1$ is π_0; any amount in excess of π_0 cannot be repaid with absolute certainty. Going back one period, by the same argument, we see that the maximum amount that can be borrowed at $T-2$ and be repaid with absolute certainty is equal to $\pi_0 + \pi_0/1 + r$. By successive backward induction, we see that the absolute maximum that a household can borrow is π_0/r: strict credit contracts naturally generate credit constraints without any need for asymmetric information or enforcement problems. If $\pi_0 = 0$ – a reasonable assumption in most cases – individuals can never hold negative wealth.[28] For credit to exist, credit contracts must allow for conditional default, that is, must mix an element of insurance with pure credit. We shall get back to this issue later.

Zeldes (1989b) examines the saving behaviour of a household facing an implicit credit constraint.[29] He shows that, for sufficiently large cash in hand, the consumption behaviour of the household is adequately approximated by the certainty equivalence model: the propensity to consume out of temporary income is approximately equal to the annuity value of the income shock (see supra, equation (3.21)). At low levels of wealth, however, consumption becomes much more sensitive to current income. At the limit, when wealth tends to zero, the propensity to consume out of current income tends to one: households who have run out of assets simply consume their current income.

Deaton (1991) extends the Zeldes (1989b) model to cases where $\pi_0 > 0$ but households cannot hold negative wealth. In this case, the credit constraint can be binding. Deaton shows that there exists a level of cash in hand x^* below which households consume all their current income. Only when cash in hand rises above x^* do households accumulate precautionary balances. Zeldes (1989a) proposes a simple test of the credit constraint hypothesis. Following Deaton (1991), he notes that if the credit constraint is not binding, household consumption must satisfy the usual Euler condition:

$$U_i'(c_{it}) = E\left[\frac{1+r}{1+\delta} U_i'(c_{it+1})\right] \tag{3.22}$$

If, in contrast, the credit constraint is binding, then:

$$U_i'(c_{it}) = E\left[\frac{1+r}{1+\delta} U_i'(c_{it+1})\right] + \lambda_t$$

$$= \frac{1+r}{1+\delta} U_i'(c_{it+1}) + \lambda_t + \varepsilon_t \tag{3.23}$$

where λ_t is the Lagrange multiplier associated with the credit constraint. If the constraint is binding, $\lambda_t > 0$; otherwise, it is 0. If utility takes the usual constant relative risk aversion form, equation (3.23) can be rewritten in terms of c_{t+1}/c_t consumption and λ_t. Since λ_t is decreasing in income, the presence of credit constraint can be tested by regressing the growth rate of consumption on household characteristics and income. Morduch (1990) applies such a test to Indian data and concludes that the presence of a credit constraint cannot be rejected among poor and middle income farmers. Only among wealthy households can the credit constraint hypothesis be rejected – a result entirely in line with Deaton (1991)'s analysis. Kang and Sawada (2002) conduct a similar test with respect to the 1997 financial crisis in Korea. They conclude that the main reason why the standard Euler equation does not hold is the presence of a credit constraint. They also conclude that the credit crunch affected households negatively. Blundell et al. (2001) further elaborate on this issue and develop a test that assesses the degree of insurance over and above self-insurance through savings. Using the PSID data from the US, they, like Mace (1991) and Cochrane (1991), uncover partial insurance, especially for transitory shocks, but reject the complete market, full insurance model.

In another article, Deaton (1990) shows that, in the presence of credit constraints, the time path of consumption is characterized by infrequent but dramatic drops in consumption that resembles famines. The rest of the time, consumption is fairly smooth in spite of large fluctuations in income. Deaton's analysis demonstrates that asset accumulation can drastically reduce fluctuations in consumption but cannot fully prevent famines. He also shows that famines only arise when households are affected by a series of successive bad shocks, a feature that has long been noted in the descriptive literature (Sen 1981).

Deaton's analysis also brings to light the fact that impatient households save even when the return on their assets is negative (Deaton 1992a). This stands in sharp contrast with a world of certainty in which households would never save when the rate of interest r is smaller than the rate of time preference δ. This theoretical prediction is consistent with the fact that poor households the world over save partly in the form of grain stocks or cash. Although grain stocks often have a positive intra-year return thanks to seasonal variations in prices, their inter-year real return is in general negative: stocks depreciate due to pests and desiccation. Similarly, cash and bank deposits typically have negative returns due to inflation. Yet poor people often hold much of their liquid wealth in the form of grain and cash.[30] Park (2000), for instance, shows that grain stocks in northern China are equivalent to several years of harvest. Lim and Townsend (1998) similarly argue that, among Indian households, grain and cash represent the major forms of precautionary saving.

3.3   RISK SHARING

So far we have discussed risk coping strategies that either seek to smooth income directly or rely on the accumulation and liquidation of assets. Our entire discussion was focused on the individual. We now turn to a more aggregate approach and consider risk sharing in a general equilibrium context.

In pre-industrial societies, and much of the Third World today, solidarity bonds often tie members of the same family, kinship group or village together. Those bonds manifest themselves in a wide variety of ways (for example Scott 1976, Posner 1980, Platteau 1991). Labour invitation and other forms of manpower assistance are an opportunity for relatives and friends to help the sick and the old (for example Moerman 1968, Cleave 1974, Feeny 1983, Watts 1983). Cost-free land (for example Norhona 1985, Matlon 1988, Gavian and Fafchamps 1996) and livestock loans (Evans-Pritchard (1940), Colson (1962), p. 170; Odegi-Awuondo (1990), Ch. six) allow the redistribution of productive assets from those who cannot use them effectively to those who have unemployed labour resources. Children that parents cannot support are taken care of, and sometimes adopted, by better-off households. Gifts, food transfers, or credit without interest allow the less successful to close the food gap. Finally, remittances from migrants increase during bad times (Evans-Pritchard (1940), p. 84, Mair (1962), p. 60, Samson (1970), Scott (1976), Posner (1980), Feeny (1983), Watts (1983), p. 124; Platteau and Abraham (1987), Ellsworth (1989), Ellsworth and Shapiro (1989), Reardon and Matlon (1989)).

In rituals, solidarity is sometimes portrayed as an instantaneous exchange of gifts.[31] In practice, however, solidarity systems are usually organized around delayed reciprocity contingent upon need and affordability.[32] In other words, solidarity is a form of mutual insurance. The person receiving assistance is not expected to give back something equivalent to what she received. What is expected from her is simply to help others in return. How much help she must provide is not entirely specified. It depends on her own circumstances at the time as well as on the situation of those calling for help.

Many authors have noted the strong relationship between the existence of solidarity mechanisms and the extreme precariousness of life in 'primitive' and other pre-industrial societies (for example Scott 1976, Posner 1980, Kimball 1988, Platteau 1991, Coate and Ravallion 1993). Even in developed economies, the occurrence of war or natural calamities revives solidarity and mutual assistance. In the words of Evans-Pritchard (1940, p.84), 'it is scarcity not sufficiency that makes people generous'. This suggests that, whenever economic and social conditions are such that individual survival is extremely uncertain without some form of mutual insurance, informal solidarity mechanisms tend to emerge naturally. These mechanisms are the focus of this section.

Formally, let s_t denote the state of the world at time t and be drawn from a finite set of possible events S_t with probability $\Pr(s_t)$. Consider a rural community constituted of N members, each with a stream of stochastic income $\pi_{it}(s_t)$ and a utility $U_i(c_{it}(s_t))$. Pareto efficiency in the sharing of risk requires that, for any set of welfare weights ω_i, individual consumption satisfies the following social planner problem:

$$\max_{\{c_{it}\}} \sum_{i=1}^{N} \omega_i \sum_{t=1}^{\infty} (1+\delta)^{-t} \sum_{s_t \in S_t} \Pr(s_t) U_i(c_{it}(s_t)) \qquad (3.24)$$

subject to the feasibility constraint

$$C_t(s_t) \equiv \sum_{i=1}^{N} c_{it}(s_t) = \sum_{i=1}^{N} \pi_{it}(s_t) \equiv \Pi_t(s_t) \qquad (3.25)$$

and a set of non-negativity constraints

$$c_{it}(s_t) \geq 0 \qquad (3.26)$$

for all s_t and all t. The set of all efficient risk sharing allocations can be traced by varying the welfare weights ω_i.

This social planner model can easily be extended to allow for accumulation. Given the existence of a riskless asset A with constant return r, the feasibility constraint becomes:

$$C_t(s_t) \equiv \sum_{i=1}^{N} c_{it}(s_t) = \sum_{i=1}^{N} (\pi_{it}(s_t) + A_{it}) \equiv X_t(s_t) \qquad (3.27)$$

where $X_t(s_t)$ denotes aggregate cash in hand.

Let $\lambda(s_t)$ be the Lagrange multiplier associated with the s_t feasibility constraint. Assuming that none of zero consumption constraints are binding, efficient risk sharing requires that:

$$\omega_i (1+\delta)^{-t} \Pr(s_t) U_i'(c_{it}(s_t)) = \lambda(s_t) \qquad (3.28)$$

Since $\lambda(s_t)$ depends only on aggregate income $\Pi_t(s_t)$ (with no accumulation) or aggregate cash in hand $X_t(s_t)$ (with accumulation), equation (3.28) implies that in a Pareto efficient allocation individual consumption can only depend on $\Pi_t(s_t)$ or $X_t(s_t)$, not on individual income.

The Pareto efficiency conditions for an interior solution can be rewritten:

$$\frac{U_i'(c_{it}(s_t))}{U_j'(c_{jt}(s_t))} = \frac{U_i'(c_{it}(s_t'))}{U_j'(c_{jt}(s_t'))} = \frac{\omega_j}{\omega_i} \qquad (3.29)$$

From equation (3.29), it is easy to see that if welfare weights and utility functions are the same for two agents i and j, then:

$$c_{it}(s_t) = c_{jt}(s_t) \qquad (3.30)$$

for all t and s_t. In this case, risk sharing is equivalent to pooling incomes and sharing them equally. If the welfare weight of individual i is higher than that of j, i's consumption is larger than j's.

The pooling of risk does not, however, require that agents mutually insure each other. To see why, suppose that one agent, say k, is risk neutral; k's marginal utility of consumption is thus constant. Equation (3.29) then implies an equalization of the consumption of all other agents across all states of the world, that is:

$$c_{it}(s_t) = c_{it}(s_t') \qquad (3.31)$$

for all i and all $s_t, s_t' \in S_t$. The risk neutral agent provides perfect insurance to all other agents; he or she plays the role of an insurance company. Equation (3.31), however, holds only for interior equilibria. For large enough shocks encountered by other agents, individual k may not have sufficient income or wealth to guarantee himself or herself a non-negative consumption. In that case, the consumption of other agents is not smoothed and the equilibrium allocation resembles one in which the 'insurance company' goes bankrupt.

Although the setup presented above has been used mainly to examine situations in which agents face both collective and idiosyncratic risk and share the latter, the presence of idiosyncratic risk is not required for insurance to take place. First, agents can find some protection from collective risk whenever attitudes toward risk differ across agents. In the presence of a risk neutral agent, for instance, agents manage to smooth their consumption perfectly provided the risk neutral agent who serves the role of insurance company has sufficiently deep pockets never to fail. Second, insurance against collective risk is even possible among agents with the same utility function and perfectly correlated incomes whenever income levels vary among agents. If agents have decreasing absolute risk aversion, for instance, it is mutually welfare increasing for agents with high average incomes to partially insure poorer agents against bad collective shocks in exchange for transfers in good states of the world. The reason is that poor agents can gain much by reducing the risk of starvation and can thus compensate rich agents for the welfare loss they incur from increased consumption volatility. Having said this, it is important to recognize that the presence of idiosyncratic risk dramatically raises the welfare gains that can be reaped through risk sharing.

The sociological and anthropological literatures abound with descriptions of insurance arrangements that resemble the kind of protection that a risk neutral agent would provide. These arrangements are often called patron-client relationships (for example Scott 1976, Platteau 1995a, Platteau 1995b) and described as implicit contracts whereby a wealthy individual provides to poorer agents protection against both idiosyncratic and collective shocks. Transfers from the poor to the rich take a variety of forms, ranging from labour services to political support. We shall discuss these arrangements more in detail below.

Equation (3.28) has been extensively used as a basis for testing efficient risk sharing as follows. Posit a functional form for $U_i(.)$, such as constant absolute risk aversion (for example Cochrane 1991, Mace 1991):

$$U_i(c_{it}) = -\frac{1}{\sigma} e^{-\sigma(c_{it}-b_{it})} \qquad (3.32)$$

where b_{it} is an individual-specific shifter that captures household characteristics and utility shocks such as disease or rituals. Equation (3.31) can be rewritten:

$$\frac{\lambda(s_t)(1+\delta)^t}{\Pr(s_t)} = \omega_i e^{-\sigma(c_{it}-b_{it})} \qquad (3.33)$$

Taking logs and summing over all community members, we obtain:

$$c_{it}(s_t) = \frac{1}{N} C_t(s_t) \frac{1}{\sigma} + (\log \omega_i - \log \omega_a) + b_{it} - b_{at} \qquad (3.34)$$

where $\omega_a \equiv 1/N \sum_{i=1}^{N} \log \omega_i$ and b_{at} is the average b_{it} in the community. Equation (3.34) indicates that consumption of individual i should be equal to average consumption, plus the difference between the log of i's welfare weight and the average log welfare weight, plus the difference between i's utility shifter and the average shifter. In other words, with constant absolute risk aversion individual consumption should respond to aggregate income and utility shocks and fully compensate for utility shocks b_{it}. A similar equation in logs instead of levels can be derived using constant relative risk aversion instead. First-differencing equation (3.34) eliminates unobservable welfare weights. If risk is shared efficiently, regressing changes in individual consumption on changes in aggregate consumption and individual income should thus yield a zero coefficient on individual income.

Following the application of this approach to US data by Altonji et al. (1992), Mace (1991), and Cochrane (1991),[33] equation (3.34) has been used by a number of authors to test whether rural communities share risk efficiently. Townsend (1994) and Morduch (2002) apply this approach to rural household data from India. They conclude that, although there is plenty of evidence that idiosyncratic variations in income are largely smoothed out, full Pareto efficiency is rejected in general. Similar results are reported for Zimbabwe by Hoogeveen (2001). According to Morduch (2002), however, efficient risk sharing cannot be ruled out within sub-groups such as castes, or for food consumption alone. Using data from Pakistan, Kurosaki and Fafchamps (2002) fail to reject efficient risk sharing among villagers but find evidence that much of the variation in incomes across villages is not shared efficiently. Kurosaki (2001a) allows for heterogeneous risk preferences across households but again rejects perfect mutual insurance. Gertler and Gruber (2002) revisit these issues with a specific focus on illness. Using data from Indonesia, they show that there are significant costs associated with illness, albeit more from income loss than from medical costs. They find very imperfect smoothing of consumption over episodes of illness, especially for severe illness that limit physical function.

These tests, however, do not provide any information as to how risk is shared. Risk sharing can be explicit, as when agents trade Arrow-Debreu securities; it can be implicit, as when they trade fiat money to equalize their consumption over states of nature. Evidence of risk pooling such as that reported by Townsend (1994), Morduch (2002), and Kurosaki and Fafchamps (2002), does not in any way constitute evidence that members of a community actively insure each other, a point that is not always made clear in the literature. We first consider implicit risk sharing, and then turn to explicit risk sharing mechanisms.

3.3.1 Implicit Risk Sharing

To see how implicit risk sharing is possible, consider an economy à la Akerlof (1985) in which each agent has an exclusive claim on the fruits falling from a coconut tree. Furthermore, suppose that agents can trade with each other using fiat currency, as in Sargent (1987), Chapter Three. Assume no credit market. As discussed in the previous section, agents can use their accumulated currency assets to smooth consumption: agents with few coconuts buy coconuts from luckier agents in exchange for fiat currency. Coconuts thus flow from high coconut agents to low coconut agents and risk is being shared without anyone explicitly recognizing that trade in coconut serves to share risk (for example Lucas 1978, Lucas 1992, Townsend 1988a, Townsend 1989).

This coconut example sounds unrealistic, but just replace 'coconut' with 'grain' and 'fiat currency' with 'livestock' and you may have a good description of an African or Indian village. The point is that, by exchanging among themselves non-consumable assets such as livestock[34] against consumable assets such as grain, villagers implicitly share risk among themselves. Similarly, by exchanging non-consumable assets for consumable assets with the rest of the world, villagers share risk with the rest of the world.

The sharing of risk via accumulation requires that markets be present for agents to trade non-consumables for consumables. Suppose, for instance, that villagers liquidate their livestock and buy grain during bad times. The extent to which this strategy enables villagers to share risk among themselves and with the rest of world depends critically on whether grain and livestock can be exchanged on the market. If they cannot, the only way villagers can protect themselves is by accumulating consumables such as grain.

In practice, market limitations are particularly serious regarding rural communities' ability to share risk with the rest of the world and thus to smooth consumption against collective shocks. If trade in grain and livestock is possible, for instance, then livestock accumulation can serve as a hedge against collective shocks. How efficiently risk is shared in this manner depends critically on the efficiency of market institutions: if the relative price of grain with respect to livestock is constant and the return to livestock is higher than the return to grain storage, then livestock is an effective hedge against drought risk. If, however, this relative price rises dramatically during droughts, as is often the case in Sub-Saharan Africa (for example Sandford 1983, Fafchamps and Gavian 1997), then the sharing of risk across communal or regional boundaries is seriously impaired. As a result, reliance on markets may increase the degree of risk a poor household faces by exposing it to a greater likelihood of entitlement failure in case of drought or famine (Dreze and Sen 1989). In this case, poor households may hide away from the market and seek self-sufficiency in food instead (Fafchamps 1992a).

Numerous studies have shown that grain and livestock markets in poor economies of the Third World are far from being efficient: prices in different locations often fail to co-move (for example Dercon 1995, Fafchamps and Gavian 1996, Shively 1996), and price differentials often exceed measurable arbitrage costs (for example Arnould 1985, Fafchamps and Gavian 1996, Baulch 1997b). The reason for this state of affairs has much to do with the thinness of rural markets, which is itself related to the low productivity of agriculture (little to sell), the large number of producers (lots of transactions), and the information and enforcement problems inherent in any market. These problems are often compounded by ill-advised government interventions in rural markets. High transactions costs de facto isolate rural communities: they lead to insufficient arbitrage and thus to high covariance between local prices and local aggregate shocks.

3.3.2 Explicit Risk Sharing

As we have seen in our discussion of precautionary saving, individual accumulation may fail to achieve perfect consumption smoothing. First, agents may run out of assets, in which case they cannot smooth; a community's capacity to share risk among its members via individual asset accumulation thus depends on the amount and distribution of wealth among its members. The poorer the community and the more unequal the distribution of wealth, the less efficient implicit risk sharing is, and thus the higher the efficiency gain from explicit risk sharing. Second, even when agents have plenty of assets, they nevertheless consume the annuity value of the income shock (Zeldes 1989b): even in a certainty equivalent world, consumption varies with current income, and there are gains from explicit risk sharing.

There are various ways in which rural communities can organize the explicit sharing of risk. To illustrate this idea, we construct a stylized model of risk sharing inspired by models of village economies developed by Townsend (1988b) and Udry (1994). Consider a group of individuals indexed by i. Let the main staple crop, such as rice, be the numeraire and let each individual be endowed with a production function $H^i(.)$ such that crop output q_{t+1}^i at the beginning of period $t+1$ is:

$$q_{t+1}^i = H^i(a_t^i, b_t^i, \varepsilon_{t+1})$$ (3.35)

where a_t^i is crop labour, b_t^i stands for cash inputs, and ε_{t+1} is a vector of all the random shocks affecting the group and its members.[35] We assume that the group cannot formally share risk with the rest of the world. Individuals have three types of assets at their disposal: grain storage s_t^i, saving on a savings account L_t^i, and currency M_t^i. Through L_t^i and M_t^i and trade in grain with the rest of the world, the village as a whole can implicitly pool risk with other villages (see above). Returns on storage are assumed to take the form:

$$(1 - \delta)\, s_t^i g^i (\varepsilon_{t+1}) \qquad (3.36)$$

where δ is a stock depreciation rate and $g_i (\varepsilon_{t+1})$ expresses the dependence of storage returns on exogenous shocks ε_{t+1}. The nominal rates of return on cash and savings accounts are 0 and r_t, respectively.

To the extent that members of the group trade all goods and labour efficiently among themselves, shadow prices of all commodities are determined endogenously through market equilibrium. These commodity prices are subject to aggregate shocks in supply and demand; idiosyncratic shocks, that is, shocks that cancel out in the aggregate do not affect market prices. This idea can formally be expressed by letting the prices on any traded commodity k depend on a vector of aggregate shocks η_t, i.e:

$$p_t^k = p^k (t, \eta_t)$$

where η_t is a subset of ε_t.

Maximizing the weighted sum of individual discounted utilities subject to a group-level budget constraint yields a Pareto efficient allocation. Let ω_i stand for an arbitrary set of welfare weights. Partition the shocks ε_t into aggregate shocks η_t and idiosyncratic shocks ϕ_t conditional on η_t; by construction, $\Pr(\varepsilon_t) = \Pr(\eta_t)\Pr(\phi_t|\eta_t)$.[36] All group-level Pareto efficient allocations can be found by varying the welfare weights ω_i in the following program:

$$\max \sum_i \omega_i \sum_t \beta^t \sum_\eta \Pr(\eta_t) \sum_\phi \Pr(\phi_t | \eta_t) U^i (c_t^i, l_t^i)$$

subject to

$$\sum_i [p_t^q (\eta_t)\, c_t^i + p_t^b(\eta_t)b_t^i + p_t^a (\eta_t)\, a_t^i] = \qquad (3.37)$$

$$p_t^q (\eta_t)\bar{q}_t(\eta_t) + (1 - \delta)\, \bar{s}_t(\eta_t) - s_{t+1} + \sum_i p_t^a(\eta_t)\, (T_t^i - l_t^i) +$$

$$p_t^M \sum_i [(1 + r^l)\, L_t^i - L_{t+1}^i + M_t^i - M_{t+1}^i]$$

where $\bar{q}_t\,(\eta_t) \equiv \Sigma_t q_t^i(\varepsilon_t)$ denotes total group output and $\bar{s}_t(\eta_t) \equiv \Sigma_i s_{tg}^i g^i(\varepsilon_t)$ denotes total grain stocks. It immediately follows from the budget constraint that money is a dominated asset and that it should not be used as a savings instrument.

Associate Lagrange multiplier λ_t with each budget constraint and Lagrange multiplier θ_t with each the credit constraint. Pareto efficiency and hence efficient risk sharing requires that:

$$\omega^i \beta^t \Pr(\varepsilon_t) U_c^i\,(c_t^i\,(\varepsilon_t), l_t^i\,(\varepsilon_t)) = \lambda_t(\varepsilon_t)\,p_t^q\,(\eta_t) \tag{3.38}$$

$$\omega^i \beta^t \Pr(\varepsilon_t)\,U_l^i\,(c_t^i\,(\varepsilon_t), l_t^i\,(\varepsilon_t)) = \lambda_t(\varepsilon_t)\,p_t^l\,(\eta_t) \tag{3.39}$$

Since the budget constraint and credit constraints are the same for all the possible realizations of ϕ_t's that correspond to a particular realization of η_t, it is easy to verify that the $\lambda(\eta_t)$ satisfies:

$$\lambda\,(\varepsilon_t) = \Pr(\phi_t \mid \eta_t), \lambda\,(\eta_t)$$

As a result, the conditions for Pareto efficiency can be rewritten:

$$w^i \beta^t \Pr(\eta_t) U_c^i(c_t^i(\varepsilon_t \mid \eta_t), l_t^i\,(\varepsilon_t \mid \eta_t)) = \lambda_t\,(\eta_t)\,p_t^q\,(\eta_t) \tag{3.40}$$

$$w^i \beta^t \Pr(\eta_t) U_l^i(c_t^i(\varepsilon_t \mid \eta_t), l_t^i\,(\varepsilon_t \mid \eta_t)) = \lambda_t\,(\eta_t)\,p_t^l\,(\eta_t) \tag{3.41}$$

for all $\varepsilon_t \mid \eta_t$. Equations (3.40) and (3.41) establish that, if risk is shared efficiently within the group, individual consumption is only a function of aggregate shocks η_t.

By the same reasoning, it follows that production choices depend only on aggregate risk:

$$\lambda(\eta_t)p_t^b(\eta_t) = \sum_\eta \Pr(\eta_{t+1})\lambda(\eta_{t+1})p_{t+1}^q\,(\eta_{t+1})\,\frac{\partial q_{t+1}^i(\eta_{t+1})}{\partial b_t^i} \tag{3.42}$$

for all b_t^i. The less concave, that is, the flatter $\lambda(\eta_{t+1})$ is as a function of η_{t+1}, the more individual production choices resemble those made by a risk neutral agent maximizing expected profit. Efficient risk sharing among members of the group thus enables agents to take more risk in crop production and, by extension, in any risk taking enterprise.

There are various ways by which efficient allocations can be supported. One approach is to integrate the group into a single entity that pools resources and solves the above social welfare problem. Efficiency can also be supported through markets for credit and insurance. To these we now turn.

3.3.3 Households and Groups

Perhaps the most universal institution for pooling resources and sharing risk is the household (for example Altonji et al. 1992, Hayashi 1995, Hayashi et al. 1996, Altonji et al. 1997, Dercon and Krishnan 2000, Browning and Lechene 2001, Diaz and Echevarria 2002, Foster 2002). In particular, Browning and Lechene (2001) estimate an intra-household model of risk sharing with Canadian data and conclude that the data are consistent with caring partners. Research from poor countries, however, shows that risk sharing among spouses is far from perfect. Dercon and Krishnan (2000), for instance, show that anthropological data from rural Ethiopia are inconsistent with perfect risk sharing among household members. Goldstein et al. (2002) obtain similar results in Ghana where they provide ample evidence that spouses do not perfectly share risk with each other. More research is needed.

As far as risk sharing is concerned, children are likely to be the primary reason for household formation. After all, one of the major motives behind household formation even in developed societies is to provide care and nurturing for children who are the most defenceless among us (Binswanger and McIntire 1987). As all parents know, children are prone to disease and accidents and they require more or less constant attention. Single parents usually find it taxing to combine a job, let alone a career, with responsible parenting. Sharing child care with others by forming a household is the preferred method for raising children the world over. When child care is particularly time consuming, for instance because kids are many, it may even be optimal for one household member to specialize in parenting and to rely on other household members for sustenance (Becker 1981). This typically results in gender casting, that is, on sets of social norms and ethical values that emphasize the special responsibility of women as mothers (Fafchamps and Quisumbing 2003). In poor rural communities, households are also the institution within which care is taken of the sick, the disabled, and the old. Retirement homes, mental institutions, and convalescence clinics are unheard of. It is within the household that people find solace when they are hit by disease and where they seek moral support when bad luck strikes.

Given the importance of households in the sharing of risk, it is not surprising that poor rural societies put a lot of emphasis on household formation in their ethical values and social practices. As anthropologists have documented in all human societies, the creation and dissolution of households are important social events that call for well attended rituals (such as birth, marriage, death). Much of family law, whether traditional or modern, can be seen as an effort to ensure that household members have a strong interest in preserving the stability of the household and in working as a team to handle shocks. In many societies, this is accomplished by providing incentives for women to specialize in taking care of vulnerable members of the household – for instance by making it difficult or impossible for women to work outside the home (for example Fafchamps 2001, Fafchamps and Quisumbing 2003). One may object to such practices on the ground that they, are inefficient and inequitable: by denying women the freedom to express their full economic potential, gender casting prevents an optimal allocation of individual talents among alternative activities. The fact remains that many societies choose to forego these allocative efficiency gains and prefer to emphasize gender casting instead. One possible explanation is that these societies attach a lot of importance to risk sharing and seek to protect those in need of assistance by casting women in the role of mothers and care givers and by nurturing among women values that emphasize compassion for children, the weak, the sick, and the old.

Legal or customary rules governing the devolution of assets upon household dissolution can similarly be seen as an effort to provide for its most vulnerable members, that is, children and, to a lesser extent, wives.[37] In developed urban societies, these concerns are expressed in the form of child care and alimony payments following divorce, for instance. Poor rural societies often have similar concerns, but express them differently. Since very few people receive regular wages from long term employment, the payment of fixed regular transfers is highly impractical. They are replaced by endowments of land or livestock that serve as a source of income through self-employment or, occasionally, through the rental of factors of production. In some cases, human capital investment replaces transfers of physical capital, as shown for instance by Estudillo et al. (2001) in the Philippines.

Given the importance of households in the explicit sharing of risk, it is not surprising to discover that the size and composition of households partly reflects the risk environment surrounding them. As Binswanger and McIntire (1987) pointed out, it is common for households in poor rural areas to span several generations and to include several nuclear households, that is, several sets of parents with their children. Combined with high fertility rates, this implies that households in poor rural areas are often large – for example, from five to eight members on average. It is not uncommon to encounter households with as many as 30 or more members; in contrast, single households are rare. The structure and organization of these large households can be quite complex and each member or nuclear unit is often granted some autonomy in managing their own affairs provided they fulfill their obligations to the common good of the household (von Braun and Webb 1989). While a detailed discussion of the internal organization of large rural households is beyond the scope of this study, certain features deserve to be mentioned. First, large households often keep a single kitchen.[38] This enables them to capture returns to scale in food preparation but also ensures that food is shared among all members. Second, large households normally keep a single granary, implying the sharing of yield risk among members. Third, members take care of each other in bad times: the sick, the disabled and the old are looked after, and the unemployed are provided with food and shelter. Finally, even though members of large households often manage certain activities individually, institutional mechanisms are present that ensure the pooling of labour resources for vital household chores such as food production. One such mechanism is the head of household's power to call upon each household member to contribute labour to the common field (von Braun and Webb 1989).[39] All these features point toward the role of households as risk sharing institutions. Foster (2002) provides some hard empirical evidence to this effect. Foster studies a sample of Bangladeshi households. Some of them reside in the same compound; others do not. By comparing health outcomes across both groups, Foster is able to tell whether co-residence serves a risk pooling purpose. Controlling for selection bias, he finds that individuals care differentially about the welfare of co-resident and non-resident family members. Specifically, it appears that the health status of co-resident family units is viewed as complementary to the health of one's own family.

The paramount role of households in risk sharing can also be seen in absentia by noting that the poorest members of society often are isolated individuals: old men and women with nobody to look after them, runaway children, physically or mentally disabled individuals who have been discarded by their family, and so on. Poverty is often associated with dysfunctional families and household separation generally leads to a lowering of standards of living. This occurs in part because returns to scale in the provision of common household goods (a home, a kitchen) are lost, but also because the reduction in risk sharing opportunities forces a less efficient allocation of resources. Kurosaki (2001b) for instance provides some evidence that the most vulnerable segments of society are those outside networks, particularly female-headed households. Morduch and Sicular (1999) argue that poverty in rural China can in part be traced back to family planning policies that led to a sharp reduction in family size.

3.3.4 Gifts and Transfers

Explicit pooling of resources may also take place, albeit in a weaker form, within larger groups. For instance, common property resources are often used partly as an asset upon which community members may draw in case of need. Swidden cultivation in East and South-East Asia, for instance, often serves as a source of food when the main rice harvest fails. Wild grains and roots similarly serve as foods of last resort.

Gifts and transfers are another important and widely studied avenue for risk sharing. For example Altonji et al. (1992), Altonji et al. 1997, Hayashi et al. 1996 study informal transfers between individuals who are altruistically linked. These are typically individuals who previously formed a household, such as parents and their children living independently. In this context, gifts and transfers are seen as an extension of what goes on within households. Hayashi (1995) obtains similar results for Japan. There is a voluminous literature documenting similar patterns in poor countries, including a large number of articles by economists (for example Lucas and Stark 1985, Ravallion and Dearden 1988, Stark and Lucas 1988, Rosenzweig and Stark 1989, Cox and Jimenez 1992, Cox et al. 1996, Cox and Jimenez 1998, Cox et al. 1998, Raut and Tran 2000, Stark and Falk 2000, Huysentruyt et al. 2002, La Ferrara 2002). In poor countries, the definition of family often extend beyond parents and their children to include distant relatives as well. Gifts and transfers between relatives or even with neighbours and friends have long been documented by other social scientists.

Much of the literature on gifts and transfers does not focus on risk sharing. Following Becker (1981), some authors such as Cox (1987) and Nugent (1990) regard intergenerational gifts and transfers as some form of quid pro quo: parents help their children when they start in life – they send them to school, equip them, give them land – in exchange for which children take care of parents when they get old.

Some authors have examined whether gifts and remittances serve an insurance role. The evidence seems to be that gifts and transfers serve some insurance purpose in the sense that they increase when times are bad for the recipient and drop when times are bad for the sender. Kang and Sawada (2002), for instance, find that among credit-constrained Korean households affected by the 1997 crisis, private transfers acted as an ex post risk coping strategy. Lundberg et al. (2000) report that Tanzanian households affected by AIDS rely on gifts and loans from others to deal with their loss.

But the bulk of the evidence suggests that gifts and transfers do not fully insure households against risk. In the rural Philippines, for instance, Fafchamps and Lund (2003) show that gifts and remittances – which come primarily from close relatives – are insufficient to deal with health crises, unemployment, and funerals. Dercon and de Weerdt (2002) report similar findings in Tanzania. Rosenzweig (1988a) shows that gifts represent a minute portion of income risk in India. Lim and Townsend (1998) and Imai (2000a) similarly show that gifts and transfers only cover a small proportion of consumption shortfalls. Among pastoralists in Southern Ethiopia,

Lybbert et al. (2000) similarly show that reciprocal transfers are surprisingly modest in view of the fact that shocks are primarily idiosyncratic. Very similar results are reported by McPeak (2002) for livestock producers in Northern Kenya.

3.3.5 Explicit Insurance

Short of pooling resources, individuals may also pool risk explicitly through mutual insurance contracts. One form that such insurance contracts may take is that of contingent claims and obligations. For instance, suppose that in state of the world s_1, Jack has 200g of rice while Jill has none. Assume that Pareto efficiency requires that both consume 100g. A mutual insurance contract simply stipulates that when Jack has 200g of rice when Jill has not, Jack gives 100g of rice to Jill. Similarly, in state of the world s_2 when Jack has nothing when Jill has a lot, Jill gives something to Jack. Promises by Jack and Jill to give each other rice in states of the world s_1 and s_2 can theoretically be traded between Jack and Jill at the beginning of time, in which case they formally resemble what general equilibrium theory calls Arrow-Debreu securities. Alternatively, Jack and Jill may agree upon a mutual insurance contract that stipulates the quantities to be given by one to the other in each state of the world. The same idea can be extended to an arbitrary number of members. Cabrales et al. (2002) present an illustrative example of such a scheme by describing La Crema, a mutual fire insurance scheme in Andorra. What makes the scheme remarkable is that it is not capitalized: members precommit to assist the fund in times of trouble but do not ex ante contribute to it.

One general problem with the kind of mutual insurance schemes described above is the difficulty of stipulating beforehand the obligations of each member in each state of the world. When the group is very large and idiosyncratic shocks are not correlated, aggregate shocks may be so small as to be ignored. In this case, a simple contract can be written that stipulates a flat and constant fee, and compensation rules that are constant over time and depend only on individual shocks. In case shocks are moderately correlated or if the group is not large, aggregate shocks do not vanish. One possibility is to make the payout rate of the mutual insurance scheme contingent on aggregate resources, but this is likely to complicate the contract. Another, simpler approach is to endow the mutual insurance scheme with an initial amount of money sufficient to ensure that the scheme does not run out of money.[40] Many social welfare programmes in developed economies closely approximate this kind of mutual insurance contracts: health and unemployment insurance, uncapitalized pension schemes, and so on. In fact, many of these programmes were initially organized as voluntary mutual insurance funds.

Some examples of explicit mutual insurance contracts and institutions can be found in poor rural societies. For instance, it is not uncommon for Sahelian villages to cultivate certain fields in common and use the harvest as a village welfare fund administered by the chief. The explicit pooling of risk is also very common among groups of fishermen (for example Plateau et al. 1985, Plateau and Abraham 1987). Sahelian farmers often form groups of three or four individuals who pool their labour resources and jointly cultivate each other's fields. In this fashion, if one of them is sick or must absent himself from work, the others can take care of his fields. Many African rural communities also have institutions whereby sick farmers can call upon others to come and harvest their farm (Fafchamps 1992b). Although these explicit risk sharing arrangements and institutions have been documented in a variety of societies and environments, they appear to be both fairly infrequent and diminishing in importance over time. Does this mean that explicit risk sharing across households is absent?

Not necessarily. Other mechanisms indeed exist that can also, at least theoretically, support Pareto efficiency. One possibility is to organize a spot market for contingent claims among village members. Let $R(\varepsilon_{t+1})$ denote a payment of R units of the numeraire if state of the world ε is realized at time $t+1$. Suppose that promises to pay $R(\varepsilon_{t+1})$ are perfectly and costlessly enforceable and that they are traded in a competitive market among village members. Consequently, the price at which promises are traded at time t only reflects current and future aggregate conditions. Formally, denote the price of a promise of one unit of numeraire in state of the world η_{t+1} by $p(\eta_t, \eta_{t+1})$. Rank states of the world such that low η_t correspond to low aggregate endowments, and high η_t to high aggregate endowments. Using equations (3.40) and (3.41), and the Euler equation of an individual capable of buying and selling promises, it can be shown that their price must be such that (as in Udry 1992, Townsend 1993):

$$p(\eta_t, \eta_{t+1}) = \Pr(\eta_t) \frac{\lambda(\eta_{t+1})p_{t+1}^q(\eta_{t+1})}{\lambda(\eta_t)p_{t+1}^q(\eta_t)} \tag{3.43}$$

λ_t denotes the marginal utility of consumption weighted over all group members. To the extent that individuals are risk averse, that grain storage is costly, and that the group is subject to aggregate shocks, λ_t is decreasing in η_t. From equation (3.43), we then see that, if there is currently a lot of grain in the economy, and thus $\lambda(\eta_t)$ is low, a promise of giving grain tomorrow can be exchanged for a lot of grain today: p is increasing in η_t. Similarly, a promise of giving grain in a bad aggregate state of the world tomorrow can be exchanged for a lot of grain today: when η_{t+1} is low, convexity of the utility function implies that $\lambda(\eta_{t+1})$ is high, and thus that p is decreasing in η_{t+1}.

The usefulness of the above construction comes from the fact that contingent promises can be bundled together into what can be referred to as credit contracts with state-contingent repayment (as in Udry 1992, Townsend 1993). To see why, define lending B_t as the price paid for an entire bundle of contingent repayment promises:

$$B_t^i = \sum_{\eta_{t+1}} \Pr(\eta_{t+1}) \, p(\eta_t, \eta_{t+1}) \sum_{\phi_{t+1}} \Pr(\phi_{t+1} | \eta_{t+1}) \, R^i(\eta_{t+1}, \phi_{t+1}) \qquad (3.44)$$

Equation (3.44) indicates that the rate of interest on a promise to pay one unit of grain in all states of the world is equal to $1/\Sigma_{\eta_{t+1}} p(\eta_t, \eta_{t+1})$; it is increasing in η_t and decreasing in η_{t+1}. Full insurance of idiosyncratic risk follows from equation (3.44). To see why, suppose that, given η_{t+1}, there are only two possible realizations, one good for i and one bad for i, each of which has equal probability. From equation (3.44), it is clear that a promise to pay one unit of grain in states $\phi_{t+1} | \eta_{t+1}$ sells for the same price as a promise to pay two units of grain only in the good state for i: price p depends only on η_{t+1}, not on ϕ_{t+1}. Since any risk averse individual would prefer the second option to the first, it is clear that optimal contingent credit repayment of this kind can serve to efficiently pool idiosyncratic risk.

Evidence in favour of the contingent credit hypothesis can be found in the works of Udry (1990), Udry (1994), Townsend (1995b), Platteau and Abraham (1987), Fafchamps and Lund (2003), and Fafchamps and Gubert (2002). Other studies such as that by Rosenzweig (1988a) and Christensen (1987) further confirm that credit among villagers in poor rural communities plays an important insurance role. Contingent informal credit can also be found among urban entrepreneurs (for example Fafchamps et al. 1994, Fafchamps et al. 1995). Several characteristics of informal credit contracts do not, however, appear consistent with the hypothesis of perfect markets for contingent contracts. For one thing, the documented magnitude of the effect of contingencies on debt repayment appears too small relative to the risks faced by. debtor and creditor. Second, informal credit contracts often stipulate zero interest, irrespective of current conditions. This feature is in contradiction with the predicted dependence of expected interest on η_t. Finally, access to contingent credit appears restricted, a feature inconsistent with the assumed market clearing property of contingent prices $p(\eta_t, \eta_{t+1})$. We shall revisit these issues in the next chapter.

3.3.6 Interlinking and Patronage

The weaving of insurance-type provisions into other contracts is another form of risk sharing that has attracted a lot of attention in the development economics literature. Contingent credit, which we just discussed, is but one example of such interlinking. Since Stiglitz's (1974) seminal article on sharecropping as a risk sharing device, the theoretical literature on land and labour markets has explored these issues in great detail (for example Braverman and Stiglitz 1982, Bardhan 1984, Bell 1988, Datta et al. 1988, Dubois 2000). Much of this literature follows from the same simple observation. Suppose two agents enter into a contractual arrangement in which one set of contractual obligations is delayed. Examples of such contracts include not only lending and borrowing but also land rentals, labour contracts, forward sale of agricultural output, supplier credit, and warranty provisions. In addition, suppose that one party to the contract is more risk averse than the other and that perfect insurance is not available through any other source. It is then in the interest of the parties to incorporate an element of risk sharing into their contract. Since the risk averse party is willing to pay for insurance, the risk neutral party can raise the expected price of the product or service they offer by sharing risk with the other party. Although much of the literature on interlinking assumes some amount of asymmetric information, the rationale for including risk sharing provisions into other transactions does not require it. The role of asymmetric information is rather to explain why parties would choose to share risk in an inefficient manner, such as through sharecropping instead of insurance.

There is limited evidence in favour of interlinking as an explicit risk sharing device used in poor rural areas (for examaple Dubois 2000, Jacoby et al. 2002). Many – though not all (Shaban 1987) – empirical studies of sharecropping, for instance, suggest that sharecropping is efficient (for examaple Sadoulet et al. 1994, Pender and Fafchamps 2002). This is in contradiction with models in which sharing crop output is a way of trading off inefficient insurance against inefficient effort (Stiglitz 1974). Evidence of explicit interlinking of insurance with other contracts is even more tenuous. In contrast, explicit interlinking has been documented in urban areas. Fafchamps (2003b), for instance, provides ample evidence of interlinking of commodity sales and credit among African manufacturers. Contractual performance in manufacturing contracts is often contingent upon shocks affecting the parties (for example Lorenz 1988, Fafchamps 1996a, Bigsten et al. 2000). In developed economies, explicit interlinking appears even more common. For example, most manufacturers, retailers, and even credit card companies offer extend warranty on consumer items; supplier credit is the norm in relations between firms and also, thanks to credit cards, between firms and consumers; and labour contracts of managers and even workers customarily include participation in the firm's profits. If anything, explicit interlinking appears less common in developing than in developed countries and in rural than in urban areas.

One possible explanation is that, in poor rural areas, explicit interlinking is replaced by long-term patronage relationships. Patronage is defined as a situation in which a wealthier member of the village provides factors of production and/or insurance to poorer villagers in exchange for a regular stream of miscellaneous services, mostly labour (for example Platteau 1995a, Platteau 1995b). The long-term multifaceted relationship that bonds a patron to his or her clients enables parties to condition actions in one aspect of their relationship upon the other party's action in another aspect – what Basu (1986) calls triadic relations. Although the spirit of the resulting interaction resembles that of interlinking, each transaction between the parties need not contain any explicit insurance. Rather, it is often the continuation of the relationship itself – and the access to credit and factors of production that it guarantees – that constitutes risk sharing.

One extreme version of patronage is labour bonding, discussed earlier. Another example is debt peonage (for example Geertz 1963, de Janvry 1981, Crow and Murshid 1994); it works as follows. An individual in difficulty borrows from a wealthier member of the community – such as a landlord, moneylender, or merchant. If all goes well, the debt is repaid and the debtor is off the hook. If the debt cannot be repaid, repayment is postponed but interest keeps accruing, possibly compounded by late interest charges. Comes a time when the nominal amount of the debt exceeds what the debtor can ever hope to repay. The debtor then becomes what is called a debt peon.[41] Formally, let $\bar{U}$ represent the expected utility to which the creditor can credibly keep a defaulting debtor. The creditor can force the debtor to accept any repayment that satisfies:

$$U(\pi_t - b_t - R_t) \geq \bar{U} \tag{3.45}$$

where π_t is the debtor's current cash-in-hand and b_t stands for unanticipated consumption needs, such as illness and ritual shocks. Equation (3.45) indicates that, as long as the utility of the debtor after repayment does not fall below $\bar{U}$, voluntary repayment of R_t is in his or her interest. Since $U'(.)$ is positive, equation (3.45) also implies that R_t is increasing in $\pi_t - b_t$. Consequently, since $\pi_t - b_t$ depends on the shocks affecting the debtor, it is in the interest of the creditor to modulate repayment R_t according to the current situation of the debtor. The repayment rule that maximizes total discounted repayment $\Sigma_{t=1}^{\infty} R_t$ is one in which $R_t = \pi_t - b_t - \underline{R}$ where $\underline{R}$ is such that:

$$U(\underline{R}) = \bar{U} \text{ or } \underline{R} = U^{-1}(\bar{U}) \tag{3.46}$$

As long as the creditor is (approximately) risk neutral and maximizes expected discounted repayments, it is optimal for him or her to perfectly smooth the debtor's welfare. Debt peonage is thus a form of insurance.[42] Under certain circumstances, it may even be optimal for the creditor to provide net flows of funds to a debt peon – in other words, to extend new loans – when $\pi_t - b_t$ is particularly low. To see why, suppose that $\bar{U}$ is the welfare level that barely guarantees survival of the debtor and his or her family. If welfare falls below $\bar{U}$, the debtor disappears. Provided that $\Sigma_{t=1}^{\infty} R_t > 0$, it is then in the interest of the creditor to keep the debtor alive by easing the debtor's temporary difficulties and raising his or her welfare to $\bar{U}$.

Equation (3.46) indicates that $\underline{R}$ decreases with decreasing in $\bar{U}$: the more the creditor can punish the debtor, the higher repayment is. In practice, the level of $\bar{U}$ depends on the creditor's capacity to foreclose on the debtor's meagre assets, to ban the debtor from employment on the creditor's farm or business, or to prohibit the debtor from purchasing goods from the creditor's store. To be effective, these threats must be credible, that is, punishment must be in the ex post interest of the creditor. Punishments such as a ban from employment on the creditor's farm or from purchase from the creditor's shop may not satisfy this requirement: after all, it is against an employer's interest to refuse workers (this may raise wages or search costs for other workers) and against a shopkeeper's interest to turn down customers (this is likely to reduce profits). Even if punishment is ex post costly for the creditor, however, it may still be in his or her interest to punish a faulty debtor if this serves to maintain a reputation for toughness and thus helps discipline other debtors (see Kreps et al. (1982) for a formalization of this idea). By the same reasoning, a creditor with numerous debtors may further lower their $\bar{U}$ by hiring thugs and using strong-arm tactics (Crow and Murshid 1994).

In order for debt peonage to persist over time, the nominal value of the debt D_t must be sufficiently high to ensure that what is owed to the creditor always exceeds $\pi_t - b_t - U^{-1}(\bar{U})$, that:

$$D_t \geq Sup\{\pi_t(s_t) - b_t(s_t) - U^{-1}(\bar{U})\} \equiv \bar{D} \qquad (3.47)$$

If inequality (3.47) is not satisfied at all t, the debt will eventually be repaid with probability one.[43] Since $\pi_t - b_t$ is stochastic, equation (3.47) implies that nominal debt is higher than expected repayment, that is, $D_t > E_{t-1}[R_t]$.[44] The fastest way for creditors to raise D_t above $\bar{D}$ is by charging a high interest rate and, if possible, late payment charges and fees. Once D_t has been raised above $\bar{D}$, the creditor can credibly extract all the surplus above $\bar{U}$ without further raising D_t; once permanent debt peonage is achieved, the creditor may even afford the luxury of appearing magnanimous by forgiving the part of the debt that exceeds $\bar{D}$.

As is clear from the above, allowing usury in an environment character-ized by widespread poverty and risk is bound to lead to debt peonage and thus the virtual enslavement of many. Societies may be fearful of the social tensions and resentment thus created and may seek to avoid the polariza-tion of society implied by debt peonage. The historical prohibition of usury both by the Catholic Church and Islam should probably be interpreted in this light. Such prohibitions, however, are inherently difficult to enforce. To see why, note that the maximum amount $\bar{R}$ that an individual can borrow is an increasing function of the nominal interest rate r charged by the cred-itor – at least up to the point where $(1+r)\,\bar{R} = \bar{D}$. For any interest rate $r < \bar{D}/\bar{R} - 1$, expected repayment is below $\bar{D}$: there are some advantageous states of nature under which the debtor does not repay all the difference between $\pi_t - b_t$ and $\underline{R}$. Let the function $R(r)$ denote this relationship, with $R(r) \leq \bar{R}$.

Now suppose that an individual is faced with a large shock such that $U(\pi_t - b_t) < \bar{U}$: his or her survival is at stake. Let r_n denote the socially acceptable (non-usury) rate of interest. If:

$$U(\pi_t - b_t + R(r_n)) < \bar{U} \tag{3.48}$$

but

$$U(\pi_t - b_t + \bar{R}) \geq \bar{U} \tag{3.49}$$

the individual will voluntarily accept a usurious loan contract. In this case, debtors willingly borrow at usurious interest rates and the socially accept-able rate of interest cannot be enforced. This example illustrates that the prohibition of usury must be accompanied by social insurance pro-grammes to be viable.

3.3.7 Sharing Risk Across Village Boundaries

So far we have discussed arrangements by which risk can be explicitly shared within the boundaries of the rural community. There also exist insti-tutions that enable villagers to share risk with the rest of the world. One such strategy is to seek the patronage of village residents who are connected to the rest of the world, such as merchants, aristocrats, or civil servants tem-porarily posted in the village. Udry (1990), for instance, points out that much quasi-credit in the villages he studied in Northern Nigeria is given out by Hausa merchants who use their outside contacts to raise funds. For Gambia, Nwuke (1998) reports that credit transactions are as likely to occur across village boundaries as within the village. Similar mechanisms are described in Watts (1983) and Crow and Murshid (1994). The individuals these authors describe can then be seen as intermediaries in the sharing of risk across village boundaries. The provision of such risk intermediation services can be an important source of social clout and political power.

Another strategy to share risk over space is simply to send village members away and ask them to help support their friends and relatives who remain in the village. Temporary and permanent labour migrations out of poor rural areas of the Third World are an extremely common and persistent phenomenon. Migrant workers go mostly to cities, mines, and plantations. Some of them move across international boundaries as well. Discussing labour migrations in detail is beyond the scope of this book but it is important to acknowledge that, in many poor rural communities, remittances from migrant workers constitute an essential part of rural incomes (for example Lucas and Stark 1985, Stark and Lucas 1988, Alderman and Garcia 1993, Adams and He 1995). Rosenzweig and Stark (1989) have argued that marriages follow a pattern similar to that of labour migrations and that the geographical matching of brides and grooms is partly motivated by income diversification motives.

Whether remittances explicitly serve the role of insurance remains an unresolved issue. Although in some cases remittances respond to shocks affecting the recipient family (Lucas and Stark 1985), in other cases they do not (Fafchamps and Lund 2003). Whether or not remittances are modulated in response to shocks should not, however, distract from the fact that remittance transfers are often essential to the survival of the recipient family. Given the cost of communicating with migrants and the difficulties and risks of transferring money across space in most Third World countries, it may be more efficient for recipients to leave the timing of remittances to the discretion of migrants and to invest at least part of the remittance money in precautionary forms of saving (Alderman and Garcia 1993). Pensions paid to retired workers, soldiers, and war veterans belong essentially to the same category as remittances, except that they are delayed wage payments that may last long after the migrant has returned to the village. In South Africa, survival in many of the former so-called bantoustans revolved primarily around remittances and pensions.

The provision of modern health services is another important form of insurance that typically involves risk sharing across village boundaries. By itself, the delivery of modern medical services to rural areas is a form of insurance since it reduces fluctuations in welfare. To see why, let utility be written $U(\pi_t, h_t)$ where π_t is monetary income and h_t is the health status of the household, itself a function of random health shocks. Normalize h_t such that 0 stands for good health. Define $b(h_t)$ as the equivalent variation associated with health status h_t, that is:

$$U(\pi_t - b(h_t), 0) \equiv U(\pi_t, h_t) \tag{3.50}$$

Function $b(h_t)$ represents the household's willingness to pay to avoid imperfect health h_t.

Suppose that, thanks to technological innovation in medicine, the health status of the household can be protected at cost $c(h_t)$. If $c(h_t) < b(h_t)$, it is in the interest of the household to incur the health cost and preserve its good health status. We have:

$$U(\pi_t, 0) \geq U(\pi_t - c(h_t), 0) > U(\pi_t, h_t) \tag{3.51}$$

Equation (3.51) shows that purchasing the health service raises the household's utility and reduces the incidence of health risk on its welfare. A contrario, if $c(h_t) > b(h_t)$, the cost of the cure is too high to justify the expense. On average, therefore, we have:

$$EU(\pi_t - \min[c(h_t), b(h_t)]) \geq EU(\pi_t - b(h_t)) \tag{3.52}$$

Voluntary purchase of health services raises welfare by reducing the incidence of health risk. Together with equation (3.51), equation (3.52) indicates that the reduction in the effect of health risk on welfare achieved via health services is a decreasing function of health cost $c(h_t)$. At the limit, if health cost is 0 for all h_t, then expected utility is $EU(\pi_t, 0)$: health risk is eliminated.

In many countries, modern health services often seek to provide health cost insurance and to redistribute welfare in addition to the health service itself. Health cost insurance can easily be added to our framework as follows. Consider a full coverage insurance scheme and let m be a constant premium such that the health insurance scheme breaks even on average, that is, such that $m = Ec(h_t)$. Clearly:

$$EU(\pi_t - m, 0) \geq EU(\pi_t - c(h_t), 0) \tag{3.53}$$

with strict inequality if the function U is concave, that is, if the household is risk averse. Health cost insurance raises welfare. In practice, it may not be optimal – or even feasible – to eliminate health risk altogether. Among poor rural populations, expensive treatments such as AZT, CAT scans, and the like are seldom cost effective in the sense that $c(h_t) > b(h_t)$. Given the choice among various insurance contracts, the rural poor are therefore likely to opt for cheaper plans that do not cover expensive treatments. These concerns are reflected in the health cost insurance plans put in place in many developing countries (Gertler et al. 1987): instead of the uncapped health insurance plans with deductibles that are encountered in most developed countries, many poor countries have opted for insurance schemes that fully pay for health care up to a certain amount, beyond which coverage stops. This approach can be a cost-effective way of providing health insurance to the poor.

Health insurance schemes often include a redistributive dimension as well, in the sense that the premium paid by some individuals i is smaller than their anticipated use of the service, that is, that $m_i < E[c(h_{i,t})]$. Of course, to break even, a redistributive scheme must collect higher premia from other individuals. In practice, evaluating the redistributive effect of health insurance schemes is complicated by the fact that many public schemes are financed by taxes, and that effective redistribution depends on the geographical distribution of health facilities and on the allocation of public funds among different types of health services (Gertler and Strum 1997). These issues are beyond the scope of this study.

Another important form of insurance available to poor rural communities is assistance from national governments and the international community (Barrett 2002). National relief organizations and NGOs have long sought to minimize the incidence of catastrophic risk such as earthquakes, hurricanes, avalanches, floods, droughts, locusts, and refugee crises. International assistance is also often provided to help governments deal with particularly acute crises – or to substitute for governments when their action is impeded by warfare or lack of funds. Prevention and protection against certain aspects of catastrophic risk are part of the mandates of several United Nations agencies, such as the UNHCR and the FAO.

However important these organizations are, evidence suggests that their effect on target populations remains small and that assistance does not always reach the neediest (Barrett 2002). For instance, Reardon et al. (1988) and Reardon et al. (1992) show that during the 1984 drought in Burkina Faso, international aid accounted for a very small proportion of the total transfers received by surveyed households. Furthermore, the geographical distribution of aid did not correspond to the welfare incidence of the drought: of six surveyed villages, the two that were worst hit received less aid than two others which were less affected. The difficulties inherent in identifying households most in need of assistance are further compounded by logistical problems. Delivering international aid to those in need is indeed often problematic because local infrastructure is not geared up to channeling large amounts of food to remote rural areas. Delivery can also be hindered by warfare and complicated by erratic movements of refugee populations. These problems are well known and need not be discussed in detail here.

Recently, new forms of explicit risk sharing contracts have been made available to the poor. These market-based interventions aim to offer hedging instruments to poor farmers in the Third World. Pioneered by the Commodity Risk Management team of the World Bank, this approach currently seeks to retail to individual producers standard price hedging instruments routinely available to international commodity traders. If successful, similar hedging contracts could be instigated to insure against weather risk or other calamities (Skees et al. 2002).

External interventions and market alternatives can potentially weaken informal risk sharing among villagers and along networks. Albarran and Atanasio (2002b), for instance, report that public transfers under the Progressa programme in Mexico crowd out private transfers. Foster and Rosenzweig (2000) similarly find that rural banks make saving easier and hence reduce the need for mutual insurance, thereby weakening informal risk sharing arrangements. Similar results are reported by Cox and Jimenez (1992) regarding social security payments in Peru and by Cox et al. (1996) in the Philippines. Crowding out is also discussed in Altonji et al. (1996) for the US.

3.4 ALLOCATION OF SCARCE RESOURCES WITHIN THE HOUSEHOLD

Whenever the risk coping strategies discussed thus far do not shelter households from the effect of risk, unpleasant choices must be made regarding the allocation of scarce resources among household members. These choices are but a reflection of the absence of better options.

3.4.1 Extreme Deprivation and Selective Mortality

When resources are extremely scarce in the sense that the survival of all household members cannot be achieved, equitable division of resources among members is inefficient. To see why, suppose that the resources π_t of a household with M members are smaller than $M\underline{c}$ where $\underline{c}$ is the minimum level of consumption to ensure survival. Equal distribution of resources means that all members would starve, since $\pi_t/M < \underline{c}$. In this case, it is clearly optimal to concentrate the available resources on certain members. As a result, one would expect mortality to be selective whenever households are subject to extreme deprivation.

Efficiency further dictates that the members of the household selected for survival should be those whose income generating potential is highest. Doing so maximizes the chances that, once the crisis that led to extreme deprivation is over, the household will be able to sustain itself. Straight application of this principle implies higher mortality among those that are otherwise unable to feed or provide for themselves. For instance, it makes little sense for a famine-stricken family to feed small children and starve adults: surviving small children could not take care of themselves once their parents are dead. By the same token, the sick, the elderly, and the disabled are low priorities for survival if resources are extremely scarce. These cruel principles are largely in line with evidence of higher mortality among young children and old people during famines (Sen 1981). These harsh realities often leave their mark on culture and tradition.[45]

3.4.2   Gender and Nutrition Gap

Efficiency considerations may similarly dictate an allocation of scarce nutrition and health resources that favours certain members of the household. For instance, it is customary in many rural societies for male adults to eat first.[46] Nutrition data similarly suggest the widespread existence of a nutrition gap in favour of males among poor communities (Strauss et al. 1993).

One possible interpretation for the priority given to adult males is that it reflects the traditional dichotomy between the productive roles of men and the reproductive roles of women. Suppose children are regarded by poor households as investments in the future. The reproductive role of women implies that female nutrition is an input in the production of children: better fed women are more likely to have healthy babies and to breast-feed them effectively (Thomas et al. 1990). Negative income shocks lower the household's willingness to invest, and hence the need to invest in female nutrition. A similar result is obtained if, at extremely low levels of income, children are regarded as luxury consumption goods. In both cases, very low entitlements result in neglected child nutrition and health and a simultaneous decrease in female nutrition.

3.4.3   School Dropouts

If low incomes can lead households to neglect child nutrition, then certainly it can induce them to withdraw kids from school in hard times. Jacoby and Skoufias (1997) and Sawada (1997) have shown that rural households are more likely to withdraw children from school not only when they are chronically poor but also when they are hit by a negative transitory income shock. The effect is particularly marked for girls. They are similarly less likely to enroll children in school. The magnitude of the transitory income shock effect is inconsistent with the certainty equivalence model, suggesting that households withdraw children from school because they are unable to smooth shocks by liquidating assets or borrowing from other villagers. Imperfect insurance thus lowers investment in human capital and has effects on long-term income distribution and on a country's capacity to innovate and modernize. These issues are revisited in Chapter Six.

4. The limits to risk coping

We have reviewed in great detail a variety of individual and collective strategies on which poor rural households rely to cope with risk. These strategies do not always work, however. In this chapter we examine some of the factors that render particular strategies ineffective. Evidence regarding the most serious constraints is also discussed.

4.1 THE LIMITS TO SELF-PROTECTION

4.1.1 Technological and Environmental Constraints

Technological and environmental constraints put limits on households' ability to reduce their exposure to risk. Income diversification may be impractical either because returns to alternative activities are too low to warrant investing in them, or because increasing returns call for specialization. Millet in the Sahel is a good example of a case in which environmental constraints limit the options open to rural households. After centuries of informal breeding by Sahelian farmers, millet has developed into an incredibly sturdy plant capable of growing extremely fast on precious little moisture and soil nutrients. Thanks to millet, African farmers have pushed the limits of cultivation further into the Sahara desert than was thought possible. The corollary of this success, however, is that no other plant can compete with millet, let alone beat it. As a result, the monoculture of millet is the norm in much of the Sahel (Matlon and Fafchamps 1989). Similar reasoning explains why drought or trypanosogmiasis resistant livestock breeds are the only ones encountered in drought or trypanosomiasis prone areas.

Pastoralism is a good illustration of a situation in which income diversification is traded off for returns to specialization. Pastoralism refers to specialized livestock raising based on long-range migrations of animals and herders (for example Smith 1975, Lovejoy 1979, Cossins 1983, Livingstone 1984). It is encountered in many semi-arid areas of the world (for example Monod 1975, Sandford 1983, Nugent and Sanchez 1989, Nugent and Sanchez 1993). Erratic rainfall both over time and over space means that animals must be moved over extremely large areas for livestock production to be feasible, let alone profitable. The need to be constantly on the move precludes most other activities or, at least, renders them costly. In practice, the thirst for income diversification is often so compelling that many pastoralists engage in some form of cultivation in spite of the high costs involved, namely, the separation of families over long periods of time (for example Monod 1975, Sandford 1983).

Flexibility is another risk reducing strategy that is subject to technological and environmental limitations. For instance, to grow grain, seeds must be planted. Once planted, they can no longer be eaten, even if rains fail and yield is zero. The extent to which precious resources must be sunk before income can be generated limits households' willingness to risk these resources. This issue is formalized in Fafchamps (1993) who shows that flexibility is lowest in dry areas because the extremely short nature of the rainy season precludes crop diversification and reduces the scope for replanting. Such concerns are often behind farmers' reluctance to adopt technologies and crop varieties that lock them into strict patterns and limit their capacity to adjust to shocks as they unfold.

By the same token, activities that require a large up-front investment reduce households' capacity to deal with shocks ex post through asset liquidation, even though they may reduce risk itself. This issue is examined in detail by Fafchamps and Pender (1997) who show that Indian households' desire to keep some liquidities reduces their willingness to invest in non-divisible risk reducing irrigation technology. To show this formally, let X_t denote cash in hand, that is, $X_t = W_t + y_t(W_t)$ where W_t is the agent's liquid wealth at the beginning of period t and $y_t(W_t)$ is the agent's realized income, which includes return to liquid wealth. Agents have access to two i.i.d. income streams with probability distributions $F(y; \tau_0)$ and $F(y; \tau_1)$ with the second stochastically dominating the first; any risk averse agent prefers the second distribution. However, moving from the first income distribution to the second requires a sunk investment k. The Belman equation after the investment has been made is:

$$V_1(X_t) = \max_{W_{t+1}} U(X_t - W_{t+1}) + \beta \int_0^\infty V_1(W_{t+1} + \tilde{y}_{t+1}(W_{t+1}))dF(\tilde{y}_{t+1}; \tau_1) \quad (4.1)$$

where $U(.)$ is the agent's instantaneous utility function and $V_1(.)$ is the agent's value function after having undertaken the irreversible investment k. Before making the investment, the agent's Belman equation is:

$$V_0(X_t) = \max\{V_0^1(X_t), V_0^0(X_t)\} \quad (4.2)$$

where $V_0^1(X_t)$ is the value of investing:

$$V_0^1(X_t) = \max_{W_{t+1}} U(X_t - k - W_{t+1}) + \beta \int_0^\infty V_1(W_{t+1} + \tilde{y}_{t+1}(W_{t+1}))dF(\tilde{y}_{t+1}; \tau_1)$$

(4.3)

and $V_0^0(X_t)$ is the value of not investing:

$$V_0^0(X_t) = \max_{W_{t+1}} U(X_t - W_{t+1}) + \beta \int_0^\infty V_0(W_{t+1} + \tilde{y}_{t+1}(W_{t+1}))dF(\tilde{y}_{t+1}; \tau_0) \quad (4.4)$$

The agent invests if $V_0^1 \geq V_0^0$.

Fafchamps and Pender (1997) show that agents with a precautionary motive for saving may want to hold liquid balances immediately after the investment is made. In other words, they may not want to spend all their liquid assets, which they keep in part to deal with emergencies, to cover the sunk cost of even a profitable investment. The rationale behind this result is easy to understand: an agent who has frozen all his assets into a single irreversible investment cannot self-insure against life's contingencies.

4.1.2   Property Rights and Asset Markets

In the preceding chapter we argued that individuals may liquidate assets in order to deal with shocks. For this approach to be feasible, individuals must have well defined and adequately protected property rights on these assets. This need not be the case. In much of Sub-Saharan Africa, for instance, land tenure systems provide fairly secure usufruct rights to farmers but prohibit land sales (for example Atwood 1990, Platteau 2000a). As a result, farming households cannot liquidate land to deal with shocks. In India, although a land market exists, very few transactions take place and creditors hesitate before foreclosing on farmers' land. Although the absence of fully individualized land rights has been accused of resulting in inefficient allocation of resources (for example Feder and Onchan 1987, Gavian and Fafchamps 1996), it may be understood as an effort to minimize the long-term divergence in incomes that Zimmerman (1993) has shown is associated with fully active land markets. In other words, laws and customs restricting land sales probably illustrate a society's effort to maintain social cohesion and preserve equality in the long run. They may also result from a desire to bar outsiders from acquiring land in the community. Restrictions on land sales need not imply less capacity to cope with risk if risk sharing institutions are provided that substitute for individual accumulation.

For similar reasons, societies may discourage labour bonding through the interdiction of slavery. Refusing to recognize and protect the property rights of slave owners significantly lowers their expected gain from labour bonding. Consider, for instance, the fate of an individual who discounts the future with discount factor delta and has voluntarily entered into an indenture contract. The contract stipulates a constant but low level of consumption $\underline{c}$ forever.[47] The bonded labourer's expected discounted utility is thus $U(\underline{c})/(1-\delta)$.

Now suppose that if the bonded labourer were to renegue on the contract, he or she would get an income π_t that evolves over time according to the following process:

$$\pi_{t+1} = \rho\pi_t + \varepsilon_{t+1} \qquad (4.5)$$

where ε is an i.i.d. shock. When the property rights of slave owners are protected by law, there is a good chance that runaway slaves will eventually be returned to their owners, probably after a good beating. In this case, running away is unlikely to be an attractive option. If slavery is illegal, however, labour bonding must be entirely self-enforcing. This in general lowers the value of bonded labourers. To see why, assume for notational simplicity that a runaway bonded labourer consumes π_t every period; his or her discounted expected future utility is thus:

$$W(\pi_t) \equiv E_t\left[\sum_{s=1}^{\infty} \delta^s U(\pi_{t+s})\right] \qquad (4.6)$$

It is clear that, as long as $\rho > 0$, $W(\pi_t)$ is an increasing function of current income π_t: high income today is correlated with high income tomorrow, and thus with high expected discounted future income.

A labourer voluntarily abides by the indenture contract as long as $U(\pi_t) + W(\pi_t) \leq U(\underline{c})/(1-\delta)$, that is, as long as the expected utility the labourer can get on his or her own is lower than what is guaranteed by the contract. If, however, $U(\pi_t) + W(\pi_t) > U(\underline{c})/(1-\delta)$, it is in the interest of the labourer to renegue on the contract. Let $\varepsilon^*(\pi_{t-1})$ be the level of ε_t such that:

$$U(\rho\pi_{t-1} + \varepsilon_t) + W(\rho\pi_{t-1} + \varepsilon_t) = \frac{U(\underline{c})}{1-\delta} \qquad (4.7)$$

For any ε_t larger than $\varepsilon^*(\pi_{t-1})$, the bonded labourer renegues on the contract. The probability of breach of contract β_t is thus $\int_{\varepsilon^*(\pi_{t-1})} dF(\varepsilon)$. Since ε^* is a decreasing function of π_{t-1}, this probability is increasing in π_{t-1}. It is clear that the probability of losing runaway slaves reduces the value of the labour bonding contract to the slave owner relative to a situation in which their property rights over slaves are externally enforced. This probability is highest when the external options of candidate bonded labourers are attractive, that is, when π_{t-1} is high, and when the chance is high that a bonded labourer will experience a shock high enough to induce breach, that is, when the variance of ε_t is high. Voluntary labour bonding is thus more likely to arise when the labour market is characterized by significant monopsony power and self-employment is unattractive.

A similar reasoning indicates that debt peonage is less attractive for lenders if usurious interest rates are prohibited by law. Indeed, it implies that it takes longer for debt to build up and thus that lenders cannot as easily enlist the assistance of the courts to seize the assets of a debtor who seeks to escape debt slavery. Usurious interest rates may still be practised, but they must then be self-enforcing: debt peons will service their debt as long as the minimum stable consumption that is guaranteed to them by the patron/lender provides them with an expected discounted utility higher than $U(\pi_t) + W(\pi_t)$. Otherwise, it is optimal for them to breach the contract. An immediate corollary is that lenders will lend less if usurious interest rates are outlawed.

We shall revisit these issues when we discuss self-enforcing risk sharing contracts and quasi-credit. What we wish to emphasize here is that the liquidation of productive assets to deal with shocks is an option that requires the existence of alienable property rights on these assets. This is not saying that allowing usury or slavery would be better for society because they result in more efficient risk sharing. It goes without saying that a minimum level of equality is in the social welfare function of many societies – as well as that of the international community – and that allocations of resources which involve slavery, usury, and high levels of land concentration are undesirable. Many societies de facto discourage distress sales of land and future labour, undoubtedly to minimize their negative social consequences. The point of this discussion is rather that, if equity objectives are to be achieved in a sustainable manner, one must take into account the natural tendency for desperate people to propose their future labour and earnings as guarantee against distress borrowing. Similarly, to achieve an equitable distribution of land, it is not sufficient to redistribute it; one must also ensure that land concentration does not re-emerge as a result of distress sales. Without a proper safety net for the poor, laudable efforts to eliminate particularly scandalous symptoms of destitution are likely to fail.

4.1.3   The Difficulties of Precautionary Saving

Households' efforts to insulate themselves against risk by accumulating assets on which they have well defined property rights are also subject to numerous constraints. The paucity of savings instruments makes it difficult and costly for them to accumulate precautionary balances. Consider, for instance, poor impatient households for whom precautionary saving is an essential risk coping strategy. As Deaton (1991) has shown, these households will save even if the return to liquid assets is negative. The reason is that their motive for saving is not to take advantage of financial opportunities but rather to set up a buffer stock that helps them smooth consumption and deal with emergencies. If the only available liquid asset has a negative return, poor households may choose to hold it anyway as a hedge against risk.

The willingness of the poor to hold assets with low or negative returns opens the door to numerous abuses. When cash balances constitute an essential part of the poor's liquid assets,'as suggested by Lim and Townsend (1998), inflation is a major tax on their meagre savings. This has potentially devastating effects on the poor's capacity to save and hedge against risk (McKinnon 1973). Rural populations fortunate enough to be located close to a bank have been shown to make an intensive use of savings and deposit accounts (Behrman et al. 1997). Rates of return offered on financial savings instruments accessible to the poor are very low in most developing countries – as well as in many developed countries. Fafchamps et al. (1995), for instance, indicate for Zimbabwe that rates of return in 1994 were around 18 per cent for savings account and around 36 per cent for money market accounts; during the same period, annual inflation reverted around 25 per cent. The example shows that small investors were receiving a negative real return on their savings while large investors with access to the money market were receiving a positive real return.

In response to the paucity of savings instruments for the poor, alternative institutions have emerged that serve their savings needs. Some of these institutions, such as rotating and savings associations (ROSCAs) have attracted a lot of attention in the recent literature (for example Besley et al. 1993, Besley and Levenson 1996, van den Brink and Chavas 1997). In their simplest form, ROSCAs are financial contracts by which a group of people pledge to periodically contribute a fixed amount to a rotating fund which is allocated to each member in turn. As Besley and Levenson (1996) have shown, this arrangement enables participants to save faster, on average, than they could on their own. Furthermore, the obligation to contribute periodically to the fund imposes a discipline on small investors that they find hard to impose on themselves. It also helps them shelter funds from competing demands by friends and relatives. ROSCAs have the added advantage of reducing the incidence of the inflation tax that investors must bear: since cash balances are not held by the group but allocated to one member and spent immediately, the group does not hold cash balances for any length of time.[48] More complicated arrangements enable participants to bid for the collected fund, thereby introducing an interest rate element into the contract.

In spite of the attention they have received, ROSCAs are probably less important for the rural poor than is often assumed. The obligation to make fixed periodic payments is ill-suited to households whose income is highly seasonal and subject to the vagaries of the weather. ROSCAs seem most popular among market traders, for whom it is a way of protecting working capital from competing consumption demands, and among salaried workers, for whom it is a way of speeding up consumer durable expenditures. ROSCAs are also rare among urban enterprises, except perhaps among small trade firms (for example Fafchamps et al. 1994, Fafchamps et al. 1995).

There are many other institutions catering to the savings needs of the poor. Many of them are discussed in Steel et al. (1997). Savings contract offered, for instance, by Ghanaian *susu* collectors resemble ROSCAs in that fixed periodic payments are stipulated, to be returned in bulk to the client at the end of a set number of payments. The only difference is that the contract is passed with an individual who takes a commission, instead of a group. Savings cooperatives are another type of institution catering to the saving needs of the poor, albeit in a somewhat more formal manner. Participants in savings cooperatives can often borrow on their own funds and those of their friends, thereby enhancing the self-insurance role of such funds. Unfortunately, prudential regulations in many developing countries are either too lax or go unenforced. As a result, many savings cooperatives turn into pyramid schemes that defraud small investors (Steel et al. 1997). In general there remains a dearth of safe and convenient savings instruments for the poor.

Whenever saving in formal or informal financial institutions is not feasible, the rural poor must save in real assets. Saving in real instead of financial assets is subject to a substantial price risk that is compounded by the poor integration of agricultural markets. Fafchamps and Gavian (1996), for instance, show that livestock markets in Niger are poorly integrated over space. The same is true for many grain markets (for example Ravallion 1986, Dercon 1995, Baulch 1997b). As a result, farmers are less able than often thought to use real assets to smooth large income shocks such as droughts. Fafchamps et al. (1998), for instance, show that Burkinabe households that were badly hit by the 1984 drought managed to absorb less than 20 per cent of their income shortfall through livestock sales. This occurred in spite of the fact that the large majority of surveyed households still held livestock after the drought. Results such as these cast serious doubt on the effectiveness of asset accumulation to deal with large weather shocks.

4.2 RISK SHARING, SELF-INTEREST, AND COMMITMENT FAILURE

We have seen that income diversification and precautionary saving are fraught with problems. Risk sharing is not devoid of difficulties either. The main reason is commitment failure.

4.2.1 Mutual Insurance with Limited Commitment

Solidarity mechanisms exist in many rural communities of the Third World. Yet in most cases, there is no formal authority to enforce them. In the past, as Posner (1981) emphasized, 'primitive' societies managed to sustain a significant degree of mutual insurance despite a weak central authority or no government at all (for example Evans-Pritchard 1940, Gluckman 1955, Colson 1962). Today, traditional local authorities, wherever they exist, have seen their power eroded by colonial governments and centralized post-colonial states. Moreover modern courts are unable to enforce mutual insurance arrangements. Indeed, such arrangements are too informal in nature. Their terms remain incompletely specified and respect for contractual obligations is extremely difficult to verify for anyone who is not party to the mutual insurance contract.

If the non-respect for mutual insurance obligations cannot be penalized by an independent court or authority, how can risk pooling be sustained? Consider the following example. Say N people agree before the agricultural season that they will pool crop output. Each promises that, in case she gets high yields, she will transfer some of her output to others. In the absence of sanction for breach of promise, however, those who actually get high yields realize ex post that it is in their advantage not to share. Thus a one shot insurance contract has no risk pooling equilibrium. (Except for non-credible promises), its unique Nash equilibrium is autarchy.

This outcome is but another illustration of the prisoners' dilemma: all realize that they can benefit from cooperation, yet all find opportunistic behaviour in their short-term interest. The theory of infinitely repeated games has shown, however, that cooperation can be supported if people are allowed to interact over a long period of time. The reason is that future periods can be used to reward cooperation and penalize opportunistic behaviour. People who breach their promise can be punished by being treated less well afterwards. The mutual insurance agreement becomes self-enforcing: it is based on voluntary participation, not on coercion.

Consider the same example in which people promise to pool crop output after harvest. This time, however, they also specify that whoever fails to respect her promise will be punished in subsequent periods. In principle, since participation in the mutual insurance scheme is purely voluntary, people could withdraw to avoid the punishment. But as long as the utility they get with the punishment is higher than what they get if they withdraw, they voluntarily accept the punishment. Consequently, the maximal punishment someone would voluntarily incur must have an expected discounted payoff that is just above the autarchy payoff.[49] Such punishment is self-enforcing and thus constitutes a credible threat. By the optimal penal code argument (Abreu 1988), a strategy profile can then be constructed specifying a cooperative path and minmax punishments for each participant. Given these punishments, people find it in their long run interest to remain on the cooperative path, that is, to give part of their crop output to others in order to avoid being punished (for example Kimball 1988, Coate and Ravallion 1993).

As Abreu (1988) has shown, more cooperation can be supported with harsher punishments. Thus, the more likely people are to starve if left to their own devices, the harsher punishment can be imposed for breach of promise, and the more mutual insurance can be achieved. When people are poor and idiosyncratic risk is important, mutual insurance significantly reduces the chance of starvation and dramatically raises people's expected utility. Consequently, solidarity mechanisms should emerge quite naturally in societies that are vulnerable to starvation and in which idiosyncratic risk is large.[50] Economic prosperity, on the other hand, undermines solidarity to the extent that it reduces individual risk of starvation. Casual empiricism confirms that informal solidarity is much stronger among the poor of this world than among the rich.

At first glance, the large number of possible equilibria that repeated games can support seems a problem. When one considers the wide variety of solidarity institutions described in the anthropology literature (e.g. Posner 1980, Platteau 1991), however, the indeterminacy of the theory turns out to be an advantage. Indeed, it is able to account for different solidarity systems springing from similar conditions. The process whereby a particular system is picked by a given society is path dependent. Since some form of negotiation is involved, the choice of solidarity arrangement is likely to be influenced by the political system of the society in question. Furthermore, symbolic representations and ethical values provide focal points – 'fair' contracts – that guide the search for an equilibrium. The end result is somewhat arbitrary. This is reflected in practice by the fact that symbolic claims (such as religion, magic powers, and superior ethnicity or caste, and so on) are often used to define social arrangements. Section 4.3 sheds a limited light on this issue, but elements of an answer as to how an equilibrium is chosen mostly lie in the political anthropology literature.

At this juncture, the reader may wonder whether the use of the theory of infinitely repeated games is warranted when it is clear that participants in a mutual insurance agreement are finitely lived. Participants, however, do not know with certainty when the contract ends, that is, when they will die. As long as, at any point in time, there remains a positive probability of survival, the formal structure of the infinitely repeated game can be preserved.[51] Nevertheless, as players get old, their probability of survival decreases. This has several consequences.[52]

Theoretically, old people may reckon that they have little time left and decide to enjoy life while it lasts. This is extremely unlikely to induce old people to neglect their solidarity obligations, however. Indeed, as they age, people become increasingly dependent on others' help and goodwill. Furthermore, the stigma associated with antisocial behaviour is likely to be transmitted to descendants. Since old people are usually taken care of by their descendants, passing onto them a poor solidarity record means endangering one's own welfare in old age.

On the other hand, younger people as a group may realize that they would benefit if old people were to be dropped from the mutual insurance system.[53] Indeed, old people are likely to be net recipients of assistance. Since their probability of survival is small, their threat to retaliate if neglected by refusing help to young people does not have much bite. The danger of young people abandoning the old is thus far more serious than that of old people neglecting their solidarity obligations.[54]

This may explain why 'primitive' and other pre-industrial societies try to compensate by granting the old a lot of political and economic power. In Sub-Saharan Africa, for instance, the clash between the old and the young has long been part of the socio-political landscape.[55] The economic power of the elders is largely based on their indirect control of their descendants' labour through direct authority over land and livestock. This partly explains why having many children is so important for most people. Old people without children are neglected unless they have the chance of finding truly altruistic help.

4.2.2 Social Insurance

We now illustrate more formally the constraints imposed on risk sharing by commitment failure. Mutual insurance is Pareto improving whenever agents are risk averse and risk is at least partly idiosyncratic. Consequently, there exist mutual insurance contracts to which agents would voluntarily agree ex ante. In other words, if $U_i(.)$ is concave and $\pi_{i,t}(s_t)$ varies across individuals, then there exist a set of contingent promises $\tau_i(s_t)$ such that:

$$EU_i(\pi_{i,t}(s_t) - b_{i,t}(s_t) + \tau_i(s_t)) \geq EU_i(\pi_{i,t}(s_t) - b_{i,t}(s_t)) \forall i \qquad (4.8)$$

with $\Sigma_i \tau_i(s_t) = 0$ for all t and s_t. Although agreeing to contract $\tau_i(s_t)$ is always individual optimal ex ante, it is never in agents' *short-term* self-interest to respect the contract whenever $\tau_i(s_t) < 0$, that is, when they are asked to assist others. Of course, if nobody ever helps others ex post, there is commitment failure: mutual insurance is not achieved and the outcome is socially sub-optimal. The question then is: what mechanism can be used to ensure that commitment failure is avoided and Pareto gains are achieved? We review three types of systems that can potentially overcome commitment failure: social insurance; family values; and long -term relationships.

Mutual insurance agreements can in principle be enforced by an external agency such as a system of laws and courts. External enforcement is indeed the rule for the multitude of mutual insurance programmes that constitute the welfare system of advanced countries. In fact, many of these countries have opted for compulsory insurance systems whereby agents' contributions are collected in the form of taxes instead of voluntary purchase of insurance contracts. A compulsory system offers the advantage of avoiding the adverse selection problem common to all insurance: agents who face a lower risk may find it cheaper to self-insure, thereby undermining the financial viability of the mutual insurance arrangement.

Poor rural communities often have compulsory arrangements as well. They mostly take the form of forced labour contributions to the provision of public goods and the constitution of welfare funds managed by the village chief or the community elders. As any form of taxation, forced labour contributions or *corvée* labour can be diverted by powerful individuals to serve their individual interests. Accusations of abuse, whether justified or not, tend to undermine the legitimacy of *corvée* labour and other social insurance institutions, and hence to raise popular resistance to taxation.

Although it is difficult to calculate how effective social insurance institutions are, observations from the field suggest that traditional social insurance systems are moribund in many rural areas of the Third World (Platteau 1991). Household surveys, for instance, hardly ever report any significant activity associated with explicit social insurance systems, such as *corvée* labour (Cleave, 1974). Other forms of labour assistance appear similarly obsolete. Using detailed labour data from Burkina Faso, Matlon and Fafchamps (1989), for instance, show that invitation labour and labour gangs, two institutions that partly serve the role of labour assistance, account only for minute amounts of labour provided by rural households. Rural sociologists and anthropologists similarly report that, in much of the Third World, social institutions meant to explicitly share risk are essentially either non-existent or devoid of content (for example Scott 1976, Popkin 1979, Poewe 1989).[56]

An alternative form of semi-formal social insurance is the reliance on charity to support the poor. Although charity can, in principle, be based on humanism and altruistic feelings towards fellow men, in practice it is often based on religious obligation. Religious taxes such as *zakat* are examples of such obligations. For social obligations originating in formal institutions and contracts, the legal use of force offers an ultimate recourse against recalcitrant individuals and thus serves as an enforcement mechanism. Religious obligations are seldom enforced in this manner. Social pressure and individual guilt are used instead. Guilt is itself nurtured through religious and family education. Although these enforcement processes are hardly formal in nature, they are activated by formally organized groups and they serve to fund social programmes that are controlled by these same groups, at least partially.

Not all religions are equally active on the social insurance front.[57] Whatever the reason for the progression of different religions among Third World populations, the fact remains that churches have taken over many social responsibilities. The emphasis on social insurance is strongest among certain Muslim brotherhoods and among evangelical churches, a factor that appears behind their recent success in making new Sub-Saharan and Latin American converts.[58] Poewe (1989), for instance, views evangelical churches in rural Zambia as a way for households to recreate traditional institutions of social insurance that had fallen into disregard. She argues that the rise of evangelical churches further undermines traditional values as new converts opt out of traditional sharing mechanisms and turn to their new 'family' instead.[59] Geertz et al. (1979) and Cohen (1969) give similar examples of the role of Muslim religious authorities in enforcing cooperation among traders.

Just like traditional institutions, religious organizations can be perverted to serve the interests of a few. Ellsworth (1989), for instance, tells the fascinating story of a Muslim holy man living in a Burkinabe village. Ellsworth traces all the gifts and transfers taking place among villagers and notices that the holy man is at the centre of a dense network of gifts. Many of these gifts are presented by villagers as charitable contributions to the holy man's social programmes. Ellsworth then notes that, although the holy man himself has very few assets, redistributes all he gets, and ostentatiously lives in a very poor house, his brother with whom he spends most of his time is quite rich and is a main recipient of the holy man's largesse. Although the brothers retain only a small portion of the money collected and quite a bit of redistribution takes place through them, the story nevertheless serves as a cautionary tale against putting too much faith in organized social insurance in a Third World rural setting.

4.2.3 Family Values

Another way for individuals to commit to sharing risk with others is by teaming up with them (Ben-Porath 1980). Marriage is such a commitment mechanism. In all societies, marriage creates an extremely strong set of contractual obligations between two people, arguably stronger than any other contract. In Western law, for instance, husband and wife owe each other help and assistance. The obligation to support a spouse in need extends beyond the dissolution of marriage, as evidenced by the practice of alimony payments. Many poor rural societies replace alimony by asset transfers but the rationale is the same: by marrying each other, two individuals incur mutual assistance obligations from which they cannot escape even upon dissolution of their union. In many cases, these obligations even carry over after death: the estate of the deceased is often obligated to assist the surviving spouse. Unless their nuptial agreement stipulates otherwise, husband and wife also often share upside risk through common ownership of assets and inheritance laws. Given the extraordinary nature of marriage obligations, it is no surprise that weddings are highly ritualized and widely celebrated affairs the world over.[60]

Parenthood is another source of mutual assistance obligation that is legally binding: in many societies, children are legally entitled to receive support from their legal parents. Although there are variations across human societies, such as in the relative hereditary rights of male and female children, it is a generally recognized *legal* principle that parents must take care of their progeny. Like marriage, parenthood obligations carry over after death or upon separation. For instance, in many legal systems it is unlawful for parents to fully disinherit their children. In Western law, children are entitled to child support from parents who have not been granted custody or even visitation rights. Similar principles can be found elsewhere.

Granting legal protection to mutual obligations within the family does not, however, guarantee that these obligations are always respected. For instance, there are circumstances such as warfare and civil strife in which legal institutions cease to function. In these cases, legal protection cannot be granted to abandoned spouses and children. Even if legal institutions are functioning, legally forcing individuals to take care of their dependants is not always easy. For instance, people may move to escape their obligations. Many poor countries lack an efficient individual identification system such as an identity card, so that it is extremely difficult to trace someone who has skipped town. Even if the person can be found, forcing them to pay is itself problematic. Poor rural dwellers have few assets that could possibly be seized, and seizing them may be counterproductive: taking away a weaver's loom will not help the weaver meet his family obligations in the future.

Unlike in developed economies, the rural poor are mostly self-employed, and if they work for a wage, it is as casual workers. Consequently, child and spouse support payments cannot be collected directly from employers. Finally, even if the person can be traced and legal obligations enforced, the protection offered by the law is not instantaneous.

Given these limitations on the legal enforcement of contracts, it is hardly surprising that family obligations are not always met. Descriptions of famines are replete with accounts of split families and abandoned children. Greenough (1982), pp. 215–25, for instance, cites examples of nuclear households breaking up during famines. Similar evidence is reported by Alamgir (1980), pp. 133–5 and 179. The 1984 Ethiopian famine, for instance, is said to have generated 100000 'orphans', many of whom were in fact separated from their parents. Similar developments could be observed in the wake of the Rwandan refugee crisis. It would be unfair to treat all separation as voluntary. After all, as Sen (1981) demonstrated, emergency work migration by able bodied males is a common risk coping strategy. The extent to which families become separated during famines is, however, a cause for concern. It shows that, when households are subjected to inordinate stress, they often fail to perform their risk sharing function.

Households also fail and separate for reasons that have nothing to do with famines, warfare, and other collective crises: for example, death, infertility, and incompatibility. When households split, the ability of their former members to deal with risk is often greatly diminished. Less able to deal with shocks, they also tend to be poorer. Studies of homeless populations, for instance, often indicate a strong correlation between dysfunctional families, risk, and destitution. Similar patterns can be found in poor rural areas. Household surveys, for example, often show that women living alone, because their husband is either dead or has left them, are systematically poorer than households in which both husband and wife are present. These examples confirm, in absentia, the important role of family in dealing with risk.

4.2.4 Informal Risk Sharing Arrangements

There are ways to minimize commitment failure other than recourse to social institutions or the legal system. One is for individuals to enter into long-term informal relationships with each other. To the extent that such relationships contain an implicit obligation to reciprocate – such as 'I am willing to help you today because I expect you to help me later' – the desire to preserve the relationship becomes its own enforcement mechanism (for example Posner 1980, Platteau 1991). Such relationship-based informal risk sharing arrangements or IRSAs are the focus of the rest of this section.

IRSAs were first formalized by Kimball (1988) and Coate and Ravallion (1993). Both use repeated games to demonstrate that an implicit agreement to share risk can be sustained through repeated interaction and thus that promises to assist others can be self-enforcing. Their argument can be generalized as follows. Consider an exchange economy in which output cannot be stored, assets cannot be accumulated, and there is no borrowing and lending from the rest of the world. People derive utility from what they consume $U_i(c_s^i)$, and at least some people are risk averse, i.e., $U_i'' < 0$ for some i's. Let $\delta \in (0, 1)$ be a common discount factor and let Q denote a sequence of action profiles or *path* of the economy. Define $\omega_i(Q)$ as agent i's discounted expected payoff along that path, that is:

$$\omega_i(Q) \equiv \sum_{t=0}^{\infty} \delta^t\, EU_i(\pi_{s,t}^i - \tau_{s,t}^i(Q))$$

where the $\tau_{s,t}^i(Q)$ refer to actual transfers at the end of each period t dictated by action profiles Q.

Following Abreu (1988), $N + 1$ strategy profiles are sufficient to span the complete set of equilibrium payoffs of this economy: one cooperative risk sharing strategy profile denoted Q^0, and one punishment strategy profile Q^k for each of the $k \in \{1, \ldots, N\}$ agents. Agents play according to Q^0 as long as nobody deviates, and switch to Q^i following a defection by agent i either to the initial path Q^0 or to any of the punishment paths Q^k. Abreu (1988) showed that, provided punishments Q^k are the harshest that can be credibly inflicted on deviant agents, adding other more complex strategies cannot expand the set of equilibrium payoffs – and thus the extent of risk sharing. Voluntary participation in informal risk sharing implies that agents cannot be maintained below the expected payoff they could guarantee themselves by exiting the risk sharing group. Since autarchy is the Nash equilibrium of the one-shot game, autarchy payoffs serve as maximum punishments:[61]

$$\omega_k(Q^k) = \frac{EU_k(\pi_s^k)}{1 - \delta} \text{ for } k \in \{1, \ldots, N\}$$

Along the equilibrium path Q^0, net transfers between agents depend not only on their own realized income but also on that of all other agents. This imposes high informational requirements as agents must monitor each other's income to spot defections (for example Fafchamps 1992b, Ligon 1998). One therefore expects IRSAs to be more prevalent among tightly knit communities where information circulates freely, such as fishing communities where the catch of the day is commonly observed, and farming communities where yields can be visually estimated by all (for example Platteau and Baland 1989, Platteau 1991).

As is well known, the set of subgame perfect equilibria of a repeated game is very large (Fudenberg and Maskin 1986). IRSAs are no exception. Kimball (1988) and Coate and Ravallion (1993) get rid of the multiplicity of equilibria by positing that a social planner picks the allocation that maximizes the unweighted sum of individual utilities subject to participation constraints. In practice, the choice of an equilibrium is likely to depend on bargaining within the risk sharing group. Bargaining power probably depends on the threat point of each member but also on their negotiating skills, ethical considerations, past experience, altruism, and ideology, as well as on the group's polity. The interplay of these factors makes the outcome hard to predict. There is no reason to believe all bargaining processes converge to the allocation picked by Kimball and Coate and Ravallion's social planner. Much can nevertheless be said about IRSAs by looking at the *set* of equilibria itself and studying how its boundary evolves as conditions change. This is the approach adopted here.

The set of equilibrium payoffs is comprised between the Pareto efficient frontier and a set of voluntary participation (VP) constraints which must be satisfied along any equilibrium path *after* the realization of *s*:

$$U_i(\pi^i_{s',t}) - U_i(\pi^i_{s',t} - \tau^i_{s',t}(Q^k)) \leq \delta\omega_i(Q^k) - \delta\omega_i(Q^i) + A_i \qquad (4.9)$$

for all $s' \in S$ and all $k = 0,1, ..., N$. Participation constraints require that, for any realization of the state of nature s', the short-run gain from deviation $U_i(\pi^i_{s',t}) - U_i(\pi^i_{s',t} - \tau^i_{s',t}(Q^k))$ must be smaller than the discounted long-run again from cooperation $\delta(\omega_i(Q^k) - \omega_i(Q^i))$. It is clear from equation (4.9) that VP constraints are never binding when $\tau^i_{s',t}(Q^k) \leq 0$. Voluntary participation is problematic only when Q^k requires an agent to help others.

Ligon et al. (2001) estimate a risk sharing model that includes a voluntary participation constraint using data from rural India and compare it with alternative models of perfect risk sharing or complete autarchy. They conclude that the limited commitment model best fits the data. Foster and Rosenzweig (2001) and Dubois et al. (2002) provide similar evidence in South Asia. Albarran and Atanasio (2002a) seek to test the existence of a voluntary participation constraint using data from Mexico. They similarly conclude that the data do not reject the presence of such constraints.

Many social scientists have argued that reciprocity is often reinforced by an ideology or culture that emphasizes the right to subsistence and the corresponding moral obligation to assist someone in need (for example Scott 1976, Brocheux 1983, Feeny 1983, Keyes 1983). To reflect this view, we have added the term $A_i \geq 0$ to capture the subjective satisfaction agents may derive from 'doing the right thing'. Alternatively, $-A_i$ can represent the guilt people may feel for reneguing on their promises. Social sanctions other than exclusion from risk sharing – such as exclusion from other forms of social interaction, shunning – are included in A_i.

The emphasis that most traditional Third World cultures put on solidarity has led some to believe that participants in mutual insurance arrangements are solely motivated by altruistic feelings and ethical principles. This view has been severely criticized by Popkin (1979) and others as much too naive. There is plenty of evidence that self-interest motivates behaviour in traditional as well as modern societies (for particularly colourful examples, see, for instance, Poewe's (1989) account of kinship in Zambia). Ethics and well understood self-interest need not be conflictual, however (Posner 1980). As equation (4.9) illustrates, they are largely complementary: VP constraints are easier to satisfy and more efficiency in risk sharing can be achieved when A_i is large, that is, when agents are altruistic or feel guilty for letting others down. This can easily be shown formally. Let $\Omega(A)$ be the set of subgame perfect equilibrium payoffs corresponding to a particular value of A for all $i \in N$. Then we have:

Proposition 4.1 *Suppose $A^1 \leq A^2$. Then $\Omega(A^1) \subseteq \Omega(A^2)$.*

Since affection is the primary source of altruism, Proposition 4.1 implies that risk sharing is expected to be strongest among members of the same family or lineage and among friends and neighbours (for example Ben-Porath 1980, Foster and Rosenzweig 1995, Ambec 1998). Altruism within the family has been studied extensively and need not be revisited here (for example Becker 1981, Cox 1987, Hayashi et al. 1991, Altonji et al. 1992, Hayashi 1995, Stark 1995, Cox et al. 1996, Hayashi et al. 1996, Altonji et al. 1997, Cox et al. 1998, Raut and Tran 2000, Stark and Falk 2000, Diaz and Echevarria 2002, Feinerman and Seiler 2002). Religious fervour also creates strong bonds between groups of converts and can serve as the basis for much mutual insurance and charity. Furthermore, the altruistic desire to help others and the ability to feel guilty for failing to do so can be cultivated through education and enhanced through personal interaction (for example Platteau 1994a, Platteau 1994b, Platteau 2000b). For all these reasons, it is not surprising that Third World communities often describe IRSAs in emotional or moralistic terms. Altruism alone, however, may be insufficient to support much risk sharing (for example Lucas and Stark 1985, Cox 1987, Altonji et al. 1992). In the remainder of this section we seek to understand when altruism and ethics are most put to the test by studying the extent to which self-interest can, on its own, support risk sharing.

4.2.5. Gifts and Risk Sharing

We begin our analysis of commitment failure in long term relationships by focusing on gifts. Formally, this means that we temporarily restrict our attention to 'stationary' strategies, that is, to strategies that depend only upon the current state of nature s, not on past transfers. Strategies are affected by the past history of play only inasmuch as defection and punishments are concerned. In this case, VP constraints take a simpler form:

$$U_i(\pi^i_{s'}) - U_i(\pi^i_{s'} - \tau^i_{s'}) \leq \frac{\delta}{1 - \delta} E[U_i(\pi^i_s - \tau^i_s) - U_i(\pi^i_s)] + A_i \qquad (4.10)$$

VP constraints (4.10) impose serious restrictions on IRSAs that can account for a number of stylized facts about gifts and risk sharing that cannot easily be accounted for in models exclusively based on altruism (for example Becker 1981, Cox 1987, Ravallion and Dearden 1988, Laferrere 2000). First of all, self-interested risk sharing cannot be supported when agents are impatient or when they do not expect to interact for long, that is, when δ is low. This is a well known property of repeated games (Fudenberg and Maskin 1986). An implication is that risk sharing based on long-term relationships is more difficult to sustain among highly mobile populations, such as urban migrants (see, for instance, Hart (1988) for evidence in Ghana). The shape of the equilibrium payoff set for various values of δ is shown in Figure 4.1.[62] The figure illustrates the well known result that the set of equilibria of a repeated game shrinks as agents get more impatient.

By pooling the resources of agents with different income streams, risk sharing can in principle redistribute incomes from agents with high average incomes to those with a low average income. Such redistribution is achieved by granting to the poor a larger share of the welfare gains from risk sharing. In this case, solidarity not only reduces temporary poverty; it also palliates chronic poverty. Self-interest, however, puts limits on redistribution that are particularly stringent if agents are impatient:

Proposition 4.2 *As δ decreases; gains from risk sharing must be shared more equally.*

Proposition 4.2, which is illustrated in Figure 4.1, implies that a redistribution of welfare is harder to achieve in communities with a short time horizon because all participants, rich and poor, then insist on receiving an equal share of the welfare gain from mutual insurance.

It has been observed that IRSAs occasionally 'break down' during famines in the sense that people most in need fail to receive assistance. Sen

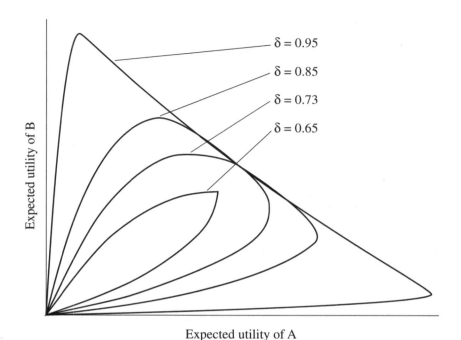

$\delta = 0.95$

$\delta = 0.85$

$\delta = 0.73$

$\delta = 0.65$

Expected utility of A

Figure 4.1   Risk sharing and impatience

(1981), for instance, notes that during the Ethiopian famine of 1974 many domestic servants were laid off by their employer even though it was clear that they would starve. The absence of risk sharing in bad times is difficult to reconcile with altruism but it can be explained by self-interest considerations (for example Altonji et al. 1992, Altonji et al. 1997, Hayashi et al. 1996). As Coate and Ravallion (1993) have shown, the discount factor required to induce an agent to share risk goes up as the income of others goes down: the lower the income of others, the harder it is to ensure voluntary income pooling. If the limited contribution that a relatively fortunate agent is willing to make is insufficient to keep others from severe hardship, then the IRSA will appear to break down.

Efficiency gains from risk sharing increase with risk and with aversion toward risk (Arrow 1971). One would therefore expect risk sharing to be more prominent when incomes are more variable and agents are more risk averse. Kimball (1988) and Coate and Ravallion (1993) indeed present simulation results in which risk sharing increases with risk and aversion toward risk. It is, however, possible to come up with examples in which the reverse is true, as illustrated in the following proposition:

Proposition 4.3 *Take any stationary IRSA in which some efficiency gains from risk sharing are realized (A1). Suppose that there exist at least one binding participation constraint for one agent, say agent i. Then:*

1. *Provided certain technical assumptions are satisfied (see proof), there exists a concave transformation of the utility function of agent i such that the participation constraint is violated.*
2. *Let N be the number of participants to the IRSA and let S be the number of possible states of the world. Then, if S ≥ 2N + 2, there exists a mean preserving spread in risk such that agent i's participation constraint is violated.*

The proof of proposition 4.3, given in the Appendix to this book, is built on the realization that two opposite forces are at work in any IRSA: an increase in risk or risk aversion raises the gains from risk sharing, thereby raising the right hand side of the VP constraints (3). But it may also increase the subjective cost of sharing risk $U_i(\pi_{s',t}^i) - U_i(\pi_{s',t}^i - \tau_{s',t}^i(Q^0))$, particularly if helping others entails one's immediate starvation.[63] Depending on the net effect of these two forces, the set of sustainable equilibria may shrink or expand. Proposition 4.3 thus helps explain why risk sharing often appears limited or non-existent among the extremely poor and the destitute. It also suggests that a reduction in average group income and an increase in income variability, for instance, because of increased population pressure or of environmental degradation, may undermine an existing IRSA.

4.2.6 Exclusion and Renegotiation

So far we have assumed that the IRSA is supported by the threat of exclusion: an agent who refuses to cooperate is excluded from the risk sharing group. This threat is not entirely credible, however, because refusing to share risk with a deviant agent penalizes the group as well. This is most easily seen in a two-person relationship: if A breaches B's trust, B should punish A by refusing to share risk with A, but doing so hurts B as well. Consequently, A could convince B to show forgiveness. By extension, we see that if the solidarity pool is small, losing one of its members means that it is less able to spread risk. Consequently, the pool is willing to renegotiate the mutual insurance contract and forgive the deviant for his or her defection. Of course, if participants anticipate that punishments will never be enforced, cooperation itself is not self-enforcing and risk sharing will not be attained. This is, in a few words, the argument made by Pearce (1987), Farrell and Maskin (1989), and Abreu et al. (1993).

It is possible, however, to find punishment paths that are renegotiation-proof. But because they are less harsh, the amount of cooperation that they can support is reduced. The idea is to build punishment paths that do not penalize non-deviant participants, that is, punishments that they wish to enforce.[64] In that case, deviants will not be able to renegotiate themselves out of their own punishment. In terms of a mutual insurance contract, it means that exclusion from the solidarity pool, even temporarily, is not a renegotiation-proof punishment path. On the other hand, fines are a form of punishment that is (weakly) renegotiation-proof. Indeed, suppose that the payment of fines is made contingent upon the state of nature: high income realizations for the punished participant result in large fines; but low income realizations still trigger assistance from the solidarity pool. Obviously, non-deviants benefit from the fines while continuing to share risk with the punished participant. Consequently they cannot be swayed away from the punishment path. From the point of view of the punished person, the payment of fines in good states of nature may still be preferable to withdrawal because protection against starvation remains provided.

To illustrate these ideas formally, we show that IRSAs can survive ex post renegotiation provided that some limits are placed on the gains that excluded agents can achieve through renegotiation. This is, for instance, the case if we require that strategies be weakly renegotiation-proof in the sense of Farrell and Maskin (1989). According to this definition, a strategy is weakly renegotiation-proof if, among its possible continuation equilibria, none strictly Pareto dominates another. This requirement ensures that non-deviant agents are not penalized along punishment paths.[65]

A simple example of weakly renegotiation-proof equilibrium is one in which deviant agents continue to share risk with the group but have to pay a (possibly contingent) fine for T periods. To illustrate how such an equilibrium can be constructed, let p_s^I stand for a vector of contingent punishment transfers that follow a defection by agent i. Along i's punishment path, the transfer rule p_s^I is followed for T_I periods, after which agents revert to the cooperative stationary rule τ_s. Then we have:

Proposition 4.4   *The strategy profile* $(\tau_s, p_s^I, \ldots, p_s^N)$ *is subgame perfect and weakly renegotiation-proof if there exist* T_I *such that, for all* $i \in N$ *and all* $s \in S$:

$$U_i(\pi_{s'}^i) - U_i(\pi_{s'}^i + \tau_s^i) \leq \sum_{t=1}^{T_I} \delta^t E[U_i(\pi_s^i + \tau_s^i) - U_i(\pi_s^i + p_s^{Ii})] \quad (4.11)$$

$$U_i(\pi_{s'}^i) - U_i(\pi_{s'}^i + p_s^{Ii}) \leq \delta^{T_I} E[U_i(\pi_s^i + \tau_s^i) - U_i(\pi_s^i + p_s^{Ii})] \quad (4.12)$$

$$U_i(\pi_{s'}^i) - U_i(\pi_{s'}^i + p_s^{Ji}) \leq \sum_{t=1}^{T_J} \delta^t E[U_i(\pi_s^i + \tau_s^i) - U_i(\pi_s^i + p_s^{Ii})] \quad (4.13)$$

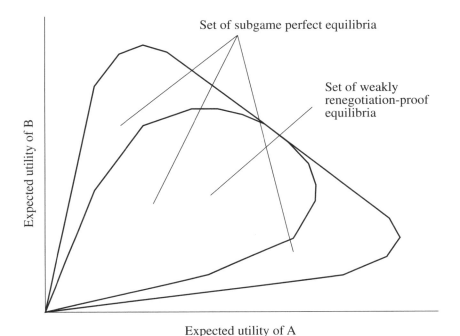

Figure 4.2   Renegotiation-proof equilibria

$$E[U_i(\pi_s^i + p_s^{Ji}) - U_i(\pi_s^i + \tau_s^i)] \geq 0 \qquad (4.14)$$

The set of weakly renegotiation-proof equilibria is illustrated in Figure 4.2.[66] Renegotiation-proofness shrinks the set of equilibrium payoffs but does not eliminate the possibility of risk sharing if agents are sufficiently patient. Asking that an IRSA be renegotiation-proof thus adds an element of realism: punishments never rely on complete exclusion and they must remain limited in time. Punished agents are requested to pay a fine that itself is contingent upon the state of nature. In practice, fines may take the form of additional requests for gifts and loans from the group. Other members of the group may also invite themselves to the table of the deviant agent, a simple but effective way of penalizing misbehaviour.

Anthropological accounts suggest that complete exclusion from the village community is rare and considered quite extreme, but there is little direct evidence on this issue.[67] Posner's (1980) review of tort law among primitive societies, however, provides convincing indirect evidence (see also Evans-Pritchard (1940), pp. 152–64). In particular, Posner emphasizes that compensation (that is, fines) are the preferred remedy for wrongdoing. Moreover, liability is strict in the sense that it punishes 'the mere act of injuring or killing another regardless of the state of mind of the injurer or the care he took to try to avoid the injury' (p. 48). In other words, compensation is due irrespective of intent. If the worst possible transgression to the duties of mutual assistance – murder – is punished by the transfer of a few cows to the lineage of the deceased, then surely minor deviations from mutual insurance obligations can similarly be dealt with. Reliance on various signals to trigger solidarity claims can also be viewed as an indirect way of punishing deviations. For instance, ostentatious consumption immediately attracts neighbours and friends who invite themselves to your table and present incessant requests for 'loans'. Failure to comply is met with anger and resentment. Such forced transfers can be viewed as fines that sanction an attempt to circumvent mutual insurance obligations.

4.3 SHARING AND POWER

IRSAs are often perceived as being fundamentally egalitarian. The idea that pre-capitalist societies are fair and equal goes back to Rousseau's 'good savage' parable. Radical thinkers have sometimes pushed this idea so far as to suggest that, thanks to IRSAs, Third World rural communities behave like village communes. The romanticized portrayal of IRSAs, especially when it is used to justify radical political options, is what motivated Popkin (1979) to expose opportunistic behaviour among Third World rural communities. The model presented here throws light on this debate.

On the side of the idealists, IRSAs have redistributive power. First, risk sharing is by definition redistributive: it takes away from those who currently have and gives to those who currently have not. Second, gifts are a non-market allocation mechanism. This has led some to believe that IRSAs are not bound by the initial distribution of endowments – that is, income streams. Third, IRSAs cultivate a solidarity ethic that can be interpreted as a favourable disposition toward redistribution. Provided that ethics and ideology are strong enough, IRSAs can potentially support Pareto efficient allocations that are more egalitarian than the initial distribution of income streams.

On the side of the sceptics, participation in IRSAs is voluntary. Even after accounting for ethics and ideology, individuals are unlikely to willingly part with a large proportion of their hard earned income without receiving something in exchange. This places considerable restrictions on the amount of redistribution that can be achieved through IRSAs. These restrictions are the focus of the following pages. We first examine the role of wealth accumulation and discuss how self-insurance via savings affects the willingness to participate in mutual insurance. We then discuss risk sharing between rich and poor agents and demonstrate that it naturally takes the form of a patron-client relationship. We then illustrate how certain individuals may derive bargaining power from unusual risk characteristics, and hence capture welfare gains from risk sharing.

4.3.1 Individual Wealth Accumulation

We have seen that individual wealth accumulation – precautionary saving – can serve as self-insurance against risk. From a theoretical point of view, wealth accumulation introduces a non-stationary element in the repeated nature of the risk sharing game. Though strictly speaking the theory of repeated games is no longer applicable, the intuition one gains from it remains a valuable source of inspiration. Self-enforcement remains the central question: is it possible to reconcile individual wealth with the self-enforcing character of solidarity? We suggest some elements of an answer.

Intuitively, accumulated wealth constitutes both a curse and a blessing for the mutual insurance system. First of all, it provides protection against many sources of risk, including collective risks like drought, war, and locusts; mutual insurance protects only against idiosyncratic risk. Accumulated wealth thus offers a form of protection that mutual insurance cannot substitute for. People with accumulated wealth are the only ones who can provide that kind of insurance. Their participation in the mutual insurance system enables it to operate also as a mechanism of intertemporal consumption smoothing. Consequently, it is in the interest of solidarity group to allow – and possibly encourage – wealth accumulation. This does not mean, however, that wealth accumulation may be encouraged in all circumstances. In particular, allowing people to accumulate wealth while others starve violates the fundamental objective of the solidarity system, which is to minimize the risk of starvation. Limits or conditions to individual wealth accumulation may thus be imposed to ensure, in the words of Scott, the right to subsistence.

There is another, more fundamental difficulty, namely: the necessity to preserve the self-enforcing character of the solidarity arrangement. Indeed, people with high realized income may be tempted to evade their solidarity obligations and instead accumulate their surplus income as individual protection against starvation.[68] Those with sufficient accumulated wealth may even defect entirely from the mutual insurance system, taking away with them what amounts to the intertemporal insurance fund of the solidarity group. How can defection be prevented in the presence of individual wealth accumulation? One possible way is to base solidarity contributions on wealth instead of current income. Addressing solidarity claims to wealthy people would 'cream off' the top wealth and hopefully prevent people from accumulating enough to escape the system. Unfortunately, creaming off top wealth has serious disincentive effects on effort. Is there a way to prevent defection without discouraging effort? Many societies seem to have found a solution to this problem, namely, granting wealthy individuals preferential treatment. To this we now turn.

4.3.2   Patron-Client Relationships

Patron-client relationships are a formal way of organizing the compensation of wealthy individuals for their continued participation in the solidarity system (for example Mair 1962, Scott 1976, Watts 1983, Basu 1986, Ellsworth 1989, Platteau 1995a, Platteau 1995b). In practice, such relationships take a variety of forms, but they can schematically be described as follows. Say there are two people, one rich, one poor. The rich person promises to help the poor in times of hardship, and in particular to insure the poor person against starvation. Since the rich person has little to gain from a risk pooling arrangement with the poor, the poor person has to reciprocate in some other way. Repeated small gifts are thus made: religious contributions, gifts to the chief, payment for metaphysical services, and so on.[69] Since the rich person often has a need for additional manpower, labour is also provided, sometimes as a form of labour insurance whereby the client is at his patron's 'beck and call'. Finally, because of the patron's ability to take advantage of economic opportunities, useful information is channeled to him. Arbitraging possibilities and other good bargains are reported by the client, as well as whatever reinforces his or her patron's economic, political and social standing.

The protection against starvation guaranteed by the patron's wealth significantly improves the expected utility of his client(s). Yet, over time, transfers of labour help the rich get richer and may lead to the concentration of wealth in their hands. For instance, household surveys in Sub-Saharan Africa often show that livestock, an essential store of wealth, is distributed very unevenly across rural households.[70] The ability of wealthier individuals to turn the mutual insurance system into an instrument of 'exploitation' – that is, of extraction of surplus – is the compensation they receive for continued participation in that system. Even though the poor may find that patrons are exploiting them, they may value security enough to accept it. Indeed, without clientelism, either solidarity would collapse altogether; or it could only survive by banning wealth accumulation[71] and therefore offering no protection against collective risk.

Clientelism can easily be accommodated within the solidarity network.

Wealthy people, because they are a source of insurance against collective risk, are very desirable to befriend. Consequently, patrons are likely to be better 'connected', and to sit at the top of a pyramid of interpersonal relationships.[72] In those circumstances, it is possible for the mutual insurance network to simplify into a single star-shaped arrangement, whereby all members of the network are connected only to the patron, and all insurance transfers coordinated by him. When that happens, the position of the patron is obviously reinforced: not only is the patron the only source of insurance against collective risk, he is also the only source of mutual insurance. More research is needed to ascertain the conditions under which centralized network patterns are likely to emerge.

To summarize, patron-client relationships provide an incentive for wealth accumulation while preserving insurance against starvation in a self-enforcing manner. In these circumstances, the ability to help others in need becomes a source of prestige and power. Social mobility takes the form of competition for clients. Lavish expenditures, public display of wealth, and prodigal assistance to the poor may simply be temporary instruments to wrest clients away from their current patron (Posner (1980), pp. 14–15). Finally, given the close ties between insurance and wealth, patrons' wealth in a sense is held for the benefit of their clients. It is not really theirs to dispense at will, and attempts to do so are likely to be met with disapproval or even revolt.[73]

The question we now ask here is whether patronage is redistributive or exploitative, that is, whether it raises or lowers the average consumption of the poor. Let us define an IRSA $\{\tau_s^i\}$ as actuarially fair for agent i if $E[\tau_s^i] = 0$ for that agent. An actuarially fair IRSA has no effect on average consumption and thus is neither redistributive nor exploitative. Decompose income π_s^i into average income x_i and an income shock e_s^i with $E[e_s^i] = 0$ for all i. Then we can show that risk sharing between rich and poor is likely to be exploitative:

Proposition 4.5 *Assume that absolute risk aversion is decreasing (A4) and tends to 0 as $x \to \bar{x} \leq \infty$ (A5). Then, unless $\tau_s^i = 0$ for all s, there exists a x^* such that, for all $x^i \geq x^*$, an actuarially fair τ_s^i violates at least one of agent i's participation constraints.*

The intuition behind proposition 4.5 is that, because of decreasing absolute risk aversion, the willingness to pay for insurance – and thus the value of any IRSA – decreases with average income x. As a result, agents that are rich enough cannot be convinced to participate voluntarily in an IRSA unless they are compensated in a way other than insurance itself. Instead of being redistributive, the IRSA must become 'exploitative': on average, it takes away from the poor and gives to the rich. Inequality in incomes is not eliminated by informal risk sharing, it is reinforced.

In practice, the poor are typically unable to make large payments to the rich. They can nevertheless buy protection in exchange for small but frequent services such as small gifts, prompt labour services (at the landlord's 'beck and call'), transfer of useful information, and provision of political support (for example Platteau 1991, Platteau 1995a, Platteau 1995b). Asymmetry in incomes thus translates into a patron-client relationship. Studies of peasant revolts indicates that 'exploitation' remains reluctantly accepted as long as landlords and rural elites continue to provide insurance and protection. Revolts arise when the rural rich move to cities and maintain the machinery of exploitation but withdraw their patronage (for example Scott 1976, Watts 1983).

Ironically for the idealist view of IRSAs, participation constraints generate more inequality than would result from market transactions, not less. To see why, suppose that a market for insurance did exist, that is, that risk sharing contracts were perfectly enforceable and did not have to be self-enforcing. Rich agents would accept any insurance contract that would guarantees them at least as much utility as they could get on their own. Agents rich enough to be (approximately) risk neutral with respect to small risks would accept any mutual insurance contract that yields a non-negative profit, that is, such that:

$$E[\tau_s^i] \leq 0 \qquad (4.15)$$

By contrast, the VP constraint for a risk neutral agent requires that:

$$E[\tau_s^i] \leq -\frac{1-\delta}{\delta}\tau_s^i \, \forall s \qquad (4.16)$$

Comparing equations (4.15) and (4.16), the rich require less compensation to share risk with the poor in the presence of perfect insurance markets than if risk sharing is achieved informally.[74] The reason is that IRSAs must be self-enforcing: the rich must accept parting with their money *after* the state of nature is known. To do so, they must see their future participation in the IRSA as at least as beneficial as the money they have to give away today. In contrast, market exchange only requires that parties find it in their advantage to transact ex ante, before the state of nature is known. Since, by definition, market transactions prevent ex post defection, extra incentives need not be provided to ensure compliance.

Equation (4.16) indicates that the expected size of future transfers is what determines the rich's immediate willingness to help the poor. If what the poor can pay on average is negligible, little insurance is provided.

Individuals with a limited ability to generate income – such as the disabled, the old, the permanently sick, orphans, widows – may thus find it difficult to get insurance through an IRSA. They may have to rely solely on altruism and ethics and live off charity. In this respect, IRSAs are fundamentally different from market economies. In both cases private incentives fail to promote social protection for vulnerable segments of society. But agents in a market economy can protect themselves against disease, disability, old age, or loss of a spouse by purchasing individual insurance beforehand. This option is not open to IRSA participants. They must rely either on others' altruism, or on their capacity to reciprocate in the future. VP constraints thus illustrate the difficulty IRSA participants may face in buying implicit insurance against, say, permanent disability through pure gift giving.

An immediate corollary of the above discussion is that if, for ideological or ethical reasons, society rejects patronage, then the rich will choose to opt out of the system and refuse to insure others. Hoff (1996) examines this situation in detail and shows that, when risk sharing is required to be actuarially fair, the size of the risk sharing group shrinks as income inequality increases. Platteau (1996, 2000b) takes this approach one step further and argues that, in many cases, the rich cannot escape the risk sharing group and its redistributive logic. Individuals who dare to invest, take risk, and innovate do not, therefore, collect the full return on their investment. As a result, Platteau argues, the risk sharing ethics stifles investment and entrepreneurship. We shall revisit these issues in subsequent chapters.

4.3.3   Power and Coalitions

The existence of asymmetries in wealth and the ensuing emergence of clientelism polarizes the solidarity network. The outcome is likely to be the emergence of a centre (or centres) and a periphery – insiders and outsiders (Popkin (1979), p. 26). People found at the periphery are of various types. Old people without descendants and widows without children often survive with great difficulty at the margin of the solidarity system. Recent settlers belonging to different ethnic groups are treated as 'outsiders'.[75] Merchants and civil servants also remain at the edge of the village solidarity network, preferring to rely on their own extra-village networks.[76]

The centre (or centres) are usually occupied by 'traditional' authorities – village chief, marabou, religious leader, traditional healer – as well as by more recent contenders – cadre, head of the cooperative, store keeper, miller, teacher. Centres are responsible for representing their community to the rest of the world. In case of a drought, for instance, it is the centre's duty to call the attention of the regional authorities and to attract as much food aid as possible. In other words, the centre is relied upon to insert itself into a regional or national solidarity network.

Since the centre is so important for the solidarity system as a whole, efforts to remove it based on the perception that it is 'feudal' and exploitative are bound to fail. The current centre may be physically eliminated, but the solidarity system will by its own internal logic strive to replace it (Bardhan (1984), pp. 176–7). The new centre may take another form – religious leader instead of traditional chief, cadre instead of landlord – but it will reappear as long as the real reasons for its emergence – that is, the need for insurance based on accumulated wealth – still exist.

To investigate these issues more in detail, we examine what happens to voluntary risk sharing if agents can form sub-coalitions. So far, equilibrium paths have been required to be individually rational: in other words it must be against the interest of any single participant in the social contract to defect. Among such equilibrium paths, however, there are situations in which a sub-group (or coalition) of participants could improve its collective welfare by withdrawing and creating its own mutual insurance arrangement. For instance, suppose that a member of the solidarity pool gets handicapped by age, disease or accident. It is of course not in his or her interest to defect. But the rest of the pool members could probably be better off without him or her.

The emergence of a mutual insurance arrangement suppose that individuals recognize that efficiency gains can be made from cooperation and negotiate a social contract in order to achieve them. If a large group of people is assumed able to define a social contract, then a fortiori one would expect smaller groups of individuals to recognize the gains they can jointly make by defecting. Consequently, equilibria should be eliminated in which sub-groups can improve their situation by jointly defecting and recreating smaller risk sharing arrangements. Call the remaining equilibria coalition-proof.

Imposing coalition-proofness seriously reduces efficiency. Consider again the above example. Ex ante, all members of the solidarity pool have some probability of becoming handicapped. Thus, all prefer a social contract that provides insurance against such risk. Yet, if coalitions form freely and costlessly, they also know that if anyone becomes handicapped, others will renegotiate a solidarity agreement exclusively among themselves. Therefore, protection will not be provided against disability, old age, and other permanent reductions of anyone's usefulness to the risk pool.[77] Whether, in practice, such coalitions can be prevented remains an open question. Obviously, the political and legal system will to a great extent impede or favour the formation of particular coalitions, and not all coalitions are equally likely to emerge.[78] Coalition-proofness raises, however, important issues and may help explain some of the features of societies in which solidarity plays an essential role. In particular, gerontocratic power structures may reflect old people's intrinsic fear of being deserted.

We now investigate these issues more formally. We assume that agents can form coalitions and threaten to split from the group and create their own IRSA (for example Bernheim et al. 1987, Bernheim and Peleg 1987). Suppose IRSA participants are free to form any coalition they want. Coalitions of agents can credibly oppose equilibria that grant their members a payoff vector strictly inferior to what they could get by forming a separate IRSA. To prevent the formation of blocking coalitions, IRSA participants must therefore be guaranteed a payoff vector that is at least as good as what they could get by splitting from the group and forming their separate IRSA. An equilibrium path that has this property is called coalition-proof.[79]

Coalition-proof equilibria are illustrated in Figures 4.3 and 4.4 in a three-person IRSA. Consider Figure 4.3 first. The set of equilibrium payoffs for each of the two-person IRSAs are presented in each quadrant. Their Pareto frontiers are given by segments AB, CD and EF respectively for agents 1 and 2, 1 and 3, and 2 and 3. Form the closed convex set $OPABQO$ by projecting the extremum points of the Pareto efficient

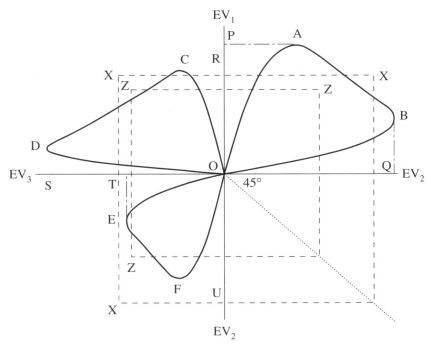

Figure 4.3   Coalition-proof equilibria

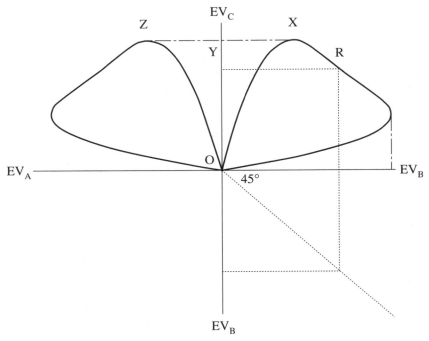

Figure 4.4   Coalitions and asymmetry

frontiers to the axes in the first quadrant. Repeat the same operation in the other quadrants to get the closed convex sets *ORCDSO* and *OTEFUO*. A three-person payoff vector is coalition-proof if it lies outside and weakly above the three convex sets *OPABQO*, *ORCDSO*, and *OTEFUO*. Points strictly inside any of these sets are not coalition-proof: a coalition of two players could achieve a better allocation on its own and can thus credibly oppose it. *X*, for instance, is coalition-proof, but *Z* is not. The same process can be applied recursively to construct the set of coalition-proof equilibria to a *N*-person IRSA.

Figure 4.4 illustrates one of the implications of coalition-proofness for risk sharing. Again, there are three agents *A*, *B*, and *C*. The income of agent *C* is negatively correlated with that of *A* and *B* but the latter two have an identical distribution of income, that is, $\pi_s^A = \pi_s^B$ for all $s \in S$. The scope for risk sharing between *A* and *B* is thus nil. If coalitions of two agents are not allowed, equilibria need only satisfy the participation constraints of each of the three agents. A point such as *M*, for instance, satisfies these requirements. Now let agents form coalitions and oppose allocations that fail to guarantee them what they could achieve by forming a separate IRSA. Any point *inside* the constrained Pareto frontier can be opposed by a coalition of agents. In this special case, most points *along* the Pareto frontiers can also be opposed by a coalition of C and one of the two agents. Take point R, for instance. At R, risk is shared efficiently between C and B but A is at his autarchy payoff. A, however, can improve his or her lot by 'bribing' C to form an A–C coalition that guarantees C a payoff higher than R and A a payoff higher than autarchy. B can, in turn, retaliate by bribing C even more, and so on. Repeating this process until convergence, we see that the set of coalition-proof equilibria of this game is the dashed line running from X to Y and from Z to Y. Along this line the expected utility of C is constant. It is the maximum that A or B in isolation could credibly promise C in order to lure him or her into forming an A–C or B–C coalition. The set of coalition-proof equilibria is non-empty even though it occurs where participation constraints are binding.[80]

When coalitions are allowed, the mere presence of an agent may confer rents to others. To see why, consider a small alteration to the preceding example and suppose that $\pi_s^B = \pi_s^A + \varepsilon$ for all $s \in S$. As long as C's payoff is greater than the maximum payoff A could credibly promise him or her, he or she prefers to remain with B. Since B's income is marginally higher than that of A, B can top any offer A can credibly make. Coalition-proof equilibria are thus those at which B and C form a risk sharing coalition and A is left in autarchy. A does not derive any gain from the game, yet A's willingness to form a coalition with C significantly increases C's bargaining power and allows him or her to extract from B most of the Pareto efficiency gains from risk sharing.

These examples illustrate that allowing coalitions may confer considerable bargaining power on some agents, particularly those whose income stream is different from the rest of the group. In his study of Nigerian villages, for instance, Udry (1990) indicates that traders are able to establish patron-client relationships with local farmers because they have an income that is less sensitive to local climatic conditions (see also Watts (1983)). The same thing can often be said of government employees, pension recipients, and households receiving large migrant remittances in farming communities (Ellsworth 1989).

Allowing the free formation of coalitions may also result in poor agents not receiving any insurance. The reason is that forming coalitions opens new avenues for the expression of self-interest. As a result, privileged members of the group can more easily oppose the egalitarian redistribution of consumption through risk sharing. Allowing coalitions, however, may promote efficiency. When coalitions are not allowed, only individuals can challenge a particular equilibrium path. Perfect equilibria can be very inefficient. By threatening to form a separate, better risk sharing group, coalitions can police IRSAs and eliminate sub-optimal outcomes. Because they bring the equilibrium path closer to the core, they also bring it closer to the allocation that would result from a perfect competitive equilibrium. The larger the risk sharing group and the more coalitions they may form, the closer coalition-proof equilibria must lie to the perfect competitive outcome and the less they can correct inequality in endowments. Achieving redistribution may therefore require that certain coalitions be combated, possibly at the risk of reducing efficiency. More generally, the degree of equity or inequity achievable via an IRSA can be manipulated through the polity by allowing certain coalitions and preventing others.

4.4   RISK SHARING AND CREDIT

In practice, gifts and transfers are seldom the dominant form of consumption smoothing in the Third World; consumption credit is typically a more important avenue for sharing risk within the community (Rosenzweig 1988a, Townsend 1994, Alamgir 1980, pp. 156–7). The resemblance between such consumption credit and market transactions is, however, largely superficial. The amounts transacted often are too small to justify court action; contracts must be self-enforcing.[81] Moreover, as recent evidence has shown, consumption credit is often implicitly combined with some form of insurance: debts can be forgiven, repayments can be postponed, and actual contractual performance typically depends on the lender's and the borrower's situation at the time of repayment (for example Platteau and Abraham 1987, Udry 1990). We now show that quasi-credit can be understood as a non-stationary strategy equilibrium of a long-term, implicit risk sharing arrangement (for example Kocherlakota 1996, Ligon et al. 2001).

4.4.1   Quasi-credit

So far we have focused on stationary strategies, that is, on strategies in which transfers depend only on the current state of nature. These strategies alone can support cooperation but less restricted strategies can achieve more. We investigate a special class of non-stationary strategies, one in which agents are individually rewarded for contributing to the group. As it turns out, this class of strategies establishes a formal link between risk sharing and credit practices.

Formally, consider strategies in which the consumption of agent i is the sum of three terms: realized income π_s^i, net transfers τ_s^i, and a reward w_t^i that, for the time being, we shall call Brownie points:

$$c^i_{s,t} = \pi^i_{s,t} - \tau^i_{s,t} + w^i_t \qquad (4.17)$$

Brownie points w^i_t can be thought of as the net wealth or goodwill capital of individual i.[82] They are not a function of the current state of nature.

Let $\pi_{s,t}$ and w_t be the vectors of individual incomes and Brownie points, respectively. Transfers $\tau^i_{s,t}$ map from the cross-product of realized incomes and Brownie points at time t into the real line, that is:

$$\tau^i_{s,t} = \Pi^i(\pi_{s,t}, w_t) \qquad (4.18)$$

Transfers depend on past history through w_t. Brownie points reward positive transfers to others, but since transfers are themselves a function of realized incomes and Brownie points, we can write the law of motion of w^i_t in the following reduced form:

$$w^i_t = W^i(\pi_{s,t-1}, w_{t-1}) \qquad (4.19)$$

Brownie points are normalized so that $\Sigma_{i \in N} w^i_t = 0$ for all t.

With these new assumptions, participation constraints can be rewritten:

$$U_i(\pi^i_{s'}) - U_i(c^i_{s'}) \leq \sum_{u=1}^{\infty} \delta^t EU_i(c^i_{s,t}) - \frac{\delta}{1-\delta} EU_i(\pi^i_s) + A_i \qquad (4.20)$$

In this new notation, stationary strategies correspond to restricted transfer functions in which $\Pi(y, w_0) = \Pi(y, w_1)$ for all y, w_0, and w_1. Since non-stationary strategies are less restrictive than pure gift giving, they should allow more risk sharing. This intuition is formalized by the following proposition:

Proposition 4.6 *Let A be the set of perfect equilibria supported by the stationary strategies and let B be the set of perfect equilibria supported by non-stationary strategies defined above. Then $A \subseteq B$.*

To illustrate that B can be strictly larger than A, consider the following simple example. Suppose there are two agents with the following concave utility function:

Consumption	1	1.5	2	2.5	3	3.5
Utility	−2	1	2	2.5	2.75	3

There are three equally likely states of the world, numbered 1 to 3. Corresponding income vectors of agents 1 and 2 are (1, 2), (2, 1), and (3, 3). Altruism is ignored, that is, $A_1 = A_2 = 0$. We compare two risk sharing schemes. The first one, which is stationary, stipulates transfers from agent

1 to agent 2 of -0.5, 0.5, and 0 in states of the world 1, 2 and 3, respectively. The second scheme is like the first in states of the world 1 and 2. But in state 3, it stipulates that an agent receives a payment of 0.5 if the previous state of the world was 1 or 2 and he or she gave a transfer to the other agent.

This payment can be thought of as contingent credit repayment. We show that the second scheme can be supported for a lower discount factor than the first. Consider the first scheme. Given the symmetry of the game, there is only one participation constraint to consider, that when one of the agents must give 0.5 to the other. Expected utilities from cooperation and autarchy are, respectively:

$$EU_i(c_{s,t}^i) = \frac{1}{3}U(3) + \frac{2}{3}U(1.5)$$

$$EU_i(\pi_s^i) = \frac{1}{3}U(3) + \frac{1}{3}U(2) + \frac{1}{3}U(1)$$

The difference between the two is $2/3$. The gain from defection is $U(2) - U(1.5) = 1$. The VP constraint is satisfied for $\delta \geq 0.6$.

Now consider the second scheme. There are two participation constraints to satisfy. The first one, as in the stationary scheme, ensures that payment is made in states of the world 1 and 2. The expected utility from Autarchy and the gain from defection are unchanged, but the expected utility from cooperation has increased because of the reward in state 3. It is now:

$$\delta[\frac{1}{3}U(3.5) + \frac{2}{3}U(1.5)] + \delta^{\frac{\delta^2}{1-\delta}}\frac{2}{3}U(1.5) + \frac{1}{6}U(3.5) + \frac{1}{6}U(2.5)$$

The minimum δ at which the participation constraint is satisfied is now 0.588. The second participation constraint makes sure that payment of 0.5 in state 3 is self-enforcing. The minimum δ at which voluntary payment is made is 0.364. The second scheme can thus supports risk sharing in bad times even when $\delta < 0.6$. More general examples can be found in Ligon et al. (2001).

As the above example suggests, quasi-credit belongs to the class of non-stationary strategies that we just discussed. To see why, let us split $\tau_{s,t}^i$ into two parts: a loan l and a pure transfer τ. Let the interest rate be r. Then:

Proposition 4.7 *For any interest rate r, and any function $W^i(y, w)$ and $\Pi^i(y, w)$, there exist a loan function $l^i(y, w)$ and pure transfer function $\tau^i(y, w)$ such that:*

$$c_{s,t}^i = \pi_{s,t}^i - l^i(\pi_{s,t}, w_t) + w_t^i - \tau^i(\pi_{s,t}, w_t) \tag{4.21}$$

$$w^i_t = -(1+r)l^i(\pi_{s,t-1}, w_{t-1}) \qquad (4.22)$$

Proposition 4.7 establishes the formal resemblance between quasi-credit and a non-stationary strategy equilibrium of a repeated risk sharing game. Quasi-credit can thus be considered as a form of insurance. Proposition 4.6 also teaches us that, in the absence of enforcement problems, efficient risk sharing could be achieved through gifts alone. It is enforcement problems that are the reason for the existence of quasi-credit: by establishing a direct link between what agents give today and what they expect to receive tomorrow, quasi-credit rewards giving over and above what pure gift giving can achieve. As a result, it is able to overcome some of the limitations imposed by participation constraints and thus raise efficiency (for example Ligon et al. 2000, Ligon et al. 2001).

Many of the features of quasi-credit that have been noted by observers of rural Third World societies (for example Gluckman 1955, Scott 1976, Popkin 1979, Platteau 1991, Basu 1986) are puzzling when quasi-credit is looked at as a regular market transaction. Treating quasi-credit as the equilibrium of a repeated risk sharing game helps explain many of these features. First, there is no sense in which the interest rate on quasi-credit contracts clears the market: as Proposition 4.7 demonstrates, the interest rate is indeterminate. This helps explain why so many Third World consumption loans between equals carry no explicit interest (for example Townsend 1994, Fafchamps and Lund 2003) and why interest rates sometimes vary wildly between transactions in the same village and time period (Udry 1990). Second, loan repayment is conditional on subsequent shocks; default and postponement are anticipated and implicitly accepted beforehand. This stands in contrast with regular credit contracts which are expected to be repaid in most if not all circumstances. Third, *access* to credit is the means by which mutual insurance is organized. Loans are therefore rationed: in order to get a loan, one must show sufficient need (Fafchamps and Lund 2003). Quasi-credit at zero interest rate is not meant to be used for investment purposes. Townsend (1993), for instance, provides evidence that investment loans in Thai villages do carry interest and are treated differently from consumption loans. Fafchamps and Lund (2003) provide similar evidence for the Philippines. Fourth, because repayment is only guaranteed by continued participation in the IRSA, quasi-credit loans are unlikely to be made to someone whose expected future contribution to or gain from risk sharing is low. Transactions are thus not anonymous but entirely personalized: that i got a loan from j does not mean that k can get a loan from j.

Many of the transfers that appear in Proposition 4.7 serve to offset credit obligations. Does it matter how these transfers take place? As Proposition

4.8 demonstrates, the answer is yes: more efficiency in risk sharing can be achieved if debt can be postponed and not simply forgiven. Let A and B be as in Proposition 4.7. Let C stand for the set of subgame perfect equilibria that can be achieved when debt cannot be rescheduled, that is, when $W(y, w_0) = W(y, w_1)$ for all y, w_0 and w_1 (A6). Then we can show that:

Proposition 4.8 $A \subseteq C \subseteq B$.

That A may $\subseteq C$ is illustrated by the example given above, in which debt could not be postponed. The example can easily be expanded to show that debt rescheduling increases the reward for giving and thus reduces the discount rate required for the participation constraint to be satisfied, in which case we would have $C \subseteq B$ as well. This is left as an exercise for the reader. Proposition 4.8 thus provides a possible explanation for why debt repayments are often postponed and rolled over instead of being simply forgiven (for example Udry 1990, Fafchamps and Gubert 2002, Fafchamps and Lund 2003).

4.4.2   Formal Credit

Although many consumption credit transactions remain informal, some, like loans from money-lenders for instance, are somewhat more formal and often include a credible threat to seek external enforcement. Since the respect for debt repayment obligations is more easily verifiable by an outside party than the state of nature on which transfers τ_s depend, there are good reasons to suspect credit contracts to be enforceable even when mutual insurance obligations are not. We now show that the possibility of external enforcement, even if imperfect, helps risk sharing. The reason is that the effectiveness of quasi-credit is limited by the requirement that credit obligations w_t^i be self-enforcing: the more debt an agent accumulates, the more tempting it is for him or her to defect from the IRSA. These limitations are reduced if credit contracts can be externally enforced.

Assume that a credible external enforcement technology exists for credit contracts. If a debtor defaults on a loan, penalties can be inflicted. Let the expected discounted utility cost of these penalties be a non-decreasing function $\bar{P}(w_t^i)$. Let us also assume that penalties are finite, i.e., that $\lim_{w \to \infty} P(w) = \bar{P} < \infty$. The participation constraint for risk sharing can then be rewritten:

$$U_t(\pi_{s'}^i) - U_t(c_{s'}^i) \leq \sum_{u=1}^{\infty} \delta^t E[V(c_{s,u}^i)] - \frac{\delta}{1-\delta} EU_t(\pi_s^i) - P(w_t^i) + A_i \quad (4.23)$$

The only difference with equation (4.22) is $P(w_t^i)$: the use of credit contracts inflicts heavier penalties on agents who defect on their risk sharing obligations. Let D be the set of perfect equilibria supported by externally enforceable credit contracts as defined in equation (4.23). Since harsher punishments support more risk sharing, we get:

Proposition 4.9 $B \subseteq D$.

External enforcement can only improve efficiency if explicit, enforceable contracts are combined with implicit risk sharing arrangements. Pure credit alone would not achieve the same result. Furthermore, external enforcement helps only if the penalty for default $P(w)$ is finite. If contractual default is never allowed, individuals never borrow more than the annuity value of their minimum income. If their minimum possible income is zero, they never become net borrowers, however small the probability of a zero income is (for example Zeldes 1989b, Carroll 1992, Fafchamps and Pender 1997).[83] In this case, consumption smoothing can only be achieved through pure gift giving. Zame (1993) demonstrates that even contingent contracts cannot, in general, be efficient unless penalties for default are not too high, that is, unless contract repudiation is tolerated in certain circumstances. Allowing debt obligations not to be met in certain cases makes credit contracts resemble quasi-credit: they de facto mix credit with insurance. Proposition 4.9 complements these earlier results by showing that insurance can in turn be made more efficient by externally imposing penalties for the non-respect of credit contracts.

Proposition 4.9 opens a large grey area between non-market transactions – the income pooling arrangements discussed in Chapter Two – and pure market transactions – contracts that are enforced exclusively through $P(w_i)$. Most real world transactions probably stand somewhere in between. There is often an implicit arrangement between parties to renegotiate the terms of the explicit contract, either by forgiving part of the debt or by postponing contractual compliance (for example Kranton 1996, Fafchamps 1996a, Fafchamps 2002). In this grey area, transactions share some of the characteristics of quasi-credit: rationing according to need; a certain indeterminacy in interest rates, solved either through individual variation in interest rate or by fixation around a focal point; de facto conditional loan repayment; and personalized, repeated transactions. They also may display characteristics that are associated with well functioning markets: limits on the individual variation of interest rates; mobility between sources of finance; free access to credit within a certain range. Although contract enforcement issues naturally raise a host of information asymmetries problems, Proposition 4.9 suggests that enforcement alone can account for many observed features of credit markets (Stiglitz and Weiss 1981) even in the presence of perfect information (see Fafchamps (1996a), and Fafchamps (2003b) for illustrations).

4.5 INFORMATION ASYMMETRIES

The contingent nature of reciprocity is necessary for it to be an effective insurance mechanism against unforeseen events, but it generates serious incentive problems (Scott 1976, p. 5). People may seek to hide, dissimulate, or misrepresent their situation of need or affordability. They also may be tempted to work less and rely on the mutual insurance system for their subsistence (for example Herskovits 1952, Popkin 1979, Poewe 1989, Platteau 1991). Pre-industrial societies have devised ways of dealing with incentive issues. In fact, many features of solidarity systems can be interpreted as ways to minimize efficiency loss, such as:

- the lack of privacy, so that consumption can easily be observed;
- the moral condemnation of greed, that is, the dissimulation of wealth;
- the redistribution of productive assets (such as land) instead of consumption to minimize shirking;
- the provision of partial or catastrophic insurance only to minimize moral hazard.

These features are discussed below in more detail.

4.5.1 Observability of Income and Wealth

In a mutual insurance system, solidarity rights and obligations depend on realized income and wealth. These are only imperfectly observable. Consequently, everyone has an incentive to underreport income and wealth in order either to be eligible for solidarity assistance, or to be dispensed from supporting others. Obviously, if individual income and wealth are entirely unobservable, there is no way opportunistic misrepresentation can be prevented and the mutual insurance system collapses. In small rural communities, however, commonly observed signals exist that are correlated with individual income and wealth. Can the solidarity system survive in those circumstances? As the theory of repeated games with imperfect monitoring has shown, the answer depends critically on how informative these signals are (Fudenberg et al. 1994).

Say signals are available that are correlated with individual realization of income or wealth. Some signals are associated with equal likelihood of either high or low income; they are not very informative. Others are associated with a high likelihood that income is high or low. Such signals can be used by the parties to the mutual insurance contract to verify each other's affordability and need. How signals are used depends on when information becomes available. If it is immediately available, it is possible to make mutual insurance transfers depend on commonly observed signals only. In that case, self-revelation of need and affordability is bypassed entirely and the danger of misrepresentation is avoided. Many manifestations of solidarity rely on such signals. For instance, transfers and gifts are more frequent at funerals and weddings (Ellsworth (1989), pp. 287, 293 and 295; Fafchamps and Lund (2003)). Of course, relying exclusively on signals can be very dangerous and costly in terms of efficiency: people may be requested to provide assistance when they actually cannot afford it, or may receive it in the absence of need.[84] Consequently, in many cases, self-revelation is allowed to partly determine solidarity transfers.

In those circumstances, parties to the mutual insurance arrangement may have insufficient immediate information to judge the veracity of insurance claims. Additional information may become available over time, however. Truthfulness may thus be appreciated ex post. Informative signals can then be used to trigger harsh but delayed punishments. Of course, as was already argued, punishments cannot be so harsh that they induce people to leave the solidarity system. Consequently, if signals are not very informative and/or are delayed far in time, and if the maximum long-term penalty is low compared to short-term opportunistic gains, misrepresentation of need and affordability cannot be prevented. In that case, the mutual insurance system can hardly operate and a self-enforcing agreement can achieve very little efficiency.

In rural communities, sources of income and forms of wealth differ significantly in their degree of observability. For instance, it is easy for an experienced farmer to guess crop yield by observing standing crops at harvest. But it is much harder to guess someone's income from migration or non-farm activity. Livestock occupies a somewhat intermediate position: it is observable when physically in the village, but mixing herds and transhumance blur the picture to a great extent. Actually, the extreme secrecy surrounding grain storage, livestock, and other assets in rural areas of the Third World is a sign that people consciously try to decrease observability of their income and wealth.

Given that crop production is the most easily observable form of income, people have an incentive to shift away from crops and to secure sources of income that are easy to dissimulate. In parts of rural Africa, it has indeed been noticed that young villagers in search of upward social mobility rarely invest their efforts in agriculture: instead, they migrate or go into trade and non-farm activities (Poewe 1989, p. 99). The temptation to dissimulate income by moving away from agriculture can be very damaging for rural communities since it endangers food security. Therefore it may be necessary to counteract it by limiting access to the village's solidarity network to those who farm and grow food crops. Those who do not grow food crops would be threatened with exclusion because they have signalled their intention to free-ride the system.

Consumption is a very powerful, yet delayed signal of income and wealth. For instance, the occurrence of large consumption expenditures is an ex post confirmation of affordability, while the absence of it confirms truthful revelation of need. The lack of privacy in pre-industrial societies allows information about consumption to circulate widely in the community (Posner 1980, pp. 6–7). Of course, consumption is a manipulable signal, and manipulation has a name: greed, that is, the avoidance of consumption as a way to misrepresent wealth so that sharing with others is minimized. The scorn and moral sanction associated with greed in many pre-industrial societies have led some observers to conclude that such societies are opposed to private accumulation of wealth (Poewe 1989, pp. 91–124). The ideas presented here suggest instead that the efficiency, and possibly the survival of the mutual insurance system are seriously threatened when it is unable to rely on consumption as an ex post signal of need and affordability. The fact that greed is ridiculed and made morally reprehensible is nothing but a proof of weakness: the mutual insurance system has to rely on non-economic incentives to try to limit opportunistic behaviour. It is not so much private accumulation of wealth that pre-industrial societies combat, but the fact that some may accumulate wealth while others are in need. In fact, pre-industrial societies welcome wealth accumulation because it is an important source of insurance against collective risk. But wealth accumulation is encouraged to take place openly, and to serve the common need for insurance. More on this issue in the section on patron-client relationships.

Finally, need can also be verified ex post if someone who has been refused assistance subsequently dies of starvation or illness. In his study of the Nuer, Evans-Pritchard (1940, pp. 152–64), mentions that someone's mere presence when a member of the community dies suddenly triggers severe punishment, irrespective of responsibility (see also Posner (1980), pp. 42–52 and the references cited therein). This can be interpreted as reflecting a very strong obligation to assist others in need: non-assistance is assimilated to murder. Examples of collective responsibility can also be interpreted in the same light: death or illness are used as a signal to trigger harsh collective punishments. Such customs ensure that someone's call for help is not taken lightly.

4.5.2   Observability of Effort

Imperfect monitoring of income and wealth is not the only incentive problem facing mutual insurance systems. Imperfect monitoring of effort may induce people to rely on others instead of working. Since the more insurance is provided, the less incentive people have to work, there is a trade-off between efficiency in insurance and efficiency in labour effort. Consequently, risk pooling may have to be limited to, say, catastrophic insurance. In Scott's (1976) words: the right to subsistence.

This can easily be illustrated with a simple example. Consider a one-period symmetric contract of full income pooling and, for simplicity, assume that it is fully enforceable and that income is observable. If effort is also observable, Pareto efficiency is achieved by requiring participants to provide the level of effort that corresponds to first best optimality. Those who deviate are heavily penalized; punishments ensure that cheating is never in a participant's best interest. Since all parties are identical and risk averse, equal distribution of income ensures the highest degree of social welfare.

If individual effort is not observable, however, moral hazard becomes a problem. Full income pooling remains Pareto efficient from an insurance point of view, but since the effort of each participant only has a marginal impact on his or her share of aggregate income, free-riding becomes a best response. Consequently, efficiency in effort is not achieved and there is under-application of effort. Formally, let the optimization problem of participant j be:

$$\max_{l_j} EU_j\left(\frac{\sum_{i=1}^{N} y_i}{N}, 1 - l_j\right)$$

subject to

$$y_i = f_i(l_i)_i \, \forall_i \in \{1, \ldots, N\}$$

where y_i stands for the income of household i, N is the total number of households, 1 total (normalized) time endowment, and l_i labour of participant i. Because of symmetry, the solution to the above also defines the Nash equilibrium contract. Dropping subscripts, individual effort is implicitly given by:

$$EU_y\frac{f'}{N} = EU_l \tag{4.24}$$

The incentive effect of insurance on individual effort is identical to that obtained in models of sharecropping, income tax, or producers' cooperatives. Here, N represents the number of parties to the contract, but equation (4.24) would be formally identical if it represented the share of output that goes to a shareholder, the marginal rate of taxation on labour income, or the number of people in a cooperative (Holmstrom 1982). In all models the effect is the same: because people do not capture the entire marginal product of their effort, they usually level off effort. Consequently aggregate output drops.[85]

Is it possible to find another contract that does better than full income pooling? An interesting alternative is suggested by Scott (1976), who insists that solidarity among peasants is characterized by guaranteed subsistence, not full income pooling. A contract aimed at guaranteeing subsistence can be constructed as follows. Set a minimum survival income. Because utility is extremely low below survival income, the largest welfare gains from insurance are achieved from the reduction in the risk of starvation.[86] Finance the minimum survival income insurance by lumpsum 'fees' levied on all players with an income realization above the survival threshold. Intuitively, such a contract improves efficiency by making participants partially residual claimants of the fruits of their efforts. If the chance of falling below the starvation income level is relatively small, financing the scheme by lumpsum fees insures that more efficiency in effort is achieved.[87] On the other hand, if the chance of falling below starvation income is high, individuals may prefer to shirk and reduce their labour effort.[88]

Formally, let $\tilde{c}$ be the fee that is charged to each member of the insurance pool. $\tilde{c}$ covers the subsistence requirements of pool participants. It therefore depends on realized aggregate income and its distribution. Let c stand for the expected value of the fee.[89] Participants are guaranteed a minimum income level y_f.[90] The optimization problem facing each member of the insurance pool is to choose a level of effort that maximizes expected utility:

$$\max_l \int_{\underline{y}}^{y_f} U(y_f - c, 1 - l)h(y)dy + \int_{y_f}^{\bar{y}} U(y(l) - c, 1 - l)h(y)dy$$

where y stands for income, l for effort, $h(y)$ *is* the pdf of y, and $(\underline{y}, \bar{y})$ is the support of y. As before, the utility function $U(.)$ is defined over income and leisure. Assume that income risk is multiplicative: $y = f(l)s$ where s is a random shock. Let $g(s)$ be the pdf of s. The first order condition for an interior optimum is:

$$-\underline{U}_l \Pr(s \leq \frac{y_f}{f(l)}) + \int_{\frac{y_f}{f(l)}}^{\frac{\bar{y}}{f(l)}} (U_y f' - U_l)g(s)ds - \bar{U} \frac{\bar{y}f'}{f(l)^2}g\left(\frac{\bar{y}}{f(l)}\right) = 0$$

where $\underline{U}_l$ stands for $U_l(y_f - c, 1 - l)$ and $\bar{U}$ stands for $U(\bar{y} - c, 1 - l)$

Totally differentiating the above with respect to l and y_f shows how, other things being equal, effort changes with the level of minimum guaranteed income. The resulting expression can be written:

$$\frac{dl}{dy_f} = \frac{-1}{SOC}\left[-U_{ly}\Pr\left(s \le \frac{y_f}{f(l)}\right) - U_y\frac{f'}{f}g\left(\frac{y_f}{f(l)}\right)\right]$$

where *SOC* stands for the second order condition of the optimization problem. The second order condition is negative at an interior optimum. Assume that the marginal utility of leisure increases with income. Then the expression in brackets is negative. Thus, for any expected insurance fee c, effort is a decreasing function of the level of minimum insured income, bringing to light the trade-off between insurance and efficiency.

More complex, non-linear contracts may be able to achieve a better balance between efficiency and insurance, but the theory of mechanism design suggests that such contracts are sensitive to slight changes in model parameters, and easily manipulated by participants if observability is not perfect (Hart and Holmstrom (1987), pp. 91–7). In other words, delicate optimal contracts are not robust. Consequently attempting to identify an optimal short-term risk pooling contract is likely to lead to counterfactual results. A more promising line of enquiry is to investigate whether repeated contracts may reduce moral hazard.

As Fudenberg et al. (1994) and Abreu et al. (1990) have shown, moral hazard could in principle be minimized, say, by the use of trigger punishment strategies. Realized output can be used as a signal for effort. Under-application of effort is more likely when output is low relative to others. Consequently, low output could trigger harsh punishment. The problem is that (1) the purpose of the mutual insurance contract is to shelter people against low output realization; (2) risk pooling can only shelter people against idiosyncratic risk. Letting low individual output relative to others trigger punishments contradicts the very purpose of the contract itself.

Other signals thus have to be found. Restricted privacy ensures a permanent check on people's actual work performance. Consumption of leisure and leisure related commodities (beer, gambling, and so on) can be used as a monitoring device. In land surplus areas of the Third World, planted acreage can also serve as a signal for effort. Of course, it is partly manipulable as people may inflate their planted acreage but fail to perform other agricultural operations in an efficient and timely fashion. Manipulation and moral hazard issues thus may also help explain why labour inputs per hectare are so low in African agriculture (for example Cleave 1974, Eicher and Baker 1982, Fafchamps 1986).

4.5.3 Ex Ante Solidarity

Another way to reduce incentive problems in ex post mutual insurance is for group solidarity to operate ex ante. While ex post solidarity compensates someone for a shortfall in income, ex ante solidarity attempts to prevent the occurrence of a shortfall. By granting access to key factors of production – land, labour, and capital[91] – ex ante solidarity minimizes costs in two ways: it reduces moral hazard; and it avoids the waste of community resources. The rationale and foundation for ex ante solidarity thus must be sought in the existence of ex post solidarity: without a right to subsistence, ex ante solidarity would not exist.

There are numerous manifestations of ex ante solidarity. Labour assistance during the cropping season, for example, is used to help the sick or the old complete farm operations on time. Indirect evidence of labour assistance can be found in Cleave (1974), pp. 169, 173–4; République du Mali (1979), p. 1; Matlon and Vierich (1982), p. G73; von Braun and Webb (1989). It is indeed more cost effective for the community to salvage crops via immediate labour assistance, instead of waiting for crops to fail and provide ex post insurance. So doing, the land and labour resources already invested in crop production by the assisted farmer are not wasted, and the cost to the group is reduced.

Another example of ex ante solidarity is land borrowing, free of charge, as practised in the West African semi-arid tropics (for example Matlon 1988, Gavian and Fafchamps 1996, Platteau 2000a). There, marginal returns to land are low (low rainfall, low soil fertility, simple technology, slow natural fertility restoration), and yields depend primarily on labour, directly via careful cultivation, and indirectly via labour investment in land fertility and water retention (manuring, ridging) (for example Prudencio 1983, Prudencio 1987). In those circumstances, it is more attractive for farmers to acquire other people's goodwill by lending out excess land, instead of cultivating it with hired manpower. Actually, attempts at direct cultivation by land rich households may face social resistance in the form of labour shirking because they violate the principles of solidarity (Woodhouse and Ndiaye n.d.). Here again the rationale is that someone short of land will also be short of food at the end of the season. A land loan is thus a way to prevent the need for food assistance, while making a full and efficient use of the labour resources and reducing moral hazard.

Of course food shortages by land poor households need not always be prevented by temporary transfers of land. Sharecropping, or providing employment to landless and land poor households may prove better alternatives, depending on the circumstances (Platteau 1991). In the absence of increasing returns to scale in agriculture, however, and provided that landlords do not have a preferred or exclusive access to key factors of production, land transfers present advantages. Indeed, they minimize moral hazard and the need for labour supervision by making tillers residual claimants of the fruits of their efforts.

Even consumption loans and food transfers can be viewed partly as manifestations of ex ante solidarity. Short-term consumption loans are very common in rural areas of the Third World (Platteau and Abraham 1987). Very often, they are used to buy food so that people may continue working until the end of the agricultural season (Christensen 1987). Such loans are sometimes made without interest; and their repayments vary with the situation of both lender and borrower (Udry 1994). Food assistance can similarly be viewed as a measure destined to prevent incapacitation due to malnutrition, thus enabling recipients to continue working. Again, the rationale is that it is cheaper for the system to transfer food now in order to reduce demands for assistance later.

4.6   RISK SHARING NETWORKS

In practice solidarity does not really operate as a group insurance. As Ellsworth (1989) and Fafchamps and Lund (2003) have shown, it rather, operates as a network in which individuals are connected to a small number of other people, who, in turn, are connected to other people (Bromley and Chavas (1989), pp. 730–2). The end result is a network of interpersonal relationships in which individuals are connected to each other either directly or indirectly.

4.6.1   The Role of Networks in Mutual Insurance

Using original data from the Philippines, Fafchamps and Lund (2003) show that efficient risk sharing is not achieved at the village level and that networks play an important role in the sharing of risk. Even within networks, however, perfect risk sharing is not achieved. Dercon and de Weerdt (2002) report similar findings in Tanzania and show that in the event of a health shock, network members cut their non-food consumption by 30 per cent while keeping food consumption roughly constant.

Lineage, kinship, neighbourhood or consanguinity are often major axes of solidarity networks, but friendship and patron-client relationships also matter (Rosenzweig 1988a). Evidence on the role of friends and relatives in coping with risk can be found in the sociological and anthropological literatures, as well as in the literature on remittances (Lucas and Stark 1985). Rosenzweig and Stark (1989) show that marriages in part respond to households' desire to form risk sharing bonds with other families in distant villages, hence suggesting that the formation of networks is itself endogenous to the risk coping process.

Compared to other disciplines, in economics the theoretical literature on networks is still in its infancy (see for instance Saloner (1985), Bala and Goyal (1998), Kali (1999), Bala and Goyal (2000), Kranton and Minehart (2000), Kranton and Minehart (2001)). The existing literature has nevertheless brought to light the limitations inherent to networks (for example Mitchell 1969, Granovetter 1995). Information channelled through networks gets distorted or filtered, sometimes by mistake, sometimes on purpose (for example Montgomery 1991, Foster and Rosenzweig 1995, Banerjee and Munshi 1999, Conley and Udry 2001, Romani 2003). Similar concerns have been expressed in the literature on industrial organizations in terms of information processing (for example Itoh 1991, Bolton and Dewatripont 1994). The enforcement power of networks is limited by the value of network links: if links can be replaced easily and costlessly, their enforcement power is weak (for example Banerjee and Munshi 1999, Fafchamps 2002). The structure of networks also influences outcome in complex ways (for example Raub and Weesie 1990, Bala and Goyal 2000, Kranton and Minehart 2001).

The fact that mutual insurance systems operate as networks can be interpreted as a result of incentive problems. Cox (1999) argues that people have a reduced ability to follow the actions of a multiplicity of characters – something he calls the 'soap opera' constraint. When the 'soap opera' constraint is binding, risk sharing crowds out information sharing for other useful purposes, such as technological innovation or contract enforcement (Barr 2000). By reducing the need for monitoring neighbours and relatives, Cox argues, formal institutions for risk sharing release the 'soap opera' constraint and thus make resources available to pursue more growth and development oriented goals.

In the absence of formal institutions, networks can also serve to economize on monitoring. Make the following two assumptions: monitoring is costly; and the cost of monitoring falls over time between any pair of individuals who actively practise solidarity. The idea behind these assumptions is that, as two individuals assist and monitor each other, over time they acquire relation specific information that allows them to monitor each other more effectively: they know each other's situation better, they have learned to read each other's facial expressions, and so on. The result of this process of learning-by-doing can be called trust.

4.6.2 The Formation of Risk Sharing Networks

Genicot and Ray (2000) present a model of endogenous group formation in risk sharing arrangements. They show that stable groups of risk sharing agents have a bounded size, hence precluding risk sharing in large groups. As a result, they also find that the degree of risk sharing in a community is generally non-monotonic in the level of uncertainty or need for insurance. This is basically because of an integer problem, that is, the number of groups of optimal bounded size that can be created in any given community.

Groups, however, need not be the way risk is actually shared. Networks may be a more accurate representation. Networks do not arise from nowhere. Yet very little is known at this point on how networks are created and how they perform their risk sharing role. de Weerdt (2002), for instance, studies who forms risk sharing networks in Tanzania and outlines the role of age and kinship, hence suggesting a learning process shaped by social constructs.

To speculate on how networks may endogenously arise, suppose we start from a situation in which mutual insurance ties do not exist. If people recognize that cooperation is Pareto improving, they will want to enter into informal mutual insurance arrangements with each other. Since they have limited resources to cover monitoring costs, they will concentrate on a limited number of informal arrangements which, over time, develop into personalized and privileged relationships based on mutual trust. This means that the process whereby the mutual insurance system is formed crystallizes it into a mesh of interpersonal relations. The process of crystallization, like many processes with dynamic increasing returns, is likely to generate multiple equilibria, path dependence, and lock-in (for example Arthur 1988, Arthur 1989, Arthur 1990). Efficient outcomes are not guaranteed. Hence the role of customs, traditions and ethics to provide focal points, guide the process, and increase the chance that it generates an efficient and fair outcome.

At its inception, the process of network crystallization is likely to take advantage of special relationships pre-existing between society members: filiation, kinship, neighbourhood, and consanguinity. Indeed, these relationships give a joint monitoring advantage to pairs of people. For instance, because of the lack of privacy in pre-industrial societies, it is hard to hide something from your neighbour or brother in law, and vice versa. By reducing monitoring costs, such relationships allow solidarity links to develop faster and stronger. Altruistic feelings between people can also serve as initial catalyst, thus in the role of filiation and friendship. Consequently, one would expect solidarity networks to largely reproduce the structure of lineage, vicinity, kinship, and consanguinity.

Networks present other informational advantages. They save on information flows and allow the day to day operation of the mutual insurance system to be decentralized. Without network, tracking the cooperative equilibria of the repeated game would actually require that large amounts of information be shared by all the members of the mutual insurance contract. Given the cost and complexity of such information flows, cooperative equilibria would probably not materialize. With networks, even the decision to punish can be decentralized: punishment by the best informed people can be used as a signal that other villagers should punish as well. Unfaithful wives, and ungrateful sons can be collectively fustigated this way.

Finally, by their decentralized nature, networks are more resilient and flexible than a global insurance pool. Births, deaths, weddings, and migrations are easily accommodated without having to renegotiate and reconsider the insurance arrangements of the entire community. Adjustments are made in a decentralized fashion, saving on renegotiation costs. Decentralization may also allow solidarity rights and obligations to remain incompletely specified without imposing an extremely complex accounting system upon the members of the insurance pool.

4.7   THE BREAKDOWN OF THE SOLIDARITY SYSTEM

The existence of solidarity networks has numerous policy implications: it affects rural welfare, as well as peasant behaviour with respect to food aid, prices, risk, technology, and new institutions. Here attention is concentrated on one of them: the prevention of destitution. When poor rural communities are hit by a major shock, say a flood, drought, or famine, the solidarity system often seems to break down (Sen 1981). Of course, it may be that, after the shock, the entire wealth of the community is no longer sufficient to ensure everybody's survival. In that case, people will die because there simply are not enough resources to support everybody. Although it is true that those who have barely enough to sustain themselves will refuse help to others, reallocating existing resources would not reduce the number of casualties. In other words, starvation is not due to the failure of the mutual insurance system.

Some evidence on the incidence of famines, however, suggests that parts of a population may suffer from severe deprivation while other segments of the same population do more than survive, and even prosper. The entitlement literature emphasizes this dimension and argues that famines are often due, not to the unavailability of food per se, but to the inability of some members of the community to lay claim to that food (for that Sen 1981, Dreze and Sen 1989). So doing, the entitlement literature also implicitly recognizes that solidarity is unable to redistribute claims on food. Can the theory of repeated games shed some light on this perplexing possibility: that, in spite of the existence of a mutual insurance system, solidarity would fail to redistribute income and food when they are most needed. The answer is yes.

Consider a rural community in which some people are better off than others. As repeated droughts and other calamities strike, people progressively liquidate their productive assets: land (if land sales are legally permitted), livestock, grain stocks, bullocks, and farm equipment. Poor people run out of alienable assets faster than rich people. They are left with unalienable assets: their own labour, experience, and skills. Depending on the circumstances, the expected discounted future value of these assets may be very low: think of herders without livestock, or farmers without land. Besides, malnutrition and disease may have diminished the ability of individuals to work and households to function. In these circumstances, the expected future contribution of poor people to the mutual insurance system is very low. They are no longer attractive partners, and nobody wishes to attract their goodwill by supporting them. Better off members of the solidarity network then find it in their collective best interest to temporarily shut poorer people off from the mutual insurance arrangement. This is more likely to happen in difficult times for everyone, when the global resources of the solidarity network are seriously reduced, and the maintenance and rehabilitation of destitutes particularly onerous.

Does it mean that poor people, knowing that they may be denied assistance when they most need it, should refuse to participate to the solidarity system? They probably do not have that option. Indeed, they need the mutual assistance system too badly in order to get through normal years to have the luxury to refuse a contract that shuts them off in bad years. All they can do is gamble their way out of poverty and destitution, and hope that 'nature' allows them to accumulate enough to be perceived as somebody worth preserving in the system.

One may wonder how coalitions of players can coordinate to exclude poor members temporarily when the mutual insurance system operates as a network. In practice, poor people are likely to have a small number of asymmetric ties with participants in the insurance pool. Being dropped by one influential member of the network may be used as a signal by others and lead them to discontinue their interpersonal relations as well. This singularly reinforces the power that patrons exercise on their poorer clients: writing them off may be a death warrant.

The ideas suggested here are consistent with some of the empirical evidence about famines. For instance, they explain how destitution can exist in societies with strong solidarity ties; and why destitutes often leave their village and come to the cities. More empirical research is needed to verify the above theory, but if true, the view of solidarity systems presented here also casts serious doubts regarding their ability to deal effectively with the old, the sick and the disabled, particularly without relatives; and with poor segments of the population in case of recurrent drought.

4.8 CONCLUSION

This chapter has focused on natural limits to the risk coping strategies of the poor. After outlining some obvious difficulties with precautionary savings, we focused primarily on informal risk sharing networks. Using concepts developed by the theory of repeated games, we gained a new understanding of many stylized features of poor rural communities. In particular, we explained how the need for intertemporal insurance favours the emergence of centres or patrons able to drain resources and information. We also saw how large external shocks may lead to the rejection of poorer people from the system. The existence of solidarity networks influences how changes in economic environment affect behaviour and welfare.

There is no contradiction between the formalization of peasant behaviour presented here and the central idea of Scott's *Moral Economy of Peasants*, namely that ethical values of pre-capitalist societies emphasize solidarity as a moral obligation and subsistence as a right. Ethics can be viewed as performing two functions: first, reduce moral hazard by attaching a moral penalty to unobservable infringements of solidarity rules; and secondly, mediate conflictual relationships between asymmetric players and provide guidance on what behaviour is fair and acceptable – in the parlance of repeated games, a focal point.

Repeated game theory, however, casts some doubts on the ability of the system to deal with the old and the disabled. Ethics, myths and political institutions there too may help mitigate problems. For instance, the cult of ancestors protects old people against neglect; and granting symbolic magical powers to mentally disabled people ensures them a role in society. Finally, peasant ethics portray the village as an idyllic place of equality and harmony, but in practice patronage and social differentiation often dominate. Thus, peasant values not only present a model of social utopia, but may also perform the function of ideology. External observers should be particularly wary of the rosy picture pre-industrial society easily paint of themselves: behind it too often lurks the extraction of a surplus from people at the lower end of the social system by people at the upper end. To this we now turn in more detail.

5. Risk and inequality

The purpose of this chapter is to provide a semi-rigorous treatment of the relationship between risk and inequality over time. There has been a lot of interest in the risk coping strategies of the poor in the recent literature but little work on the relationship between these strategies and inequality (Fafchamps 1999b). Some have begun to suspect that certain risk coping strategies further impoverish the poor (for example Sen 1981, Dasgupta 1993). Labour bonding and debt peonage are examples that we have discussed earlier (for example de Janvry 1981, Srinivasan 1989). Patronage, that is, the protection of the poor by the rich in exchange for labour and services, is also suspected of perpetuating poverty (for example Platteau 1995a, Platteau 1995b).

The purpose of this chapter is to clarify the relationship between inequality and risk. Our objective is to understand how wealth accumulation and risk sharing affect the evolution of inequality over time. We ignore possible feedback effects between inequality and social choices (Benabou 2000). Mookherjee and Ray (2000) have shown that, in a generic model with human capital accumulation, persistent inequality can arise. Multiplicity of steady states may also occur if human capital is indivisible. A similar result is obtained in Durlauf (1996) in a model where wealth feeds back into educational investment through the finance of local public schools. Here we abstract from human capital issues. The persistence of inequality is studied in detail for the US in Arrow et al. (2000). We focus, here on poor agrarian economies.

Instead of analysing on a single model in detail, we provide a rapid overview of various modeling frameworks. This approach has the merit of identifying key trade-offs. Results presented here should be seen as preliminary and tentative. To keep things manageable, we focus on a two-agent economy and ignore incentive issues and asymmetric information. Agents are infinitely lived. Returns to wealth are taken to be deterministic but, unlike many models of long-term inequality, income is stochastic. Five concepts of inequality are distinguished: in marginal utility, consumption, income, cash-in-hand, and wealth.

We begin by showing that when risk sharing is perfect, inequality in welfare is constant over time. This is hardly a novel result, but it implies that perfect risk sharing eliminates social mobility. This might be a 'good' thing if welfare is distributed equitably. But it is hardly equitable if the constant distribution of welfare is highly unequal. We also examine the constraints that voluntary participation in mutual insurance imposes on redistribution.

Next, we assume risk sharing away and examine how inequality evolves over time when agents accumulate an asset. We distinguish between three canonical situations. We first assume that asset accumulation is unbounded and the asset yields a positive return. In this case, wealth can be thought of as capital. We show that inequality converges to a single value over time. If agents have different propensities to save, the share of total wealth in the hands of the more thrifty agent converges to 1. If agents have identical savings functions, inequality converges to an arbitrary level that depends on the path of income realizations.

We then consider what happens when the asset yields a zero or negative return. Grain storage is an example of such an asset. Here, the only motive for holding wealth is precautionary saving. In this case, there is no persistent inequality; agents switch rank as a function of income realizations. Inequality is nevertheless correlated over time. This correlation is higher when the asset return is higher (that is, less negative).

Next we examine the situation when wealth yields a positive return but is in finite supply. Land is an example of such an asset. Manpower can also, in principle, be accumulated via indenture contracts. We find that, in this case, persistent inequality naturally arises if one agent is more thrifty than the other. Persistent inequality may also arise even if agents have identical savings functions provided their savings rate increases with wealth. In this case multiple equilibria may obtain, especially if the return to the asset is high or the asset stock is large. Initial conditions or early realizations of income select which equilibrium the economy gets locked into. Societies might seek to prevent this kind of polarization by closing down markets in such assets. One possible example is the prohibition of land sales that prevails over most of the countryside in Sub-Saharan Africa (for example Atwood 1990, Platteau 1992). Another example is slavery, which is now prohibited everywhere but was legal in many places a couple of hundred years ago. Many European immigrants, for instance, financed their voyage to America through indenture contracts.

We then return to risk sharing in the presence of assets. With perfect risk sharing, welfare inequality is constant across time. But, as is well known, much indeterminacy arises in the definition (and packaging) of assets. For this reason, we focus on the accumulation of net wealth and ignore credit. We find that for continued participation to mutual insurance to be voluntary, welfare inequality must be consistent with agents' assets and incomes. A redistribution of assets may thus be necessary to support a particular level of inequality. This implies that asset inequality must remain 'close' to welfare inequality.

In the following section, we introduce imperfect commitment. The end result is a hybrid situation half-way between the risk sharing model and the pure accumulation model. One interesting result is that, if risk aversion is high for poor agents but low for rich ones, risk sharing with imperfect commitment is most likely to take the form of patronage. We find that, with imperfect commitment, patronage on average takes away from the poor. In this case, risk sharing becomes a factor of polarization as it makes inequality more likely and more persistent.[92] Patronage does, however, protect the poor from starvation so that for the poor it is preferable to less wealth inequality but no risk sharing. This might explain why patronage relations tend to arise endogenously in a variety of contexts, even after asset redistribution (de Janvry et al. 2001).

To further understand polarization, in the last part of this chapter we take a closer look at the lower end of the wealth ladder and focus on factors affecting the existence of a debt trap.

5.1   A STYLIZED ECONOMY

We begin with an infinitely lived, two-agent economy. Throughout the chapter, we use the superscript $i \in \{1, 2\}$ to denote the agent and the subscript t to denote the time period. Aggregate variables appear without i superscript. Utility is written $U_i(c_t^i)$. For simplicity, we assume that the common discount factor is unity. Each agent i derives a random stream of income $\{y_t^i\}$ on a finite support $(0, \bar{y}]$ with $\bar{y} < \infty$. We also assume that the probability of zero income is 0. Aggregate income y_t is defined $y_t = \sum y_t^i$.

Each agent is endowed with a vector of assets. Some of these assets are marketable, such as grain; others cannot be traded, such as entrepreneurship. The value of marketable assets is called wealth and denoted W_t^i. Wealth can be accumulated. In contrast, non-traded assets denoted Z^i cannot be accumulated and are constant over time. The institutional framework determines which assets are marketable and which are not. The prohibition of indenture contracts, for instance, means that manpower is not a marketable asset – although its product, work, can be traded. Wealth yields a return γ which, for simplicity, we assume constant over time and individuals. This return can be positive or negative. When $\gamma > 0$, we say that wealth is productive; when $\gamma \leq 0$, we say that wealth is storable but unproductive. Examples of productive wealth include land, manpower, and capital. Examples of storable but unproductive wealth include grain, water, and minerals.[93] Income is a function of marketable and non-marketable assets:

$$y_t^i = \omega^i(Z^i, \theta_t) + \gamma W_t^i \qquad (5.1)$$

where θ_t denotes the state of nature at time t. Income is random through the dependence of function $\omega^i(.)$ on θ_t. We assume here that θ_t is uncorrelated over time. In the remainder of this chapter, we refer to $\omega^i(Z^i, \theta_t)$ as labour income and to γW_t^i as wealth income. Cash-in-hand X_t^i is defined as $X_t^i \equiv y_t^i + W_t^i$.

The object of the chapter is to investigate how wealth accumulation and risk sharing affect inequality. We distinguish five concepts of inequality: in marginal utility, consumption, income, cash-in-hand, and wealth. Since there are only two agents, inequality can be represented as the ratio between the two agents. Inequality ratios are written as the letter N_t^z where z denotes the variable over which the ratio is computed. For instance, inequality in income is written:

$$N_t^y \equiv y_t^2/y_t^1 \tag{5.2}$$

Similarly, inequality in consumption, cash-in-hand, and wealth are written $N_t^c \equiv c_t^2/c_t^1$, $N_t^x \equiv X_t^2/X_t^1$, and $N_t^w \equiv W_t^2/W_t^1$. For reasons that will become apparent when we discuss risk sharing, it is also useful to define a measure of welfare inequality as the ratio of marginal utility:

$$N_t^u \equiv U_1'(c_t^1)/U_2'(c_t^2) \tag{5.3}$$

If $U(c) = \log(c)$, then $N_t^u = N_t^c$. In general N_t^c tends to track N_t^u and can thus be thought of as a money-metric measure of inequality in instantaneous welfare.[94] While four of the inequality measures are non-problematic, N_t^w is not defined when $W_t^1 = 0$.[95] This is taken into account in subsequent sections.

The purpose of this chapter is to characterize what long-term inequality looks like and how it evolves over time. We also seek to relate the different measures of inequality to each other. As is clear from the notation, inequality measures vary over time and with the state of nature. Much of this chapter is thus concerned with the probability distribution of inequality measures. We focus primarily on long-term – or steady state – inequality and thus seek to uncover the asymptotic (steady state) unconditional distribution of inequality measures. To reflect this fact, steady state inequality measures are written without time subscript. For instance, $\Pr[N^y]$ denotes the probability distribution of steady state income distribution. The unconditional expected value of N^y is denoted $N_e^y \equiv E[N^y]$, and similarly for the other inequality measures.

We also wish to study the extent to which inequality endures over time. In particular we focus on the steady state correlation between N_t^y and N_{t+1}^y or, more precisely, on the relationship between N_t^y and $E[N_{t+1}^y | N_t^y]$.

Suppose that

$$E[N^y_{t+1}|N^y_t] = \rho N^y_t + \delta N^y \qquad (5.4)$$

If, for instance, $\delta = 0$ and $\rho = 1$,

$$E[N^y_{t+1}|N^y_t] = N^y_t \qquad (5.5)$$

inequality follows a random walk: inequality today is likely to persist tomorrow. If, in contrast, $\rho = 0$ and $\delta = 1$, we have

$$E[N^y_{t+1}|N^y_t] = N^y \qquad (5.6)$$

which implies that inequality is short-lived. In general, the closer to 1 ρ is, the more persistent inequality is.

We proceed as follows. We first examine a number of simple, limit cases. Then we introduce complications. Limited commitment is discussed in Section 5.5. To characterize the distribution of inequality measures, we rely on a combination of algebraic and simulation methods. In all cases, we seek to relate different types of inequality to each other.

5.2   NO MARKETABLE ASSETS

We begin by assuming that marketable assets are absent and thus that accumulation is not feasible: $W^i_t = 0$ for all i and t.[96] Income is labour income only: $y^i_t = \omega^i(Z^i, \theta_t)$. It follows that $\Pr[N^y_t] = \Pr[N^y]$: the unconditional probability distribution of income inequality is at its steady state in all t; there is no transition period. It also follows that $N^x_t = N^y_t$ since $y^i_t = X^i_t$. The unconditional expectation of income inequality simply is:

$$E[N^y] = E\left[\frac{\omega^2(Z^2,\theta_t)}{\omega^1(Z^1,\theta_t)}\right] \qquad (5.7)$$

This means that a more talented individual has a higher income on average. Since income is a function of never changing assets, there is no social mobility in incomes. We also see that, since we have assumed that the θ_t shocks are uncorrelated over time, conditional and unconditional income inequality are equal:

$$E[N^y_t|N^y_{t-1}] = E[N^y] \qquad (5.8)$$

Any deviation from expected income inequality $E[N^y]$ is short-lived.

Inequality in consumption depends on whether income risk is shared or not. If risk sharing is not possible, then $c_t^i = y_t^i = \omega(Z^i, \theta_t)$. In this case, $N_t^c = N_t^y$ and shares all the properties of N_t^y. If, in addition, utility has the form $U(c) = \log c$, we also have $N_t^u = N_t^y$. In a world with no accumulable assets, no risk sharing, and relative risk aversion close to unity (that is, log utility), income inequality summarizes all there is to know about welfare inequality.

Suppose, in contrast, mutual insurance contracts are perfectly and costlessly enforceable. Perfect competition thus reaches an efficient allocation. Pareto efficiency in the sharing of risk dictates that

$$\frac{U_1'(c_t^1)}{U_2'(c_t^2)} = \frac{U_1'(c_{t'}^1)}{U_2'(c_{t'}^2)} \equiv k \text{ for all } t \text{ and } t' \tag{5.9}$$

where k is a constant equal to the ratio of welfare weights (for example Cochrane 1991, Mace 1991, Altonji et al. 1992). Since $U_1'(c_t^1)/U_2'(c_t^2) \equiv N_t^u$, it follows that welfare inequality N_t^u is constant over time with $N^u = k$. This is true even though N_t^y varies from period to period: welfare inequality is divorced from income inequality.

With perfect pooling of risk, individual consumption is only a function of aggregate income. This implies that, if aggregate income y_t is constant over time, consumption is constant as well. If the economy is subject to collective shocks, inequality in consumption varies in a deterministic fashion with aggregate income. But the distribution of welfare is unchanged, that is, there exist monotonic functions of individual consumptions c_t^1 and c_t^2 (the marginal utility functions) such that the ratio of these functions is constant across time and states of nature. Thus, even though individual consumption and welfare might change over time (as aggregate resources expand or dwindle), inequality remains constant in some fundamental sense.

When agents have identical preferences with constant relative risk aversion, N_t^c remains constant over time even in the presence of aggregate shocks.[97] Consumption inequality $N_t^c = (N^u)^{\frac{1}{k}}$, with $N_t^c = N^u$ if $U(c) = \log(c)$. For other utility functions, N_t^c might change slightly over time and states of nature. But within this framework, N_t^c can be thought of as an approximation to N^u, which is the relevant welfare measure in our economy.

Although hardly novel, this result implies that perfect risk sharing, as could be achieved for instance via a perfect insurance market, would freeze welfare inequality to a permanent level. This might be socially acceptable if this level is relatively egalitarian. There are many Pareto efficient allocations in our stylized economy. But nothing guarantees that the Pareto efficient allocation selected by a competitive market equilibrium would be socially acceptable. This probably explains why there is a lot of public intervention in social insurance and why many insurance schemes pursue redistribution objectives. Some are even worded not as insurance but as anti-poverty programmes. Because insurance also determines welfare inequality, it is likely to be combined with redistribution so that it does not itself become the source of inequality.

This raises the issue of how much redistribution can be sustained if participation in risk sharing is voluntary. Not all risk sharing arrangements can be sustained in a decentralized market. The main constraint imposed by a decentralized market equilibrium is ex ante voluntary participation: agents must find it in their interest to participate in a risk sharing arrangement/to purchase an insurance contract. If this condition is not satisfied, agents would be better off by consuming their individual income.[98] This simple observation implies that agents who could guarantee themselves a higher utility in autarchy must in general have a higher level of utility with risk sharing.

Risk sharing does not preclude redistribution. Suppose we wish to achieve equality in expected consumption, that is, we wish to attain $E[N^c] = 1$. If $E[N^y] = E[N^c]$, attaining equality is non-problematic since reversion to autarchy – $c_t^i = y_t^i$ – would result in equality. We can thus define redistribution as the difference between $E[N^y]$ and $E[N^c]$. With taxation/forced participation in mutual insurance, any level of N^u is sustainable. This not true of decentralizable arrangements. Voluntary participation in any mutual insurance contract puts bounds on how far N^u (and thus $E[N^c]$) can stray from $E[N^y]$ and thus on the level of equality that can be achieved.

For instance, if all agents have the same utility function, agents with higher expected earnings must be ensured higher consumption. This puts a bound on $E[N^y] - E[N^c]$. Consumption inequality is thus, in general, a function of unalienable assets Z^i. The only case in which voluntary participation might induce agents with higher expected earnings to accept less consumption than agents with lower expected earnings is if the former are much more risk averse than the latter. By the same reasoning, we see that the more risk averse agents are, the more they are willing to accept a redistribution of average consumption in exchange for better insurance. We revisit these issues in Section 5.5.

These results are summarized in the following proposition:

Proposition 5.1 *In the absence of accumulable assets:*

1. *The distribution of income inequality is at its steady state in all periods:* $\Pr[N_t^y] = \Pr[N^y]$ *for all t.*
2. *If income shocks are uncorrelated, conditional expected inequality in income is constant:* $E[N_t^y | N_{t-1}^y] = E[N_t^y] = E[N^y]$.

Proposition 5.2   *Without risk sharing:*

1.   *Inequality in consumption is equal to inequality in income: $N_t^c = N_t^y$.*
2.   *Expected long-term inequality in consumption is constant: $E[N^c] = E[N^y]$*
3.   *With log utility, inequality in welfare is equal to inequality in income: $E[N^u] = E[N^y]$.*

Proposition 5.3   *With perfect risk sharing:*

1. $N_t^u = N^u$: *welfare inequality is constant; there is no social mobility.*
2. $N_t^c = G(y_t)$ – *inequality in consumption is a deterministic function of aggregate income.*
3. $N_t^c = N^c$ *if $y_t = y$ or if $U_i(c) = \log(c)$ or if $U(c) = \dfrac{c^{1-R}}{1-R}$ for $i = \{1, 2\}$.*

Proposition 5.4   *With voluntary participation in risk sharing:*

1.   *$E[N^c]$ is a non- decreasing function of $E[N^y]$ if all agents share the same utility function (up to an affine transformation).*
2.   *The more risk averse agents are, the more redistribution $E[N^y] - E[N^c]$ can voluntarily be achieved, and the closer $E[N^c]$ can be brought to unity (equality in expected ratio of consumption).*

5.3   ACCUMULATION WITH NO RISK SHARING

We now allow for wealth accumulation by assuming the existence of marketable assets. In this section, we focus on the case where explicit risk sharing is not possible – perhaps because a market for insurance does not exist. Agents potentially have two motives for saving: precautionary saving and growth in consumption – prudence and patience (Kimball 1990). If the return on marketable assets is negative, prudence is the only motive for saving (Deaton 1991). Throughout we assume that there is no borrowing.

5.3.1   Unbounded Accumulation

We first examine the case where $\gamma > 0$. Provide agents save enough, they can accumulate indefinitely. At the limit, their wealth becomes so large that income is entirely dominated by the return to wealth γW_t^i which, by assumption, is non-stochastic. Consequently, as wealth becomes large, income shocks have less and less effect on consumption. This implies that inequality is asymptotically deterministic. We now show this more rigorously.

We first must establish conditions under which people save enough for wealth to grow indefinitely. We need $E[W^i_{t+1}|W^i_t] > W^i_t$. Suppose, for instance, that agents save a constant proportion s of their income $y^i_t = \omega^i + \gamma W^i_t$. We have:

$$
\begin{aligned}
E[W^i_{t+1}|W^i_t] &= E[s(\omega^i + \gamma W^i_t) + W^i_t] \\
&= sE[\omega^i] + s\gamma W^i_t + W^i_t > W^i_t
\end{aligned}
\tag{5.10}
$$

which is satisfied for any $s > 0$. If each agent chooses their level of saving by maximizing its expected discounted utility subject to a budget constraint, we obtain an Euler equation of the form:

$$
U'_i(c^i_t) = (1 + \gamma)E[U'_i(c^i_{t+1})]
\tag{5.11}
$$

where the intertemporal discount factor drops out since, by assumption, agents do not discount the future.[99] We see from the above equation that the marginal utility of income must fall, on average, over time – which implies that consumption must rise and thus that assets must be accumulated (Deaton 1991). This establishes that when $\gamma > 0$ and agents do not discount the future, indefinite accumulation obtains.

Having established that both agents accumulate, we now turn to the characterization of long-term inequality in wealth N^w_t. Since agents always hold positive assets, at least after a while, the distribution of N^w_t is well defined.[100] We note that, as both agents become wealthier, labour income becomes a vanishingly small proportion of their cash-in-hand. Savings thus becomes almost deterministic and the path of individual wealth converges to a deterministic path. This is illustrated in Figure 5.1 which plots three possible paths of N^w_t for a fully symmetrical model with a constant saving rate. The only difference between the paths is the sequence of labour income shocks. To facilitate interpretation, we graph wealth shares $W^2_t / W^1_t + W^2_t$ instead of N^w_t. We see that all paths eventually converge to a single share.

How inequality evolves over time depends on the relative savings rate of both agents. If one agent saves faster than the other, wealth inequality N^w_t diverges permanently, either tending to infinity (if agent 2 saves more) or to 0 (if agent 1 saves more). If agents save at the same rate, their wealth asymptotically grows at the same rate: the ratio of their wealths tends to a constant. Wealth inequality tends to a constant (see Figure 5.1). This is true even if their labour income processes are different because, when wealth is large enough, labour income does not matter anymore. This finding is reminiscent of Polya urn processes (Arthur et al. 1994). Wealth inequality N^w_t follows a random walk with smaller and smaller increments. Initial realizations of income determine the speed with which wealth is initially accumulated, and thus the process of initial differentiation. As time passes,

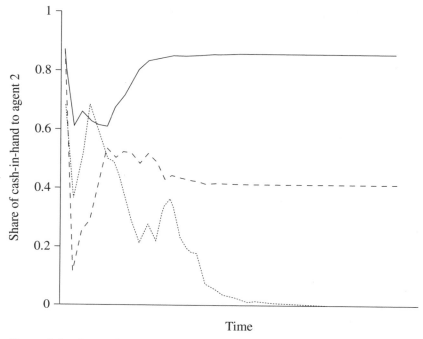

Figure 5.1   Inequality over time for three realizations of labour income

however, changes in wealth inequality (that is, in the ratio of wealth levels) become smaller and smaller as income – and thus savings – become progressively dominated by wealth. Inequality in wealth converges to an asymptotic value N^w. This is illustrated in Figure 5.1.[101]

This implies that the conditional distribution of N^w_{t+1} gets more and more narrowly defined around N^w_t as time passes. There is 'lock-in': changes in inequality becomes smaller and smaller over time. Even though both agents might have had the same economic opportunities ex ante, over time they diverge so that, with time, their economic prospects become highly contrasted. At the limit, relative prosperity becomes permanent. Social mobility – that is, the chance of changing one's rank – disappears over time.

Which value N^w_t converges to is path dependent: if agent 1 is lucky early on, he or she gets a head-start, and vice versa. Ex ante, there are many possible asymptotic values N^w can take – essentially any value between zero and infinity. Are all these values equally likely? In general the answer is no. To characterize the ex ante (unconditional) distribution of N^w we need to impose more structure on the model. The distribution of N^w is also complicated by the fact that it is a ratio. It is easier to characterize the distribution of the share of total wealth $S_t^w \equiv W_t^1/W_t^1 + W_t^2$. By construction, $S_t^w \in [0, 1]$. Since N_t^w converges to a single value, so does S_t^w.

With identical non-traded assets $Z^1 = Z^2$, independent income shocks, identical initial wealth $W^1 = W^2$, and identical utility functions $U^1(.) = U^2(.)$, both agents are ex ante equivalent and their economic opportunities are the same. If agents have equal initial endowments and identical preferences, it should be possible to show that $E[S^w] = 0.5$. The realized value of S^w, however, can take any value between 0 and 1. In the symmetric case, agents have equal opportunities ex ante but once inequality sets in it gets reinforced over time.

Having characterized the distribution of wealth inequality, we now turn to other inequality measures. By definition, we have $N_t^x = (\omega_t^2 + (1+\gamma)W_t^2)/(\omega_t^1 + (1+\gamma)W_t^1)$ and $N_t^y = (\omega_t^2 + \gamma W_t^2)/(\omega_t^1 + \gamma W_t^1)$. As W_t^1 and W_t^2 tend to infinity over time, both ratios tend to N_t^w. We thus have $\lim_{t\to\infty}\|N_t^x - N_t^w\| = \lim_{t\to\infty}\|N_t^y - N_t^w\| = 0$: inequality in cash-in-hand and in income tends to inequality in wealth. Of course, since wealth increases without bounds, inequality is not synonymous with poverty: at the limit, both agents are infinitely wealthy.

Given that there is no risk sharing, each agent consumes exclusively from their own cash-in-hand $X_t^i \equiv y_t^i + W_t^i$. Let $c^i(X_t^i)$ denote the consumption function of individual i. We have $N_t^c = c^2(X_t^2)/c^1(X_t^1)$. Suppose that both consumption functions are asymptotically linear, for example, that $\lim_{x\to\infty} c^i(X) = k^i X$. In this case, $\lim_{t\to\infty}\|N_t^c - (k^2/k^1)N_t^x\| = 0$: inequality in consumption tends to a multiple of wealth inequality.

More generally, there exists a function of wealth inequality $f^c(N_t^x)$ to which consumption inequality converges: $\lim_{t\to\infty}\|N_t^c - f(N_t^x)\| = 0$.[102] This implies that, at the limit, the ratio of consumption is a function of the ratio of wealth. The same reasoning applies to welfare inequality, that is, there exists a function $f^u(N_t^x)$ such that $\lim_{t\to\infty}\|N_t^c - f(N_t^x)\| = 0$. Inequality in wealth leads to inequality in consumption and in welfare. Other conclusions apply as well: path dependence; lock-in; ex ante unpredictability of long-term inequality. When both agents asymptotically save at the same rate, all inequality measures converge to a single number.

These results can be summarized as follows:

Proposition 5.5 *With unbounded accumulation ($\gamma > 0$), we have:*

1. $\lim_{t\to\infty}\|N_t^x - N_t^w\| = \lim_{t\to\infty}\|N_t^y - N_t^w\| = 0$
2. *There exists a function $f^c(N_t^x)$ such that $\lim_{t\to\infty}\|N_t^c - f(N_t^x)\| = 0$.*
3. *There exists a function $f^u(N_t^x)$ such that $\lim_{t\to\infty}\|N_t^u - f(N_t^x)\| = 0$.*
4. $\lim_{t\to\infty} Var[N_{t+1}^w|N_t^w] = 0$, $\lim_{t\to\infty} Var[N_{t+1}^x|N_t^x] = 0$, $\lim_{t\to\infty} Var[N_{t+1}^y|N_t^y] = 0$, $\lim_{t\to\infty} Var[N_{t+1}^c|N_t^c] = 0$, $\lim_{t\to\infty} Var[N_{t+1}^u|N_t^u] = 0$.

5. *Ex ante, N^w is a random variable $\in (0, \infty)$. By extension, the same applies to other inequality measures.*
6. *If agents asymptotically save at the same rate, all inequality measures converge to a single number $N^w \in (0, \infty)$.*
7. *If agents asymptotically save at a different rate, all inequality measures converge either to 0 (if agent 2 saves less than 1) or to ∞ (if agent 2 saves more than 1).*

5.3.2 Bounded Accumulation with Unproductive Assets

The situation is very different if $\gamma < 0$. In this case, wealth accumulation is costly. Agents engage in it only to insure themselves against income shocks – the precautionary savings motive. This case is more relevant for poor or preindustrial societies where opportunities to invest are few and returns to assets are low.

Accumulation in such models has been analysed elsewhere (for example Zeldes 1989b, Deaton 1990, Deaton 1991, Deaton 1992a). Assets are known to follow a renewal process. As long as accumulated wealth is positive, it follows a random walk. For sufficiently large negative shocks, agents deplete all their wealth, at which point the process is 'renewed', that is, it forgets the past and starts anew. How much accumulation takes place depends on the marginal propensity to save (MPS) out of cash-in-hand. Kimball (1990) has shown how the MPS is related to the third derivative of the utility function via what he calls 'prudence', defined as $\phi \equiv - U'''/U''$. Other things being. equal, more prudent agents – higher ϕ – save more.

We seek to characterize the distribution of cash-in-hand, income, and consumption. In this model as in the previous one, all inequality measures are closely related. This is because, in the absence of risk sharing, an agent's consumption depends exclusively on individual cash-in-hand X_t^i. Inequality in cash-in-hand thus translate into inequality in consumption and welfare. However, because agents use wealth to smooth consumption, inequality in consumption is typically much less than inequality in wealth (for example Paxson 1992, Townsend 1994).[103]

We begin by noting that, since income is bounded, wealth is also bounded. This is because $\gamma < 0$. To see why, let $\bar{\omega}^i$ denote the maximum level of labour income. The maximum rate at which wealth can accumulate is when agents save all and income is always at its maximum. $W_{t+1}^i = \bar{\omega}^i + (1 + \gamma) W_t^i$. Since $\gamma < 0$, we see that wealth cannot exceed $-\bar{\omega}^i/\gamma$.

Inequality in cash-in-hand N_t^x in general follows an AR1 stochastic process between 0 and ∞. This is because income realizations induce random changes in the wealth of both agents. If an agent gets a temporarily high cash-in-hand level, he or she saves and his or her wealth goes up. The opposite is true if realized cash-in-hand is low. Cash-in-hand inequality is thus a transient phenomenon: since each agent's wealth is bounded from above and from below, all agents eventually run out of funds in finite time. This implies that no agent can indefinitely stay ahead of the other. By this reasoning, the distribution of N_t^x is stationary. By extension, all inequality measures have stationary distributions. Unlike in the case with infinite accumulation, there is no lock-in here.

Can we be more precise and characterize the distribution of some of the inequality measures? Consider consumption inequality. If agents were perfectly able to smooth consumption thanks to precautionary saving, consumption would be constant as well as consumption inequality. This outcome, however, is generally not achievable. The next best outcome is if preferences are quadratic and households face no credit constraint. In this case, certainty equivalence applies and agents respond to income shocks by consuming the annuity value of their total wealth (for example Hall 1978, Zeldes 1989b).

In our case, the annuity value of a (finite) income shock is 0 since agents' rate of time preference is 0.[104] The annuity value of wealth is also 0 since, with $\gamma < 0$, wealth is expected to be eliminated in finite time. We therefore get the standard permanent income result: when the rate of time preference is 0, agents consume their average income $E[\omega^i(Z_t^i, \theta_t)]$ which is also the annuity value of wealth. In the more general case, Zeldes (1989b) has shown that, when wealth is sufficiently large, consumption tends to the certainty equivalent level of consumption for a large enough level of wealth. This is true for any (reasonable) utility function and holds even if agents cannot incur a negative net worth. Applying these ideas to our economy, we see that when the wealth of both agents is large, N_t^c tends to $E[\omega^2(Z_t^2, \theta_t)]/E[\omega^1(Z_t^1, \theta_t)]$: consumption inequality is a function of inequality in expected labour income.

In general, N_t^c is not constant. When cash-in-hand is large for both agents, certainty equivalence approximately holds and fluctuations in consumption – and thus in consumption inequality – are quite small. As Zeldes (1989b) and Carroll (1992) have shown, however, certainty equivalence is violated when wealth is small and agents cannot borrow (as we assume here). In this case, a shortfall in cash-in-hand results in a drop in consumption – and a temporary increase in consumption inequality. Since these shortfalls can affect both agents, we would expect consumption inequality to fluctuate around $E[\omega^2(Z_t^2, \theta_t)]/E[\omega^1(Z_t^1, \theta_t)]$ and to be correlated over time (through the dependence of current consumption on accumulated wealth). The precise distribution of consumption inequality, however, is difficult to characterize without imposing more structure on the model. Figure 5.2 uses numerical simulation to illustrate how inequality in labour

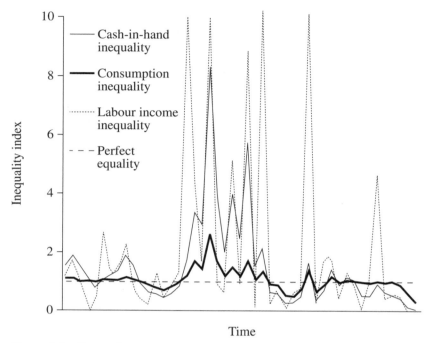

Figure 5.2   Inequality over time with precautionary saving only

income, cash-in-hand, and consumption evolve over time.[105] We see that, thanks to precautionary saving, inequality in consumption is always less than inequality in cash-in-hand or in labour income.

Regarding correlation in inequality over time, we first note that, in the absence of correlation in labour income, correlation in cash-in-hand inequality depends on how much agents accumulate. If they accumulate a lot, the correlation is high; if they accumulate little, the correlation is low. Consequently any factor that favours accumulation also favours the correlation of inequality over time. This means, for instance, that inequality is more persistent when the propensity to save is higher. By the same token, the correlation between N_t^x and N_{t+1}^x depends on γ. If γ is very negative, wealth dissipates rapidly and $Cor[N_t^x, N_{t+1}^x]$ is low: a wealth advantage does not last long. If γ is close to 0, the reverse is true. At the same time, if both agents accumulate more, they are better able to withstand shocks, and consumption inequality fluctuates less on average.

Second, we note that the more cash-in-hand is correlated over time, the more consumption is correlated as well. This is because consumption is a monotonically increasing function of cash-in-hand: $c_t^i = c^i(X_t^i)$ with $c'(X) > 0$ for all X. As a result, a high correlation between x_t^2/x_t^1 and x_{t+1}^2/x_{t+1}^1 results in a high correlation between $c^2(X_t^2)/c^1(X_t^1)$ and $c^2(X_{t+1}^2)/c^1(X_{t+1}^1)$. Since welfare inequality depends on consumption, the same observation applies to N_t^u.

Combining the two above observations, we note that factors that raise accumulation reduce the variance of consumption and welfare inequality but raise persistence in inequality. This is illustrated in Figure 5.3 again using numerical simulation: when γ is lower – and accumulation less – consumption inequality is more variable but it is less correlated over time.[106]

Results can be summarized as follows:

Proposition 5.6 *With bounded accumulation ($\gamma < 0$) and no discounting, we have:*

1. *All inequality measures are stationary Markov processes.*
2. *All inequality measures move together.*
3. *N_t^c fluctuates around $E[\omega^2(Z_t^2, \theta_t)]/E[\omega^1(Z_t^1, \theta_t)]$.*

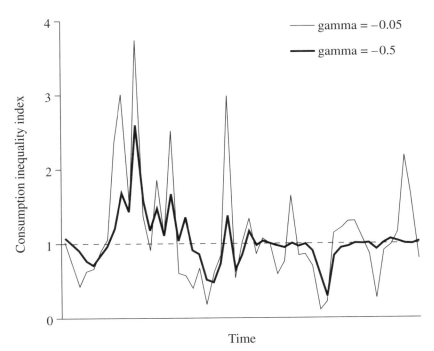

Figure 5.3   Consumption inequality and return on savings

4.   *Var*$[N_t^x]$, *Var*$[N_t^y]$, *Var*$[N_t^c]$ *and Var*$[N_t^u]$ *are non-decreasing functions of* γ.
5.   *Cor*$[N_t^x, N_{t+1}^x]$, *Cor*$[N_t^y, N_{t+1}^y]$, *Cor*$[N_t^c, N_{t+1}^c]$ *and Cor*$[N_t^u, N_{t+1}^u]$ *are increasing functions of* γ.

Part 1 above means that inequality is a transient phenomenon. Part 2 means that inequality in non-traded assets Z^i has a permanent effect on inequality. Parts 3 and 4 mean that easier accumulation reduces fluctuations in inequality but raises persistence in inequality. There is a trade-off between social mobility and vulnerability.

5.3.3   Accumulation with Assets in Fixed Supply

In the previous subsection, agents accumulate assets independently of each other. Grain storage is an example of wealth that fits nicely in this model. Other types of wealth, such as land, do not fit as nicely. In this subsection, we consider accumulable assets that are in fixed supply, that is, such that $W_t^1 + W_t^2 = \bar{W}$. Land is one possible example, provided there exists a sales market for land (Takasaki et al. 2000). Another possible example is manpower in societies that allow voluntary indenture contracts (Srinivasan 1989). In general, we assume that $\gamma \geq 0$, that is, that the asset is productive. The case where $\gamma = 0$ corresponds to the island economy is discussed in Sargent (1987), Chapter Three.

   We begin by focusing on asset inequality. Other inequality measures ultimately depend on how the fixed asset is shared. When the asset is in fixed supply, we can no longer ignore relative prices: the price p_t at which the asset is turned into consumption varies to clear the asset market. This singularly complicates the model because fluctuations in asset prices introduce uncertainty in real asset returns and generate a speculative motive for holding wealth. In the discussion that follows, we mostly ignore these complications.

   Saving is now a function of cash-in-hand and asset price: $W_{t+1}^i = s^i(\omega_t^i, W_t^i, p_t)$. To simplify the presentation, we assume that the savings function is separable so that:

$$W_{t+1}^i = \frac{s^i(\omega_t^i, W_t^i)}{g(p_t)} \qquad (5.12)$$

with $\partial s^i / \partial \omega^i \geq 0$ and $\partial s^i / \partial W^i \geq 0$. With this assumption, the market clearing condition $W_t^1 + W_t^2 = \bar{W}$ yields the following expression for asset inequality (expressed here as a share):

$$S_{t+1}^w \equiv \frac{W_{t+1}^2}{W_{t+1}^1 + W_{t+1}^2} \qquad (5.13)$$

$$= \frac{s^2(\omega_t^2, W_t^2)}{s^1(\omega_t^1, W_t^1) + s^2(\omega_t^2, W_t^2)}$$

$$= \frac{s^2(\omega_t^2, S_t^w \overline{W})}{s^1(\omega_t^1, (1 - S_t^w)\overline{W}) + s^2(\omega_t^2, S_t^w \overline{W})}$$

For comparison with earlier sections, $N_t^w = S_t^w/(1 - S_t^w)$. The advantage of the above formulation is that the asset price has been factored out. What the above expression shows is that future asset inequality depends on current inequality: when S_t^w is large, saving by agent 2 tends to be large relative to agent 1. This is because agents save from cash-in-hand and large wealth raises cash-in-hand. This process may lead to self-reinforcing inequality – what we call polarization. The question is under what conditions polarization arises.[107]

This can be answered by examining the law of motion of S_t^w given above. The analysis is complicated by the fact that the ω_t^i's are random variables so that the law of motion of S_t^w is stochastic. We focus on the relationship between S_t^w and $E[S_{t+1}^w]$. We note that

$$E[S_{t+1}^w] \simeq \frac{s^2(E[\omega_t^2], S_t^w \overline{W})}{s^1(E[\omega_t^1], (1 - S_t^w)\overline{W}) + s^2(E[\omega_t^2], S_t^w \overline{W})} \tag{5.14}$$

Consequently the relationship between S_t^w and $E[S_{t+1}^w]$ can be studied by studying the above difference equation. Figure 5.4 illustrates what it looks like depending on the curvature of the savings function.[108] The two agents are assumed to have the same savings function. Two curves are shown. The one with a nearly linear (low curvature) savings function intersects the 45 degree line at 0.5 from above. This means that if the fixed asset is shared equally at time t, it tends to be shared equally at time $t+1$ as well. Deviations from equality tend to correct themselves over time: at low S_t^w leads to a higher $E[S_{t+1}^w]$ and vice versa. Income shocks push S_{t+1}^w up or down a bit, but inequality always gravitates around $S_t^w = 0.5$. There is a single steady state distribution of assets. Polarization does not arise. If agents have different savings rates, polarization arises: the thrifty agent eventually gets most of the asset. This finding is reminiscent of what we found with unbounded accumulation: the share of total wealth owned by the thrifty agent rises over time, although in this case it does not converge to 1 unless the savings rate of the other agent falls to 0 for low enough wealth. However, there is still a single steady state distribution.

The story is different in the case of the high curvature savings function. Here, the curve intersects the 45 degree line three times, corresponding to three zeros of the difference equation.[109] The middle intersection is unstable because it is cut from below. This means that, starting from equal

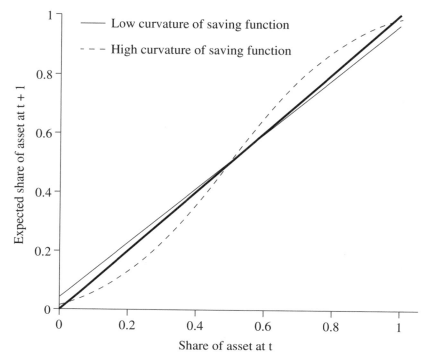

Figure 5.4   Law of motion of inequality with fixed total asset

distribution of assets, small differences in income realizations induce
differentiation: one agent is able to accumulate more than the other. There
are therefore two steady state distributions of assets: one in which agent 1
owns most of the asset, and one in which agent 2 is the wealthy agent. There
is polarization even though agents are symmetrical, that is, have the same
preferences and the same expected labour income.

Multiple steady state distributions are simulated in Figure 5.5.[110] Two
alternative paths of S_t^w are shown. The only difference between the two is
the sequence of labour income shocks. Which long-term distribution of
inequality is chosen depends on initial realizations of labour income. When
agent 2 is lucky early on, he or she is able to accumulate more of the fixed
asset and to gain a permanent advantage. The reverse is true if agent 1
enjoys high income draw at the beginning. There is path dependence. These
results are similar to those reported by Carter and Zimmerman (2000) for
a more complicated simulated economy. Multiple equilibria arise even if
labour incomes are strongly correlated across agents, although this corre-

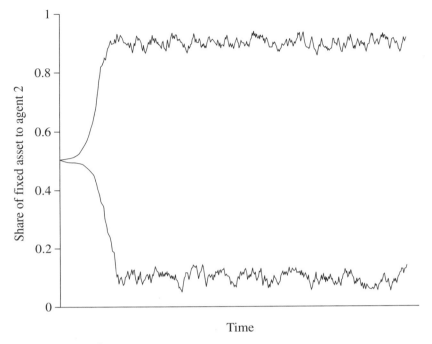

Figure 5.5   Polarization

lation may delay the polarization process starting from an egalitarian distribution.

The corollary of path dependence is that the starting point – 'history' – matters. If, for exogenous reasons, an agent has most of the wealth to start with, multiplicity of equilibria disappears. The only steady state distribution is the one that favours this agent.

The above framework enables us to investigate the factors that favour multiple equilibria and thus polarization among otherwise identical agents. We have already seen that polarization is more likely when the savings rate increases sharply with cash-in-hand. In fact, polarization cannot arise if the savings rate is constant and identical for both agents. In this case we have:

$$E[S_{t+1}^w] \simeq \frac{sE[\omega_t] + sp_t(1+\gamma)S_t^w \overline{W})}{sE[\omega_t] + sp_t(1+\gamma)(1-S_t^w)\overline{W} + sE[\omega_t] + sp_t(1+\gamma)S_t^w \overline{W})} \quad (5.15)$$

$$= \frac{sE[\omega_t] + sp_t(1+\gamma)S_t^w \overline{W}}{2sE[\omega_t] + sp_t(1+\gamma)\overline{W}}$$

which is linear in S^w_t. The intuition behind this result is that for multiple steady state distribution to arise, accumulation must get reinforced over time.

It can also be shown that all factors that increase wealth income relative to labour income favour multiple equilibria. This is true of an increase in γ or $\bar{W}$ or of a decrease in $E[\omega^i]$. The reason is that when the income from wealth is small, differences in wealth may not be sufficient to cause a large differentiation in savings rate. As a result, polarization does not arise.

Turning to the conditional (steady state) distribution of inequality, results from the previous section apply here as well: the more remunerative wealth is, the more correlated inequality is over time. The rationale is the same.

Having clarified how wealth evolves over time, the extension to consumption and welfare is straightforward. In the absence of risk sharing, consumption is simply a function of individual cash-in-hand. Inequality in wealth results in inequality in cash-in-hand and thus in consumption and welfare. Consequently, all that has been said about polarization and multiple equilibria in asset inequality applies to consumption and welfare as well.

Our findings can be summarized as follows:

Proposition 5.7   *Suppose $W^1_t + W^2_t = \bar{W}$ and $\gamma \geq 0$. We have:*

1. *All inequality measures move together.*
2. *Multiple steady state distributions of inequality can arise if the savings rate increases with wealth. This is true even if agents have identical savings function and distribution of labour income. This is true even if labour incomes are strongly correlated.*
3. *When multiple steady state distribution exists, initial conditions may have a permanent effect on the distribution of inequality.*
4. *Multiple steady state distributions are more likely if:*
    (a) the savings rate increases more rapidly with wealth;
    (b) the return to wealth γ is high;
    (c) total fixed wealth $\bar{W}$ is large;
    (d) expected labour income $E[\omega^i]$ is small.

Although it is perilous to interpret the above results literally since they were obtained in a highly stylized model, they may provide an explanation for the apparent difficulty of durably affecting land inequality. It has indeed been observed that land inequality often worsens after land reform. Using a complex simulation model, Zimmerman (1993) explains this outcome in terms of credit constraints and perverse fluctuations in land prices. The above model generalizes these insights.

Using data from Ethiopian pastoralists, Lybbert et al. (2000) provide some evidence of how the process described here may work out in practice. The accumulable asset is livestock. The availability of common access pasture de facto limits the size of the aggregate herd (Fafchamps 1998). The authors provide evidence of non-convex wealth dynamics: herders who have lost too many animals find it extremely difficult to restart a herd. Many must leave livestock raising altogether. Similar observations have been made regarding pastoralists elsewhere. This suggests the existence of poverty traps partly due to competition for a common resource – here, common posture.

In this section we have interpreted the accumulated factor as land. Other interpretations are feasible as well. If indenture contracts are allowed, then agents can sell their future labour in exchange for immediate consumption. This has the effect of raising $\bar{W}$ and thus the likelihood of multiple equilibria and thus of polarization among otherwise identical agents. For this reason, certain societies might decide to 'close' or 'outlaw' markets for productive assets in order to prevent inequality. For such measures to be effective, however, alternative channels must exist that enable agents to smooth consumption. If such channels are non-existent, labour bonding and distress sales of land may be the next best alternative (for example Srinivasan 1989, Fafchamps 1999b). Labour bonding contracts are revisited in the next section because indentured labourers would normally be insured against risk (that is, they get a constant albeit low consumption) after they begin working as landed workers.

5.4   ACCUMULATION AND RISK SHARING

We now consider wealth accumulation and risk sharing together. We begin by assuming that risk sharing contracts are perfectly and costlessly enforceable. The case with unbounded accumulation is ignored since, in the long run, both agents have infinite wealth and self-insure perfectly. We therefore consider what happens if agents can save in the form of an unproductive asset such as grain stocks. This is the Arrow-Debreu world studied for instance by Udry (1994) and Townsend (1995b). With complete markets, the Pareto efficient outcome can be sustained. This outcome ensures that

$$\frac{U_1'(c_t^1)}{U_2'(c_t^2)} = \frac{U_1'(c_{t'}^1)}{U_2'(c_{t'}^2)} = k \text{ for all } t \text{ and } t' \tag{5.16}$$

where k is a constant that depends on the ratio of welfare weights of each agent. An immediate corollary of the above is that, with assets and perfect risk sharing, welfare inequality is constant over time: $N_t^u = k$. Wealth and income distribution are inconsequential for welfare distribution.

We now turn to consumption inequality. Along the equilibrium path, individual consumption fluctuates only as a function of aggregate cash-in-hand $X_t \equiv X_t^2 + X_t^2$: if X_t is high, both agents consume a lot; if X_t is low, both agents consume little. Purely idiosyncratic fluctuations in income do not affect consumption. If the utility function takes a constant absolute risk aversion form, $N_t^c = N_t^u = k$ (for example Cochrane 1991, Mace 1991, Altonji et al. 1992). If the utility function has constant relative risk aversion, it is the ratio of the log of consumption that is constant. More generally, N_t^c is an increasing function of N_t^u.[111]

Next we note that if the economy is subject to collective income shocks, the precautionary savings motive applies: it is in the interest of all agents collectively to accumulate grain to protect themselves against future collective shortfalls. The rules governing the accumulation of precautionary saving are the same as those discussed earlier (for example Zeldes 1989b, Kimball 1990, Deaton 1991), except that when they pool risk agents do not need assets to insure against idiosyncratic risk. The level of aggregate saving should, in general, be lower with risk sharing. We denote the (efficient) aggregate savings function $s(X_t)$. The higher collective risk is, the more aggregate saving we expect (provided agents' preferences are prudent; Kimball (1990)).

Can we say something about wealth inequality over time? To this we now turn. There is a difficulty because the distinction between credit, wealth, and insurance is indeterminate in equilibrium. All that matters is the level of cash-in-hand in the economy X_t, the aggregate savings function $s(X_t)$, and the consumption splitting rule k. Many different contract combinations can deliver the first best solution: Arrow-Debreu securities/fully contingent contracts; a combination of credit and insurance contracts (Lucas 1978); and insured credit contracts (Udry 1994). This point has been made before and need not be revisited here. For the remainder of this section, we focus on the case with a combination of credit and insurance.

Even if we restrict our attention to a particular set of contracts, the distribution of wealth among agents is still indeterminate. This is because any distribution of wealth is compatible with any constant ratio of marginal utilities provided it is combined with the correct insurance contract. Put differently, it does not matter who 'owns' the wealth. This is because, whatever the distribution of wealth, insurance contracts can be found to ensure that the existing cash-in-hand is distributed among agents so as to satisfy Pareto efficiency.

To reduce indeterminacy, we add a new incentive constraint, namely, that insurance contracts are renegotiation-proof. By this, we mean that at the beginning of each period, agents must regard insurance contracts as individually rational ex ante. (Commitment failure, that is, ex post voluntary participation is ignored here; it is discussed later.) An example of an insurance contract that violates this ex ante participation constraint is a contract that stipulates that agent 1 transfers consumption to agent 2 in all states of the world. For agent 1 to accept to continue an insurance contract, he or she must provide agent 1 with some expected future benefits.

Formally, let $\tau(X_t^1, X_t^2)$ be the transfer from agent 1 to agent 2 that is stipulated in the contract if individual cash-in-hand are X_t^1, X_t^2. The continuation payoff of a participant is defined by the following Belman equation:

$$V_i(X_t^i) = \max_{W_{t+1}^i} U_i(X_t^i + \tau^i(X_t^1, X_t^2) - W_{t+1}^i) + EV_i(\omega^i(Z_i, \theta_{t+1}) + (1+\gamma)W_{t+1}^i)$$

$$(5.17)$$

where transfers $\tau^i = -\tau$ if $i = 1$ and $\tau^i = \tau$ if $i = 2$.[112] The autarchy continuation payoff is:

$$\tilde{V}_i(X_t^i) = \max_{\tilde{W}_{t+1}^i} U_i(X_t^i - \tilde{W}_{t+1}^i) + E\tilde{V}_i(\omega^i(Z_i, \theta_{t+1}) + (1+\gamma)\tilde{W}_{t+1}^i) \quad (5.18)$$

Ex ante voluntary participation requires that:

$$E\tilde{V}_i(X_t^i) \leq EV_i(X_t^i) \quad (5.19)$$

Arrangements that satisfy the ex ante participation constraints belong to the core (Hildenbrand 1974).

This requirement somewhat restricts the range of insurance contracts, but not entirely. This is because, whenever all agents are risk averse, they are willing to pay for insurance. If all agents are risk averse, they are all willing to pay, which means that there are many insurance contracts that satisfy the ex ante participation constraint – that is, belong to the core. One category of contracts that always satisfy the participation constraint – even if one or more agents are risk neutral – is the set of contracts that are actuarially fair. For the purpose of this chapter, an actuarially fair contract is when the expected payment from one agent to the others is zero, that is, when $E[\tau(X_t^1, X_t^2)] = 0$. For the remainder of this section, we restrict our attention to actuarially fair contracts.

This is still not sufficient to tie down wealth distribution. This is because, in the presence of assets, credit is redundant.[113] All that matters is agents' net wealth. This is immediately apparent from the above voluntary participation constraints: all that matters is net wealth/cash-in-hand X_t^i. Consequently, from now on we ignore credit and use the term 'assets' to refer to net wealth.

With all these additional assumptions, we now seek a characterization of insurance and wealth distribution as the level of transfers and current and future assets that satisfies voluntary participation constraints and ensures that $U_1'(X_t^1 - \tau(\theta_t) - W_{t+1}^1)/U_2'(X_t^2 - \tau(\theta_t) - W_{t+1}^2) = k$ for all θ_t and $E[\tau(X_t^1, X_t^2)] = 0$ in all periods. A full characterization of such plan is beyond this chapter (see for example Lucas 1978, Prescott and Mehra 1980). But a few preliminary insights are worth mentioning.

First, voluntary participation in risk sharing requires that wealth be aligned with desired consumption. Failure to align the two will either violate voluntary participation constraints or the actuarial fairness requirement. To see why, suppose that this is not case: agent 1 is expected to enjoy more consumption but have less wealth. Since agent 1 has a lower income (wealth generates income), this means that on average he will need to receive more from agent 2 in order to raise his consumption.

There are two cases to consider. First suppose that future savings requirements remain unchanged. Giving more to agent 1 will violate the actuarial fairness requirement. Second, suppose that future saving is adjusted to satisfy the actuarial fairness requirement: agent 1 is asked to save less (to leave more for consumption); agent 2 is asked to save more. This solves the problem for the current period but results in a violation of the voluntary participation constraint in subsequent periods – a richer agent 2 is more likely to opt out of an insurance arrangement – or runs into a feasibility constraint when all the wealth of agent 1 is exhausted.

An immediate corollary is that wealth must be aligned with intended distribution of consumption for a risk sharing arrangement to be renegotiation-proof. This is but an application of the second welfare theorem: initial wealth determines consumption inequality. Another way of saying this is that N_t^w is an increasing function of N_t^c. Since income is a function of wealth, we also have that N_t^y *is* an increasing function of N_t^c.

It is difficult to be more explicit given that the level of aggregate wealth varies with collective shocks. But one remarkable consequence of efficient risk sharing is that welfare inequality N_t^u does not change over time. Inequality measures such as N_t^c, N_t^y, N_t^x, and N_t^w may change with X_t but rankings do not change.

The incompatibility of social mobility with efficiency in risk sharing means that societies face a trade-off between perfect insurance and equality of chances. Put differently, they must choose between permanent poverty for some and permanent prosperity for others but protection against idiosyncratic shocks; and social mobility, that is, the opportunity for ranks to change over time. This conflict should not come as a surprise: after all, the rich are not insured if they may lose their status. For them social mobility is not Pareto efficient. Consequently an efficient risk sharing system is always geared towards the preservation of the social status quo.

Our findings are summarized as follows:

Proposition 5.8   *With asset accumulation and perfect risk sharing:*

1. N^u *is constant over time. Other measures of inequality may change over time.*
2. *Credit is redundant; only net wealth matters.*
3. N_t^c, N_t^y, N_t^x, *and* N_t^w *are all non-decreasing functions of* N^u.
4. N_t^c, N_t^y, N_t^x, *and* N_t^w *must remain 'close' to* N^u *for risk sharing to be renegotiation-proof.*

5.5 IMPERFECT COMMITMENT

In the previous section we assumed that risk sharing/insurance contracts can be perfectly and costlessly enforced. As argued by Posner (1980) and Platteau (1991), this need not be a reasonable assumption for poor communities. In the absence of external enforcement, risk sharing must be self-enforcing. This requires adding ex post voluntary participation constraints of the form:

$$\tilde{V}_t(X_t^i) \leq V_t(X_t^i) \tag{5.20}$$

Other sources of market imperfections (such as the information asymmetries discussed in Fafchamps (1992b) and Ligon (1998)) are ignored here. For a detailed analysis of risk sharing with imperfect commitment, see Kimball (1988), Coate and Ravallion (1993), and Fafchamps (1999a). Ligon et al. (2000) and Ligon et al. (2001) present models with wealth accumulation. Our purpose here is not to present imperfect commitment models in detail but rather to discuss their implications for inequality over time.

We begin by noting that if ex post participation constraints are never binding, we are back to the previous section: risk sharing is efficient and N_t^u is constant over time. Next, if participation constraints prevent any risk sharing (that is, all $\tau^i(X_t^1, X_t^2) = 0$ for all X_t^1, X_t^2), then we are back to Section 5.3. A world with imperfect commitment is thus in between the two.

Ligon et al. (2000) discuss how N_t^u evolves over time when commitment constraints are binding. Following Kocherlakota (1996), they show that N_t^u stays constant as long as constraints are not binding. When a constraint becomes binding for one agent, N_t^u changes so as to incite the agent to voluntarily remain in the risk sharing arrangement. After this jump, N_t^u remains unchanged until another commitment constraint becomes binding. If there exist ratios of marginal utility such that constraints are never binding, then the economy converges to one of these ratios, after which time N_t^u remains constant. If not, then the economy stochastically cycles across a finite set of marginal utility ratios – and hence a set of N_t^u. To the extent that risk sharing is optimized subject to commitment constraints, Kocherlakota (1996) and Ligon et al. (2001) further show that the set of N_t^u among which the economy randomly cycles is as close as possible given the constraints. Thus, even though inequality changes over time, it changes just by as much as is necessary to satisfy voluntary participation.

These results show that, the more efficient risk sharing is, the more persistent poverty is. Any departure from efficient risk sharing allows for social mobility, with the natural restrictions discussed in Section 5.3. Of course, if risk sharing is initially egalitarian, imperfect commitment may take the economy away from an egalitarian distribution of welfare. In this sense, imperfect commitment can generate social differentiation. But the opposite is also possible: imperfect commitment and the rise of opportunism may erode asymmetric risk sharing arrangements that traditionally guarantee more welfare to specific individuals, such as nobles, high castes, village chiefs, and the like.

One issue of interest is the emergence of patronage as a natural outcome of risk sharing arrangements with imperfect commitment. To see how this is possible, first note that, in the presence of imperfect commitment, rankings may change over time. This means that certain agents accumulate more assets than others, even if the distribution was initially egalitarian. Suppose that absolute risk aversion falls with cash-in-hand. Then it can be shown that agents that have accumulated sufficient wealth will refuse actuarially fair contracts (Fafchamps 1999a). For their ex post participation constraint to be satisfied, they must receive more than they give on average. We call this situation 'patronage', in other words, a situation in which a rich agent offers insurance and protection to poor agents in exchange for constant payments and services (for example Platteau 1995a, Platteau 1995b).

If we allow for patronage, ex post participation constraints should be easier to satisfy in sharply polarized societies provided that asset accumulation is sufficient to reduce absolute risk aversion to negligible levels among the rich while very poor households become extremely concerned by risk. To see why, consider our two-agent economy and assume that agent 1 has all the economy's wealth W and sufficient income to be risk neutral. Agent 2, in contrast, faces a lot of income risk and is desperate to purchase insurance. It is clearly in the interest of agent 1 to become a patron and to serve as 'insurance company' for agent 2. If agent 2 is sufficiently patient, it is in his or her interest to pay agent 1 in exchange for the (credible) promise of protection against negative income shocks.

To demonstrate this point, consider the following example. Utility is linear except in the vicinity of 0 (e.g., below 1/4), where it falls to $-\infty$. This is meant to represent the fear of starvation. Incomes are (2,0) and (0,2) with probability 1/2. Total wealth is 100, return to wealth is 10 per cent. Here we assume that the rich agent has a discount factor of 0.5. First suppose that both agents have equal wealth. Since they can both insure themselves for survival, they are unwilling to pay for future insurance. Consequently, risk sharing does not take place. Next, suppose that agent 1 has all the wealth and agent 2 has nothing. Now agent 2 is concerned about survival. His promise to pay for insurance is thus credible. The ex post participation constraint of agent 1 is:

$$\tau_1 \leq \left[-\frac{1}{2}\tau_1 + \frac{1}{2}\tau_2 \right] \frac{0.5}{1 - 0.5} \qquad (5.21)$$

where τ_1 is the transfer from agent 1 to agent 2 in the first state of the world (when agent 2 has an income of 0), and τ_2 is the transfer of agent 2 to agent 1 in state 2 (when agent 2 has an income of 2). The maximum transfer agent 1 agrees to pay must satisfy $\tau_1 = \tau_2/3$. Given this constraint, the maximum agent 2 is willing to pay is an amount that ensures his or her constant consumption:

$$2 - \tau_2 = 0 + \tau_1 \qquad (5.22)$$

The solution is $\tau_1 = 1/2$. This example illustrates that the fear of starvation by the poor may trigger patronage albeit imperfect commitment prevented risk sharing among agents with equal wealth.

From the point of view of inequality dynamics, patronage is interesting because it enables the rich to accumulate more and the poor to accumulate less. This is because, on average, the rich receive net transfers from the poor. The precise form of inequality fostered by patronage depends on the returns to wealth and whether aggregate wealth is bounded or not. If returns to wealth are positive and unbounded, patronage is only a transient phenomenon: even poor agents save so that, in the long run, they no longer need to purchase insurance from the patron.

If returns to wealth are negative, patronage reinforces the tendency towards inequality. But polarization is not an absorbing state because aggregate wealth gets depleted in finite time with probability one. In this configuration, patronage arises and survives for a while until aggregate wealth is spent to deal with a large (or series of) collective shock(s), at which point it disappears because impoverished patrons cannot promise sufficient protection and extract net payments from others. If returns to wealth are positive but aggregate wealth is bounded, patronage makes polarization more likely.

A similar possibility arises if returns to wealth are positive but total wealth is fixed. In this case, patronage indirectly raises the return on wealth for the rich, hence making multiple equilibria more likely. This is but an application of Proposition 5.4.

These findings can be summarized as follows:

Proposition 5.9   *With imperfect commitment:*

1. *If ex post voluntary participation constraints are never binding, risk sharing is efficient and there is no social mobility, that is, N^u is constant over time.*
2. *If ex post voluntary participation constraints are always binding, models discussed in Section 5.3 apply.*
3. *If risk aversion is high for agents without assets but low for agents with assets, risk sharing is more likely in polarized societies, where it takes the form of patronage.*
4. *Other things being equal, patronage makes inequality in wealth and consumption more likely and long lasting, while protecting the poor from starvation.*

5.6   RISK AND POVERTY TRAP

5.6.1   Poverty Trap and Inequality

So far, in our discussion of wealth dynamics we have assumed that poverty is not an absorbing state: someone with no assets can, given time, accumulate his or her way out of poverty. This assumption was crucial in our discussion about social mobility in a world with precautionary saving. In this section we discuss the possibility that the poor may not escape poverty. The existence of poverty traps would dramatically affect our discussion of inequality over time: if individuals without assets at one point in time find it impossible to accumulate, then asset poverty becomes an absorbing state; agents cannot 'rebound' from it.

The existence of poverty traps has dramatic effects on the dynamics of inequality. Suppose that agents are infinitely lived or, equivalently, that a poverty trap is inherited across generations. Further suppose that accumulation is bounded. Then the laws of martingales predict that, in finite time, everyone (but one in the case of fixed aggregate wealth) eventually falls into the trap. This is true provided that there is no wealth trap. Indeed, a wealth trap would preclude certain individuals (or dynasties of individuals) from falling back into poverty after they have achieved a high enough level of wealth.

Translated in terms of inequality, the existence of poverty traps generates strong predictions. In the case of unbounded accumulation, agents can only fall into the trap early on; once they have accumulated enough wealth, falling back is no longer possible (with income bounded from below). Only individuals unlucky enough to fall into the trap early on would remain permanently poor. This would imply a dramatic rise in inequality over time.

In the case of bounded accumulation with unproductive assets, everyone eventually falls into the poverty trap. The long-term equilibrium is thus one in which everyone is poor. In the case of bounded accumulation of an asset in fixed supply – such as land – the existence of poverty traps must imply the existence of at least one wealth trap: for $N - 1$ agents to be trapped in poverty, the Nth agent must permanently hold all assets. Long-term inequality then depends on the form of wealth traps: if $\bar{W}$ is the minimum required to be in a wealth trap, then long-term inequality is such that one person holds all the fixed assets while all the others are poor. In contrast, if W/k is the threshold for a wealth trap, then there is room for k agents to be rich while the rest are permanently poor.

5.6.2 The Causes of a Poverty Trap

Because of its dramatic effect on inequality, it is important to investigate what could cause poverty traps and under which conditions they may arise. The literature has proposed many different reasons for poverty traps (for example Dasgupta 1993, Arrow et al. 2000). Some have emphasized the difficulty for the poor to save: if their income is below what is needed for survival, they cannot save at all and remain permanently poor. As their nutritional and health status deteriorates as a result of poverty, they may fall into what some call extreme poverty or destitution, which is a state of complete dependency on immediate nutritional needs. Such low consumption is usually not sustainable and, sooner or later, leads to death. From the formal point of view of the study of dynamic inequality, therefore, destitution by itself does generate a class of permanently poor since it is but a short lived state. Only if destitution is inherited would it affect long-term inequality. To the extent that extremely poor people cannot successfully raise children, we find it unlikely that destitution, by itself, would extend over generations.

Others have emphasized various psychological and sociological processes by which the poor internalize their condition to make it more bearable and fail to even conceive of escaping poverty (for example Montgomery 1993, Arrow et al. 2000). These processes, if inherited, may explain poverty traps of longer duration. Here, we revisit some of the issues discussed earlier in this volume and focus on another possible cause of poverty trap, namely the debt trap – of which debt peonage and labour bonding are but two manifestations (for example de Janvry 1981, Bardhan 1984, Srinivasan 1989, Genicot 2002).

5.6.3　Debt Trap

The debt trap refers to a situation in which an agent has accumulated so much debt that he or she can never repay it.[114] The debt trap is not a phenomenon limited to poor countries. Bissuel (2003), for instance, states that around 200000 French households are currently so heavily indebted that they have no likelihood of ever repaying. People living in poor countries are potentially more at risk of falling into a debt trap. This is because, due to the presence of risk, they are often unable to cover their basic consumption needs. When this happens, theory predicts that they would be willing to borrow even on very disadvantageous conditions. This is because being permanently poor tomorrow is preferable to starving today.

To understand how someone can fall into a debt trap, we construct a simple principal-agent model of contingent loan repayment. This model is largely inspired by the literature on sovereign debt where debt repayment is often renegotiated (for example Eaton and Gersovitz 1981, Kletzer 1984, Eaton et al. 1986, Grossman and Van Huyck 1988). Throughout, borrower and lender are denoted by the superscripts b and l, respectively. The model is recursive. Assets are ignored. The stock of debt at the beginning of period t is denoted D_t. During period t, borrower and lender each incur an income shock s_t^i, $i = \{b, l\}$.[115] Repayment is written R_t. The instantaneous utility of the borrower is written $U_b(c_t^b)$ with $c_t^b = y_t^b - R_t = \bar{y}^b + s_t^b - R_t$. The utility of the lender is $U_l(c_t^l)$ with $c_t^l = \bar{y}^l + s_t^l + R_t$. In both cases, $\bar{y}^i$ denotes the expected income of agent i. For simplicity, we assume that incomes are iid. Negative consumption is not feasible, i.e., $\bar{y}^b + s_t^b \geq R_t$. This means that the borrower cannot repay in period t more than his or her current income.

In each period, borrower and lender renegotiate debt repayment. We begin by assuming that the lender has all the bargaining power. We revisit this assumption later in this section. Repayment by the borrower is voluntary in the sense that agreeing to the lender's conditions must leave the borrower better off than breaking the relationship. We call breaking the relationship a default. We assume that, in case of default, the lender can credibly inflict legal and extra-legal penalties denoted $P_t \geq 0$. In general, these penalties depend on the stock of debt so that $P_t = P(D_{t+1})$ with $P' \geq 0$. Legal penalties primarily take the form of court action. Examples of extra-legal penalties include recourse to 'loan enforcers' and exclusion from other social intercourse (Spagnolo 1999). If penalties are not credible, $P_t = 0$ (Fafchamps 1996a).

With these assumptions, the model takes the form of an agent-principal model:

$$\max_{R_t, D_{t+1}} U_l(\bar{y}^l + s_t^l + R_t) + \beta^l \, EV_l(D_{t+1}) \text{ subject to} \qquad (5.23)$$

$$U_b(\bar{y}^b + s_t^b - R_t) + \beta^b \, EV_b(D_{t+1}) \geq U_b(\bar{y}^b + s_t^b) + \beta^b \, EV_b(0) - P(D_{t+1}) \; \forall t$$

$$\bar{y}^b + s_t^b \geq R_t \; \forall t$$

where the first inequality is the voluntary participation constraint and the second is the feasibility constraint. Parameters β^l and β^b are the discount factors of the lender and borrower, respectively. We assume that the borrower worries about starvation, that is, $\lim_{c \to 0} U_b(c) = -\infty$. In this case, the second constraint is superfluous. Since the borrower's utility is monotonically decreasing in R_t and the penalty is monotonically non-decreasing in D_t, it is always in the lender's interest to choose R_t and D_{t+1} such that the voluntary repayment constraint is binding.

If $P(D) = 0$ for all D, repayment is still possible but only if the lender provides insurance. Bulow and Rogoff (1989b) derive a similar result for sovereign debt. In this context, the optimal debt contract becomes fully contingent and resembles an insurance contract (Grossman and Van Huyck 1988). If the lender is risk neutral, the optimal repayment schedule is such that the borrower's consumption is constant. The expected gain to the borrower is an increasing function of the borrower's willingness to pay for insurance, that is, of his or her risk aversion. Only if the borrower is risk neutral is expected repayment 0 (Fafchamps 1999a). If the lender is risk averse, the optimal debt contract resembles mutual insurance: when the lender receives a negative shock, repayment is higher and debt falls faster (Ligon et al. 2000).

When computing $EV_l(D_{t+1})$, the lender takes into account the possibility of future default. But in the model (5.23), it is never in the lender's interest to force the borrower into actual default. This is because we have implicitly assumed that the lender does not benefit from imposing the penalty. In this case, the lender's payoff is highest if he or she continues extracting regular debt repayment R_t from the borrower. This situation is what some have described as debt peonage: the borrower is a 'prisoner' of the lender and obligated to permanently repay a never-extinguished debt. Note, however, that if $P(D)$ is 0 or close to 0 for all D, the lender must provide insurance to the borrower otherwise $EV_b(D_{t+1}) < EV_b(0)$ and default occurs. Only if $P(D)$ is high enough can positive payments be extracted in all states of the world (Bulow and Rogoff 1989a).

If the lender directly benefits from imposing the penalty, default eventually occurs. Let $Q(D_t)$ be the lender's payoff if the penalty is imposed.

Suppose that there exists a high enough D_{t+1} such that $EV_l(D_{t+1})$ $< EV_l(0) + Q(D_{t+1})$. Then it is always in the lender's interest to set D_{t+1} such that:

$$EV_l(D_{t+1}) < EV_l(0) + Q(D_{t+1}) \qquad (5.24)$$

For any finite $P(D_{t+1})$, default is ensured by setting R_t at the highest possible level – so that $U_b(\bar{y}^b + s_t^b - R_t)$ tends to $-\infty$. In this case, the voluntary repayment constraint is violated and default occurs. Labour bonding – that is, a defaulting borrower becomes the slave of his or her lender – is an example of such situation (Genicot 2002). The lender may also perceive a high utility from punishing the borrower out of anger or spite (Becker and Madrigal 1994).

What the above discussion has made clear is that, without additional restrictions on the relationship between D_t, R_t, and D_{t+1}, the model instantaneously results in either debt peonage or labour bonding. This is because the lender has too much power. Restrictions on the relationship between D_t, R_t, and D_{t+1} may come from various sources. Laws regarding usury and admissible contractual penalties for late payment set a cap on the speed with which the debt can rise. The lending contract may also specify beforehand what fees and interest charges are assessed in case of non-payment. For instance, if the maximum admissible interest rate is r^{max}, then the lender faces an additional constraint:

$$D_{t+1} \leq (D_t - R_t)(1 + r^{max}) \qquad (5.25)$$

If such a constraint is present, it is always in the interest of the lender to set $D_{t+1} = (D_t - R_t)(1 + r^{max})$ since this maximizes future repayments. If r^{max} is high and D_t is large relative to what the borrower can pay, the nominal debt increases exponentially and eventually exceeds the value of all future payments the borrower can ever make.[116] When this happens, debt peonage or labour bonding again obtain. Societies may seek to prevent this occurrence by forbidding usury.

Competition in the credit market also imposes limits on the speed at which debt can accumulate. If the borrower can borrow from other sources at a rate $r < r^{max}$, any attempt by the lender to impose r^{max} leads the borrower to borrow D_t elsewhere at rate r to pay off his debt to the lender. This ensures that the borrower does not incur the default penalty $P(D_t)$. In the perfect competition case, r is equal to the riskless interest rate plus a risk premium (for example Kletzer 1984, Grossman and Van Huyck 1988). As the borrower's debt increases relative to his or her ability to pay, the risk premium increases as well so that, even in a perfect competitive economy, an unlucky borrower eventually ends up as a debt peon – not to a particular lender but to the collectivity of lenders. To prevent this occurrence, many societies have bankruptcy laws for corporations. Except for the US, however, most societies do not recognize individual bankruptcy, in which case past debts are never extinguished and debt peonage is legally possible.[117] In this case, debt is only extinguished by the death of the debtor.[118]

Having clarified the factors that affect the path of debt repayment, we turn to the debt contract proper. For a lender and a borrower to voluntarily enter in a debt contract, they must both benefit from it. For the lender, this means that $V_l(D_0) \geq V_l(0)$: lending yields more utility. If the lender is risk neutral, this boils down to:

$$\sum_{t=1}^{\infty} \beta_l^t E[R_t] \geq D_0 \text{ or} \qquad (5.26)$$

$$\frac{E_0[R]}{D_0} \geq \frac{1 - \beta_l}{\beta_l}$$

The borrower must also agree to the contract. This requires that

$$V_b(0) \leq V_b(D_0) \qquad (5.27)$$

where $V_b(D_0)$ internalizes the fact that, in some future state of the world, the borrower may want to default and incur the penalty (Fafchamps 1996a). If repayment is too high, the borrower prefers not to borrow. The same occurs if repayment is insufficiently flexible so that default is likely, and if the penalty for default is high. By the same token, a contract with rigid repayment is not attractive to a borrower who faces a lot of income risk. A borrower may nevertheless accept a disadvantageous contract if he or she is very impatient (for example, in the case of a drug addict, or a compulsive gambler) or if he or she is on the brink of starvation, so that money today is worth much more than money tomorrow. For this reason, we expect poor people facing a lot of uninsured risk to voluntarily enter into debt contracts leading to debt peonage or labour bonding.[119]

There is, however, one last important wrinkle on the story. If the default penalty $P(D_t)$ is small or zero, the borrower may avoid a debt trap if insurance is available from sources other than the lender. Voluntary debt peonage or labour bonding requires that alternative sources of protection against risk be absent. To see why, suppose unlucky borrowers can instantly find another person who can and is willing to provide the same level of mutual insurance. Further suppose that this person does not inherit the lender's claim on the borrower, so that the relationship with this new partner starts with a 'clean slate'. In this case, the unlucky borrower receives the same level of insurance as with the old lender but does not incur the cost – debt peonage. This point was initially made by Bulow and Rogoff (1989b) regarding sovereign lending but applies equally well to our case.

It is important to recognize the conditions that make debt peonage impossible or unlikely. First, the initial lender's claim must not be passed over to the new partner. Whether or not this is the case depends on the way society regards the initial lender's claim. If it is viewed as legitimate, new partners may refuse to assist the unlucky borrower to escape the consequences of his or her actions. Social norms and ethical values are thus likely to affect whether or not escape from debt peonage is possible. By the same token, if lenders collude not to undermine each other, escape will also not be possible. Of course, this begs the question of how collusion can be sustained over time, but this is another story.

Second, the new partner must be able to provide insurance that is comparable to that offered by the initial lender. Because there is a cost associated with debt peonage, insurance need not be exactly as good for the borrower to switch allegiance. But it has to be good enough. An immediately corollary is that if only the lender is capable of offering the needed insurance, then voluntary debt peonage is self-enforcing. This is precisely the patronage situation described by Platteau (1995a) and Platteau (1995b) and discussed in the previous chapter, except that here it takes the form of a debt trap.

Third, access to insurance from the new partner must be fast enough. Suppose that time is required to form a trust bond with a new partner before full mutual insurance can take place. Further suppose that the borrower has not already formed such bonds. Then securing an alternative source of insurance by forming a new bond is not instantaneous. In this case, the delay may be sufficient to deter switching. An immediate corollary is that individuals with few bonds are more likely to fall into a debt trap – a prediction that appears in line with what we know of destitution in rich countries, for instance. Put differently, transition into permanent poverty and destitution is more likely for individuals with little or no social network capital.

A second corollary is that individuals will seek to avoid ever falling into a debt trap by forming and maintaining bonds with potential sources of insurance. This is the issue of endogenous network formation we discussed at the end of the previous chapter. More empirical research is needed in this area. What is clear, however, is that even people with many bonds can fall into permanent poverty if these bonds are severed or destroyed by external events. War, for instance, can force people to relocate, thereby losing contact with their precious partners. As we have seen, famines can generate similar movements of population, thereby triggering similar consequences. Illness and accidents can also claim the lives of partners or make them poor sources of insurance. For these reasons, we expect social network capital – and shocks to it – to be key long-term determinants of people's transition into a debt trap or debt peonage situation.

Although there has been a lot of research on the determinants of chronic poverty, there is a dearth of research on the relationship between distress sale of assets, labour bonding, debt trap, and permanent poverty. An exception is the work of Fafchamps and Gubert (2002) who examine debt repayment practices among a sample of rural Filipino households. The data were collected from 200 rural households during three visits covering a nine month period. Detailed information relative to all loans and loan repayment was collected. Data were also collected on shocks affecting respondents and their lenders.

As in Udry (1994), they find that loan repayment depends on shocks affecting both lender and borrower. But the form contingent repayment takes is not what is usually assumed, for instance, a reduction in the amount repaid. Their results indicate instead that debt rescheduling is the dominant form of contingency: borrowers delay repayment when they are hit by a shock, and accelerate repayment when the lender is hit by a shock. These results are consistent with Udry's (1990) description of informal lending in Northern Nigeria. In contrast, when the debt is paid, the difference between the amount contracted and the amount repaid is in general small and need not depend on shocks. Debt roll-over is uncommon. Although some loans are made at usurious interest rates, the authors find no evidence of debt trap in the survey area. There is, however, some evidence that debtors unable to repay in cash volunteer their labour as repayment. As far as we can judge, this practice does not seem to be associated with labour bonding in the survey area. Not having found evidence of debt in this particular area does not, of course, preclude its existence in other parts of the world. More research is needed – microcredit – especially at a time when lending to the poor is seen as a remedy to poverty.

5.7 CONCLUSION

In this chapter we have examined how risk, accumulation, and insurance affect inequality. The main findings are that there are trade-offs between insurance and social mobility, and between asset markets and social polarization. We find that, in the presence of imperfect commitment, mutual insurance might be easier to sustain in the form of patronage in unequal societies. We also find that, when wealth is made of assets in fixed supply, such as land or manpower, trade in these assets naturally leads to an unequal distribution of welfare and income. For this result to arise, the savings rate must increase with cash-in-hand. Factors that favour accumulation, such as a high return on wealth or a large aggregate stock of wealth, also favour inequality.

From an equity point of view, there might therefore be a rationale for shutting down certain asset markets, in other words, those for which supply is finite. This is because allowing accumulation is likely to result in polarization. This conclusion applies primarily to land, manpower, mineral resources, and the environment. With the possible exception of mineral resources, these are also the markets in which restrictions on market transactions are most widespread. In contrast, the accumulation of unbounded resources such as equipment, skills, and knowledge does not raise similar fears although, in the long run, they also lead to persistent inequality. These assets are also those that are essential for growth.

Developed societies are adamantly opposed to slavery – even if it is voluntary. Yet, the US has a student loan programme that require graduates to work in the Army for a set number of years. Unlike other labour contracts for which employees can never be forced to work, military personnel who do not report for work are regarded as having deserted. Student loans by the military are thus a modern form of indenture contracts – with the caveat that they are used to accumulate education. These loans are acceptable while other indenture contracts are not. This suggests that society intuitively understands the distinction between bounded and unbounded assets and the implication for inequality.

This chapter also suggests that shutting down certain asset markets can only be effective in reducing inequality if it is combined with access to actuarially fair insurance. If a starving person cannot sell his or her future workforce in exchange for survival today, patronage is likely to arise as a substitute (for example Srinivasan 1989, Platteau 1995a). Given that patronage favours polarization, the end result is not very different. This implies that programmes to eradicate inequality must imperatively combine asset redistribution with access to fair insurance. This is particularly true in pre-industrial societies where aggregate accumulation is small or non-existent. Redistribution of assets is not, by itself, sufficient to durably eliminate inequality.

Our analysis also offers some caution to those who see the provision of insurance mechanisms as a solution to poverty. The theory is quite clear: perfect insurance freezes inequality. An insurance system based on voluntary participation – such as a market based approach for instance – cannot eliminate inequality. It might raise the welfare of the poor by providing protection against shocks, but it will not in general eliminate inequality that is already there.[120] A tax based system might be necessary to build redistribution into the insurance system. Combating inequality thus requires policy tools other than insurance. In some cases, organizing insurance might even worsen the long-term prospects of the poor by reducing social mobility.

This chapter leaves many questions unanswered. One issue of interest is the interface between accumulation, inequality, and growth. Most engines of growth require the accumulation of something – equipment, skills, knowledge. It is therefore widely recognized that economic development is intimately related to aggregate accumulation. The distribution of wealth across the population is also likely to affect the pace of growth (Aghion et al. 1999).

This issue has received a lot of attention in the literature as far as the accumulation of human capital is concerned (for example Becker and Tomes 1979, Galor and Zeira 1993, Maoz and Moav 1999, Mookherjee and Ray 2000). The literature has also examined the relationship between risk taking, credit markets, and growth (for example Banerjee and Newman 1991, Banerjee and Newman 1993, Aghion and Bolton 1997, Piketty 1997). Less attention has been devoted to capital accumulation and returns to scale (for example Stiglitz 1969, Freeman 1996). For instance, if production is subject to increasing returns to scale, the concentration of capital in a few hands would ensure faster growth than a more egalitarian distribution. The same reasoning applies to human capital: if the highest returns are in technology transfer, a few highly trained individuals who can introduce technology from elsewhere might better favour growth than a large number of workers with a little bit of training. Factors that influence the evolution of wealth inequality over time, such as returns to assets, income correlation, and patronage, may thus affect growth as well (in addition to being influenced by it). These issues need more research.

6. Risk and development

So far we have discussed how the rural poor deal with risk. We now focus on the relationship between rural poverty, risk, and economic development. The poor's inability to deal with risk does not only have welfare effects. It also reduces a society's capacity to accumulate, innovate, and develop. Risk thus contributes to creating a vicious circle of poverty. A proper understanding of the interaction between risk and poverty is essential to identify the obstacles to growth and development in poor rural societies. This chapter discusses several mechanisms through which poverty and vulnerability hurt growth.

6.1 NUTRITION AND HUMAN CAPITAL

It has long been recognized that poverty is detrimental to the accumulation of human capital, and in particular to health, nutrition, and education. It is hardly novel to point out that the poor are malnourished. In fact, malnutrition is often used as an indicator of poverty, if not synonymous with it, and the provision of adequate nutrition is at the core of many efforts to combat poverty (World Bank 1986). In this section we revisit some of these issues and reinterpret them in relation to risk and risk coping strategies. Given the voluminous literature on these issues, we limit ourselves to a brief survey of the salient themes.

6.1.1 Fertility and Infant Mortality

In Chapter Two we stressed that health risk is one of the major risk factors faced by the rural poor and that it disproportionately affects children. As a result, child mortality is high in most rural areas of the Third World, although it has been steadily declining thanks to vaccination campaigns and the provision of simple health care. Because the poor rely on their children for old age support, it has been argued that the poor compensate for high infant mortality by having more children in order to ensure a minimum number of surviving offspring (Datta and Nugent 1984, Nugent 1985, Rosenzweig and Wolpin 1985, Nugent 1990, as well as Chakrabarti et al. 1993 and the references cited therein). High fertility, in turn, raises population pressure both within the household and in society at large, leading to a Malthusian trap both at the individual and the aggregate level.

There are several problems with this line of argument. First the logic of the story is partly defective. If people have children to ensure old age support, then the main driving force behind increased demographic pressure ought to be adult mortality, not child mortality. The reason is that, while adult mortality cannot be 'corrected' ex post, most infant and child mortality can.[121] To see why, consider the following hypothetical example. Suppose that adult mortality is zero but child mortality is 250/1000, that is, a child has a 25 per cent chance of dying before the age of five. A couple has calculated that, by the time they reach old age, they need two surviving offspring, no more, to take care of them. Clearly, the optimal strategy is for the couple to have two children at the outset and to wait to see what happens. Only if one of the kids dies before the age of five is it optimal for the couple to have another child, and so on until two children reach the age of five. Except for some possible overshooting if menopause is reached before two surviving kids have been obtained, this strategy will result in two surviving children.[122] Of course, in this stylized example the realized fertility rate of the couple depends on child mortality: any child death is matched by an additional birth (Bongaarts and Cain 1981). But the number of surviving children – and thus population pressure – is not sensitive to the child mortality rate.[123] Only an increase in *adult* mortality would induce risk averse parents concerned with old age support to compensate by having more children, resulting in an average number of surviving adults greater than two, and thus in an increase in population pressure. As this example illustrates, infant and child mortality are unlikely by themselves to lead to a Malthusian trap; adult mortality, however, can.

Second, the empirical evidence on Malthusian traps is largely inconclusive (for example Dasgupta (1995) and the references cited therein). For one thing, currently developed countries managed to dramatically expand their population while growing rapidly. In contrast, there are several examples of developing countries or regions that drastically reduced fertility rates and population growth without noticeable impact on growth (such as Kerala, Sri Lanka). Recent work by demographers suggests that fertility behaviour might best be understood in terms of net fertility, that is, in terms of the number of surviving children per woman. There is indeed ample historical evidence that net fertility is responsive to perceived income opportunities: when they abound, as was the case historically in the Americas, net fertility rises; when they are stationary, net fertility is by and large just sufficient to ensure a constant population (Lee 1987). If this interpretation is correct, increases in net fertility should be seen mostly as a response to perceived increases in income opportunities such as those generated by the opening of a land frontier or by urbanization and industrialization (for example Wilson and Airey 1999, Wilson 2001). This issue deserves more investigation.

   Third, the micro evidence on the relationship between poverty and fertility is also largely inconclusive (for example Dasgupta 1995, Wilson and Airey 1999). Empirical evidence suggests that in poor villages the relationship might well run in a direction opposite to what is normally assumed, wealthier households having more children not less. This appears to be the case whenever children are an important source of labour for cultivation and livestock herding: households with more abundant resources are induced to have more offspring because the children can participate in farm work and are more easily provided for (for example Grootaert and Kanbur 1995, Basu and Van 1998). Only when opportunities arise to significantly raise the expected earnings of children through better education and nutrition does a trade-off arise between the quantity and quality of the children a couple might optimally have. If the returns to human capital are sufficiently high *and* adult mortality sufficiently low, investing in a small number of highly educated and well nourished children becomes optimal (Becker et al. 1990). The high cost of schooling might, however, preclude the poor from investing in child quality, leaving them the only option of investing in quantity – at least as long as they have enough land and livestock to provide for them. This might lead to a two-tiered situation, in which wealthy, urban based, market oriented parents invest in a few well educated kids, rural based, subsistence oriented parents invest in many uneducated kids, and low income households invest in children hardly at all. We revisit these issues below when we discuss human capital. For the time being, let us simply point out that the micro evidence on the relationship between poverty and fertility does not support a general monotonic relationship between rural poverty and high fertility.

   Finally, many rural societies have invented an institutional response to the need for old age support. Although it is possible to find in poor villages elderly people without descendants who live in deep poverty, it is erroneous to assume that old age support is only ever provided by direct descendants. In many cases, the extended family is involved as well. Individuals without descendants can anticipate their need for old age support by cultivating the goodwill of other relatives. In other words, the extended family provides a framework within which replacements for missing offspring can be found. Many societies formalize offspring replacement through the practice of adoption, thereby strengthening the bonds between a childless couple and its adopted offspring. The very existence of these institutions – extended family and formal adoption – suggests that poor rural societies have devised insurance mechanisms against the loss of offspring, thereby reducing the need for excess fertility.

6.1.2 Nutrition, Health, and Vulnerability to Shocks

Poor health has an immediate effect on poverty because it makes it difficult or impossible for people to work. Pandey (2001), for instance, shows that illness reduces the labour supply of Indian households and affects their production choices. Sauerborn et al. (1996) report similar findings regarding loss of labour for Burkina Faso and argue that in the busy season sick households tend to postpone or ignore treatment, with possible adverse consequence later on. Health shocks also have long-term consequences.

Without doubt the most dreadful consequence of poverty is that income and health shocks often lead to early death. This is true for children, as discussed in the above subsection, but also for adults and the elderly. Early demise may follow from someone's inability to command sufficient food, clothing, and shelter for day-to-day survival, or from someone's incapacity to receive proper medical care to deal with a treatable disease. Famines are examples of shocks that affect an entire group's capacity to provide for itself. In practice today, famines and other emergency situations often result or are seriously aggravated by warfare and civil unrest, as the examples of the 1984 Ethiopian and Sudanese famines illustrate. Epidemics such as – HIV/AIDS, malaria, measles, and tuberculosis – the worst killer diseases in Sub-Saharan Africa – are examples of health shocks that affect many individuals in the same population.

There are long lasting effects of shocks other than death. Stunting, a serious deficit in height, is the result of improper nutrition during childhood. Children who are raised in households subject to severe even if temporary shocks, and who consequently receive insufficient food, may suffer permanent consequences in the form of reduced height. In addition, stunting is generally believed to be correlated with poor health and to raise the risk of complication during pregnancies (see, however, Payne and Lipton (1994) for a dissenting opinion). Even if stunting is not associated with poor health, it nevertheless reduces an individual's body size and strength. Indeed, short size has empirically been associated with lower productivity in farming and livestock activities (for example Foster and Rosenzweig 1993, Foster and Rosenzweig 1996, Fafchamps and Quisumbing 1999, Fafchamps and Quisumbing 2003). Disease can similarly reduce someone's ability to cope with subsequent health shocks, especially if left untreated. Consequently, inability to cope with health risk at a moment in time leads to increase vulnerability in the future.

Poor populations subject to repeated shocks have a high incidence of stunting and high physical vulnerability to diseases (Payne and Lipton 1994). These deficiencies reduce the population's capacity to produce and accumulate (Fogel 1990), hence making it difficult to get itself out of poverty. Although one should be careful not to fall victim to economic determinism – after all, all countries were once poor, including the rich of today – poverty makes development difficult in ways that are hard to anticipate for well fed, healthy development experts in the field and project managers in their offices.

By increasing the vulnerability of individuals or groups to health and income shocks, poverty leads to higher morbidity and mortality and a higher incidence of stunting, chronic poor health, famines, and destitution. These undoubtedly have an adverse effect on the stock of human capital and talent in a given society. They also disrupt families and make it difficult for children to receive the nutrition and schooling they need. None of these observations are new, but they serve to emphasize that poverty by itself seldom leads to death or disease. Except in cases of extreme destitution, the proximate, cause of death or poor health is always an identifiable income or health shock. It is not poverty that kills or incapacitates, but the vulnerability to shocks that is generated by poverty.

From this realization, it follows that welfare can be improved dramatically by decoupling poverty from vulnerability. This is important because eradicating poverty is a difficult and lengthy task. Realizing that the most visible and least desirable consequences of poverty can be eliminated or at least minimized without eliminating poverty itself opens new avenues for intervention.

6.1.3 School Attendance and Risk

Since the seminal work of Schultz (1961), the role that human capital, and especially education, play in the development process has received a lot of attention (for example Barro and Sala i Martin 1992, Mankiw et al. 1992). Microeconomic empirical work suggests that, in poor rural areas, the returns to education are highest in non-farm activities (for example Jolliffe 1996, Yang 1997, Fafchamps and Quisumbing 1999). Some evidence indicates that it might also be significant in farming, especially when new technologies are introduced (for example Lockheed et al. 1980, Phillips 1987). The poor's capacity to invest in schooling is thus an important factor of long-term success in the development of rural areas of the Third World.

Yet, not only do poor rural households find it hard to stay well nourished and healthy, they also have to struggle to put their children in school. Money for school fees, books, and uniforms is hard to come by. Furthermore, children's time is valuable because they often contribute to household work, participating in livestock and farm activities as well as to household chores (for example Grootaert and Kanbur 1995, Fafchamps and Quisumbing 2003). Since borrowing on future income is difficult if not impossible in virtually all economies – but especially in those where adult mortality is high – poor parents cannot always afford to send their children to school. This depresses the human capital of their offspring and tends to replicate their own poverty across generations.

Recent empirical work has refined the above picture by bringing out the role that shocks play in school attendance. Jacoby and Skoufias (1997) and Sawada (1997) have indeed shown that children's propensity to join school and to drop out of school responds not only to chronic poverty but also to transient shocks. Kurosaki (2001b) reports similar findings. In their study of intergenerational mobility in schooling, Binder and Woodruff (2002) find that the Mexican economic crisis of the mid 1990s can explain some of the slowdown in educational progress. Edmonds (2002) reports an increase in school attendance and a drop in child labour among new recipients of an income transfer in South Africa. Further discussion of the relationship between child labour and income is found in Basu and Tzannatos (2002) and Wahba (2002). The evidence provided by Sawada (2002) further indicates that the effect of transitory income shocks on school entry and dropout rates is higher than that of permanent income. This result suggests that households' incapacity to handle temporary shocks in income is a more important determinant of school attendance than poverty itself. These findings have important policy implications. They suggest that programmes aimed at helping poor parents handle emergencies may be more cost effective in keeping poor children in school than programmes aiming either at reducing poverty itself or at reducing school costs for the poor as a whole. It might be more cost effective to reduce school fees selectively for those parents who face temporary difficulties.

6.2 RISK AND TECHNOLOGICAL INNOVATION

We have seen that one of the ways by which the rural poor cope with risk is by choosing activities and techniques of production that keep income variations to a minimum. One potential consequence of such a strategy is that the poor will resist technological innovations that raise the mean and variability of income at the same time. This simple observation has received a lot of attention and resistance to risk taking has been blamed for many of the failures to induce poor villagers to adopt technologies developed for them (for example Eicher and Baker 1982, Feder et al. 1985).

This section revisits these issues and briefly summarizes the implications of risk aversion for technology adoption and extends it to market risk. It also reviews the available evidence for and against risk aversion as an impediment to innovation and market participation.

We begin with a discussion of risk aversion and production choices. We continue with a review of the trade-off between specialization and diversification. Next, we debate commercial farming and the reliance on the market in poor rural areas. We conclude with a brief discussion of technological uncertainty and learning.

6.2.1 Production Choices and Risk

We have seen in Chapter Three that one way for poor farmers to reduce the income risk they face is to make production choices that reduce the variance of their net income. As Sandmo (1971) elegantly demonstrated, one effect of risk aversion on production choices is to reduce effort. To see why, consider a producer with indirect utility $V(y, p)$ where p is a vector of consumption prices that, for the moment, we assume constant. The value of output is stochastic and is written $\tilde{\theta}x$ where $\tilde{\theta}$ is a combination of multiplicative yield risk and output price risk. The producer faces a cost function $C(x)$ which is increasing in x and concave, that is, with decreasing returns to scale (as would be the case if there is a fixed factor). Assuming that no insurance is available and that sufficient funds are available to finance production, the decision problem of the producer can be written:

$$\max_{x} E[V(y, p)] \qquad (6.1)$$

subject to

$$y = \tilde{\theta}x - C(x) + U \qquad (6.2)$$

where U denotes unearned income (such as remittances, pension, rental income). The first order condition is:

$$E[V'(\tilde{\theta} - C'(x))] = 0 \qquad (6.3)$$

If the producer is risk neutral, utility is linear in income, which implies that V' is constant. The first order condition then boils down to:

$$C'(x) = \mu \qquad (6.4)$$

where μ is shorthand for $E[\tilde{\theta}]$. In this case, optimality requires that marginal cost equal expected marginal revenue. A similar result is obtained if the producer is risk averse but complete insurance is available, so that production decisions are decoupled from producer preferences (see Chapter Three, Section 3.3.2, 'Explicit Risk Sharing').[124]

However, if the producer is risk averse, then expected output x will be lower than it would be if complete insurance were available or if the producer was risk neutral. To see why, note that, since $V(y, p)$ is concave in y when the producer is risk averse, $V'(y, p) \leq V'(E[y], p)$ whenever $\tilde{\theta} \geq \mu$, and vice versa. Consequently,

$$V'(y, p)(\tilde{\theta} - \mu) \leq V'(E[y], p)(\tilde{\theta} - \mu) \tag{6.5}$$

for all $\tilde{\theta}$. If inequality (6.5) is true for all $\tilde{\theta}$, then we can take expectations of both sides and write:

$$E[V'(y, p)(\tilde{\theta} - \mu)] \leq V'(E[y], p)E(\tilde{\theta} - \mu)] = 0 \tag{6.6}$$

where the right hand side of the inequality is zero since, by definition, $\mu \equiv E[\tilde{\theta}]$. Now, from the first order condition $E[V'(y, p)p] = E[V'(y, p)C'(x)]$, we can write:

$$E[V'(y, p)(p - \mu)] = E[V'(y, p)(C'(x) - \mu)] \tag{6.7}$$

Combining equation (6.7) with inequality (6.6) we get:

$$C'(x) \leq \mu \tag{6.8}$$

Since the cost function is concave, the value of x that satisfies inequality (6.8) must be smaller than the value of x that satisfies the equality $C'(x) = \mu$. Consequently average output x is smaller without complete insurance than with it. Sandmo's (1971) result implies that producers without perfect insurance will underproduce, and hence underinvest in production and underpurchase inputs relative to what would be dictated by the maximization of expected profit. The poorer producers are and the less access they have to insurance, the more concave $V(y, p)$ will be, and the lower x will, in general, be.[125]

Sandmo's (1971) contribution has been widely received among economists working on technology adoption by poor farmers as a convincing story to explain resistance to technological innovation and underinvestment in production enhancement. If one abstracts from the purchase of new technologies and investment in durable productive resources, the evidence does not, however, strongly support Sandmo's conclusion: poor rural households do not appear to systematically underproduce given their productive resources and the absorptive capacity of the market for agricultural products (Walker and Ryan 1990). This should not be surprising. After all, at some fundamental level, Sandmo's result is counterintuitive: if people are poor and are concerned about survival, the solution is clearly not to underproduce. So what is it about Sandmo's result that is misleading?

One issue is the assumption that consumption prices are constant. We get back to it below, but it is not central to our critique of the common interpretation of Sandmo's result. More important are Sandmo's assumptions about how output is produced and how production is financed. The model presented above makes two fundamental – though hidden – assumptions. First it assumes that all inputs are marketed so that only their market value, summarized in $C(x)$, matters. If, in contrast, output is produced primarily with labour and that a complete labour market does not exist, then Sandmo's model is inappropriate. If the choice facing farmers is enjoy leisure now and starve later, or produce now and survive, then most farmers will choose to produce. Furthermore, the higher the risk they face, the harder they are likely to work. This can be formalized by rewriting the above model as in Fafchamps (1993):

$$\max_{l} E[V(y, p, l)] \qquad (6.9)$$

subject to

$$y = \tilde{\theta}(T - l) + U - C \qquad (6.10)$$

where l stands for leisure, T for total time endowment, and C for minimum consumption. We have assumed for simplicity that output is linear in labour. The utility function $V(y, p, l)$ can be understood as the result of a two-step optimization process: in the first period the producer chooses how much to work – and thus how much leisure l to consume; in the second period the producer chooses how to spend earned and unearned income on consumption. Solving for the second period optimization process yields the conditional indirect utility function $V(y, p, l)$ (see Epstein (1978), Epstein (1980) for details).

The first order condition of the above optimization problem is:

$$E[V_y \tilde{\theta}] = E[V_l] \qquad (6.11)$$

From equation (6.11), straightforward comparative statics yields:

$$\frac{dl}{dC} = \frac{E[V_{yl}] - E[V_{yy}\tilde{\theta}]}{SOC} \qquad (6.12)$$

Since the second order condition is necessarily negative at an interior optimum and since V_{yy} is negative whenever the producer is risk averse, we see that a sufficient condition for leisure consumption to decrease as the minimum consumption requirement C increases is that $V_{yl} \geq 0$, that is, that the marginal utility of leisure is non-decreasing in non-leisure consumption y – a natural assumption if leisure is a normal good. In fact, it is even possible for the marginal utility of leisure to be decreasing in y and still have leisure decreasing in C provided that the producer is sufficiently risk averse. Translated into English, this result implies that poor villagers will produce more, not less, if they face a higher risk of starvation.

A second hidden assumption in Sandmo's model is that input costs can be financed with output: Sandmo's model indeed contains no additional liquidity or credit constraint requiring that:

$$C(x) \leq B \tag{6.13}$$

where B is the amount of cash the producer has access to. This is akin to assuming either that credit is available to finance all input purchases, or that producers are sufficiently wealthy to finance these costs from their own pocket. When inputs are not purchased but provided directly by the household, such as owned land, family labour, manure from own livestock, and draught power from own animals, constraint (6.13) is unlikely to be binding. But when farmers are presented with new technologies for which up-front cash outlays are required, such as fertilizer, improved seeds, animal traction equipment, irrigation pumps, and the like, these conditions are unlikely to be satisfied and constraint B is likely to bind for poor farmers. Consequently, poverty coupled with credit market imperfections constitutes a working hypothesis for why poor farmers do not adopt new technology that is more intellectually appealing than aversion toward risk.

There is, however, another modification of Sandmo's model that is quite relevant in practice, namely, one emphasizing bankruptcy risk. Sandmo's model implicitly assumes that production costs can always be financed out of output or out of wealth/unearned income U. Indeed, for Sandmo's model to be rigorously correct, one must assume either that consumption can become negative – an impossibility – or that income and U are *always* sufficient to cover $C(x)$, that is, that the producer never goes bankrupt. These conditions are seldom satisfied in the case of poor farmers considering spending cash on a new agricultural technology. Even assuming that credit is available to finance input purchases, poverty still means that there is little wealth or unearned income to pay the debt in case of crop failure. What happens to a producer without enough assets to pay the debt then determines their willingness to borrow money to purchase inputs.

To begin with, if lenders insist on full payment under all circumstances, they will refuse to lend to a producer who does not already have enough assets to purchase the inputs. In other words, if lenders refuse to bear any default risk, poor borrowers will de facto be rationed out: since they cannot promise to repay for certain, they cannot enter into a contract that requires full repayment in all circumstances. Only producers who already have assets can borrow; borrowers can never hold a negative net wealth (Carroll 1992). Notice that rationing arises without any imperfect information; it is simply a consequence of the fact that producers cannot give what they do not have.

Next, suppose that default is allowed but that lenders insist on recouping as much of the amount borrowed as possible. In this case, when the value of crop output falls below the value of the debt, the producer is forced to consume nothing.[126] To capture the fact that consuming nothing or close to nothing is a very unpleasant occurrence, let the utility of zero consumption be a large negative number, say, $-H$. Let the cumulative distribution of random income y be written $F(y)$ and let the support of y be $[0, \bar{y}]$ with $\bar{y}$ possibly $+\infty$. The producer's optimization problem now is:

$$\max_{x} - H\Pr(y \leq C(x)) + E[V(y, p)|y > C(x)] \tag{6.14}$$

subject to

$$y = \tilde{\theta}f(x) - C(x) \tag{6.15}$$

For notational simplicity we have assumed that the interest rate is 0, so that debt repayment equal $C(x)$. To focus on debt repayment, unearned income U is assumed to be 0.

The above model is not very different from Sandmo's. All it does is to bring into the open the probability of bankruptcy: $-H\Pr(y \leq C(x))$. The first order condition becomes:

$$-HC'(x)\frac{\partial\Pr(y \leq C(x))}{\partial x} + E[V'(y, p)(\tilde{\theta} - C'(x))|y > C(x)] = 0 \tag{6.16}$$

Note that if $f(0) = y > 0$, that is, survival can be attained without purchased input x, then only if $C(x) = 0$ does the first term – the effect of input expenditures on the probability of bankruptcy – disappear.[127] This is different from Sandmo's model because it implies that even if the producer is risk neutral, that is, if $V(y, p)$ is linear in y, the producer still behaves in a risk averse manner, in other words refrains from using the amount of inputs x that maximizes expected profits. The reason is that the producer fears bankruptcy. In fact, if $-H = -\infty$, it is optimal for the producer not to purchase any input x at all *even if* lenders are willing to lend.

The difference between Sandmo's general result that risk averse producers purchase less inputs and our conclusion that producers who fear bankruptcy purchase less inputs might appear minute. In fact, however, it is crucial for policy design. In our model, what producers are worried about is not so much variations in income but the probability that realized income may be so low as to endanger the survival of the household. If this is a fair characterization of poor producers' fears about purchased inputs, it implies that if a mechanism can be found that provides credit AND eliminates the risk of bankruptcy, poor producers will be willing to purchase cash inputs. Such mechanisms in fact exist. Here are three examples.

The first example is that of sharecropping. In many sharecropping contracts it is common for the landlord to provide some of the cash inputs and to take part of the output as compensation (for example Braverman and Stiglitz 1986, Shaban 1987, Dubois 2000, Jacoby et al. 2002). This contractual arrangement does not eliminate risk for the producer, but it provides credit: the inputs are given at the beginning of the cropping season, they are repaid at harvest. Furthermore, it eliminates bankruptcy risk: if crops fail, nothing is paid.[128] In spite of initial fears regarding landlords' willingness to invest in new technology (Bhaduri 1973), the bulk of the evidence now indicates that sharecropping is an effective way of delivering input credit to producers (for example Braverman and Stiglitz 1986, Gavian and Teklu 1996, Jacoby et al. 2002).

The second example is taken from the input delivery practices of agricultural marketing boards during and after the colonial period in Sub-Saharan Africa.[129] It was common practice for agricultural marketing boards to provide farmers with agricultural inputs at the beginning of the season and to recoup the cost of these inputs at harvest time. Since many of these marketing boards had a monopsony on the cash crop they were responsible for, producers could not abscond from the credit they had received by selling to someone else.[130] This method of recouping input credit de facto meant that farmers were responsible for input costs only up to the value of their cash crop output. The method by which this was accomplished varied (sometimes input costs were simply deducted from a pan-territorial output price, sometimes villagers as a group were held collectively responsible for the payment of inputs used in their village) but the end result was the same: in case of crop failure, producers paid nothing. The simple fact that producers complained bitterly any time this principle was violated serves to stress its importance.

The third example comes from contract farming. In many ways, contract farming resembles what agricultural marketing boards do: they provide affiliated growers with seeds and inputs and promise to purchase all or part of their output, at which time inputs are paid. The crop itself serves as collateral for the inputs and the contractor often has the right to harvest the crop to recoup the cost of the inputs.[131] Although in theory contractors could seek to recover all input costs on growers' assets in case of crop failure, they hesitate to do so not to antagonize their growers. So, de facto, growers pay nothing in case of crop failure.

These three input delivery schemes have two features in common: payment at harvest, and no payment in case of crop failure. Otherwise the details of input repayment vary a lot from one example to the next – in the sharecropping example, costs are paid as a share of harvest; in the agricultural marketing board example, costs are deducted from the output price or paid jointly by villagers; in contract farming, costs are deducted from the value of the harvested crop. That much variation suggests that these contractual details are less important than the two principles listed above. Similar principles can be successfully applied to other technology delivery schemes, such as animal traction equipment.[132]

6.2.2 Diversification and Specialization

In the preceding subsection we have argued that aversion toward risk and a desire to smooth consumption are not, by themselves, a convincing explanation for poor farmers' reluctance to purchase new inputs. Credit constraints and concerns about bankruptcy are probably a more accurate way of thinking about the obstacles poor farmers face when adopting agricultural practices that require the use of purchased inputs. In this section, we argue that risk aversion is an excellent explanation for another often observed feature of technology adoption by poor farmers, namely, partial adoption.[133]

The attractiveness of partial adoption follows from the portfolio argument discussed in Chapter Three: if the incomes generated by different technologies are only imperfectly correlated, producers can reduce the total variation of their aggregate income by combining several crops and technologies on their farm. In fact, if crops and techniques of production are characterized by constant returns to scale, the portfolio argument would dictate that any risk averse farmer ought to plant all the crops and varieties and use all the techniques of production that are not stochastically dominated by others.[134] Thus, if new technologies are divisible, farmers' desire to smooth consumption should make them more willing to adopt *more* new technologies than if they were risk neutral. Put differently, poor farmers' desire to smooth consumption favours – not hinders – the adoption, albeit partial, of new technologies as long as they are divisible. In contrast, risk neutral producers would concentrate on the single crop or technology, whether new or old, which has the highest expected return. Based on this reasoning, and abstracting from the issue of purchased inputs discussed in the previous subsection, if consumption smoothing is the main determinant of technology choice, risk averse farmers should adopt any new technology that comes along provided its risk profile differs from what they currently cultivate. On the other hand, risk neutral farmers should only adopt the new technologies that yield a higher return. Unless one is willing to assume that the new technologies proposed to Third World farmers are always superior to what they currently grow – a proposition that is doubtful given the quality of what often comes out of agronomic research stations in poor countries – one would expect risk averse farmers to be on average more receptive than risk neutral farmers, not less, to new technology. Put differently, the probability that a producer would adopt an arbitrary new technology on at least part of its fields is higher for risk averse than risk neutral farmers as long as the new technology does not require large cash expenditures up front.

Of course, this conclusion holds only if the new technology is divisible, that is, if it does not benefit from returns to scale. In case the technological innovation has fixed costs (such as those of tractors) or requires a reorganization of production that is not favourable to diversification (such as a large irrigated scheme), then the desire to smooth consumption clearly operates against adoption. The reason is that the desire to diversify dilutes some of the gains from adoption. By the same token, even if adoption takes place, poor farmers' diversification strategy still works against full specialization, hence implying that the full gains from innovation are not captured. Partial adoption is the rule, which dilutes the gains not only from innovation but also from learning about the new technology. The same can be said of income diversification strategies that encompass multiple farm and non-farm activities: by spreading their attention too thin, households fail to capture all the gains from specialization in a single activity. This is the price society pays for portfolio diversification.

To summarize, risk averse farmers' desire to diversify their portfolio of crops and activities has two opposite effects on technology adoption. On the one hand it makes them more receptive to new technologies that have a different risk profile, hence favouring adoption. On the other hand, it makes them less willing to specialize in a single activity or crop, even if it generates a higher income on average. Reluctance to specialize, in turn, reduces the gains from adoption and hinders it, particularly if the new technology benefits from increasing returns to scale. One should thus not blame the desire to smooth consumption for non-adoption of divisible technologies; risk aversion should only be blamed for partial adoption. An immediate corollary is that if a divisible technological innovation, such as an improved seed or chemical fertilizer, is not adopted at all by poor farmers, one should first look towards credit constraints and fear of bankruptcy as likely explanations, not toward a desire to diversify.

6.2.3 Technological Uncertainty and Learning

There is another type of uncertainty that is generated by new technology, namely, uncertainty regarding its income distribution. When a technical innovation is introduced in a new environment, it is typically unclear how it will perform and interact with local conditions. Experimentation is required to assess the probability distribution of the new technology. Some experimentation is typically undertaken by research organizations who then disseminate the results via extension agents. But in practice, farmers often feel the need for additional experimentation to investigate how the new technology interacts with their other activities and whether it performs in local conditions as advertised by extension agents. They also need to learn how to use the new technique.

This process of learning and experimentation is costly and time consuming. The question then arises of who is more likely to undertake this process, and whether poverty and risk aversion hinder it. It has been argued that poor risk averse farmers are unlikely to experiment because of the risk associated with it. The arguments presented in the previous subsection indicate that this intuition is partly misleading. The desire to diversify ought to make poor risk averse farmers quite willing to experiment on a small scale. The first reason is that, since risk averse farmers are more likely to adopt a new technology (see above), they are also more likely to find experimentation attractive. The second reason is that experimentation itself is a form of risk diversification, and thus ought to be perceived as attractive as long as it can be undertaken on a small scale and does not raise any serious financial concerns. One would therefore expect even the poorest of farmers to experiment with new seeds on tiny parcels. If this does not take place, other explanations must be sought, as for instance mistrust of the information provided by extension agents and the widespread belief that extension agents promote ill-adapted technologies and agronomic practices.

There are, however, circumstances in which learning and experimentation are non-divisible. Migration to the city is an example of an experimentation process which is difficult to undertake in a small scale manner (unless it is sufficiently close to allow an easy commute) and thus may discourage very poor farmers. Only for sufficiently large households with good connections in the city do migration prospects become attractive – unless of course the local situation has deteriorated so much that survival is a stake. These predictions are, by and large, consistent with observation.

The switch to animal traction is also largely non-divisible because draught animals have to be bought and trained and equipment has to be purchased before experimentation can begin. In these circumstances it is conceivable that a technology that is suitable ends up not being adopted because the learning process itself is too risky. This problem has typically been dealt with in two different ways. One approach has been to subsidize an otherwise comprehensive and rigid package. Success has been limited and debt recovery disappointing, hence precluding replication (for example Sargent et al. 1981, Eicher and Baker 1982). A second approach, which seems to have worked better, has been to focus on very small scale animal traction, for instance using a single donkey instead of a pair of oxen, and to allow farmers to adopt only parts of the package, such as a cart or a weeder (for example Sargent et al. 1981, Jaeger 1986). The arguments presented here suggest that the success of the second approach is probably due to the fact that it breaks the innovation into smaller components and brings experimentation within the reach of poor farmers.

Given the risk and potential benefits of large scale experimentation, one may wonder whether poor farming communities have found institutional ways of disseminating information about technology. After all, the results of experimentation and learning are at least partially non-rival in nature: once someone has figured out how to grow a particular crop in a particular environment, others can copy the technique without subtracting from the innovator's welfare.[135] Extension programmes which have focused their technology dissemination efforts on large, more receptive farmers, have often justified their approach by implicitly assuming the existence of village institutions for the sharing of knowledge. If successful, early adopters, it was argued, would trigger copycats and the technology would trickle down to the entire community (for example Norman 1978, Eicher and Baker 1982, Griliches 1988, Foster and Rosenzweig 1995). Recent work, however, casts some doubt on the existence of efficient channels for the dissemination of new technologies at the community level (Conley and Udry (2001) and personal communication from David Widawski, IRRI). Poor farmers seem to know much less about each others' production techniques than is often assumed and are often quite individualistic in their approach to farming. If technology information circulates at all among farmers, it appears to be in processed form and along networks of friends and relatives rather than in an efficient community based manner. These findings, although preliminary, caution us not to put too much faith in the idea that non-divisibilities during learning and experimentation are irrelevant because the knowledge acquired by innovators circulates efficiently within the community.

6.3   COMMERCIAL CROPS vs. SUBSISTENCE FARMING

In many cases, farmers cannot make full use of the technologies that are proposed to them without shifting, at least partially, to commercial crops and moving away from subsistence farming, if only to be able to pay for purchased inputs. Yet, agricultural censuses and household surveys often show that cash crops are grown principally by large farmers.[136] This section investigates the relationship between poverty, risk, and self-subsistence. A proper understanding of this relationship is indeed essential if the rural poor are to leave their cocoon and integrate into the global economy.

Several explanations have been proposed for the positive relationship between cash crop orientation and farm size. Some argue that farmers differ in their ability to sustain risk and that crop choices are but the consequence of differences in income risk aversion (for example Binswanger 1980, Shahabuddin et al. 1986). Others invoke the presence of credit constraints, lumpy investments, technological differences, and differentials in relative factor costs across farms (for example Feder 1980, Feder 1985, Eswaran and Kotwal 1986). These explanations contain elements of truth but they are not based on the fundamental difference between food crops and cash crops, namely that food crops can be consumed while cash crops cannot. A third explanation takes this difference as starting point and notes that in the absence of food markets, Third World farmers have to be self-sufficient in basic staples (de Janvry et al. 1991). In that case, farmers allocate land to cash crops only if their food security is guaranteed (Chapter Three). This explains why large farmers are more cash crop oriented than are small ones.

The trouble with the latter explanation is that, in most poor villages today, food markets do exist. Yet it can be shown that, even when food markets are present, only wealthier farmers are likely to grow cash crops (Fafchamps 1992a). The starting point is that, because of high transport costs and low agricultural productivity, rural food markets are thin and isolated (for example Timmer 1986, Dercon 1995, Shively 1996, Barrett 1997). Consequently, farmers are confronted with food prices that are volatile and highly correlated with their own agricultural output. Since basic staples constitute a large share of total consumption and have low income elasticity, farmers are adamant in protecting themselves against food price risk. In most cases, this is optimally achieved by emphasizing food self-sufficiency. Wealthier farmers, however, spend proportionally less on food. By the same reasoning, they also prefer to allocate proportionally less of their land to food crops.

To show this formally, let the producer's maximization problem be written:

$$\max_{L_i} EV(y, p) \tag{6.17}$$

subject to

$$y = \sum_{i=1}^{N} \pi_i L_i, \ 0 \le L_i \le \bar{L} \ \forall i \text{ and } \sum_{i=1}^{N} L_i = \bar{L} \tag{6.18}$$

where, as before, $V(y, p)$ is the indirect utility function, y is agricultural income, and p the vector of consumption prices. Then $\pi_i = p_i q_i$ is the revenue per acre of crop i, $\bar{L}$ is the producer's endowment of the fixed factor of production, and L_i is the amount of the fixed factor allocated to crop i. Combining first order conditions for an interior optimum, one gets the usual series of equations $E[V_y \pi_i] = E[V_y \pi_j]$ for all i and j.[137]

Consider a first order expansion of the marginal utility of income around average income $\bar{y}$ and prices $\bar{p}$:

$$V_y \simeq \bar{V}_y + \sum_{k=1}^{M} \bar{V}_{y p_k} (p_k - \bar{p}_k) + \bar{V}_{yy}(y - \bar{y}), \tag{6.19}$$

where M is the set of consumed goods and $\bar{V}x$ stands for $V_x(\bar{y}, \bar{p})$. Let Ψ equal $-\bar{y} \bar{V}_{yy}/\bar{V}_y$, the coefficient of relative risk aversion with respect to income variability at $(\bar{y}, \bar{p})$ (Newbery and Stiglitz 1981). Totally differentiating Roy's identity, we get:

$$V_y \simeq \bar{V}_y [1 - \sum_{k=1}^{M} \bar{q}_k \left(\frac{\eta_k}{\bar{y}} - \frac{\Psi}{\bar{y}}\right) (p_k - \bar{p}_k) - \frac{\Psi}{\bar{y}}(y - \bar{y})] \tag{6.20}$$

where $\bar{q}_i$ and η_i are respectively quantity consumed and income elasticity of consumption at $(\bar{y}, \bar{p})$. Multiplying by π_i and taking expectations, the above expression becomes:

$$E[V_y \pi_i] \simeq \bar{V}_y \left\{ E[\pi_i] - \sum_{k=1}^{M} s_k (\eta_k - \Psi) E\left[\pi_i \left(\frac{p_k}{\bar{p}_k} - 1\right) \right] - \Psi E\left[\pi_i \left(\frac{y}{\bar{y}} - 1\right) \right] \right\} \tag{6.21}$$

where s_k stands for the consumption share of good k at average prices and income $\bar{p}_k \bar{q}_k / \bar{y}$. In order to simplify the above expression, let the expected revenue per acre of one of the crops, say $E[\pi_n]$, serve as numeraire. Plugging equation (6.21) into first order condition $E[V_y(\pi_i - \pi_j)] = 0$, dividing by $\bar{V}_y$ and by numeraire $E[\pi_n]$, and defining m_i as $E[\pi_i]/E[\pi_n]$, the following equation is derived:

$$(m_i - m_j)(1 + \Psi) \tag{P}$$

$$+ \sum_{k=1}^{M} CV_{p_k}(m_j \rho_{\pi_j p_k} CV_{\pi_j} - m_i \rho_{\pi_i p_k} CV_{\pi_i}) s_k (\eta_k - \Psi) \qquad (Q)$$

$$- \Psi \frac{E[(\pi_i - \pi_j) y]}{\bar{y} E[\pi_n]} \simeq 0 \qquad (X)$$

where CV stands for coefficient of variation and ρ for coefficient of correlation. This equation must hold for all interior i and j. It is dimension-free and therefore homogeneous of degree zero in all prices and revenues.

The final step is to obtain an explicit expression for crop portfolio choices. Let l_i stand for $L_i / \bar{L}$. The farm income per acre can then be written as $\Sigma_{k=1}^{N} l_k \pi_k$. Manipulating expression (X) in the above equation and multiplying through by $\Sigma_{k=1}^{N} l_k m_k$, a system of $N-1$ independent linear equations with N unknowns l_k is obtained. The system is identified by adding the constraint that crop shares sum to one.

When there are only two crops, say 0 and 1, the optimal crop portfolio can be solved explicitly as:

$$l^* \simeq \min\left(1, \max\left(0, \frac{-(P+Q) + \Psi S}{(m-1)(P+Q) - \Psi T}\right)\right) \qquad (6.22)$$

where l stands for l_1 and m for m_1. $E[\pi_0]$ serves as numeraire. We have:

$$T = CV_{\pi_0}^2 + m^2 CV_{\pi_1}^2 CV_{\pi_0} CV_{\pi_1}, \quad S = m\rho_{\pi_0 \pi_1} CV_{\pi_0} CV_{\pi_1} - CV_{\pi_0}^2 + m - 1.$$

Except for an approximation error, the optimal crop portfolio has thus been expressed as a function only of parameters that have an intuitive content: expenditure shares, income elasticities, relative risk aversion, ratio of expected returns, coefficient of variation of prices and revenues, and the correlation between prices and revenues.

6.3.1   Effect of Consumption Preferences on Crop Choices

The relationship between crop choices and consumption preferences is now analysed in detail when two crops are produced. Crop revenues are assumed independent of the price of non-produced consumption goods. In order to further simplify notation, write $CV_{p_i}(\rho_{\pi_0 p_i} CV_{\pi_0} - m\rho_{\pi_1 p_i} CV_{\pi_1})$ as A_i for $i = 0, 1$.

First, consider how crop portfolio l^* changes with consumption shares. Totally differentiating the first order condition, the sign of dl^*/ds_i is the same as the sign of $A_i(\eta_i - \Psi)$. Four cases are possible, depending on whether A_i is positive or negative and whether income elasticity η_i is larger or smaller than the coefficient of income relative risk aversion. The sign of A_i depends on whether $Cov(\pi_j, p_i)$ is greater or smaller than

$Cov(\pi_i, p_i)$. Generally the covariance between the price of one crop and the revenue of the other is smaller than the covariance between price and revenue of the same crop (see infra). Consequently, the usual situation is that:

$$\frac{dl_i}{ds_i} > (<)0 \text{ iff } \eta_i < (>)\Psi.$$

Income relative risk aversion is often believed to lie between one and, say, four (for example Binswanger 1980, Newbery and Stiglitz 1981, Binswanger and Sillers 1983). Suppose that crop i is a staple food and that the other crop is not consumed, in other words is a cash crop. In that case, the income elasticity of crop i is unlikely to be greater than one. Therefore, in the most usual situation, and other things being equal, a risk averse farmer, whose share of food in total expenditure is large will produce proportionally more food than a similarly risk averse farmer whose share of food in total expenditure is small. Only farmers with a low share of food in total expenditures *will devote a significant amount of resources to cash crop production.* The result is reversed when the coefficient of relative income risk aversion is smaller than the income elasticity of food, a condition satisfied for instance by risk neutral farmers for whom food is a normal good.

Next consider the effect that the income elasticity of demand has on crop portfolio. Using the same argument as above, it follows that:

$$\frac{dl_i}{d\eta_i} < (>)0 \text{ iff } Cov(\pi_i, p_i) > (<)Cov(\pi_j, p_i) \tag{6.23}$$

Thus when $Cov(\pi_i, p_i) > Cov(\pi_j, p_i)$, the producer reduces production of a crop for which his income elasticity is large. The reason is that when consumption prices and crop output are correlated positively, growing a particular crop serves as insurance against consumption price uncertainty. But high income elasticity leads to a high expected utility *gain* from price variability (Turnovsky et al. 1980). Consequently, a producer with high income elasticity for a particular crop will find it in his interest to be *less* insured and therefore to grow less of that crop.

The effect of income risk aversion on crop portfolio can similarly be approximated. The sign of $dl*/d\Psi$ is the same as the sign of:

$$-A_0 s_0 - A_1 s_1 + m - 1 - \frac{S - lT}{1 + l(m - 1)}$$

which is the combination of two effects: a direct portfolio effect captured by $m - 1 - s - lT/1 + l(m - 1) = Cov(y, \pi_0 - \pi_1)/\bar{y}E[\pi_0]$; and a consumption effect captured by the $A_i s_i$ terms.

The sign of the consumption effect again reflects the fact that growing a crop whose revenue is positively correlated with consumption prices is a form of insurance. Consequently, more risk averse farmers will seek to insure themselves against consumption price risk by increasing the production of consumed crops, provided that the covariance condition is satisfied and that the direct portfolio effect is not too strong.

The balance between the direct portfolio effect and consumption effect in general depends on the model parameters. It is worth pointing out, however, that the consumption effect may lead to the 'perverse' result that *a more risk averse person chooses to produce more of the risky crop.* Whether or not such a situation arises depends critically on the share of the risky crop in consumption and on the covariance between price and revenue from that crop: the larger the share and the larger the covariance, the more likely a more risk averse producer is to shift production toward the risky crop.

Finally the three comparative static experiments can be combined to look at the effect that a rise in land assets, wealth, or expected income has on the crop portfolio. Because of the assumption of constant returns to scale, differences in farm size have no effect on expected yields. They only affect portfolio decisions via their incidence on consumption shares, demand elasticities, and risk aversion.

Consider the case of interest in which farmers grow a food and a cash crop, income relative risk aversion is constant, and changes in income elasticities are small and can be ignored. Letting subscript f stand for food, the effect of an increase in wealth or expected income has the same sign as $A_f s_f / y \, (\eta_f - 1) \, (\eta_f - \Psi)$.

What is the most likely sign of the above expression? As has already been argued, the covariance condition necessary for $A_f s_f$ to be positive is likely to hold for staple foods because of their low price elasticity. The income elasticity for staple food can be large for poor households, but it is likely to remain below unity; that is, richer households are likely to spend a smaller fraction of their income on staple food. Finally, poor rural households facing various sources of risk, but with few insurance mechanisms to rely on, are likely to be risk averse. Thus, the most likely relationship between wealth (that is, farm size) and cash crop emphasis is *positive*. This is also the most commonly observed situation.

Possible – but unlikely – configurations of parameters exist in which small farmers are more cash crop oriented. One is when risk aversion is low: $\Psi < \eta_f < 1$, a condition unlikely to hold among Third World small farmers. Another is when the self-consumed good is a luxury: $1 < \eta_f < \Psi$. This may occur in special circumstances, for instance when farmers produce a cash crop as well as a 'noble' cereal such as rice or wheat but consume partly a purchased, inferior cereal such as sorghum or millet. Then poor farmers may indeed choose to produce more cash crop in order to purchase the inferior cereal.[138] Other possible candidates as high-income-elasticity agricultural products are fruits and vegetables, meat, dairy, oilseeds, and spices, at least over some income range. Their share of total expenditures, however, is likely to remain small and the consumption effect on crop portfolio limited.

6.3.2   Market Integration and Food Self-Sufficiency

The main reason why food prices in poor rural areas are highly variable is because rural food markets are thin and isolated (for example Timmer 1986, Dercon 1995, Minten 1995, Barrett and Dorosh 1996, Shively 1996, Baulch 1997a, Baulch 1997b). They are thin because of low agricultural productivity and, hence, low marketed surpluses; they are isolated because of poor infrastructure and high transportation costs. This process is compounded by the fact that the very thinness of markets induces rural households and communities to aim for self-sufficiency, thereby further reducing interaction with the rest of the world. Food price volatility is thus an essential ingredient in a vicious circle of rural poverty that runs from low productivity to low marketed surplus to thin markets to volatile food prices to no specialization in high value cash crops to low productivity. To illustrate how this essential process operates, we simulate the effect of changes in market environment on crop portfolio using the model developed above. We begin by specifying the stochastic market structure and then present simulation results.

6.3.3   Modelling Correlation between Prices, Revenues and Output

To simulate the effect of market integration on crop choices, we first need to specify the relationship between supply and demand. We assume a fixed market demand from the rest of the world, with a constant price elasticity and we ignore possible general equilibrium effects. Given these assumptions, we can express prices and revenues as functions of both the random production shocks and the underlying demand characteristics. Assume that Q, the aggregate market supply, and q, individual output, are imperfectly correlated. Let $\hat{p} = a\bar{Q}^{-\kappa}$ denote the price corresponding to the average quantity supplied $\bar{Q}$; it is *not* in general equal to the average price. Parameter κ, is the inverse of the price elasticity of demand. Using Taylor expansions (as in Mood et al. (1974), p. 181), one gets:

$$E[p_i] = E[a\bar{Q}^{-\kappa}] \simeq \hat{p}(1 + \frac{1}{2}\kappa(\kappa + 1)CV_{\bar{Q}}^2) \qquad (6.24)$$

$$V[p_i] = V[a\bar{Q}^{-\kappa}] \simeq \hat{p}^2 \kappa^2 CV_Q^2 \qquad (6.25)$$

Mean and variance of revenue, and correlation between price and revenue, can similarly be approximated as:

$$E[\pi] = E[a\bar{Q}^{-\kappa}q] \simeq \hat{p}\bar{q}(1 + \frac{1}{2}\kappa(\kappa+1)CV_Q^2 - \kappa\rho_{Qq}CV_QCV_q) \qquad (6.26)$$

$$V[\pi] \simeq \hat{p}^2\bar{q}^2(CV_q^2 + \kappa^2 CV_Q^2 - 2\kappa\rho_{Qq}CV_QCV_q) \qquad (6.27)$$

$$\rho_{\pi p} \simeq \frac{\hat{p}^2\bar{q}(\kappa^2 CV_Q^2 - \kappa\rho_{Qq}CV_QCV_q)}{\sigma_\pi\sigma_p} \qquad (6.28)$$

Examination of equation (6.28) indicates that, for most values of the demand elasticity and the correlation between individual output and aggregate supply, correlation between price and revenue is positive. Only when demand is very elastic and individual output very highly correlated with aggregate output does the correlation between price and revenue become negative. Those two conditions are unlikely to be met simultaneously, particularly in poor rural areas. Consequently, the covariance condition necessary for many results of the previous subsection is met in most cases. Equation (6.21) combined with equations (6.27) to (6.28) forms the basis of the simulations presented below.

6.3.4 Simulation Results

Having formalized the market structure, we are ready to simulate the integration of the producer into a larger market, either via trade liberalization (such as removal of restrictions to trade such as check points and road blocks), or by the integration of the village economy into a larger regional or national market (for instance via better transportation facilities or an improved marketing system). Market integration confronts the producer with entirely new market demand schedules for his crops and affects average price, price elasticity, price variance, and the correlation between prices and revenues. For agricultural products, one expects the price elasticity of market demand to be higher in large integrated markets than in small isolated markets. The reason is that markets covering a lot of geographical and sectoral diversity offer more substitution possibilities. The variance of prices, on the other hand, is likely to decline with market integration. Indeed, the major cause of yield variability is weather, and in a large geographical market aggregate supply will blend local disturbances that are partly uncorrelated. Finally, correlation between individual weather conditions on separate farms is likely to decrease with the distance separating them. Consequently the correlation between individual and aggregate output is also likely to decrease with market integration, thereby reducing the price and revenue correlation.

Numerical simulations examine the effect of changes in (relative) output prices; variance of aggregate food output; correlation between revenue and price; elasticities of aggregate demand; and correlations between crop revenues. Parameters used for the simulations are chosen to represent a typical Third World farming household (for example Fafchamps 1985, Fafchamps 1986, Matlon 1977, Binswanger 1980): high variance of individual as well as aggregate output (coefficient of variation = 0.6), high correlation between individual and aggregate output (0.7), and low price elasticity of demand (0.5).

Households have the choice between growing a food crop (good 0) and a non-consumed cash crop (good 1). For simplicity, cash crop revenue is assumed independent from food price. Three hypothetical households are considered: the first does not consume any of its production and consumes food produced (or industrially processed) elsewhere; the second spends a moderate share (30 per cent) of its income on locally produced food; and the third allocates a major share (80 per cent) of its income to self-produced food. All households are assumed moderately risk averse.

The first household represents a fully commercialized farmer. The second is partially commercialized but not entirely reliant on the market for their food consumption. The third is a household that hardly grows any cash crop at the initial parameter values, is essentially self-sufficient in food, and sells any food surplus on the market in order to satisfy minimal non-food needs. Given their consumption pattern, farmer 1 is likely to be richer and larger, and farmer 3 to be poorer and smaller. The simulations may also be thought of as contrasting crop portfolio behaviours predicted by univariate (household 1) and multivariate (household 2 and 3) expected utility models.

Results show that a change in the cash crop's average price has the expected supply response effect. There is a difference between the three households, however, in that poor households are less prone to produce the cash crop to start with. Therefore, richer households may respond to a price increase by allocating significantly more resources to cash crop production while poorer households remain entirely concentrated on the food crop. In other words, larger farms have a higher elasticity of cash crop supply response.

Higher food prices induce poor producers to revert to self-subsistence much faster than do fully commercialized farmers. Smaller farms thus have a higher price elasticity of food production.

An increase in food price variance, keeping average price constant, has a non-monotonic effect on output (Figure 6.1). All three households initially increase food production as a result of a small increase in variance of food

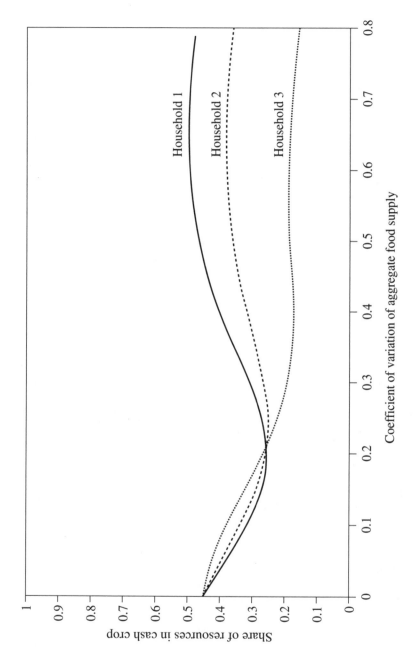

Figure 6.1   Effect of the variance of the food price

prices, but their reaction to further increases in that variance is different. As food prices continue becoming more volatile, market oriented households finally revert to cash crop production because higher variance increases expected revenue. The volatility of food prices increasingly hurts poor households, however, and induces them to maintain a high level of food self-sufficiency. Less correlation between individual and aggregate food output has a small positive effect on cash crop production among commercialized farmers, but only a small and ambiguous impact on poor farmers.

Changes in the price elasticity of market demand faced by producers affect crop choices in a non-linear way via their impact on expected revenues and the covariance matrix between prices and revenues. Results show that a large increase in demand elasticity for the cash crop (Figure 6.2) does not eliminate the difference in crop emphasis between the three households. Since, from the point of view of the producer, a fixed price is similar to an infinitely elastic demand, this suggests that fixing the price of a cash crop need not be sufficient to induce small farmers to grow it. On the other hand, fixing the price of the *food* crop (Figure 6.3) is a very effective way of dramatically reducing differences between farms as well as of increasing the cash crop production of small farmers. Finally, a decrease in correlation between crop revenues has no impact on crop choices in the absence of consumption effects (household 1), but encourages slightly more emphasis on cash crops when consumption effects are important (Figure 6.4).

To summarize, these results suggest that market integration progressively diminishes the need for food self-sufficiency. As better roads and transportation equalize price movements across a larger regional or international market, food prices ought to become increasingly dissociated from local supply and demand conditions. All the effects of market integration – a lower variance in food prices, less covariance between individual output and aggregate supply, a more elastic demand because of substitution and international trade possibilities – reduce an individual's rationale for food self-sufficiency.

6.3.5 Policy Implications

In many developing countries, cash crops are by definition already integrated in international markets while food markets remain local in nature. Food market integration would thus reduce price variance and the correlation between individual and aggregate output. It is also likely to increase the market price elasticity of food demand and to decrease the correlation between crop revenues. Results presented in the previous subsection suggest that these effects combine to decrease small farmers' need to rely on their own food production. Promoting food market integration by investing in

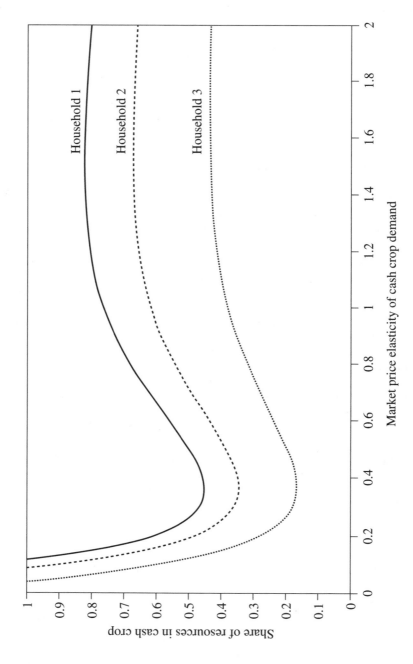

Figure 6.2 Effect of the market price elasticity of the cash crop

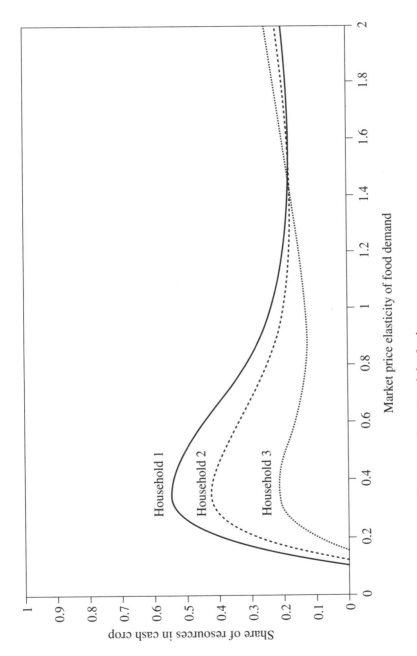

Figure 6.3 Effect of the market price elasticity of the food crop

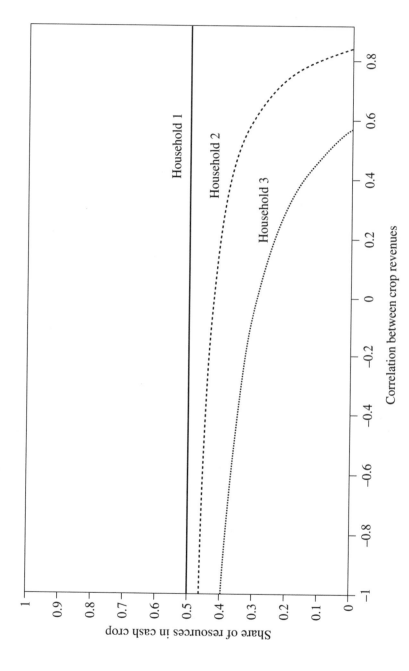

Figure 6.4   Effect of the correlation between crop revenues

roads and transportation, and removing institutions or policies impeding domestic trade, are therefore essential in order to allow crop specialization. Agricultural resources freed from staple food production may possibly be used more efficiently producing cash crops. Less concern for food self-sufficiency would also increase farmers' supply response to cash crop price incentives.

The analysis presented above also suggests that a similar outcome may be achieved or strengthened by selling food at controlled prices in villages. The Indian government, for instance, has used state owned retail outlets to pursue a cheap food policy in rural areas. It would be worthwhile reviewing the effect of that policy in light of the ideas presented here. To summarize, *food* market integration via reduced trade restrictions, better roads and transportation, and/or government food shops can be a powerful tool to boost cash crop production and to increase responsiveness of small farmers to price incentives. For many Third World countries with debt service problems, this may be an effective way of generating badly needed foreign exchange.

The analysis presented here also has a number of policy implications regarding technological change. The effect of successful technological innovations through farmers' incomes has already been explored in detail in Section 6.2, where it was concluded that producers with higher incomes are likely to put more emphasis on cash crop production. Hence, other things being equal, technological change should boost cash crop production by raising incomes.

Technological change in agriculture, however, is often crop-specific. The model presented here throws new light on the issue of crop bias in agricultural research. Improving cash crop productivity, as many African countries have done (Eicher and Baker 1982), will fail to reach the many farmers who, for food security reasons, are unable to allocate a significant amount of resources to cash crop production. Besides, it would favour only better-off farmers who are in a position to grow cash crops.

At the same time, however, improving food crop productivity has limited potential for agricultural growth if food markets are not better integrated. Indeed, as long as food markets remain isolated by government policies, difficult transportation, and high marketing costs, households will prefer to allocate the freed resources to cash crop production as soon as food security is satisfied. This may lead to the paradoxical situation in which improved food production technology ends up favouring cash crop production.

The latter problem has several consequences. First, limiting technological improvements to cash crops is counterproductive. Even if a country's only objective is to increase cash crop production, a certain amount of resource saving innovation is required to alleviate food security concerns of poor households with loosely integrated food markets. Consequently, even in countries that rely heavily on cash crops for foreign exchange generation, and which typically seek to maximize cash crop production, productivity increases should be sought in both cash and food crop production.

Second, at least in some countries, food crops also have the potential to become cash crops given the proper market environment and infrastructure (for instance Kenya or Zimbabwe). The model presented here suggests that combining food market integration with increased food crop productivity has a good chance of success. Indeed, it would directly address farmers' food security concerns, and at the same time promote a global increase in agricultural output. Whether such an option is feasible depends in part on the national and international market for the specific types of food that a country or region is able to produce. For instance, semi-arid regions that can only produce coarse cereals with low income elasticities probably must wait for the emergence of a sufficiently large local market for animal feed.

6.4   PRECAUTIONARY SAVING AND INVESTMENT CONSTRAINTS

It has often been claimed that risk averse producers unable to insure themselves against income shocks tend to shy away from risky activities (for example Pratt 1964, Arrow 1971, Sandmo 1971). This idea has been used to explain why poor producers find it difficult to invest in production enhancing technologies. However, as argued earlier, this apparently simple and straightforward explanation evaporates once subjected to intense scrutiny – at least in the way it is customarily described and modelled. The main reason is that it ignores the fact that the poor have developed ways of dealing with risk. In the presence of complete or incomplete insurance, aversion toward risk is not the appropriate concept.

An alternative explanation for the poor's difficulty in investing has been the existence of credit constraints. This approach similarly ignores the time dimension: when faced with a profitable investment opportunity, the poor may be unable to invest today but they can in principle save to undertake the investment at a later date. Poverty, per se, thus fails to explain why investment does not take place in the long run. In this section we propose an alternative approach that combines the risk aversion and the credit constraint ideas into a single dynamic model. We investigate the extent to which poor households are discouraged from making highly profitable but non-divisible investments and we show that poverty, credit, saving, and risk are closely related.

The intuition behind our approach can be summarized as follows. Poor farm households have at least two motives for saving: to insure against income shortfalls, and to self-finance profitable investments when credit is not available. If returns to savings are low, they may find it difficult to accumulate enough wealth to finance a large non-divisible investment, even if it is highly profitable. They remain trapped in poverty (for example Nurkse 1953, Lewis 1954). Investment irreversibility may also serve as an additional deterrent to investment. A reversible investment can be turned into liquidities should the household face an external shock beyond what can be handled with other accumulated wealth. An irreversible investment, on the other hand, detracts permanently from the household's liquid wealth and thus impinges on its ability to self-insure. A household with a precautionary motive for holding wealth may thus treat irreversible and reversible investments differently. In particular, the wealth threshold at which it is willing to make a reversible investment may be below that at which it makes an irreversible investment.

To illustrate these concepts, we construct and simulate a stochastic dynamic programming model of savings and investment. The model shows the role that non-divisibility and irreversibility play in investment decisions.

It has long been recognized that poor farmers in the Third World find it hard to finance large, lumpy investments (McKinnon 1973). Credit constraints are commonly regarded as the major explanation for this state of affairs and much emphasis has been put in the literature on the role that credit constraints play in farm size distribution and investment patterns (for example Feder 1985, Eswaran and Kotwal 1986, Iqbal 1986, Carter 1988). Credit constraints may result from interest rate restrictions (for example McKinnon 1973, Shaw 1973, Gonzalez-Vega 1984), from asymmetric information (Stiglitz and Weiss 1981), or from enforcement considerations (for example Bell 1988, Pender 1996, Fafchamps 2003b). In addition, in a risky environment farmers may choose to avoid credit if the penalties for default are sufficiently severe. Regardless of the reason, farmers in developing countries must thus often self-finance a large share of the investments they make. Trying to determine what impact this has on their ability to make a highly profitable but non-divisible and irreversible investment the object of this section.

A key question is why poor farmers who lack access or willingness to use credit do not choose to save in order to self-finance highly profitable investments. One possible explanation is that they find it hard to save. Often contributing to the difficulty are government interest rate restrictions and other policies that keep the returns to savings low (McKinnon 1973). Such policies were in place in India during the 1970s and 1980s, the period of the present study (Pender 1992). Being constantly faced with life threatening situations for which poor farmers must liquidate their meagre assets, the argument goes, they can never accumulate enough to finance a large investment. We investigate this possibility directly by examining the saving and investment behaviour predicted by models of precautionary saving.

A second possible explanation is that the irreversibility of well construction operates as a disincentive to invest. As Epstein (1978) stressed early on, flexibility, that is, the capacity to revise certain decisions assumes an important role in a multi-period setting. Fafchamps (1993), for instance, estimates a three-period structural model of labour allocation decision in semi-arid farming and demonstrates that flexibility differently affects farmers' decision to plant and weed. Dixit (1989) and Dixit and Pindyck (1994) have shown that it may be optimal for an investor faced with a (partly or totally) irreversible investment to wait until more information is available on the investment's profitability. By investing now, the investor indeed loses the option to collect more information and make a better decision later.

The situation we are interested in is different in that little or no new information is gained over time about the profitability of the investment. Investment irreversibility may nevertheless affect the investor's decision if the investor has a precautionary motive for saving. By waiting, the agent is better able to use liquid wealth to cope with income shortfalls. Tying all their money into an illiquid asset may generate an unbearable risk. The trade-off between a higher return on wealth and better consumption smoothing may thus generate a liquidity premium, that is, a level of precautionary savings deemed comfortable enough for the investment to take place. The liquidity premium might, however, be zero if the investment itself reduces risk, as is typically the case for irrigation.

Hints that irreversibility matters can be found in Rosenzweig and Wolpin (1993). Using household survey data from semi-arid India, the authors show that poor farmers are less likely to invest in irrigation equipment than in bullocks despite the fact that the return on the former is higher than, that on the latter. The reason is, they argue, that bullocks can be sold when the need arises while pumps cannot. We revisit this issue and attempt to quantify the effect that irreversibility and credit constraints have on farmers' willingness to undertake a large, non-divisible investment.

6.4.1 Investment and Precautionary Saving

We begin by developing a model of self-financed, non-divisible investment. The model combines a continuous decision – how much to save – with a discrete choice – whether to invest in a well or not. The possible effect of irreversibility is explicitly taken into account. We consider an agent who faces two possible i.i.d. income streams with probability distributions $F(y; \tau_0)$ and $F(y; \tau_1)$. By building a well at cost k, the agent can exchange an income stream $F(y; \tau_0)$ against the income stream $F(y; \tau_1)$. Parameter vectors τ_0 and τ_1 thus characterize the shape of the income distribution without and with a well, respectively. Income is restricted to the positive quadrant, i.e. $y \in [0, \infty)$. We consider two cases, one in which the agent cannot recoup investment cost k and revert to $F(y; \tau_0)$ – the irreversible case – and one in which they can – the reversible case. We begin with the irreversible case.

6.4.2 A Model of Irreversible Non-Divisible Investment

Let X_t stand for the agent's cash on hand at time t, that is:

$$X_t = W_t + y_t(W_t)$$

where W_t is the agent's accumulated wealth at the beginning of year t and y_t is his or her realized net income from all sources at the end of year t, which is a function of liquid wealth at the beginning of the period. After the investment, the optimization problem facing the agent is summarized by the following Belman equation:

$$V_1(X_t) = \max_{W_{t+1}} U(X_t - W_{t+1}) + \beta \int_0^\infty V_1(W_{t+1} + \tilde{y}_{t+1}(W_{t+1})) dF(\tilde{y}_{t+1}; \tau_1) \quad (1)$$

Instantaneous utility $U(.)$ is continuous and concave and exhibits decreasing absolute risk aversion: the agent thus has a precautionary motive for saving (Kimball 1990).

We further assume that $U(c) > -\infty$ for all $c \geq 0$ – but is $-\infty$ or not defined for $c < 0$: the agent cannot have negative consumption. This implies that, as Zeldes (1989b) and Carroll (1992) have shown, the agent optimally decides never to borrow beyond the annuity value of his or her minimum possible income. We further assume that, under both income streams, the minimum possible income is 0. Then, along the optimal path the agent never is a net borrower: if creditors insist on being paid under any circumstance, then an agent with a minimum income of zero will not be able to become a net debtor and net borrowing can not be used to smooth consumption. An alternative interpretation is to postulate that there is a penalty for breach of contract and that the penalty is so severe that the agent chooses not to incur debt. (The same argument applies to strictly enforceable contingent contracts – Zame (1993).) Whether the agent is refused credit because he or she cannot repay in all possible states of the world, or fears the possible consequences of default, the result is the same. Of course, if default is allowed, credit can be used to provide insurance (for example Eaton and Gersovitz 1981, Kletzer 1984, Grossman and Van Huyck 1988).

Let δ be the agent's rate of time preference, i.e., $1/1 + \delta \equiv \beta$. If we further assume that δ is greater than the return on liquid wealth, the agent is a natural dissaver: he or she saves for the sole purpose of smoothing consumption (for example Kimball 1990, Deaton 1991). As argued in Deaton (1990), Deaton (1992a), and Deaton (1992b), countless poor consumers, particularly in Third World countries, find themselves exactly in this predicament. Now consider the agent's decision before the investment has taken place. Formally, the agent computes his or her expected utility under two alternative scenarios: invest now, or wait until later. In case he or she invests now, his or her expected utility is:,

$$V_0^1(X_t) = \max_{W_{t+1}} U(X_t - k - W_{t+1}) + \beta \int_0^\infty V_1(W_{t+1} + \tilde{y}_{t+1}(W_{t+1}))dF(\tilde{y}_{t+1}; \tau_1)$$

(6.29)

In case he or she chooses to wait, her expected utility is:

$$V_0^0(X_t) = \max_{W_{t+1}} U(X_t - W_{t+1}) + \beta \int_0^\infty V_0(W_{t+1} + \tilde{y}_{t+1}(W_{t+1}))dF(\tilde{y}_{t+1}; \tau_0)$$

(6.30)

The agent chooses to invest if $V_0^1(X_t) > V_0^0(X_t)$. The value function $V_0(X)$ corresponding to the no-investment situation can thus be found by solving the following Belman equation:

$$V_0(X_t) = \max\{V_0^0(X_t), V_0^1(X_t)\}$$

(6.31)

It can be shown that the option to invest in the future is valuable even though, unlike in Dixit and Pindyck (1994), no new information is gained about the investment's profitability:

Proposition 6.1

1. *If the return to the investment is such that there exists a level of wealth at which the agent would want to invest, then the option to invest raises the agent's ex ante utility.*
2. *An agent given the option to wait may defer investment compared to an agent who must invest now or never.*

In Proposition 6.1 we assume that a sufficiently wealthy individual would want to invest. But, depending on the parameters of the model, it may be optimal for him or her never to invest. If, for instance, $F(y; \tau_0)$ stochastically dominates $F(y; \tau_1)$, then investing is not optimal since it would reduce the agent's expected utility for any initial level of cash on hand. The converse is not true, however: even if $F(y; \tau_1)$ stochastically dominates $F(y; \tau_0)$, investment will not take place if the agent has insufficient wealth, that is, if $X_t < k$. Sufficient (but not necessary) conditions for investment to be a valuable option are, first, that the investment is profitable, that is, yields a positive expected return:

$$\int_0^\infty ydF(y; \tau_1) - \int_0^\infty dF(y; \tau_1) > rk \tag{A1}$$

where r is the expected return on liquid wealth W_r. The second condition is that the agent is asymptotically risk neutral, that is:

$$\lim_{c \to \infty} \frac{cU''(c)}{U'(c)} = 0 \tag{A2}$$

If these two conditions are satisfied, then the existence of a level of cash on hand is guaranteed above which the agent invests and one (possibly the same) below which he or she refrains from investing:

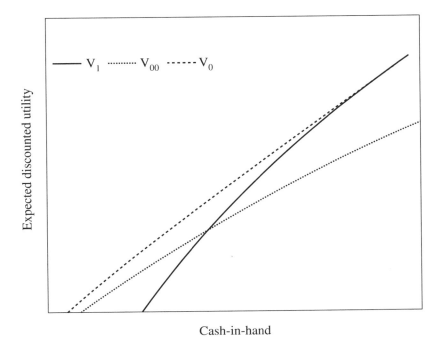

Figure 6.5   Value of investment option

Proposition 6.2

1. *Given (A1-2), there exist at least one x^* such that $V_0^0(x^*) = V_1(x^* - k)$.*
2. *If x^* is unique, for all $x > x^*$, the agent invests, and for all $x < x^*$, the agent does not invest.*
3. *If x^* is not unique, let $\bar{x}^*$ and $\underline{x}^*$ be the largest and smallest x^*, respectively. Then, for all $x > \bar{x}^*$, the agent invests, and for all $x < \underline{x}^*$, the agent does not invest.*

In the remainder of this section, we focus our attention on the simple case in which there is a level of wealth at which investing is optimal. Let X^* be the minimum level of cash in hand at which the investment takes place – that is, such that $V_0^0(X^*) = V_1(X^* - k)$. We then define the *liquidity premium P* as the amount of liquid wealth that the agent wishes to hold immediately after the investment:

$$P \equiv arg \max_{W_{t+1}} U(x^* - k - W_{t+1}) + \beta \int_0^\infty V_1(W_{t+1} + \tilde{y}_{t+1}(W_{t+1})) dF(\tilde{y}_{t+1}; \tau_1)$$

The liquidity premium acts as a deterrent to investment because the agent must accumulate not only the cost of the investment itself but also the amount of liquid wealth he or she wishes to hold as precautionary saving.

6.4.3   Precautionary Saving and Reversible Investment

The cost of irreversibility can be found by considering the reversible case. Formally, the latter case can be seen as an extension of the irreversible case. In each period, the agent can be in one of two states: with or without the investment. Each of these states has its own value function. The value functions, in turn, reflect the fact that, before deciding on consumption, the agent may invest and pay k, or liquidate the investment and receive k. Intermediate cases in which divestment is possible, but at a cost can be analysed in a similar manner. We thus get a system of two Belman equations:

$$\bar{V}_0(X_t) = \max\{\bar{V}_0^0(X_t), \bar{V}_0^1(X_t)\} \tag{6.32}$$

$$\bar{V}_1(X_t) = \max\{\bar{V}_1^1(X_t), \bar{V}_1^0(X_t)\} \tag{6.33}$$

where:

$$\bar{V}_0^0(X_t) = \max_{W_{t+1}} U(X_t - W_{t+1}) + \beta \int_0^\infty \bar{V}_0(W_{t+1} + \tilde{y}_{t+1}(W_{t+1})) dF(\tilde{y}_{t+1}; \tau_0)$$

$$\tag{6.34}$$

$$\bar{V}_0^1(X_t) = \max_{W_{t+1}} \ U(X_t - k - W_{t+1}) + \beta \int_0^\infty \bar{V}_1(W_{t+1} + \tilde{y}_{t+1}(W_{t+1}))dF(\tilde{y}_{t+1}; \tau_1)$$

(6.35)

$$\bar{V}_1^1(X_t) = \max_{W_{t+1}} \ U(X_t - W_{t+1}) + \beta \int_0^\infty \bar{V}_1(W_{t+1} + \tilde{y}_{t+1}(W_{t+1}))dF(\tilde{y}_{t+1}; \tau_1)$$

(6.36)

$$\bar{V}_1^0(X_t) = \max_{W_{t+1}} \ U(X_t + k - W_{t+1}) + \beta \int_0^\infty \bar{V}_0(W_{t+1} + \tilde{y}_{t+1}(W_{t+1}))dF(\tilde{y}_{t+1}; \tau_0)$$

(6.37)

As before, $\bar{V}_0^1(X_t) = \bar{V}_1(X_t - k)$ and $\bar{V}_1^0(X_t) = \bar{V}_0(X_t + k)$. This system can be solved simultaneously by backward induction. The liquidity premium for a reversible investment can similarly be defined as:

$$\bar{P} \equiv arg \max_{W_{t+1}} \ U(x^* - k - W_{t+1}) + \beta \int_0^\infty \bar{V}_1(W_{t+1} + \tilde{y}_{t+1}(W_{t+1}))dF(\tilde{y}_{t+1}; \tau_1)$$

(6.38)

$P - \bar{P}$ represents the option cost of irreversibility. It is clear that, if the return on the non-divisible investment is certain and investors face credit constraints, the cost of irreversibility $P - \bar{P} \geq 0$. When the return to investment is variable, however, $\bar{P}$ need not be 0. To see why, note that when the investment is reversible, $\bar{P} + k$ is the level of precautionary saving. As Dreze and Modigliani (1972) and Kimball (1990) have shown, this level is an increasing function of the variance of income when absolute risk aversion is decreasing. Thus, the higher the variance of income after investment, the higher $\bar{P}$. For a sufficiently high variance of the post investment income process, therefore, $\bar{P} > 0$. A contrario, if undertaking the investment reduces the variance of income and the investor is credit constrained, then $\bar{P}$ may be zero. In that case, P alone constitutes a good indicator of the cost of irreversibility. Finally, $\bar{P}$ cannot exceed P: irreversibility can only raise the liquidity premium in the presence of credit constraints and a precautionary motive for saving. If $P = 0$, then $\bar{P} = 0$ as well.

Reversibility does not imply that the savings behaviour of the agent is unaffected by the presence of a non-divisible, high return investment. As Pender (1992) has shown in the certainty case, in the presence of credit constraint the agent's willingness to save increases in the vicinity of the threshold level of wealth k – even if it means momentarily accumulating wealth at a rate of return inferior to δ. The reason is that the agent anticipates the benefits from higher returns and strives to reap them. Pender (1992) shows that a low return on saving may have a perverse disincentive effect on investment because it makes it difficult for a credit constrained agent to accumulate enough to undertake the investment (McKinnon 1973). The presence of a liquidity premium reinforces this argument: not only do agents have to accumulate enough to invest, they must also build up a sufficient buffer stock of liquid wealth. A low return on liquid wealth thus has a disincentive effect of on an agent's willingness to accumulate and invest that is compounded by the presence of a liquidity premium.

6.4.4   Poverty, Shocks, and Investment

Using the ICRISAT data from India, Fafchamps and Pender (1997) econometrically estimate a model of irreversible investment in wells. Investments in individual wells for irrigation offer a perfect opportunity to study the effect of non-divisibility and irreversibility on investment behaviour. The ICRISAT data have been widely used to study issues relative to consumption smoothing and wealth accumulation patterns (for example Rosenzweig 1988a, Rosenzweig 1988b, Morduch 1990, Rosenzweig and Wolpin 1993, Townsend 1994, Pender 1996, Morduch 2002). They are particularly well suited for our purpose because most of the assumptions made by our model are satisfied: villagers are known to be risk averse (Binswanger 1980) and impatient (Pender 1996); they are poor and face a lot of risk (Walker and Ryan 1990); they are unable to fully insure through mutual insurance and credit arrangements (for example Townsend 1994, Morduch 2002); they are unable to fully finance the cost of well construction through credit (Pender 1992); and they buy and sell assets to smooth consumption (for example Rosenzweig and Wolpin 1993, Lim and Townsend 1998).

Estimation results by Fafchamps and Pender (1997) yield estimates of an intertemporal discount rate of 18 per cent and estimates of relative risk aversion reverting around 1.8–3.1, somewhat high but not altogether implausible given the low income levels in the area (Walker and Ryan 1990). The model fits observed behaviour fairly well, given the panel nature of the data. Using an Euler equation approach and assuming a constant relative risk aversion coefficient as we do here, Morduch (1990) estimated the coefficient of relative risk aversion in the same village to be 1.39. Discount rate estimates are all well above 5 per cent and vary between 17 per cent and 29 per cent. These values are lower but of the same order of magnitude as the median discount rates measured by Pender (1996) using experimental games in two of the ICRISAT villages. Discount rates are not a direct measure of the pure rate of time preference δ since they are affected by consumption smoothing motives as well. But if we account for seasonal effects and income shocks, the existence of high discount rates in semi-arid India (median values between 50 per cent and 60 per cent in most experiments) is consistent with a rate of time preference as high as estimated here.

6.4.5 Credit Constraints and Poverty Trap

Armed with estimates of risk aversion and discount rate, we are now in a position to ascertain whether the precautionary motive for saving plays a significant role in surveyed households' reluctance or inability to invest in well construction. Using the parameters estimated by Fafchamps and Render (1997), we simulated the threshold cash on hand and liquidity premium at which a poor household invests in a large irreversible investment such as an irrigation well. The threshold cash on hand is found iteratively as the X^* at which the following equation is satisfied:

$$\max_{W_{t+1}} U(X^* - k - W_{t+1}) + \beta \int_0^\infty V_1(W_{t+1} + \tilde{y}_{t+1}(W_{t+1}))dF(\tilde{y}_{t+1}; \tau_1) \qquad (6.39)$$

$$\max_{W'_{t+1}} U(X^* - W'_{t+1}) + \beta \int_0^\infty V_0(W'_{t+1} + \tilde{y}_{t+1}(W'_{t+1}))dF(\tilde{y}_{t+1}; \tau_0)$$

The liquidity premium is simply W_{t+1} at, the solution of equation (6.39).

Results show that for a highly profitable investment such as an irrigation well in the ICRISAT villages, the liquidity premium is positive but small: once they reach the required threshold cash on hand, households are predicted to invest almost all their wealth in digging the well. For most households, irreversibility constitutes a relatively minor impediment to investment. This is not the case, however, for less profitable investments. Simulation results then show that some households may never invest in the well. For those who invest, the liquidity premium can amount to a large proportion of the investment cost and the threshold cash in hand goes up by a significant percentage. In this case, irreversibility clearly deters investment, the reason being that poor investors do not want to freeze all their liquid wealth in a fixed asset.

For sufficiently poor households, the combination of the indivisible nature of the investment and the desire to retain some liquid wealth after the investment has been undertaken makes it extremely difficult to accumulate the threshold wealth necessary for investment. In simulations based on the parameters estimated by Fafchamps and Pender (1997), the threshold cash on hand at which households without a well would consider investing is equivalent to more than three times their average pre-investment income, and is over twice their average cash on hand after harvest. Many households thus fail to undertake the investment in irrigation simply because they are unable to accumulate enough wealth to cover the investment cost. To verify this possibility, the income and saving patterns of a household with the average characteristics of Fafchamps and Pender's sample were simulated. One hundred simulations were conducted, each of them fifty years long. Results indicated that in none of these one hundred simulations does the household accumulate enough to invest in the well. Households appear trapped – in a probabilistic sense – in poverty: because their income is low, they are too concerned about their immediate survival to accumulate much, they never manage to have enough to undertake an indivisible but highly profitable investment, and they remain poor.

Simulation results nevertheless indicate that poor households attempt to save for the well. The liquid savings for households facing the option to invest in the well were simulated and compared with those of hypothetical households without that option. On average, households with the option to construct a well save 40 per cent more than identical households without it. These results are consistent with theoretical propositions derived by Pender (1992): the poor attempt to save for the well, but accumulating enough is simply too hard for most of them.

To test whether credit can help households out of poverty, the simulations were redone assuming that the household can borrow part of the value of the investment at a low interest rate. Debt repayment is assumed forgiven in bad years.[139] Results show that in almost all the simulations, investment takes place. The waiting time to investment is long, however: 19 years on average for investing households. The reason is that, with borrowing, the threshold cash on hand is less half of what it is without borrowing. This puts the investment within the range of what households can afford with moderate savings after a good cropping season.

To check whether subsidizing credit plays an important role, the simulations were redone assuming that borrowed funds carry a higher (real) interest rate. Results indicate a reduction in investment, but the rate charged on borrowed funds must be raised substantially before all investment disappears. From this we conclude that what matters is not so much the cost of credit but rather its availability. To successfully promote well construction, credit must bring investment within the reach of poor households. These results are in line with the success of programmes such as the Grameen Bank (Pitt and Khandker 1996).

McKinnon (1973) and Pender (1992) argue that higher returns on liquid wealth can make investment possible by encouraging households to save. To investigate this possibility, the model is simulated with higher returns to liquid wealth, as could be achieved, for instance by a deregulation of interest rates on savings accounts. Simulation results confirm McKinnon and Pender's theoretical intuitions but they also indicate that, in this particular case, a sizeable increase in returns to liquid wealth is required before a noticeable rise in investment materializes.

6.4.6   Poverty, Investment, and Non-Divisibility

In this section we investigated whether poor farmers are discouraged from making highly profitable investments which are non-divisible and irreversible. We constructed a model of irreversible investment by an agent with a precautionary motive for saving. Simulations conducted with estimated parameters suggest that many poor farmers may find themselves trapped in poverty due to their inability to accumulate enough wealth to self-finance the construction of an irrigation well. Risk aversion per se does not explain the reluctance to invest: farm incomes with a well stochastically dominate incomes without. Irreversibility constitutes a small additional deterrent to investment.

These results demonstrate empirically the magnitude of the inefficiency and inequity caused by poor households' inability to finance profitable but non-divisible investments. An investment yielding a high real rate of return was foregone by most households who were, in effect, forced to accept a lower return on divisible liquid wealth. In the context of financial repression common in many developing countries, such an outcome is consistent with concerns raised by McKinnon (1973), Shaw (1973) and others in the 1970s. They also suggest the importance for poor farmers of having access to remunerative savings opportunities (for example McKinnon 1973, Pender 1992).

This section also presents the advantage of integrating the theory of precautionary saving with that of credit constraints and irreversible investment under risk. A similar approach can be applied to other investments in which non-divisibility may serve to deter investment by poor households, such as human capital accumulation, or firm creation and expansion. Irreversibility is a feature common to many economic decisions. Investment in schooling, human fertility, and the construction of a production unit, for instance, are all situations in which decisions cannot be reversed. Partial irreversibility is even more widespread as many decisions can only be reversed at a cost: for instance, those concerning migration, purchase of durables, purchase of equipment. This section has shown that agents with a precautionary motive may refrain from incurring any of these irreversible investments.

6.5   RISK SHARING AND RISK TAKING

The poor are not only less able to take risk because they do not have the financial and human capital required to invest; they are also less willing to bear additional risk. Mutual insurance with other villagers may reduce some of these inhibitions and encourage risk taking. The sharing of risk, however, also dilutes incentives for risk taking, especially if the egalitarian social norms on which solidarity is founded force the redistribution of success as well as failure cit (for example Platteau 1996, Platteau 2000b). Allowing less egalitarian forms of risk sharing, such as patronage, eliminates this problem but creates other difficulties, the most important one being the tendency for the poor to further impoverish themselves. The net effect of mutual insurance on risk taking is thus ambiguous. This section delves into these issues in more detail.

6.5.1   Norms of Risk Sharing in Rural Communities

It has been argued that norms of risk sharing that are prevalent in poor rural communities operate as wealth redistribution mechanisms and, as such, discourage the rural poor from saving and investing. In a couple of recent papers, Platteau and Hayami (1996) and Platteau (1996) revisit these issues and go as far as proposing a division of pre-industrial agrarian societies into two groups. The authors argue that Asian-type societies are those in which norms of risk sharing do not impose an excessive tax on returns to effort, individual accumulation is allowed and encouraged, and development takes place. In contrast, African-type societies have norms of risk sharing that impose an excessive tax on returns to effort, thereby discouraging individual accumulation and holding back development.[140] To explain why this might be the case, Platteau and Hayami (1996) bring to the fore geographical and technological factors that have shaped rural societies. Platteau (1996) adopts a Boserup (1965) style argument and notes that population density determines techniques of production such as irrigation. By reducing crop risk, Platteau argues, irrigation means that returns to effort are more easily identifiable. Consequently, the cultural representations of societies with irrigation recognize more clearly a link between effort and outcomes.

Although there is probably an element of truth in the idea that risk sharing discourages accumulation, the claim that this process might account for the relative performance of entire continents is, I believe, unreasonable. The truth is more complex and requires that we disentangle the sharing of income and consumption risk from the redistribution of wealth. To address these issues, we first discuss the circumstantial evidence regarding individualism and accumulation in poor societies in general and in Africa in particular. Next, we revisit some of the conceptual underpinnings of the relationship between risk sharing, risk taking, and investment. We continue with a detailed discussion of asymmetric forms of risk sharing, also called patronage, and their relationship with investment and development.

6.5.2 Circumstantial Evidence on Individualism

Let us begin by saying that there is little doubt that most people in poor rural societies anywhere, including Sub-Saharan Africa, recognize that individual effort raises income. If they did not, it is hard to see why they would work at all. Fafchamps and Minten (1999) indeed show that, if anything, poor traders are more individualistic and less inclined to share risk with others than large traders. The claim that the rural poor in certain parts of the world do not work hard because they do not see a relationship between effort and income is too far fetched – at least stated in these general terms.

Second, it is difficult to believe that people's desire to accumulate wealth and power is less strong in some parts of the world than in other parts of the world because of social norms emphasizing redistribution. There is indeed plenty of circumstantial evidence that poor rural areas are not immune to individualism and opportunism (for example Popkin 1979, Poewe 1989). The history of Africa, just like any other part of the world, provides ample – and often unsavoury – evidence of accumulation and greed, including a long history of slavery (for example Hopkins 1973, Watts 1983, Bayart 1989, Shillington 1989). In areas with a low population density and where shifting cultivation is practised, individual land property rights are costly to enforce (Binswanger and McIntire 1987).[141] Accumulation then historically takes a different form, in other words the control over 'bodies' through slavery, labour bonding, and polygamy. In contrast, where labour is plentiful power comes from the accumulation of other means of production such as land and cash. The fact that accumulation in low population density/high enforcement cost areas takes a different form from other areas may have been misinterpreted as a sign that accumulation is less important. This is probably erroneous, although it is important to recognize that the accumulation of control over bodies is not achieved by the same means as the accumulation of land and financial wealth. This may have implications regarding investment and development that we discuss below.

6.5.3 Risk Sharing, Investment, and Saving

Platteau and Hayami (1996) argue that risk sharing decreases investment because it taxes success. This is forgetting that risk sharing also reduces the cost of failure. As we have discussed earlier, poor producers might be deterred from investing in new technologies and market opportunities because they are concerned about downside risk, that is, the possibility that they might not survive a bad shock. By protecting producers from the worst consequences of shocks and ensuring their survival, risk sharing ought to favour investment and risk taking for the same reasons that formal insurance, venture capital, derivative markets, and portfolio diversification favour investment in developed economies. In other words, we should expect the insurance dimension of risk sharing to favour investment and risk taking, not discourage them. Even if risk sharing mechanisms tax success, their net effect on development could be positive.

Risk sharing might, however, reduce the need for precautionary saving and thus lower aggregate saving (see Chapter Three). Although this is probably true, one should keep in mind that precautionary balances must be kept in liquid form to serve their purpose. This implies that what the rural poor save to deal with risk is in general kept in grain stocks, small livestock, cash, jewellery, and deposit accounts (see Chapter Three). The need for liquidity means that the poor will be willing to save in instruments that have a low or even negative return, such as grain stocks carried over from year to year, and cash in inflationary economies. Such forms of investment are not necessarily efficient from society's perspective, so that reducing precautionary saving might improve allocative efficiency.

Furthermore, as we have argued earlier, precautionary balances are unlikely to finance the purchase of large, non-divisible investments. For the same reason, they are unlikely to be invested in highly risky projects. Consequently, the reduction in precautionary saving that one would expect to result from better sharing of risk need not subtract from investment and risk taking. A fall in precautionary saving might seriously hurt investment only if financial institutions exist that permit the poor to keep their wealth in liquid form while channeling the mobilized resources to high risk, high return investments. Such financial intermediaries are typically lacking in poor rural areas and when they are present they do not always protect small depositors against aggregate financial risk.

In addition, risk sharing may decrease precautionary savings against idiosyncratic risk but accumulation is still required to deal with collective risk: when a drought hits a region, pooling risk with neighbours and friends does not make more food available locally. In these circumstances, it would be foolish for rural communities to set up risk sharing arrangements that discourage any type of accumulation. In fact, such a community would not survive very long in the harsh conditions faced by most poor rural communities of the world today.

Communities might, however, restrict accumulation by some and favour accumulation by others. Too much accumulation by the lower echelons of rural society might indeed challenge the established social order in ways that are deemed undesirable by the higher echelons of society or even by society at large, if they fear the social and political unrest that would follow an erosion of, say, the power of village chiefs. To prevent this from happening, the rural establishment may seek to expropriate successful individuals from the fruits of their success. This process, however, is distinct from the idea of risk sharing per se and it must be analysed separately. To this we now turn. We begin with a discussion of patronage.

6.5.4 Patronage and Inequality

Risk sharing between individuals of different income potential need not lead to an equalization of their ex post consumption levels. In fact, one would expect the rich to refuse sharing risk in ways that reduce their expected utility. It can even be shown (see Chapter Four) that a sufficiently risk neutral individual will always oppose even a balanced (that is, non redistributive) mutual insurance scheme. A fortiori, such an individual would reject a scheme that calls for net expected transfers from the rich to the poor (see also Hoff (1996)). Risk sharing can, however, be organized in such a way as to compensate the rich for insuring the poor. This arrangement is called patronage and was already discussed in Chapter Four (see also (e.g. Platteau 1995a, Platteau 1995b)).

In patronage, the rich collect the equivalent of an insurance premium from the poor, usually in the form of frequent small payments and services. Extreme forms of patronage include debt peonage and labour bonding, but patronage can also take a more benign, paternalistic form. Irrespective of the form it takes, however, patronage naturally reinforces inequality in society (see also Carter and Zimmerman (1996)). It is thus false to argue that risk sharing inhibits risk taking and accumulation: patronage as a form of risk sharing in fact favours the accumulation of wealth by a few who then patronize less fortunate members of society. The key issue is thus whether societies may fear the concentration of wealth and power that is likely to result from the unchecked development of patronage.

6.5.5 Egalitarian Norms

As discussed in Chapter 5, Part I, unchecked accumulation of factors of production in societies with a lot of risk can totally modify the social structure and rapidly lead to a highly differentiated and highly conflictual society. In anticipation, societies may try to prevent the excesses of factor accumulation by imposing egalitarian norms. One way is to institute rituals that periodically waste all wealth, such as the *potlach* rituals among Northeast native American tribes and other rituals that call for the massive consumption of food, beer, and livestock at regular intervals. This works well in static societies; but of course it is no good in a growing society where capital must be accumulated. Another way to do so is to prevent transactions on factors of production through, for instance: the prohibition of slavery, indentures, and labour bonding; the prohibition of usury, to reduce debt peonage (see Chapters Four and Five); and the prohibition of land sales to people from outside or even inside the community, as is common in much of Africa (for example Atwood 1990, Platteau 1995c, Gavian and Fafchamps 1996). These issues were discussed in detail in Chapters Four and Five.

Yet another way to discourage the accumulation of assets is to encourage patronage – of the arts, of the church, and of the poor (Ellsworth 1989). So doing, the physical wealth of the rich gets redistributed periodically. In practice, however, patronage is seldom an avenue to egalitarianism. Giving away one's wealth often amounts to investing in a relationship that can become a source of additional wealth in the long term. Unless one recognizes the long-term benefits the rich derive from patronage, it might be erroneously concluded that it is a tax imposed on the wealthy.

In societies where patronage is the dominant avenue to upward social mobility, wealth is often seen as returns to help and networks, not returns to effort and risk taking. A wealthy person is someone who has helped many, can help them again and can count on their gratefulness. Fafchamps and Minten (1999), and Fafchamps and Minten (2002), for instance, show that relationships and social capital are essential to success in grain trade because it gives access to trade credit and regular supplies and facilitates the conduct of business. Similar examples can be found in the political economy literature under the name of prebendalism (Bayart 1989). The reason why patronage is an avenue to individual prosperity is that giving obligates the other party to reciprocate, and that what is reciprocated is more valuable to the patron than what is given away. Whenever these conditions are satisfied, giving is nothing but an investment in social capital and it becomes a route to power.

6.5.6 Social Structure and Patronage

That patronage is encouraged need not imply that it is encouraged for everyone: certain individuals may not be recognized as having the right to become a patron. This is hardly surprising since patronage is a source of power. Those in power will probably resent any intrusion on their territory and seek to protect their dominant position. To that effect, norms of social stratification are likely to be invented that make it difficult to challenge power – such as castes, nobility, hereditary chiefdom, and so on. Current patrons may also attempt to undermine challengers by siphoning off, in the name of risk sharing and egalitarianism, any extra wealth that could potentially be used to create a concurrent network of clientelistic relationships.

If successful, these attempts undoubtedly tax risk takers and innovators who are not members of the rural elite. But it would be ill-advised to blame risk sharing for this state of affairs: self-preservation of power is the reason. Besides, even in the absence of risk sharing institutions and egalitarian norms, the rich and powerful are likely to protect their power by whatever ways are available to them, such as by restricting access to land, credit, and labour and by imposing an extra corruption burden on outsiders. These are manifestations of power struggle, not of risk sharing.

6.5.7 Patronage, Accumulation, and Returns to Scale

It should be clear that patronage per se need not work against accumulation by society at large. Abstracting for a moment from social capital, patronage reduces the concentration of individual wealth since it forces the redistribution of material goods from those who have to those who have not (see, however, Ellsworth (1989)). But redistribution by itself does not eliminate wealth. The question then is, does the existence of norms of redistribution of material wealth serve as a disincentive to accumulation by individuals?

We have already discussed the favourable role that the insurance provided by risk sharing should have on investment. We now focus on the role of accumulation as a source of prosperity. Since the redistribution of material wealth implied by patronage and norms of redistribution operates as a tax on economic success, it appears that the existence of patronage ought to reduce incentives to accumulate. Incentives to accumulate thus appear smaller than they would be in an idealized capitalist society. This is forgetting that patronage gives access to power and enables individuals to accumulate social capital. The prestige and connections acquired through gift giving require that material wealth be generated, if only to be redistributed. It is thus far from clear that a patronage system creates less incentive to produce and invest than a more individualistic system where economic agents consume the material wealth they generate. A patron cannot succeed without 'stuff' to give away and, to the extent that giving is the source of power, patronage is probably as potent a stimulant for output as capitalism.

The problem created by patronage is elsewhere. In a society with norms of redistribution of material wealth, it is difficult for single individuals to accumulate large quantities of investable funds. In the absence of returns to scale, this is not problematic: financial capital gets redistributed and facilitates the creation of myriads of small enterprises – what is commonly known as the informal sector (Fafchamps 1994). If returns to scale are decreasing, the redistribution of financial capital is even efficiency enhancing from a social welfare point of view. However, the dilution of capital brought about by patronage makes it difficult to take advantage of investment opportunities that benefit from large economies of scale, such as automobile manufacturing or steel mills. The reason is that no single individual is able to accumulate enough money to make large scale, nondivisible investments. Incrementalism is the rule.[142] Consequently, one would expect societies where patronage is strong to experience difficulties forming a domestic capitalist class and financing large scale investments with local private funds. A natural response to this state of affairs is likely to be increased state intervention. Many poor countries, in Sub-Saharan Africa and elsewhere (such as Indonesia), fit this description fairly well, except that they often have an ethnically foreign business class (Fafchamps 2000). Prebendalism and political networks of clientelism can thus be seen as efforts by patronage based societies to enlist the help of the state to mobilize large scale resources and capture economies of scale. Whether these efforts are ultimately successful in bringing about sustainable growth in large scale business remains a hotly debated question (for example World Bank 1981, World Bank 1993).

There is, however, a form of capital the accumulation of which is facilitated by patronage and risk sharing, namely, social capital in the form of networks. Returns to social capital are highest in information intensive activities such as trade (for example Fafchamps and Minten 1999, Fafchamps and Minten 2002), but the available evidence suggests that they are also present in manufacturing (for example Fafchamps 2000, Barr 2002). An immediate corollary is that societies in which patronage and thus social capital (networks, trust) are strong should prosper in activities that are intensive in social capital such as trade. The available evidence indeed suggests that merchant networks are strong even in countries with little or no large scale manufacturing, such as most Sub-Saharan African countries (for example Bauer 1954, Jones 1959, Cohen 1969, Meillassoux 1971, Amselle 1977, Staatz 1979). Similar forces operated in the ancient world (e.g. Braudel 1986, Putnam et al. 1993, Greif 1993, Greif 1994) and are at work in other parts of the world as well, as evidenced by the success of ethnic Chinese communities throughout East and South East Asia.

Whether or not patronage and norms of redistribution are detrimental to accumulation and growth thus depends on the relative roles of financial and social capital in the development process: if finance is the key constraint, then patronage is detrimental to growth; if, however, social capital is ultimately more important, then patronage can potentially play an important role in linking up key economic actors and building up essential economic networks. Experience suggests that large scale investments are not a foolproof recipe for growth, as the Stalinist experiment in Russia and Korea's recent problems have shown. Good international contacts and the capacity to build local networks are also important (for example Piore and Sabel 1984, Putnam et al. 1993). Given time, patronage based societies might build the international links that are essential for access to information and markets in developed countries. When they do, they will undoubtedly surprise us.

7. Conclusion

We now take stock of what we have learned about the relationship between risk, rural poverty, and economic development. We also make suggestions regarding future work and policy intervention. A special emphasis is put on identifying current gaps in knowledge and areas where empirical work is most needed to support or vindicate recent theoretical developments.

7.1 WHAT WE HAVE LEARNED

We have learned that risk affects the rural poor in numerous and profound ways. The magnitude and range of shocks that affect rural populations of the Third World is without comparison in developed economies. Perhaps the only way to describe it to people who have never been there is to compare it to a war economy: death strikes at random a large proportion of the population, especially children; the provision of health services is either non-existent or insufficient; trade with the rest of the world is difficult so that many commodities are rationed or unavailable and local prices are erratic; food is at times very scarce; and steady wage employment is non-existent so that people must make a living from self-employment in little jobs. To deal with such a harsh environment, people are equipped with very little in terms of advanced technology and accumulated assets. Financial institutions are either absent or inefficient and expensive, and in many places, inflation is rife so that the cost of hoarding money is high.

In response to these extremely difficult conditions, rural societies have developed sophisticated ways to cope with risk. These multi-faceted strategies include: settling relatively safe areas; breeding plants and species that survive in difficult environments; diversifying sources of income; preserving flexibility and keeping options open; accumulating precautionary saving; forming strong and large households; seeking the protection of the rich and powerful; and sharing risk with a large network of friends and relatives. These strategies are subject to serious technological, environmental, and economic constraints that limit their effectiveness. Furthermore, rural societies often prohibit individually rational options such as distress land sales, labour bonding, and debt peonage, because they would generate unacceptable inequality and social tension in the long run.

Commitment failure seriously limit society's capacity to share risk. Institutions have developed that provide partial solutions to this problem. Corvée labour can be used by traditional chiefs to set up a village welfare fund. How effective such efforts are ultimately depends on the leadership and integrity of the chiefs themselves. A similar comment can be made about the social programmes of numerous churches and NGOs. Family law, whether modern or traditional, establishes a strong bond between spouses and between parents and children and penalizes those who seek to avoid their family responsibilities. Family values are a key element of the rural poor's strategy to deal with risk; loyalty to the family is seen as a fundamental civic virtue. The failure to abide by these values often results in personal disaster.

Commitment failure is also mitigated by forming long-term relationships with networks of friends and relatives. These relationships, however important in helping the poor deal with risk, are not perfect: self-interest motives introduce distortions that preclude a fully efficient sharing of risk. Widespread reliance on quasi-credit contracts instead of income pooling or contingent transfers is a sign that self-interest and commitment failure shape the form taken by mutual insurance. Efforts to minimize incentive problems induced by information asymmetries also reduce the effectiveness of mutual insurance, for instance by limiting coverage to observable events or providing partial insurance to limit moral hazard. Moral norms and village ideologies can be seen as attempts to penalize inefficient opportunistic behaviour and to induce truthful information revelation and, hence, to mitigate the perverse effects that self-interest and information asymmetries have on mutual insurance.

In Chapter Five, we have learned that there are trade-offs between insurance and social mobility, and between asset markets and social polarization. We also found that, when wealth is made of assets in fixed supply such as land or manpower, trade in these assets naturally leads to an unequal distribution of welfare and income. For this result to arise, the savings rate must increase with cash-in-hand. Factors that favour accumulation, such as a high return on wealth or large aggregate stock of wealth, also favour inequality.

From an equity point of view, there might therefore be a rationale for shutting down certain asset markets, in other words those for which supply is finite. This is because allowing accumulation is likely to result in polarization. This conclusion applies primarily to land, manpower, and mineral and environmental resources. With the possible exception of mineral resources, these are also the markets in which restrictions to market transactions are most widespread. In contrast, the accumulation of unbounded resources such as equipment, skills, and knowledge does not raise similar fears although, in the long run, they also lead to persistent inequality. These assets are also those that are essential for growth.

Our analysis also offers some caution to those who see the provision of insurance mechanisms as a solution to poverty. The theory is quite clear: perfect insurance freezes inequality. An insurance system based on voluntary participation – such as a market based approach for instance – cannot eliminate inequality. It might raise the welfare of the poor by providing protection against shocks, but it will not in general eliminate inequality that is already there. A tax based system might be necessary to build redistribution into the insurance system. Combating inequality thus requires policy tools other than insurance. In some cases, organizing insurance might even worsen the long-term prospects of the poor by reducing social mobility.

We have also learned that the relationship between risk, poverty, and economic development is complex but that our understanding of the underlying processes has progressed dramatically with recent theoretical and empirical advances. We argued that rural poverty by itself is unlikely to raise net fertility, that is, the number of surviving children per woman. We argued that chronic poverty, by itself, seldom leads to starvation – except in cases of extreme destitution. Its negative impact on welfare comes mostly from the fact that it dramatically raises the vulnerability of individuals and households to adverse shocks. The effects of these shocks manifest themselves not only in terms of short-term and long-term nutritional status but also in terms of morbidity and mortality rates. The evidence further suggests that populations that are ill and poorly fed cannot operate effectively and fail to reach their full potential. We also reported recent evidence indicating that the poor find it difficult to keep their children in school. As in the case of nutrition and health, the role of income shocks was also brought to light in the sense that a single negative income shock appears to have as much negative effect on schooling as permanent poverty (Sawada 1997).

Next, we discussed the relationship between rural poverty, risk, and technological innovation. We argued that Sandmo's (1971) traditional explanation for the poor's reluctance to invest in risky technologies – namely, their aversion to risk – does not survive close scrutiny. In its stead, we propose a distinction between several distinct processes. First, we argue that if inputs are provided by the producer himself or herself, such as land, labour, and livestock manure, Sandmo's reasoning no longer applies: faced with the choice between enjoying leisure now and starving later or investing time in a risky activity such as crop production, risk averse households naturally choose to take risks and produce. Second, if production requires purchased inputs such as improved seeds, fertilizer, or pesticides, poor households might refrain from producing not because they are risk averse but more simply because they do not have sufficient funds. Furthermore, even if they have access to credit for these inputs, they might still refrain from purchasing because they fear bankruptcy. In this case, it is not so much the variance of output per se that is an issue but rather the fact that output might be insufficient to cover input costs. We provided three examples of mechanisms that provide credit for modern inputs and eliminate the risk of bankruptcy without eliminating production risk. These mechanisms have been successfully used for input delivery in different contexts, suggesting that bankruptcy risk might be a more useful concept to understand technology adoption than risk aversion.

Next, we turned to the diversification argument and noted that the poor's desire to diversify ought to favour adoption of new technologies. In fact, based on the diversification argument alone, we argued that risk averse farmers should be more – not less – likely to adopt new technologies that are divisible and do not require massive cash outlays. Only when the new technology is non-divisible (such as a tractor, animal traction) does risk aversion operate against adoption. The desire to diversify was also seen to operate against full specialization in a single technology, whether old or new. As a result, diversification reduces the gain from technological innovation. One should therefore not blame risk aversion per se for the non-adoption of divisible technologies such as fertilizer and improved seeds.

We then discussed the relationship between poverty, risk, and experimentation with new technologies. We noted that, by the diversification argument, poor farmers ought to be quite willing to experiment with new techniques of production as long as this can be done on a small scale. The reason is that new technologies provide new avenues for diversification and that diversification has more value for risk averse producers. However, when experimentation and learning are non-divisible, they conflict with the poor's desire to diversify, which singularly reduces their appeal. To summarize, we identified the non-divisibility of technology and its learning process as a major stumbling block on the road to adoption by poor farmers. The variance of output appears, by itself, unimportant, except inasmuch as it raises fears of bankruptcy. The main factors that hinder technology adoption by poor risk averse farmers thus appear to be: large cash outlays, loss of diversification after adoption, and large risk during experimentation and learning.

Next we focused on the observed regularity that larger farmers in the Third World are more cash crop oriented and smaller farmers more food crop oriented. Using a simple model of crop portfolio decision with income and consumption price risk, we showed that conditions prevailing in rural communities of the Third World tend to reproduce the observed relationship between farm size and cash crop cultivation. The intuition behind the

approach was simple: rural food markets in poor countries are thin and isolated, leading to a high variance in food prices and a high covariance
between individual and market supply. Staple consumption, on the other
hand, is essential for survival. Consequently, staple food expenditures have
a low income elasticity. The combination of both elements leads to a situation in which food *security* at the household level is best achieved by a high
degree of food *self-sufficiency*. Large farmers differ from small farmers not
only in better access to credit and their better ability to sustain risk, but also
in the lower share that staple foods represent in their total consumption
expenditures. The model presented in Chapter Six suggested that this alone
can account for the observed regularity between farm size and cash crop
cultivation.

We then proceeded to illustrate how market integration progressively
diminishes the need for food self-sufficiency. As better roads and transportation equalize price movements across a larger regional or international
market, food prices become increasingly dissociated from local supply and
demand conditions. All the effects of market integration – a lower variance
in food prices, less covariance between individual output and aggregate
supply, a more elastic demand because of substitution and international
trade possibilities – were shown to reduce an individual's rationale for food
self-sufficiency. Our analysis also predicted that large farmers would have a
higher price elasticity of cash crop supply, and that small farmers would
have a higher price elasticity of food crop production. The integration of
food markets thus appears an essential ingredient to agricultural modernization.

We then turned toward credit constraints and precautionary saving.
What motivated our analysis was the simple observation that, although the
poor might not afford a non-divisible investment today, by saving enough
they ought to afford it tomorrow. Consequently, credit constraints ought to
constitute only a temporary obstacle to investment. We argued that this
observation is correct but very misleading. To that effect, we showed that,
when the poor use their limited liquid wealth to smooth consumption and
deal with consumption shocks, they might resist investing all of it in an irreversible investment. We showed that this was the case even if investing
results in an income stream that stochastically dominates the original distribution of their income. In other words, resistance to investment had
nothing to do with risk aversion as normally defined: in a Sandmo (1971)
setup (see above), any risk averse individual would choose the income
stream that stochastically dominates the others; this is not the case when
the investment is irreversible and the poor save for precautionary reasons.

Using parameters estimated from samples of investments in wells by
Indian farmers, we showed that poor individuals with a precautionary

motive for saving find it very hard to save enough to finance a large lumpy investment. The reason is that income and consumption shocks nearly always hit them before they have had the time to accumulate enough for the investment. This is true even though the poor respond to the presence of an investment opportunity by saving more. As a result, the probability of investing is very low and the average time to investment extremely long. To summarize, although the law of martingales implies that eventually everyone invests, 'eventually' can be an awfully long time – much too long to wait for.

The link between poverty and low investment apparent in these results is reminiscent of 'vicious circle' and 'big push' theories of development propounded decades ago by Nurkse (1953), Lewis (1954), Nelson (1956), and others. Modern versions of these theories can be found in Gaylor and Ryder (1989), Murphy et al. (1989), Fafchamps and Helms (1996) and Barro and Sala i Martin (1995). These issues deserve more empirical research at the village and household level.

In the final part of Chapter Six, we discussed the relationship between risk sharing and risk taking. In Chapters Three and Four we saw that the sharing of risk among members of a rural community is an important way by which the poor deal with external shocks. The end of Chapter Six examined whether the sharing of risk serves as a disincentive to invest, as some have recently argued. We first pointed out that the insurance component of risk sharing ought to favour investment, not deter it, for the simple reason that better insured investors are less vulnerable to unfavourable investment outcomes and thus are more prone to invest. Risk sharing is, however, likely to reduce the need for precautionary saving. Consequently, members of risk sharing networks ought to lower their holdings of liquid wealth. We nevertheless pointed out that liquid assets are still necessary to deal with collective shocks, and thus that precautionary saving would still be required. In addition, we know that precautionary saving is often kept in a form that is both highly liquid and not very productive. Unless the poor save mostly at the bank and financial intermediation is efficiently organized, a lowering of precautionary saving is unlikely to significantly reduce productive investment.

Next we discussed how norms of wealth redistribution coupled with the need to share risk with others leads to patronage systems in which the better off protect the weaker members of society against adverse shocks. We noted that communities subject to lots of external shocks might fear the concentration of wealth that would naturally arise, were asset and credit markets allowed to freely develop. We pointed out that, in order to ensure long-term social cohesion, these communities might come up with egalitarian norms that prohibit certain types of transactions and require the redistribution of material wealth. We argued, however, that these norms need not preclude the accumulation of social capital in the form of networks of reciprocal obligations and debts of gratitude.

We then investigated whether egalitarian norms of redistribution dilute incentives to invest. We noted that generating material wealth is essential to build up social networks of patronage through redistribution. Consequently, incentives to invest and create wealth exist as long as patronage as a form of social upward mobility is an option open to everyone. It remains unclear, however, whether these incentives are as strong as those that exist when individual consumption of material wealth is the primary objective of success. Incentives to invest may nevertheless be lowered if certain individuals are not allowed to rise socially. In this case, 'taxation' by society in the form of forced redistribution, theft, and pilferage becomes a potent disincentive to accumulation and risk taking. That this might be an issue in many poor rural areas of the Third World is implied by the fact that ambitious young men and women often leave the countryside and go to the city where there are fewer obstacles to individual success. The rigidity of social structure might thus be an obstacle to risk taking, especially by young individuals more open to modern techniques of production. In this sense, progress might indeed be held back.

We concluded Chapter Six by noting that patronage as a system of social stratification makes it difficult for single individuals to accumulate large sums of money. Consequently, large investments are not undertaken. If returns to investment are decreasing or constant, this is not a problem: redistribution of material wealth facilitates the creation of myriads of microenterprises, which is precisely what we observe in many poor countries. However, the dilution of capital brought about by patronage makes it difficult to take advantage of investment opportunities that benefit from economies of scale. Social stratification based on patronage is thus likely to be inimical to large scale industrialization. In contrast, patronage favours the accumulation of social capital, an essential ingredient in trade. Patronage based societies might thus constitute a favourable breeding ground for trade based activities, provided the right kinds of contacts can be established with the outside world.

7.2   WHAT WE DO NOT KNOW

We have learned a great deal about risk coping by the poor but there is still a lot we do not know. Casual observation tells us that patterns of settlement partly match the relative safety of specific environments in terms of human and livestock health. Migration studies show that the poor move out of unwelcoming areas in large numbers and travel far and wide in search of better living conditions. We also know, simply by watching television, that drought, warfare, and other natural catastrophes throw scores of people on the roads in search of safety. Yet it is not fully understood what makes people live where they live.

It is more and more obvious that, in due time, large areas of the earth that are currently populated will eventually be depopulated, in particular wide tracts of inhospitable mountain, desert, marshes, and rainforest. Eventually, people will move, as they should, away from fragile, marginal areas toward lands suitable for urban settlement and intensive agriculture. This movement should be understood in order to be facilitated. It is where people are not moving that pockets of rural poverty will remain the longest. Efforts to stabilize poor populations on fragile lands are ill advised as they contribute to the perpetuation of rural poverty.

The recent abundance of theoretical and empirical work on precautionary savings has brought to light the role of asset accumulation as a hedge against risk. It has shown that the poor are willing to save, even at negative interest rates, and thus that they are penalized by inflation and by financial repression that keeps returns on savings accounts artificially low. Although there has been a lot of work on credit markets in poor rural areas, there is a dramatic dearth of work on savings and on the use of financial instruments by the rural poor. The few empirical studies that exist, however, show that the provision of financial institutions in rural areas helps the poor save. Reconstruction of cash balances of rural households, although highly speculative, indicates that money may be a more important savings instrument than is often recognized. Precious little is known on how the rural poor use money and other financial instruments. More work is needed so that adequate savings instrument can be provided.

Economists are only beginning to recognize the paramount importance that the household formation process has on poverty. In this study, it has been argued that one of the primary functions of households is to form teams of people who can deal with shocks together and help each other in difficult times. It has also been hypothesized that households can be broken by traumatic events and that the dissolution of households almost always has negative repercussions on its former members. Yet very little is known on how households form and, even more importantly, how they break apart. Rural household surveys typically follow existing households and ignore isolated individuals who eke a living at the margin of rural communities or join the ranks of a highly mobile urban proletariat. Households that break apart are often dropped from survey rosters and no information is collected on the fate of their former members. As a result of these biases, we know very little about the effect of household dissolution on poverty and risk coping. The little bit that we know, however, is troubling: female headed households in rural areas are nearly always worse off than households where both spouses are present. More work is needed to understand the factors that favour stable and successful households in spite of external shocks.

We also need to better understand how resources are allocated within households themselves. The evidence suggests that households deal with shocks by reallocating scarce resources to their productive members. Women seem to pay the price of such a strategy because their traditional function is reproduction, and investment in children is a low priority when a household can barely feed its current members. More research is needed to confirm that this interpretation is correct and that it can account for the often observed nutrition deficit of poor rural women. In particular, we may wish to find out whether these nutrition and health outcomes are optimal and desirable from the point of view of women themselves.

Recent work has shown that networks of long-term relationships help mitigate commitment failure not only in risk sharing, but also in other forms of exchange. The importance of networks has long been recognized in other social sciences but the time has now come for economists to examine the role that networks play in the sharing of risk. More needs to be known on how networks are formed and how they fall apart. It is indeed becoming increasingly clear that individuals with few friends are at a disadvantage in a rural world fraught to danger. Social network capital should thus be viewed as a crucial factor affecting and being affected by poverty and shocks.

Much recent work on risk coping by the poor has been extremely naive regarding the role of inequality and power. Yet observers of poor rural societies consistently warn us that desperate people will do anything to buy time, including mortgaging their own future. We have seen that the sharing of risk between the rich and the poor has a natural tendency to become exploitative and to foster inequality. We need to take a harder look at the interplay between power and risk. Judging by the legal prohibitions many rural societies have come up with to discourage distress sale of productive assets such as land and labour, these issues are important to the people involved and they deserve empirical enquiry.

Finally, although we have made much progress in our understanding of individual risk coping strategies, we still know very little about how they interact with each other. One issue that has received some attention is that of the relationship between individual asset accumulation and explicit risk sharing. We have seen that much pooling of risk can be achieved when individuals hold precautionary savings and can trade their assets for consumption goods in perfectly competitive markets. We have also argued that self-interest may discourage individuals from participating in risk sharing arrangements if the expected gains they make from sharing risk are not commensurate with what they are asked to contribute. Intuitively, this creates a tension between risk sharing and precautionary saving: if the latter is easy and cheap, this lowers the expected gain from explicit risk sharing, and thus the contributions individuals are willing to make to help others. One may therefore fear that introducing better precautionary savings instruments can undermine existing risk sharing arrangements. This issue deserves more theoretical and empirical investigation.

Regarding the effect of risk and rural poverty on economic development, we have cast doubt on the idea that the poor's concern for old age security increases fertility rates net of infant and child mortality. We believe that efforts to ensure the old age security of the poor, although favourable to their welfare, are unlikely to have a significant effect on demographic pressure. This issue deserves further investigation.

Recent research indicates that temporary income shocks are as damaging for school attendance as chronic poverty. This suggests that school dropout rates could be dramatically curtailed by helping the poor deal with temporary shocks. Future research should seek to assess the best way to achieve this purpose in a financially sustainable manner.

We have demonstrated that the idea that the poor resist innovation simply because they are risk averse is far too simplistic. A better understanding of the available theory and empirical evidence suggests instead that the poor worry not so much about the variation of income per se, but rather about keeping a sufficient buffer of liquid assets to deal with emergencies. Consequently, they are unlikely to invest whatever assets they have in inputs and equipment that must be paid for up front. Our analysis suggests that successful dissemination of purchased inputs requires a combination of credit and insurance. Further investigation is needed to identify input delivery systems that are well adapted to the needs of poor producers.

We have argued that the poor's desire to diversify ought to make them quite receptive to divisible technologies such as seeds, fertilizer, and pesticides. Instead of encouraging the adoption of combined packages on a whole farm, the analysis presented here suggests that experimentation with small quantities on small plots is a better way of getting poor producers interested in new technology. This issue requires empirical confirmation. We have also shown that food price volatility raises poor farmers' concerns for food self-sufficiency. More research is needed to measure how strong these concerns are and how much they distort production choices.

Finally, in Chapter Six, we argued that societies which impose norms of material wealth redistribution favour patronage as a mode of social differentiation. We further indicated that, if this is the case, norms of redistribution ought not to be perceived as obstacles to saving and investment because generating material wealth is necessary to build one's social network. Whether this is true in practice requires serious empirical investigation. More work is also required to identify the types of social capital that is most necessary for growth.

7.3   WHAT LOCAL GOVERNMENTS CAN DO

Keeping in mind that there are still many unresolved issues regarding risk coping by the poor, what we already know or strongly suspect suggests a number of policy interventions. We discuss them briefly here.

1. It is important that governments do not stop natural migration and resettlement out of marginal areas. In the past, governments have often been tempted to fixate populations in what is perceived to be their traditional habitat. Scarce national resources would be better spent developing high potential areas and encouraging people to move there. This means draining marshes, clearing forests, setting up irrigation infrastructure, and building roads into areas with a high agricultural potential. Inciting people to relocate into such areas also requires vigorous efforts to eradicate malaria, trypanosomiasis, and other parasitic human and livestock diseases.
2. By the same token, governments should stop trying to move rural populations to marginal zones in ill-advised 'relocation schemes', such as the development of the Amazon, the new economic zones in Vietnam, or forced resettlement in Ethiopia.
3. In countries where high agricultural potential areas are non-existent or already overcrowded, such as some of the Sahelian countries or the Rwanda-Burundi region of Africa, agriculture may be unable to absorb population growth. In this case, governments may want to consider either helping their surplus population to emigrate abroad, or anticipating the growth of the urban periphery and the need to provide poor urban migrants with decent public services.
4. We saw that, under conditions of extreme duress, the poor may adopt risky or even suicidal strategies. One such example is the chaotic movements of famine-stricken people in search of food along roads and across country boundaries. These movements are often dangerous, as they separate families and put them at the mercy of bandits and rogue armies. Relief efforts should try to anticipate these movements by distributing aid before panic sets in and households leave

their village. This requires, for instance, the continued presence of famine early warning systems and the existence of well defined procedures and relief agencies equipped and trained to deal with emergencies at short notice.

5. Governments should move away from an exclusive emphasis on rural credit and turn to rural savings. This is particularly relevant given evidence that the rural poor rely less on livestock sales to deal with risk than was previously believed. Adequate savings instruments should thus be made available to the poor. This requires setting up clear and rigid prudential guidelines for rural savings and loan associations, and penalizing those who profit by establishing pyramid schemes that defraud the poor.

6. Governments should be cautious when promoting institutions that encourage poor people to borrow. Advances in credit delivery such as group lending have led to a rapid increase in lending to the poor. The analysis presented here suggest that doing so is likely to force at least some proportion of the poor into a debt trap. To avoid this outcome, steps should be taken to protect the poor from permanent insolvency. This is difficult to accomplish while at the same time ensuring sufficient repayment incentives for those who can repay.

7. Governments should renounce using the inflation tax to finance their deficit. Financial repression is counterproductive in that it lowers the return that the poor get on their precautionary saving.

8. Governments should favour the geographical integration of grain and livestock markets. Barriers to trade across regional and international boundaries should be removed and road blocks should be dismantled. Veterinary services should be provided to herders in a cost-effective manner.

9. Governments should focus the provision of health services on prevention and the delivery of cost-effective health services. They should also favour the provision of safe drinking water. Expensive treatments such as those required by AIDS patients are beyond the reach of most poor countries. Until a cheap treatment for AIDS becomes available, scarce resources are better used for the prevention and treatment of curable tropical diseases, such as malaria, measles, bronchitis, tetanus, gastro-intestinal infections, and the like.

10. Governments should launch campaigns to eradicate malaria and other parasitic diseases. Due to the public good nature of eradication, only a massive coordinated campaign can succeed.

11. Wild animals and their habitat are reservoirs of dangerous diseases and parasites. Elephants, wild buffaloes, and crocodiles are also notorious for trampling crops and killing children every year. Governments

should ensure that efforts to protect wildlife do not impose too high a cost on neighbouring communities.

12.   Governments should provide a safety net for those who have fallen outside the protection of village level, relationship based risk sharing arrangements. This includes orphans, abandoned and runaway children; old people without relatives to care for them; permanently disabled individuals rejected by their family; and victims of domestic violence. These programmes must be designed in such a way that they do not generate perverse incentives and undermine family solidarity.

13.   Governments should pursue agricultural intensification and seek new products and new international markets for their products. In the long run, rural poverty can only be eradicated by economic development.

14.   Policy instruments such as relief scholarship programmes should be developed and tested that help the poor bring and keep their children in school in spite of temporary exogenous shocks. School based feeding programmes may also assist in keeping children in school in spite of consumption shortages, thereby opening an important way for governments to provide insurance to the poor while improving human capital.

15.   Governments should seek to eliminate exploitative forms of relationships between rich and poor. Child labour in sweat shops and child prostitution are examples of such practices that have attracted a lot of public attention lately. Eradicating these practices is complicated by the fact that the poor may willingly accept exploitation as the only way to survive. In the case of child labour, poor parents may effectively 'sell' some of their children to feed the rest of the family or finance their way out of poverty. In these circumstances, repression alone is unlikely to work, and may even make things worse. What is needed is a comprehensive effort to help victims overcome the circumstances that led to exploitation in the first place.

16.   The suspicion that women bear the brunt of food shortages at the household level has implications for food targeting, especially during famines, but also on a more regular basis. For instance, governments should open food-for-work and other public works schemes to the participation of women.

17.   Delivery systems for purchased inputs should include two essential components: a credit component, so that the liquid wealth of the poor remains at their disposal to deal with income and consumption shocks; and a contingent default clause, so that nothing has to be paid if output is zero. Methods should be investigated that achieve these objectives without generating too much opportunistic default.

18.   The dissemination of divisible inputs such as improved seeds and fer-

tilizer ought to encourage small scale experimentation by the poor instead of pushing large comprehensive packages.

19. The integration of food markets should be pursued through better roads and transportation and the removal of policies and institutions impeding domestic trade such as road blocks and cross-regional trade barriers. Government sponsored shops providing cheap food may also provide a partial answer to small farmers' food self-sufficiency concerns.

20. Because of their concern for food security, technological change in cash crops alone will fail to attract small farmers. Agricultural research should concentrate on promising food crops as well as cash crops.

21. Credit is the principal avenue through which the poor can invest in large non-divisible assets such as irrigation equipment. Credit need not cover the entirety of the investment cost, nor does it require a subsidized interest rate. What appears more important is that debt relief be made available when adverse shocks occur, and that access to credit be as predictable and widespread as possible, so that the minute the poor have accumulated enough liquid assets, credit is granted without delay and the investment is undertaken. Otherwise, liquid wealth will dissipate due to exogenous shocks.

22. Investment can be facilitated by putting better saving instruments at the disposal of the rural poor. Although the poor are typically willing to hold onto liquid wealth in spite of negative returns, low returns on the poor's savings make it harder for them to accumulate enough to invest and are thus detrimental to growth.

23. Government should seek to bring credit closer to the poor by experimenting with various forms of contingent or insured credit. How this can be achieved is still unclear at this point, but it may involve a combination of flexibility in debt repayment, innovative use of collateral, and group lending.

24. Efforts should be made to ensure that the rural structure is willing to accept the success of entrepreneurs and innovators. Oppression by the old and the powerful is not conducive to rural investment and entrepreneurship.

25. Efforts to dismantle patronage networks and to favour Western-style individualism are probably futile as they undermine risk sharing institutions that are deemed important by the societies concerned. One should instead strive to invest in the kind of social capital that is most needed for growth.

7.4   WHAT THE INTERNATIONAL COMMUNITY CAN DO

The role of the international community is twofold. First it serves a redistributive role by assisting governments of poor countries take care of the poorest and most vulnerable segments of their population. In performing this role, the international community should strive not to let the domestic political debates of rich countries dictate what kind of assistance is given to poor countries. Laudable concerns for the fashionable moral principles of the day too often lead developed countries to patronize their weaker Southern neighbours and impose upon them whatever political agenda is most in vogue at home. For instance, scandals about the funding of political organizations in developed countries spills over into condemnation of corruption abroad. Concerns for women and the environment translate into gender and environmental conditionality. This conditionality is often embraced by recipient countries – and imposed by donors – with a great deal of hypocrisy. Such patronizing behaviour is unbecoming of international relations between sovereign countries. Besides, the lesson givers seem to forget that, not long ago, they were themselves corrupt, kept women in a state of dependence, and pillaged their environment for profit. The international community should learn not to let the domestic political agenda of rich countries get in the way of assistance to the poor.

The international community serves a second, more important role: the provision of international public goods. Here are some examples of practical ways in which it can help the rural poor:

1.   The international community should continue to serve its role of planet-wide risk sharing and help governments deal with massive crises triggered by natural and man-made catastrophes: droughts, warfare, genocide, floods, earthquakes, and so on. The effectiveness of these efforts could be improved if the collaboration of local governments can be secured beforehand, that is, via the establishment of local relief agencies with the right expertise in targeting and delivery. This requires long term collaboration with local authorities.

2.   Relief efforts of the international community are often jeopardized by military conflict on the ground. It might be worth exploring the idea of penalizing the hindrance of relief operations and the diversion of relief aid for political or military gain. Indeed, interfering with relief efforts often results in unnecessary death and suffering, sometimes more so than warfare itself (as in Biafra, Ethiopia in 1984, Southern Sudan). Making it an international crime to divert or prevent the dis-

tribution of food aid would pave the way for the newly created International War Crimes Tribunal to seize itself of such cases. This would reinforce the protections that are already imparted by treaty to international bodies such as the International Red Cross and HCR.

3. More funds should be channeled into research for a malaria vaccine. It is a scandal that malaria resistance to new prophylactic drugs spreads very quickly even though these drugs are in practice only used by a tiny proportion of the population. It is as if nobody cared as long as a new generation of drugs can be found in time to protect the wealthy. Clearly, the rural poor will be protected from malaria only when a suitable vaccine is discovered and produced in large enough quantities to reduce production costs.

4. Research on an AIDS vaccine is also a top priority. HIV has become a Third World disease and current treatment is outside the reach of the rural poor. Only a cheap vaccine can improve the situation of millions of villagers in Uganda, Tanzania, Zaire, Botswana and elsewhere.

5. A massive international campaign to eradicate malaria by the year 2050 should be launched. This effort could be the single most important contribution to reducing the risk faced by the rural poor in Sub-Saharan Africa.

6. A similar effort should aim at eradicating trypanosomiasis (a livestock disease) from West Africa.

7. Locust control efforts should be continued and revitalized.

8. Peace keeping efforts should be pursued more vigorously. The international community should condemn and stigmatize practices of powerful nations whereby they arm factions and groups in poor countries to serve their geopolitical interests.

9. More funds should go to research on high potential tropical crops such as maize, rice, and cassava. Fewer resources should be wasted on breeding millet and other crops that only grow in marginal areas. In the long run, millet and sorghum will probably only be used as livestock feed.

10. The international community should assist the efforts of governments of developing countries to gain free access to developed countries for their agricultural products. It is contradictory for developed countries to ask poor countries to increase their agricultural exports while at the same time protecting their domestic markets from what the rural poor could credibly export, that is, grain, meat, sugar, vegetable oils, animal feed, fruits, and vegetables.

11. The international community should help poor countries steer away from inflationary policies that hurt the poor by reducing the value of their meagre savings. One avenue to explore is the establishment or

expansion of currency agreements such as the CFA Franc zone, or the 'dollarization' of developing countries, such as the one proposed by Chile. This, of course, assumes that the problems inherent in such agreements can be dealt with satisfactorily.

Notes

1. Many authors, for instance, implicitly assimilate risk coping to consumption smoothing (for example Cochrane 1991, Mace 1991, Townsend 1994, Morduch 2002).
2. A Muslim holiday.
3. Strictly speaking, one could argue that ritual and utility risks are one and the same. One's inability to buy drugs for a sick child or to consume a sheep at Tabaski leads to a loss of welfare. Both thus induce people to incur certain expenditures to smooth their utility. Economists, however, have traditionally paid a lot of attention to utility risk, but, unlike anthropologists, they have largely ignored ritual risk. This legacy of neglect militates in favour of making the distinction.
4. For example Bardhan (1984), Reardon (1997), Foster and Rosenzweig (1996), and Foster and Rosenzweig (1993). There are some exceptions (such as Dutta et al. 1989, Schaffner 1995).
5. See, however, Hart (1988), Fafchamps (1996a), Fafchamps (1997), Bigsten et al. (2000), and Fafchamps et al. (2000) for evidence of contractual risk in urban areas.
6. This is hardly surprising given that many of the resettled people were weakened by malnutrition and that a cholera epidemic was rampant among them. It is estimated that, of the one million people forcibly relocated in the wake of the 1984 Ethiopian famine, between 50000 and 100000 died within a year.
7. Irrigation dams and canals often increase the risk of malaria and other parasitic diseases.
8. See, for instance, Eddy (1979) and Comité Ad Hoc Chargé de l'Elaboration d'un Code Rural (1989) for evidence of a steady northward movement of sedentary settlement in Niger since the turn of the century.
9. If certain inputs are chosen after observing π_j, then we redefine q_j as being the return to activity j net of optimally chosen ex post inputs. If production is subject to constant returns to scale, the optimal factor mix does not depend on the scale of production and the unit cost of production is constant. In this case, l_j is proportional to the amount of any of the factors used in producing good j.
10. Assuming, for the time being, that the agent cannot issue securities, that is, buy insurance.
11. ICRISAT Burkina Faso data.
12. Pirates' attacks on boat people fleeing war and persecution in South East Asia during the 1980s have been well documented in the press.
13. Think of the US Savings and Loans scandal, for instance.
14. Formally, this is but an application of the general principle that open loop optimization is inferior to closed loop.
15. Many plants adapt to seasons by developing what agronomists call photo-sensitivity: their maturation is sensitive to the duration of the day. Consequently, their output performance depends on the time of the year at which they are planted: if they flower too early or too late, they will not yield as much grain. As a result, photo-sensitive varieties have a narrower planting window than non photo-sensitive varieties.
16. Matlon and Fafchamps (1989), for instance, report that 73 per cent of non-harvest crop labour on millet goes to weeding. Similar percentages are reported for other crops. The importance of weeding is a consequence of the switch from long to short bush fallows: the disparition of forest and savannah cover favours the proliferation of parasitic weeds such as *striga*, thereby imposing an externality on farmers. See, for instance, Boserup (1965) and Pingali et al. (1987) for a discussion.
17. Unvoluntary slavery – for example, slave raids – is a distinct phenomenon that is ignored

here. We also abstract from the fact that powerful people may use their monopoly power as food suppliers or employers of last resort to artificially raise food prices and lower wages in bad times, thereby inciting more people to voluntarily propose themselves as bonded labourers.

18. In practice, the survival level of food intake may be below that required for someone to work. This complication is ignored here.

19. The argument can be extended to finite time bonded labour, but assuming an infinite contract simplifies the notation. Historically, indenture contracts for US and Canadian immigrants were of finite duration. The discussion of whether labour bonding is credible or not, is postponed until Chapter Three.

20. The example can easily be extended to the case where shocks and wages follow a Markov process.

21. Setting up a market for bonded labourers – that is, introducing slavery – raises the expected value from bonded labour since it introduces an additional option. This issue is ignored here.

22. Mauritania is a case in point: it has had no less than three successive legal reforms declaring slavery illegal.

23. For simplicity, human capital is here taken as given and unchanged over time. The model can be generalized to allow for human capital accumulation as well; see for instance Sawada (1997) and Jacoby and Skoufias (1997).

24. Although this result does not appear as such in Kimball's analysis, it follows immediately from his work.

25. A similar argument can be found in Roumasset (1976).

26. See, however, Paxson (1993), Chaudhuri and Paxson (2001), and Carter (1997).

27. In fact, the ability to borrow without limit is implicit in the certainty equivalent model, see for example Hall (1978).

28. They can, however, borrow against non-divisible productive assets such as land or buildings. Banks' insistence on collateral is consistent with the idea that households cannot hold negative wealth.

29. Although a credit constraint is not explicitly imposed on the model, the requirements that consumption be non-negative and that all debt contracts be paid with certainty ensure that the agent cannot hold negative net worth.

30. The reader will note a close similarity between precautionary saving and Keynes' liquidity motive for holding money.

31. In anthropology, the substantivist school has given a lot of attention to solidarity rituals and reciprocal gifts. See Polanyi (1944) and the references cited in Posner (1980) and Platteau (1991). Those rituals 'stage' reciprocity and reassert the bonds that link the villagers and/or the lineage together. They are a way to symbolically 'live' solidarity as an everyday reality. At the same time, however, those rituals often portray village solidarity the way villagers would like it to operate, but not necessarily the way it actually works. As argued by Popkin (1979) and Watts (1983), granting too much attention to these rituals and their underlying egalitarian ideology may lead to overestimating the efficiency and redistributive performance of actual solidarity mechanisms.

32. There are exceptions, as for instance when hunters share a good kill, and fishermen the day's catch. See, for instance, the study of the Poovar fishermen of South India by Platteau and Baland (1989) and Platteau and Abraham (1987); and of the Dakar fishermen by Sow (1986).

33. Cochrane (1991) tests whether illness results in lower aggregate consumption. He concludes that short illnesses are fully insured while long illnesses are not. Strangely, however, Cochrane fails to account for the possibility that sick individuals may require *additional* consumption expenditures to deal with health care costs.

34. Poor rural dwellers are, in general, extremely reluctant to consume their animals in bad times; they might seek to sell them instead, as the calorie price of meat nearly always exceeds that of grain (see above). This is particularly true for large animals, perhaps less so for small stock such as goats, pigs, and chicken. See Sen (1981) and Fafchamps (1998) for a discussion.

35. Certain of these shocks such as individual sickness may not affect crop output directly but to keep notation compact we let ε_l stand for all the shocks affecting the village and its members.

36. To keep the notation simple, we assume that the distribution of shocks is i.i.d. over time. It can be shown that results are unchanged if shocks are correlated over time.

37. The fact that, in many societies, wives are perceived as economically vulnerable is largely a consequence of gender casting: encouraging women to specialize in the provision of care within the household implies that they develop skills that have little market value (Becker 1981). To ensure that women find the provision of household care in their long-term interest, they need to be compensated for specializing in non-market skills when the household breaks down.

38. In fact, 'eating from the same pot' is the most commonly used defining feature of a household unit.

39. The allocation of labour within the household can lead to conflicts of interest among members and result in inefficiencies; see for instance Udry (1996), and Jones (1986).

40. Or, at least, nearly never.

41. The exact meaning of the Spanish term 'peón' appears to lie somewhat between that of 'peasant' and 'serf'.

42. Formal models of debt peonage as described here can be found in the literature on sovereign debt (for example Eaton and Gersovitz 1981 Kletzer 1984, Grossman and Van Huyck 1988).

43. This results from the law of martingales.

44. The situation in which the nominal amount of the debt does not represent what creditors expect to receive formally ressembles what, in the sovereign debt literature, is called debt overhang. Data on secondary markets for sovereign debt provide ample evidence of discrepancy between the face value of a debt and its valuation by creditors (for example Kyle and Sachs 1984, Cohen 1990). See Fafchamps (1996b) for a detailed discussion of the determinants of this discrepancy.

45. In Ethiopia, for instance, it is customary not to name a child until it has attained two years of age.

46. This is true, for instance, in Northern Ethiopia where children eat after their parents. Not so long ago, in much of rural Europe the head of the household would be served first and other members next; the wife would serve the meal and eat later.

47. At the cost of additional but straightforward notation, the same argument can be extended to finite duration indenture contracts.

48. Inflation incidence within the group, however, varies between those who receive the money early and those that receive it late. Even in the absence of inflation, ROSCAs reduce the amount of money held in the economy and thus the amount of seignorage paid by agents. Although ignored in the current literature, these issues are probably important, as evidenced by the fact that, as a rule, poor economies often are cash-poor.

49. This does not mean that someone can never be brought temporarily below the autarchy payoff. Indeed, as Abreu et al. (1986) have shown, frontloading punishments is often optimal in games with discounting, because it allows harsher punishments. Optimal punishment paths involve pushing the deviant player below the one shot minmax payoff for a while before reverting to a long-term cooperative equilibrium.

50. Assuming that society members are able to coordinate their actions to achieve an efficient mutual insurance agreement. Obviously some level of social stability is required for coordination to emerge. Political or social unrest, or the rapid structural transformation of society may hinder individual efforts toward coordination.

51. This is achieved by combining the probability that the game will continue with the players' discount factor. See Kreps (1990), pp. 505–6.

52. Cox (1987) models transfers between generations based on altruism and exchange without using the theory of repeated games nor recognizing the incentive problems associated with such transfers.

53. This is not a figure of speech. In some hunter-gatherer tribes, old people who can no longer walk are simply left behind to die.

54. In fact, in at least one primitive society it is reported that the young are reluctant to share their food with the old because it is unlikely that the old will reciprocate in the future. See Holmberg (1969), pp. 151–3.
55. See for instance Sankara's attempts to shake the power of elders in rural Burkina Faso.
56. Although some social scientists argue that these social institutions have gone out of fashion due to the rise of capitalism and individualism (Scott 1976), it is unclear whether they ever were truly effective (for example Popkin 1979, Fafchamps 1992b). Accounts of the past workings of social institutions are indeed subject to memory and age bias and to the idealization of the past.
57. Animist beliefs, for instance, aim at putting people in communion with their immediate physical environment; consequently, they create a strong identification with a particular geographical setting. As a result, animists may not share a sense of community with humanity as a whole and feel no charitable inclination toward people outside their immediate kin group. In contrast, religions such as Buddhism, Christianity, and Islam are open to all men and women and strive to build a sense of community that bypasses geographical distinctions. In fact, one may argue that large religions developed precisely as a response to the need for a cement to keep larger communities together. This need is strongest in urban areas where animist references become meaningless and lead to unhealthy cleavages among people. The penetration of outside religions such as Islam and Christianity into Sub-Saharan Africa through cities is in line with this observation. These observations are essentially speculative, however. Rigorous evidence on the relationship between religion and risk sharing is largely non-existent.
58. The emphasis on social programmes also seems to have been instrumental in the political clout gained by Islamic fundamentalist movements such as the Palestinian Hamas, the Algerian Islamic Salvation Front, and the Lebanese Hezbollah.
59. For a model of this process, see for instance the one developed by Hoff (1996) to deal with mutual insurance. We discuss Hoff's model more in detail below.
60. The fact that marriage laws may be unwritten and enforced through traditional courts using traditional procedures does not subtract from their legal nature.
61. This does not mean that permanent exclusion is the only possible form of punishment. The expected discounted payoff of a punished agent cannot fall below his or her expected discounted autarchy payoff, otherwise the agent would defect from the punishment path. But punishments can be front-loaded (Abreu 1986): the payoff of the punished agent can temporarily be brought below the autarchy payoff provided that the punishment phase is limited in time.
62. Figure 4.1 was constructed by computer simulation, using stationary strategies and assuming that $A = 0$, $N = 2$ and $U_i(y) = \log(y)$.
63. Unless starvation is already certain, in which case sharing does not make any difference.
64. The informed reader will notice that it is the concept of weakly renegotiation-proofness as defined by Farrell and Maskin (1989) that is used here.
65. Continuation payoffs need not be (constrained) Pareto efficient, however: they may be dominated by continuation payoffs of paths other than Q^0. Deviant agents are thus assumed unable to challenge the status quo and propose a new equilibrium path. In the case of IRSAs, this seems a reasonable restriction given that the equilibrium strategy often is a social norm: renegotiation out of it is likely to prove difficult (for example DeMarzo 1992, Abreu et al. 1993, Ambec 1998).
66. Figure 4.2 was constructed using a numerical simulation based on the equations for Proposition 4.4 for a two-person IRSA.
67. The informed reader will have noticed one of the ironies of attempting to apply repeated game theory to real-life situations. In equilibrium, the threat of credible punishment is sufficient to prevent deviation. Consequently, punishments should never be observed. In the presence of imperfect monitoring, events may trigger punishment paths even though nobody deviated from the cooperative path. This may allow punishments to be observed, but they will remain rare occurrences.
68. The temptation is stronger if wealth generates income, that is, if it is not simply hoarded as jewellery or food stocks.

69. See, for instance, Scott (1976), Platteau (1991), Platteau (1995a), Platteau (1995b), and Greenough (1982), pp. 207–15. Ellsworth (1989) presents numerical evidence that members of the village establishment receive net transfers from poorer members of the community.
70. Gini coefficient for livestock ownership is usually greater than 0.5. See Fafchamps (1986), p. 18.
71. For instance by organizing the wasteful elimination of grain surplus in ceremonies and beer festivals.
72. See Ellsworth (1989) for evidence that wealthier people have denser networks as evidenced by reciprocal gift relationships.
73. Scott's account indeed suggests that peasant revolts in South-East Asia occurred when landlords relocated themselves in the cities and invested in non-rural activities.
74. Given our sign convention, agents receive a compensation when τ_s^i is negative.
75. In West Africa, Fulani herders and Mossi settlers are examples of ethnic groups that manage to live at the periphery of rural solidarity networks.
76. Hausa merchants, for instance, often reside in villages outside of their ethnic boundaries. Solidarity between them and the villagers is minimal. See Eddy (1979) for examples.
77. Formally, this does require outright exclusion. Such people can be kept in the system, but the insurance benefits they can lay claim to are essentially reduced to nothing.
78. For instance, see Watts (1983) for an in depth study of the interaction between the polity, informal solidarity, and hunger in Northern Nigeria.
79. Requiring that equilibria of repeated games be robust with respect to any coalition of agents is akin to requesting that it belong to the core or the stable set of feasible cooperative outcomes. By construction, perfect equilibria are robust with respect to 'coalitions' of a single agent since they satisfy VP constraints.
80. It is easy to verify that the core of the corresponding market economy is a single point at which C gets all the gains from trade.
81. In that, consumption credit formally resembles the way sovereign debt contracts have been modelled in the literature (for example Eaton and Gersovitz 1981, Kletzer 1984, Grossman and Van Huyck 1988).
82. w_i^j need not be expressed in monetary terms. In the *hau* system of exchange discussed by Sahlins (1972), for instance, goodwill takes a purely symbolical form.
83. The only exception is when an agent's utility without the loan is already $-\infty$. Desperation can lead agents to borrow under threats of extreme punishment if they do not repay.
84. The African movie *Le Mandat* by the Senegalese director Ousmane Sembene is a perfect illustration of this danger. In the movie, the fact that a man receives a money order from a migrant relative is used by all as a signal to trigger immediate solidarity claims. In the end, the man is unable to collect the money and is ruined.
85. It is difficult if not impossible to prove that an increase in N decreases effort in all possible cases. The reason is that, depending on the parameters of the model, decreasing effort at some levels of N might increase the chance of low levels of income sufficiently to outweigh the disutility of effort. See for instance Salanié (1997) and Singh (1989) for a discussion in the sharecropping case.
86. Starvation cannot be entirely prevented, however, as long as there remains the possibility that the average income of the entire group falls below the survival threshold.
87. Note that the first best level of effort with the solidarity scheme need not be the same as the individually optimal level of effort without it. Indeed the income and risk reduction effects of the scheme may reduce the supply of labour.
88. Remember that symmetry is assumed here. In an asymmetric situation, poorer households would have a much greater chance than richer households of finding it in their interest to rely exclusively on welfare. As with all insurance models, asymmetries raise the possibility of adverse selection.
89. The insurance pool is assumed large enough that the covariance between $\bar{c}$ and individual income can be ignored.
90. Again for simplicity, the distribution of aggregate income is assumed such that the minimum income level is attainable in all circumstances.

91. See Platteau (1991), pp. 121–9 and the references cited therein. Providing jobs to relatives and friends can be viewed in the same light.

92. Here we do not use the term polarization to describe the distribution of income at a given point in time, as in Estaban and Ray (1994) and Zhang and Kanbur (2001), but as a differentiation process whereby persistent inequality endogenously arises among otherwise equal agents.

93. Storable wealth can, over a short period, yield a positive return. But, unlike productive assets, it has to be destroyed in order to produce something else.

94. To be a satisfactory measure of inequality, N_t^u needs to be normalized in some way. One possibility is to set $U_1'(c)/U_2'(c) = 1$ for some level of consumption c, for example, average consumption. In practice, $\bar{N}_t^u$ is most useful when both agents have the same utility function.

95. To ensure that income inequality is always defined, we assume that $\Pr[\omega^i(Z^i, \theta_t) = 0] = 0$. This also ensures that N_t^x is always defined. We also assume that $U(0) = -\infty$ so that zero consumption is never optimal. Since income is never 0, positive consumption is always feasible and N_t^c is always defined. Utility is assumed continuously differentiable so that N_t^u is always defined as well. In contrast, N_t^w need not be defined if $W_t^1 = 0$.

96. This means that N_t^w is not defined. Consequently, it is ignored in this section.

97. We have $U(c) = c^{1-R}/1 - R$. Differentiating with respect to c and replacing in the definition of welfare inequality, we obtain $N_t^u = (c^1/c^1)^R$. When $U(c) = \log(c)$, $N_t^u = c^2/c^1$. Since $N_t^c \equiv c^2/c^1$, we see that whenever N_t^u is constant, so is N_t^c.

98. The allocation must be in the core (Hildenbrand 1974).

99. If agents discount the future, indefinite accumulation obtains if the return on the asset is higher than the rate of intertemporal preference.

100. Starting from zero assets, it is possible that low initial realization of income triggers no accumulation. We ignore these complications here and focus on the long-run distribution of N_t^w only.

101. Figure 5.1 is constructed using a convex savings function (lower savings rate at low values of cash-in-hand). Both agents have the same savings function. Labour incomes are independent and uniformly distributed. Three paths are generated corresponding to three sets of labour income realizations. With a constant savings rate, the distribution of convergence shares S^w is more concentrated around 0.5. This is because lucky labour income early on provides less of a headstart in wealth accumulation.

102. To see why, note that in the long run, the path of inequality depends less and less on income, that is, converges to a deterministic path. Consider the deterministic path of cash-in-hand inequality. Along this deterministic path, to each inequality ratio corresponds a ratio of consumption.

103. Because wealth can fall to 0 for both agents, the distribution of N_t^w is not strictly speaking defined. For this reason, we ignore it here and focus instead on inequality in cash-in-hand. The latter is always defined since income can never be 0.

104. Ignoring the case where labour income follows a random walk. Here the distribution of labour income is assumed stationary.

105. As in Figure 5.1, the savings function is convex (lower savings rate at low levels of cash-in-hand). This is meant to reproduce the shape of Zeldes' consumption function. Both agents have the same savings function. Labour income is independently distributed.

106. Settings for Figure 5.3 are identical to those of Figure 5.2, except that the value of γ is varied.

107. In this model as in Banerjee and Newman (1991), the rich have a less risky income stream than the poor. But in contrast to their work, we do not consider risk taking as an entrepreneurial activity.

108. To compute this Figure, we use a savings function of the form $S(\omega, W) = e^{\alpha(E[\omega]+(1+\gamma)W)} - 1$. Parameter α determines the curvature of the savings function: the higher it is, the more convex savings. Values of α are respectively 0.02 and 0.2 for the low curvature and high curvature savings functions reported in the Figure.

109. This curve resembles Azariadis's (1996) analysis of country-level poverty traps (see his Figure 2c). Our interpretation is quite different, however. In Azariadis, poverty traps

exist for each country independently from any interaction between them. Here, the trap arises from the interaction between the two agents.

110. The savings function is the same as for Figure 5.4. Here $\alpha = 0.04$.

111. Conditional on the total cash-in-hand in the economy.

112. Here we assume that savings decisions can be decentralized. This is because insured decision makers face the same returns to wealth as the group. Consequently, their savings decisions are consistent with the social planner's optimum.

113. Agents who borrow to finance productive investments have a positive net worth. Most credit observed in practice goes to agents with positive net worth, that is, to a household to purchase a home or firms to purchase equipment.

114. In the sovereign debt literature, a similar concept exists under the name of debt overhang (Krugman 1988).

115. Consumption shocks such as a sickness that requires health expenditures can be treated as utility shocks as in for instance Mace (1991), Cochrane (1991).

116. Examples of this kind of situation can be found in sovereign debt contracts when nominal debt is sold at a discount on secondary markets.

117. To our knowledge, the Philippines do not have personal bankruptcy laws.

118. In some societies, for example that of the ancient Romans, debt is inherited.

119. Adding asymmetric information to the model does not drastically affect predictions regarding debt traps. If shocks s_t^b and s_t^l are not observable, lenders cannot condition repayment on s_t^b. Leaving repayment at the discretion of the borrower creates moral hazard, since it is in the interest of the borrower to falsely report shocks to abscond from repaying the debt. In this case, rigid repayment may be optimal. But the lender may provide imperfect insurance by giving the borrower some limited discretion regarding the timing of repayment, such as to let arrears accumulate up to a given ceiling or to allow delays of up to 60 days – provided the borrower is in 'good standing', that is, has not abused this flexibility in the past. This discretion works like a line of credit or overdraft facility. It can improve upon a rigid repayment schedule by providing limited insurance to the borrower. Banks often operate in this manner. They typically combine a loan with an overdraft facility. The loan has a rigid repayment schedule, but the overdraft facility gives the borrower a certain discretion in the timing of repayments.

120. Unless the rich's willingness to pay was quite high to start with and they were asked to pay much more for insurance than the poor. With assets, this is unlikely to be the case because then the rich can self-insure.

121. Infant mortality is traditionally defined as the proportion of children who die before the age of one; child mortality is the proportion of children who do not attain the age of five.

122. As the couple approaches menopause without two children aged five or above, the possibility arises that both or one of the two children might die after they can be replaced. In this case, the couple might choose to overshoot whenever it approaches menopause without two offspring aged five or above. As a result of overshooting, the average number of surviving offspring might slightly exceed two, but not by much because the overwhelming majority of couples would have two surviving offspring by the time they reach menopause.

123. Except just before menopause, when a couple without two surviving children may optimally choose to overshoot.

124. Note that even if perfect insurance markets exist, complete insurance need not exist: the economy might be subject to collective shocks it cannot insure against. In this case, residual risk remains and producers are predicted to behave in a risk averse manner even though insurance markets are perfect (Kurosaki and Fafchamps 2002).

125. Although this statement is intuitively appealing, more stringent conditions about the curvature of the utility function are in fact needed for it to be true. See for instance Diamond and Stiglitz (1974), Dreze and Modigliani (1972), and Dardanoni (1988).

126. Or close to nothing if, as is often the case by law, creditors cannot foreclose on everything the debtor has.

127. To be fully rigorous, we need another technical assumption, namely that the distribution of θ has not mass point at 0.
128. In fact, there is evidence that even when the harvest is poor although not zero, tenants are also dispensed to share output with the landlord (for example Dutta et al. 1989, Singh 1989).
129. Cotton marketing boards in West Africa are a good illustration of these practices (Roberts 1996).
130. Although some invariably tried, especially nearby porous borders like that between Senegal and Gambia.
131. In fact, certain contracts stipulate that harvesting is done by the contractor themself.
132. In this case, repayment of the equipment is spread over several years and producers get a repayment holiday if they can show they were hit by an adverse shock (ILO 1984).
133. By partial adoption we mean adoption of a crop or technology over only a portion of the farm or for some of the time. We do not mean the adoption by farmers of only certain parts of a package that is proposed to them. Debundling by farmers of ready-made technological packages is a sign of experimentation and should be encouraged.
134. More precisely, if N moments are required to fully characterize crops' distribution function and no crop/technique is stochastically dominated by other crops or combination of other crops /techniques, then farmers ought to plant N crops/use N techniques.
135. Except for the possible reduction in purchase price, a problem which can, at least in theory, be solved by compensating – the village equivalent of patents.
136. See, however, Matlon (1977) for a counter example.
137. Corner solutions are ignored. The reason is that conditions leading to an increase (decrease) in level of an interior L_i are the same as those making it more (less) likely for a null L_i to become positive or for an interior L_i to become equal to $\bar{L}$. Thus, any conclusion reached for interior L_i's quite naturally extends to non-interior ones.
138. Situations where this may be the case are irrigated perimeters along the Niger, Gambia (Kargbo 1985), or Senegal rivers (Morris and Newman 1989). Whether reversals are actually observed deserves more research. In Matlon's (1977) study of Northern Nigeria, small farmers produce proportionally more cash crop and less food than middle size farmers. Unfortunately, the evidence required to show that this unusual pattern could be explained by consumption risk alone is not available.
139. This assumption is essential, otherwise agents optimally decide not to incur debt (see supra)
140. Some of the same arguments have already been used to explain the relative performance in South-East Asian countries. See, for instance, the largely inconclusive controversy between Scott (1976) and Popkin (1979).
141. Latin America is an exception to this rule: historically, land has been plentiful but the state has protected the property rights of large landowners, thereby creating a class of landless peasants in spite of land abundance.
142. A good illustration of incrementalism is the mass of unfinished houses that dot the landscape of most developing countries.

Appendix: Proofs of propositions

Proof of Proposition 4. 1: Each point on the boundary of the equilibrium set can be found by maximizing one agent's expected utility subject to satisfying all participation constraints and maintaining other agents at a given expected utility level. By varying the expected utility of other agents and by repeating the process for all agents, we can span the whole boundary of the equilibrium set. Now, participation constraints with A^1 are a restricted version of participation constraints with A^2. Therefore, by Le Chatelier principle, the maximum expected utility with A^2 lies weakly above what can be achieved with A^2 for all expected utility levels of other agents. Every point on the boundary of $\Omega(A^1)$ thus lies weakly below every point on the boundary of $\Omega(A^2)$. This proves the proposition. Strict inclusion occurs whenever δ and A^1 are low enough for some participation constraints to be binding. A strictly higher A^2 then is sure to release the binding participation constraints somewhat and to strictly enlarge the set of equilibria. ■

Proof of Proposition 4.2: For any given IRSA τ_s^i, the right hand side of the voluntary participation constraint VP decreases with δ. Consider an arbitrary agent i and state of nature s. Let δ fall to the point where the VP constraint is binding for that i and s. In order to further decrease δ while still ensuring payment of τ_s^i, agent i has to be compensated in other states of nature s'. Compensation by other agents is possible as long as some of their participation constraints are not binding. A lower δ thus forces agents who contributed little and whose participation constraints were therefore less binding, to contribute more. If δ drops further, eventually no agent is left without binding participation constraint. ■

Proof of Proposition 4.3: We drop i subscripts for simplicity of exposition.

Part 1: *(Case 1)* If $U_i(y) > -\infty$ for all $y > -\infty$, assume that there exists a binding participation constraint for that agent at which he or she does not get his or her highest possible income (A2). *(Case 2)* If $\lim_{y \to y^*} U_i(y) = -\infty$ for $y^* > -\infty$, assume that agent i prefers the probability of a $-\infty$ utility tomorrow a $-\infty$ utility today (A3). If utility is undefined below a particular value of y, set it equal to $-\infty$. Let $\tilde{y}$ denote the realized income of agent *i* at the binding participation constraint. Let X stand for the right hand side of the participation constraint $V(\tilde{y}) - V(\tilde{y} - \tilde{\pi})$. Since the constraint is binding and there is risk sharing (A1), the right hand side of the participation constraint is strictly positive and $X > 0$. Construct a concave transformation of $V(y)$ as follows: for all $y \geq \tilde{y}$, lease $V(y)$ unchanged; for all $y < \tilde{y}$, rotate agent *i*'s utility by a factor $k > 1$, i.e., *i*'s utility becomes $kV(y) - (k - 1)V(\tilde{y})$.

Case 1:   With this new utility function, the right hand side of the participation constraint becomes kX: the utility loss of complying with IRSA obligations has been stretched by a factor k. The right hand side of the participation constraint after the transformation of $V(y)$ can be decomposed into three parts:

$$(k - 1)V(\tilde{y})[\Pr(y \leq \tilde{y}) - \Pr(y - \pi \leq \tilde{y})] +$$
$$k \int_{y}^{\tilde{y}} [V(y - \pi) - V(y)]ds + \int_{\tilde{y}}^{\bar{y}} [V(y - \pi) - V(y)]ds$$

Let the three terms of the above sum be denoted A, kB, and C. The right hand side of the participation constraint before the transformation was simply $B + C$. By (A2), $C \neq 0$. The participation constraint after the transformation is violated iff $A + kB + C < kB + kC = kX$, that is, iff $k > A/C - 1$. Since A and C are constants that do not depend on k, such a k always exists.

Case 2:   If $\lim_{y \to y^*} V(y) = -\infty$ for y* $> -\infty$, then as one increases k, agent *i*'s utility may fall to $-\infty$ for income realizations in the support of π_s, or for possible consumption realizations $\pi_s - \tau_s$. When this happens *i*'s expected utility falls to $-\infty$ and the construction that we used in case 1 no longer works. It is still possible, however, to pick a k large enough that the utility agent *i* derives from contributing $\tilde{\pi}$ is $-\infty$. Then, by (A3), the participation constraint is violated. ∎

Part 2:   Let ω_s stand for the probability that the realized state of the world is $s \in \{1, 2, \ldots, S\}$. By assumption, $1 > \omega > 0$ for all s. Let s' be the state of the world when the participation constraint is binding and let Z_i be the value of the binding participation constraint $V(\pi_{s'}) - V(\pi_{s'} - \tau_s^i)$. Introduce the following notation:

$$A_s^i \equiv V(\pi_s - \tau_s) - V(\pi_s)$$
$$\mu^j = \frac{1}{S} \sum_{s=1}^{S} \omega_s \pi_s^j$$

$$\sigma^j = \frac{1}{S} \sum_{s=1}^{S} \omega_s (\pi_s^j - \mu^j)^2$$

Furthermore, let Ω be the vector of probability weights $(\omega_s, \omega_{s'}, \ldots, \omega_{s'})$, B^i be the vector $(B_1^i, \ldots, B_S^i)$, Φ be the vector of income means $(\mu^1, \ldots, \mu^N)$, Σ be the vector of income variances $(\sigma^1, \ldots, \sigma^N)$, 1 be a vector of ones, and Ξ and Ψ stand for the SxN matrices of incomes and squared deviations from income mean.

We know that

$$\Omega' B^i = Z^i$$
$$\Omega' \Xi = \Phi'$$
$$\Omega' \Psi = \Sigma'$$
$$\Omega' 1 = 1$$

We want to show that it is possible to find another set of probability weights $\hat{\omega}_s$ such that each agent faces the same expected income, the variance of each agent's individual income has increased, and agent i's participation constraint is violated. Formally we want to find a vector $\hat{\Omega}$ such that

$$\hat{\Omega}' B^i = Z^i + \epsilon$$
$$\Omega' \Xi = \Phi'$$
$$\hat{\Omega}' \Psi = \Sigma' + \Gamma'$$
$$\hat{\Omega}' 1 = 1$$

where $\epsilon > 0$ is a scalar and Γ is a vector of strictly positive numbers. The above can be rewritten:

$$\hat{\Omega}' [B^i \Xi \Psi 1] = [Z^i + \epsilon, \Phi', \Sigma' + \Gamma', 1] \tag{B1}$$

Let ρ be the rank of the matrix $[B^i \Xi \Psi]$. Clearly, ρ cannot exceed $2N + 2$. Thus if $S \geq 2N + 2$, there exists at least one set of probability weights (several if the inequality is strict) such that equation (6) is satisfied for any arbitrary ϵ and Γ. Since by assumption the initial probability weights ω_s are all strictly positive, the linearity of equation (B1) implies that there exists a set of numbers ϵ and Γ such that equation (B1) is satisfied and $\hat{\omega}_s \geq 0$. ∎

Proof of Proposition 4.4: Equation (4.4) guarantees that punishments deter ex post defection from the cooperative path τ_s. Equation (4.5) ensures that punishments are self-enforcing for the punished agent. Equation (4.6) ensures that each agent $i \in N$ is deterred from defecting on the punishment of another agent $j \neq i$. Equation (4.7) guarantees that punishments are not dominated by other paths and thus are weakly renegotiation-proof. Other participation constraints are never binding and can be ignored.∎

Proof of Proposition 4.5:   We drop i subscripts for simplicity of exposition. Define p_s as the scalar that satisfies

$$V(x+\epsilon_s) - V(x+\epsilon_s - p_s) = \frac{\delta}{1-\delta} E[V(x+\epsilon_{s'} - \tau_{s'}) - V(x+\epsilon_{s'})] \quad (7.1)$$

p_s is the willingness to pay for the reduction in risk generated by the IRSA; that willingness to pay depends on the realized state of the world s. Because of decreasing absolute risk aversion, p_s decreases with x for all s (Pratt 1964).

In the limit, when absolute risk aversion is 0, equation (4.1) boils down to:

$$p_s = -\frac{\delta}{1-\delta} E\tau_s \quad (7.2)$$

which is 0 if the IRSA is actuarially fair. Thus $\lim_{x\to\infty} p_s = 0$. Now consider a particular $\tau_s > 0$. By assumption, τ_s satisfies i's participation constraint when $x = \bar{x}$. As $x\to\infty$, however, it does not since willingness to pay has dropped to 0. Therefore, by the continuity of equation (4.1), there must exist an x^* such that:

$$V(x^* + \epsilon_s) - V(x^* + \epsilon_s - \tau_s) = \frac{\delta}{1-\delta} E[V(x^* + \epsilon_{s'} - \tau_{s'}) - V(x^* + \epsilon_{s'})]$$

This establishes the proof.∎

Proof of Proposition 4.6:   Similar to that of Proposition 4.1.∎

Proof of Proposition 4.7:   Set

$$l^i(\pi_s, t, w_t) = -1/(1+r)W_i(\pi_s, t, w_t)$$
$$\tau^i(\pi_s, t, w_t) = \pi^i(\pi_s, t, w_t) - l^i(\pi_s, t, w_t)$$

∎

Proof of Proposition 4.8:   Apply Le Chatelier principle as in Proposition 4.6.∎

Proof of Proposition 4.9:   Equation (4.14) is a restricted version of equation (4.15). Apply Le Chatelier principle as in proposition 4.6.∎

Proof of Proposition 6.1:
To see why Part (1) holds, let $V_{00}(x)$ denote the agent's value function if the investment were not allowed. Ex ante, having the option to invest cannot make the agent worse off than $V_{00}(x)$. The agent's expected utility if he or she were to invest today is $V_0^1(x)$ which, by construction, is equal to $V_1(x - k)$. We have shown that the agent cannot or does not want to borrow. Consequently, for $x < k$, $V_1(x - k)$ is not defined or $-\infty$. If the investment is profitable enough, $V_1(x - k)$ must eventually cross $V_{00}(x)$. These concepts are illustrated in Figure 6.5.

Suppose that the agent was made a once and for all offer to invest today. $V_1(x - k)$ is the value of using the option; $V_{00}(x)$ is the value of not investing. If $V_1(x - k)$ and $V_{00}(x)$ cross, say at x^*, then the agent invests if $x > x^*$ and does not invest if $x < x^*$. Now suppose that the agent can invest either today. or tomorrow. If he or she invests today, he or she gets the same utility from investment $V_1(x - k)$ as before. Suppose he or she decides to wait and chooses an optimal level of W_{t+1}, given that he or she will have the option to invest tomorrow. Let the value of that choice be denoted $\bar{V}_0^0(x)$. Since he or she still has the option to invest tomorrow, the utility he or she will get from a given level of cash on hand x tomorrow is the sup of $V_{00}(x)$ and $V_1(x - k)$. Denote that utility $\bar{V}_0$. Clearly $E\bar{V}_0$ is larger than EV_{00}. By equation (3), it therefore must be that $\bar{V}_0^0(x) \geq V_{00}(x)$ for all x: tomorrow's option to invest raises the agent's utility.

Prolonging the time during which the agent may decide to invest can only further increase his or her ex ante utility. To see why, suppose the agent is given three periods during which investment is possible. Consider the first period. His or her payoff if she invests immediately is unchanged; it is $V_t(x - k)$. If he or she waits, his or her utility tomorrow is:

$$\bar{V}_0(x) = \max\{(\bar{V}_0^0(x), V_1(x - k)\}$$

It is clear that $\bar{V}_0(x) \geq \bar{V}_0(x)$ which was itself $\geq V_{00}(x)$. We can thus apply the same argument as before: by equation (6.37), the utility of waiting has increased further. Applying the same logic recursively, it is clear that the option to invest raises the agent's utility above $V_{00}(x)$ even when the investment is not undertaken. It cannot, however, raise the agent's utility above what it would get by investing immediately.

Part (2) immediately follows from the following argument. Consider an agent who can invest either today or tomorrow. In the proof of proposition 1, we saw that $\bar{V}_0^0(x) \geq V_{00}(x)$. This means that $\bar{V}_0^0(x)$ cuts $V_1(x - k)$ above x^* – say at x^{**}. There is therefore a range of values of cash on hand for which an agent without the option to wait would invest while an agent who can wait would prefer to (see also Figure 6.5). By the proof of proposition

1, $V_0^0(x)$ can only be raised further when more options are added. Adding options can therefore only increase the range of cash on hand values over which it is preferable to wait.∎

Proof of Proposition 6. 2:   Let $V_{00}(.)$ be, as before, the value function when the investment is not allowed. For $x = 0$, $V_1(x - k)$ is $-\infty$. Given (A2), for $x \to \infty$, $V_1(x - k)$ and $V_{00}(x)$ are approximately linear. Therefore, by (B1), $V_1(x - k)$ is then greater than $V_{00}(x)$. Given that instantaneous utility is continuous and concave, both V_1, and V_{00} are continuous (and concave). Then they must intersect at least once. Using the same backward induction argument used in proposition 6.1, it is possible to show that $V_1(x - k)$ and $V_0^0(x)$ must also intersect. This proves the first part. If they intersect only once, say at x^*, then $V_1(x - k) > V_0^0(x)$ for all $x > x^*$ and vice versa for all $x < x^*$. This proves the second part. The last part follows because, as was shown above, for a large enough x $V_1(x - k) > V_0^0(x)$, and vice versa for a low enough x.∎

Bibliography

Abreu, Dilip, 'Extremal Equilibria in Oligopolistic Supergames', *Journal of Economic Theory*, 1986, *39*, 191–225.

——, 'On the Theory of Infinitely Repeated Games with Discounting', *Econometrica*, 1988, *56*, 383–96.

——, D. Pearce, and E. Stacchetti, 'Optimal Cartel Equilibria with Imperfect Monitoring', *Journal of Economic Theory*, 1986, *39*, 251–69.

——, ——, and ——, 'Toward a Theory of Discounted Repeated Games with Imperfect Monitoring', *Econometrica*, 1990, *58 (5)*, 1041–63.

——, ——, and ——, 'Renegotiation and Symmetry in Repeated Games', *J. Econ. Theory*, 1993, *60(2)*, 217–40.

Adams, Richard H. and Jane J. He, *Sources of Income Inequality and Poverty in Rural Pakistan*, Washington, DC: Research Report 102, IFPRI, 1995.

Aghion, Philippe and Patrick Bolton, 'A Theory of Trickle-Down Growth and Development', *Review of Economic Studies*, 1997, *64*, 151–72.

——, Eve Caroli, and Cecilia Garcia-Penalosa, 'Inequality and Economic Growth: The Perspective of the New Growth Theories', *Journal of Economic Literature*, 1999, *37*, 1615–60.

Akerlof, George A., 'Discriminatory, Status-based Wages Among Tradition-Oriented, Stochastically Trading Coconut Producers', *J. Polit. Econ.*, 1985, *93(2)*, 265–76.

Alamgir, Mohiuddin, *Famine in South Asia: Political Economy of Mass Starvation*, Cambridge, MA.: Oelgeschlager, Gunn and Hain Publ., 1980.

Albarran, Pedro and Orazio Atanasio, 'Empirical Implications of Limited Commitment: Evidence from Mexican Villages', 2002a. (mimeograph)

—— and Orazio P. Atanasio, 'Do Public Transfers Crowd Out Private Transfers? Evidence from a Randomized Experiment in Mexico', Technical Report, WIDER Discussion Paper No. 2002/06, Helsinki 2002b.

Alderman, Harold and Marito Garcia, *Poverty, Household Food Security, and Nutrition in Rural Pakistan*, Washington, DC: International Food Policy Research Institute, Research Report Vol. 96, 1993.

Altonji, Joseph G., Fumio Hayashi, and Laurance Kotlikoff, 'The Effects of Income and Wealth on Time and Money Transfers between Parents and Children', Technical Report, NBER Research Working Paper 5522, 1996.

——, ——, and Laurence J. Kotlikoff, 'Is the Extended Family Altruistically Linked? Direct Tests Using Micro Data', *Americal Economic Review*, 1992, *82(5)*, 1177–98.

——, ——, and ——, 'Parental Altruism and Inter Vivos Transfers: Theory and Evidence', *Journal of Political Economy*, 1997, *105(6)*, 1121–66.

Ambec, Stefan, 'A Theory of African's Income-Sharing Norm with Enlarged Families', 1998. (mimeograph)

Amselle, Jean-Loup, *Les Négociants de la Savanne*, Paris: Editions Anthropos, 1977.

Arnould, Eric J., 'Evaluating Regional Economic Development: Results of a Marketing Systems Analysis in Zinder Province, Niger Republic', *J. Developing Areas*, 1985, *19*, 209–44.

Arrow, Kenneth J., *Essays in the Theory of Risk Bearing*, Chicago: Markham Publ. Co., 1971.

Arrow, Kenneth, Samuel Bowles, and Steven Durlauf, *Meritocracy and Economic Inequality*, Princeton NJ: Princeton University Press, 2000.

Arthur, Brian W., 'Self-Reinforcing Mechanisms in Economics', in *The Economy as an Evolving Complex System: SFI Studies in the Sciences of Complexity*', P.W. Anderson, K.J Arrow and D. Pines (eds), 1988.

——, 'Competing Technologies, Increasing Returns, and Lock-In by Historical Events', *Economic Journal*, 1989, *99*, 116–31.

——, 'Positive Feedbacks in the Economy', *Scientific American*, 1990, pp. 92–9.

Arthur, Brian W., Yuri M. Ermoliev, and Yuri M. Kaniovski, 'Strong Laws for a Class of Path-Dependent Stochastic Processes', in *Increasing Returns and Parth Dependence in the Economy*, Ann Arbor, MI: University of Michigan Press, 1994, pp. 185–201.

Atwood, David A., 'Land Registration in Africa: The Impact on Agricultural Production', *World Development*, 1990, *18, No.5*, 659–71.

Azariadis, Costas, 'The Economics of Poverty Traps — Part One: Complete Markets', *Journal of Economic Growth*, 1996, *1*, 449–86.

Bala, Venkatesh and Sanjeev Goyal, 'Learning from Neighbors', *Review of Economic Studies*, 1998, *65(3)*, 595–621.

—— and ——, 'A Non-Cooperative Model of Network Formation', *Econometrica*, 2000, *68(5)*, 1181–229.

Banerjee, Abhijit and Kaivan Munshi, 'Market Imperfections, Communities, and the Organization of Production: An Empirical Analysis of Tirupur's Garment-Export Network', 1999. (mimeograph)

Banerjee, Abhijit V. and Andrew F. Newman, 'Risk-Bearing and the Theory of Income Distribution', *Review of Economic Studies*, 1991, *58*, 211–35.

—— and ——, 'Occupational Choice and the Process of Development', *Journal of Political Economy*, 1993, *101(2)*, 274–98.

Bardhan, Pranab, *Land, Labor and Rural Poverty*, New York: Columbia University Press, 1984.

Barr, Abigail, 'Social Capital and Technical Information Flows in the Ghanaian Manufacturing Sector', *Oxford Economic Papers*, 2000, *52(3)*, 539–59.

——, 'Enterprise Performance and the Functional Diversity of Social Capital', *Journal of African Economies*, 2002, *11(1)*, 90–113.

Barrett, Christopher B., 'Liberalization and Food Price Distributions: ARCH-M Evidence from Madagascar', *Food Policy*, 1997, *22(2)*, 155–73.

——, 'Food Security and Food Assistance Programs', in *Handbook of Agricultural Economics, Volume 2*, Bruce Gardner and Gordon Rausser (eds), Amsterdam: Elsevier Science BV, 2002.

—— and Paul A. Dorosh, 'Farmers' Welfare and Changing Food Prices: Nonparametric Evidence from Rice in Madagascar', *American Journal of Agricultural Economics*, 1996, *78*, 656–69.

——, Mesfin Bezuneh, Daniel C. Clay, and Thomas Reardon, 'Heterogeneous Constraints, Incentives and Income Diversification Strategies in Rural Africa', 2001. (mimeograph)

Barro, Robert J. and Xavier Sala i Martin, 'Convergence', *J. Polit. Econ.*, 1992, *100*, 223–51.

—— and ——, *Economic Growth*, New York: McGraw Hill, 1995.

Basu, Kaushik, 'One Kind of Power', *Oxford Econ. Papers*, 1986, *38*, 259–82.

—— and Pham Hoang Van, 'The Economics of Child Labor', *American Economic Review*, 1998, *88(3)*, 412–27.

—— and Zafiris Tzannatos, 'The Global Child Labor Problem: What Do We Know and What Can We Do?', 2002. (mimeograph)

Bauer, P.T., *West African Trade: A Study of Competition, Oligopoly and Monopoly in a Changing Economy*, Cambridge: Cambridge University Press, 1954.

Baulch, Bob, 'Testing for Food Market Integration Revisited', *Journal of Development Studies*, 1997a, *33(4)*, 512–34.

——, 'Transfer Costs, Spatial Arbitrage, and Testing for Food Market Integration', *American Journal of Agricultural Economics*, 1997b, *79(2)*, 477–87.

Bayart, Jean-François, *L'Etat en Afrique: La Politique du Ventre*, Paris: Fayard, 1989.

Becker, Gary S., *A Treatise on the Family*, Cambridge, MA.: Harvard University Press, 1981.

—— and Vicente Madrigal, 'The Formation of Values with Habitual Behavior', 1994. (mimeograph)

—— and Nigel Tomes, 'An Equilibrium Theory of the Distribution of Income and Intergenerational Mobility', *Journal of Political Economy*, 1979, *87(6)*, 1153–89.

——, Kevin M. Murphy, and Robert Tamura, 'Capital, Fertility, and Economic Growth', *J. Polit. Econ.*, 1990, *98*, S12–S37.

Behrman, Jere R., Andrew D. Foster, and Mark R. Rosenzweig, 'Dynamic Savings Decisions in Agricultural Environments With Incomplete Markets', *Journal of Economic and Business Statistics*, 1997, *15(2)*, 282–92.

Bell, Clive, 'Credit Markets and Interlinked Transactions', in *Handbook of Development Economics*, Hollis Chenery and T.N. Srinivasan (eds), Amsterdam: North Holland, 1988.

Ben-Porath, Yoram, 'The F-Connection: Families, Friends, and Firms and the Organization of Exchange', *Population and Development Review*, 1980, *6(1)*, 1–30.

Benabou, Roland, 'Unequal Societies: Income Distribution and the Social Contract', *American Economic Review*, 2000, *90(1)*, 96–129.

Bernheim, B. Douglas and Bezalel Peleg, 'Coalition-Proof Nash Equilibria: II. Applications', *Journal of Economic Theory*, 1987, *42*, 13–29.

——, ——, and Michael D. Whinston, 'Coalition-Proof Nash Equilibria: I. Concepts', *Journal of Economic Theory*, 1987, *42*, 1–12.

Besley, Timothy and Alec R. Levenson, 'The Role of Informal Finance in Household Capital Accumulation: Evidence from Taiwan', *Econ. J.*, 1996, *106(434)*, 39–59.

——, Stephen Coate, and Glenn Loury, 'The Economics of Rotating Savings and Credit Associations', *Amer. Econ. Rev.*, 1993, *83(4)*, 792–810.

Bhaduri, A., 'A Study of Agricultural Backwardness under Semi-Feudalism', *Economic Journal*, 1973, *83*, 120–37.

Bigsten, Arne, Paul Collier, Stefan Dercon, Marcel Fafchamps, Bernard Gauthier, Jan Willem Gunning, Anders Isaksson, Abena Oduro, Remco Oostendorp, Cathy Patillo, Mans Soderbom, Francis Teal, and Albert Zeufack, 'Contract Flexibility and Dispute Resolution in African Manufacturing', *Journal of Development Studies*, 2000, *36(4)*, 1–37.

Binder, Melissa and Christopher Woodruff, 'Inequality and Inter-generational Mobility in Schooling: The Case of Mexico', *Economic Development and Cultural Change*, 2002, *50(2)*, 249–67.

Binswanger, Hans P., 'Attitudes Towards Risk: Experimental Measurement Evidence in Rural India', *Amer. J. Agric. Econ.*, 1980, *62(3)*, 395–407.

—— and John McIntire, 'Behavioral and Material Determinants of

Production Relations in Land-Abundant Tropical Agriculture', *Econ. Dev. Cult. Change*, 1987, *36(1)*, 73–99.

—— and Mark R. Rosenzweig, 'Behavioral and Material Determinants of Production Relations in Agriculture', *Journal of Development Studies*, 1986, *22, No. 3*, 503–39.

—— and Donald A. Sillers, 'Risk Aversion and Credit Constraints in Farmers' Decision-Making: A Reinterpretation', *Journal of Development Studies*, 1983, *20*, 5–21.

Bissuel, Bertrand, 'Surendettement: Jean-Louis Borloo veut une reforme radicale', *Le Monde Hebdomadaire*, 2003, *No. 2830 du 1 février 2003*, page 6.

Blundell, Richard, Luigi Pistaferri, and Ian Preston, 'Partial Insurance and Consumption Dynamics', 2001. (mimeograph)

Bolton, Patrick and Mathias Dewatripont, 'The Firm as a Communication Network', *Quarterly Journal of Economics*, 1994, *109(4)*, 809–39.

Bongaarts, John and Mead Cain, *Demographic Responses to Famine*, New York: Population Council, 1981.

Boserup, Ester, *The Conditions of Agricultural Growth*, Chicago: Aldine Publishing Company, 1965.

Braudel, Fernand, *Civilization and Capitalism*, New York: Harper and Row, 1986.

Braverman, A. and J.E. Stiglitz, 'Sharecropping and the Interlinking of the Agrarian Markets', *American Economic Review*, 1982, *72*, 695–715.

—— and J. Stiglitz, 'Cost-Sharing Arrangements under Sharecropping: Moral Hazard, Incentive Flexibility, and Risk', *Americal Journal of Agricultural Economics*, 1986, *68(3)*, 642–52.

Brocheux, Pierre, 'Moral Economy or Political Economy? The Peasants Are Always Rational', *J. Asian Stud.*, 1983, *42(4)*, 791–803.

Bromley, Daniel W. and Jean-Paul Chavas, 'On Risk, Transactions, and Economic Development in the Semiarid Tropics', *Economic Development and Cultural Change*, 1989, *37(4)*, 719–36.

Browning, Martin and Valerie Lechene, 'Caring and Sharing: Tests Between Alternative Models of Intra-Household Allocation', 2001. (mimeograph)

Bulow, Jeremy and Kenneth Rogoff, 'A Constant Recontracting Model of Sovereign Debt', *J. Polit. Econ.*, 1989a, *97(1)*, 155–78.

—— and ——, 'Sovereign Debt: Is to Forgive to Forget?', *Amer. Econ. Review*, 1989b, *79(1)*, 43–50.

Cabrales, Antonio, Antoni Calvo-Armengol, and Matthew O. Jackson, 'La Crema: A Case Study of Mutual Fire Insurance', 2002. (mimeograph)

Carraro, Ludivico, 'Vulnerability, Poverty and Ability to Smooth Consumption: A Theoretical Model and its Empirical Analysis in Ethiopia', 1999. (mimeograph)

Carroll, Christopher D., 'The Buffer-Stock Theory of Saving: Some Macroeconomic Evidence', *Brookings Papers on Econ. Activity*, 1992, *2*, 61–156.

Carter, Michael R., 'Equilibrium Credit Rationing of Small Farm Agriculture', *Journal of Development Economics*, 1988, *28*, 83–103.

——, 'Environment, Technology and the Social Articulation of Risk in West African Agriculture', *Economic Development and Cultural Change*, 1997, *45(2)*, 557–90.

—— and Frederick J. Zimmerman, 'Inequality and Growth in Latin America: A Microeconomic Analysis', 1996. (mimeograph)

—— and Frederick J. Zimmerman, 'The Dynamic Cost and Persistence of Asset Inequality in an Agrarian Economy', *Journal of Development Economics*, 2000, *63(2)*, 265–302.

Chakrabarti, Subir, William Lord, and Peter Rangazas, 'Uncertain Altruism and Investment in Children', *American Economic Review*, 1993, *83(4)*, 994–1002.

Chaudhuri, Shubham and Christina H. Paxson, 'Smoothing Consumption under Income Seasonality: Buffer Stocks vs. Credit Markets', 2001. (mimeograph)

Christensen, Garry, 'The Influence of Agro-Climatic Conditions on Rural Credit: Evidence from Burkina Faso', 1987. (mimeograph)

Cleave, John, *African Farmers: Labor Use in the Development of Smallholder Agriculture*, New York: Praeger, 1974.

Coate, Stephen and Martin Ravallion, 'Reciprocity Without Commitment: Characterization and Performance of Informal Insurance Arrangements', *J. Dev. Econ.*, 1993, *40*, 1–24.

Cochrane, John H., 'A Simple Test of Consumption Insurance', *J. Polit. Econ.*, 1991, *99(5)*, 957–76.

Cohen, Abner, *Custom and Politics in Urban Africa: A Study of Hausa Migrants in Yoruba Towns*, Berkeley, CA: University of California Press, 1969.

Cohen, Daniel, 'Debt Relief: Implications of Secondary Market Discounts and Debt Overhangs', *World Bank Econ. Review*, 1990, *4(1)*, 43–53.

Collier, Paul, 'The Macroeconomic Repercussions of Agricultural Shocks and their Implications for Insurance', Technical Report, WIDER Discussion Paper No. 2002/46, Helsinki, 2002.

Colson, Elizabeth, *The Plateau Tonga of Northern Rhodesia (Zambia)*, Manchester: Manchester University Press, 1962.

Comité Ad Hoc Chargé de l'Elaboration d'un Code Rural, *Plaquette Code Rural*, Niamey, Niger: Ministère de l'Agriculture et de l'Environnement, 1989 (version provisoire).

Conley, Timothy and Christopher Udry, 'Social Learning through

Networks: The Adoption of New Agricultural Technologies in Ghana', *American Journal of Agricultural Economics*, 2001, *83(3)*, 668–73.

Cossins, Noel, 'Production Strategies and Pastoral Man', in 'Pastoral Systems Research in Sub-Saharan Africa', Addis Ababa: ILCA (ed.), 1983.

Cox, Donald, 'Motives for Private Income Transfers', *J. Pol. Econ.*, 1987, *95(3)*, 508–43.

——, 'Informal Networks, Institutions and the Soap Opera Constraint', 1999. (mimeograph)

—— and Emmanuel Jimenez, 'Social Security and Private Transfers in Developing Countries: The Case of Peru', *World Bank Economic Review*, 1992, *6(1)*, 155–69.

—— and ——, 'Risk Sharing and Private Transfers: What about Urban Households?', *Economic Development and Cultural Change*, 1998, *46(3)*, 621–37.

——, Zekeriya Eser, and Emmanuel Jimenez, 'Motives for Private Transfers Over the Life Cycle: An Analytical Framework and Evidence from Peru', *Journal of Development Economics*, 1998, *55(1)*, 57–80.

——, Bruce E. Hansen, and Emmanuel Jimenez, 'Are Households Altruistic? Private Transfers in a Laissez-Faire Economy', 1996. (mimeograph)

Crow, Ben and K.A.S. Murshid, 'Economic Returns to Social Power: Merchants' Finance and Interlinkage in the Grain Markets of Bengladesh', *World Develoment*, 1994, *22(7)*, 1011–30.

Daniels, Lisa, *Changes in the Small-Scale Enterprise Sector from 1991 to 1993: Results from a Second Nationwide Survey in Zimbabwe*, Bethesda, MD: Gemini Technical Report No. 71, Gemini, 1994.

Dardanoni, Valentino, 'Optimal Choices Under Uncertainty: The Case of Two-Argument Utility Functions', *Economic Journal*, *98(39)*, 429–50, 1988.

Dasgupta, Partha, *An Inquiry into Well-Being and Destitution*, Oxford: Clarendon Press, 1993.

——, 'The Population Problem: Theory and Evidence', *Journal of Economic Literature*, 1995, *33*, 1879–1902.

Datta, Samar K. and Jeffrey B. Nugent, 'Are Old-Age Security and the Utility of Children in Rural India Really Unimportant?', *Population Studies*, 1984, *38*, 507–9.

——, ——, Asher Tishler, and Jone lin Wang, 'Seasonality, Differential Access and Interlinking of Labour and Credit', *J. Devel. Studies*, 1988, *24(3)*, 379–93.

de Janvry, Alain, *The Agrarian Question and Reformism in Latin America*, Baltimore, MD: Johns Hopkins University Press, 1981.

——, Marcel Fafchamps, and Elisabeth Sadoulet, 'Peasant Household

Behavior with Missing Markets: Some Paradoxes Explained', *Economic Journal*, 1991, *101(409)*, 1400–17.

——, Gustavo Gordillo, Jean-Philippe Platteau, and Elisabeth Sadoulet, *Access to Land, Rural Poverty, and Public Action*, Oxford: Oxford University Press, 2001.

de Weerdt, Joachim, 'Risk-Sharing and Endogenous Network Formation', Technical Report, WIDER Discussion Paper No. 2002/57, Helsinki, 2002.

Deaton, Angus, 'Saving in Developing Countries: Theory and Review', *World Bank Econ. Rev.*, 1990, *Proceedings of the World Bank Annual Conference on Development Economics 1989*, 61–96.

——, 'Saving and Liquidity Constraints', *Econometrica*, 1991, *59(5)*, 1221–48.

——, 'Household Saving in LDCs: Credit Markets, Insurance and Welfare', *Scand. J. Econ.*, 1992a, *94(2)*, 253–73.

——, 'Saving and Income Smoothing in Côte d'Ivoire', *J. African Economies*, 1992b, *1(1)*, 1–24.

—— and Ron Miller, 'International Commodity Prices, Macroeconomic Performance, and Politics in Sub-Saharan Africa', *Journal of African Economies*, 1996, *5(3)*, 99–191, Supplement Part I.

Dekker, Marleen and Hans Hoogeveen, 'Bride Wealth and Household Security in Rural Zimbabwe', *Journal of African Economies*, 2002, *11(1)*, 114–45.

Delgado, Christopher L., *Livestock Versus Foodgrain Production in Southeast Upper Volta: A Resource Allocation Analysis*, Univ. of Michigan, 1979. Livestock Production and Marketing in the Entente States of West Africa, Monograph No. 1.

DeMarzo, Peter M., 'Coalitions, Leadership, and Social Norms: The Power of Suggestion in Games', *Games and Economic Behavior*, 1992, *4(1)*, 72–100.

Dercon, Stefan, 'On Market Integration and Liberalisation: Method and Application to Ethiopia', *Journal of Development Studies*, 1995, *32(1)*, 112–43.

——, 'Income Risk, Coping Strategies, and Safety Nets', *World Bank Research Observer*, 2002, *17(2)*, 141–66.

Dercon, Stefan and Joachim de Weerdt, 'Risk-sharing Networks and Insurance against Illness', CSAE WP No 2002-16, 2002, Department of Economics, Oxford University, Oxford.

—— and Pramila Krishnan, 'Income Portfolios in Rural Ethiopia and Tanzania: Choices and Constraints', *Journal of Development Studies*, 1996, *32(6)*, 850–75.

—— and ——, 'In Sickness and in Health: Risk-Sharing within

Households in Rural Ethiopia', *Journal of Political Economy*, 2000, *108(4)*, 688–727.

Diamond, Peter A. and Joseph E. Stiglitz, 'Increases in Risk and in Risk Aversion', *Journal of Economic Theory*, 1974, *8*, 337–60.

Diaz, Antonia and Christina Echevarria, 'Solidarity, Transfers, and Poverty', *Review of Development Economics*, 2002, *6(3)*, 337–50.

Dixit, Avinash, 'Entry and Exit Decisions Under Uncertainty', *J. Polit. Econ.*, 1989, *97(3)*, 620–38.

Dixit, Avinash K. and Robert S. Pindyck, *Investment Under Uncertainty*, Princeton, NJ: Princeton University Press, 1994.

Dreze, Jacques H. and Franco Modigliani, 'Consumption Decisions Under Uncertainty', *J. Econ. Theory*, 1972, *5*, 308–35.

Dreze, Jean and Amartya Sen, *Hunger and Public Action*, Oxford: Clarendon Press, 1989.

Dubois, Pierre, 'Assurance Complète, Hétérogénéité des Préférences et Métayage au Pakistan', *Annales d'Economie et de Statistique*, 2000, *0(59)*, 1–35.

——, Bruno Julien, and Thierry Magnac, 'Risk Sharing with Formal and Informal Contracts: Theory, Semi-Parametric Identification and Estimation', 2002. (mimeograph)

Durlauf, Steven N., 'A Theory of Persistent Income Inequality', *Journal of Economic Growth*, 1996, *1(1)*, 75–93.

Dutta, Bhaskar, Debraj Ray, and Kunal Sengupta, 'Contracts With Eviction in Infinitely Repeated Principal-Agents Relationships', in *The Economic Theory of Agrarian Institutions*, P. Bardhan (ed.), Oxford: Clarendon Press, 1989.

Eaton, Jonathan and Mark Gersovitz, 'Debt with Potential Repudiation: Theoretical and Empirical Analysis', *Review Econ. Studies*, 1981, *XLVIII*, 289–309.

——, ——, and Joseph E. Stiglitz, 'The Pure Theory of Country Risk', *European Econ. Review*, 1986, *30*, 481–513.

Eddy, E., *Labor and Land Use on Mixed Farms in the Pastoral Zone of Niger*, University of Michigan, 1979. Livestock Production and Marketing in the Entente States of West Africa, Monograph No. 3.

Edmonds, Eric V., 'Is Child Labor Inefficient? Evidence from Large Cash Transfers', 2002. (mimeograph)

Eicher, Carl and Doyle Baker, 'Research on Agricultural Development in sub-Saharan Africa: A Critical Survey', in MSU International Development Paper No. 1, Michigan State University, 1982.

Ellsworth, Lynn, *Mutual Insurance and Non-Market Transactions Among Farmers in Burkina Faso*, University of Wisconsin, 1989. Unpublished PhD thesis.

—— and Kenneth Shapiro, 'Seasonality in Burkina Faso Grain Marketing: Farmer Strategies and Government Policy', in *Seasonal Variability in Third World Agriculture*, David E. Sahn (ed.), Baltimore: Johns Hopkins University Press, MD: 1989.

Epstein, Larry G., 'Production Flexibility and the Behavior of the Competitive Firm Under Price Uncertainty', *Review of Economic Studies*, 1978, *140(2)*, 251–62.

——, 'Decision Making and the Temporal Resolution of Uncertainty', *International Economic Review*, 1980, *21(2)*, 269–83.

Estaban, Joan-Maria and Debraj Ray, 'On the Measurement of Polarisation', *Econometrica*, 1994, *62(4)*, 819–51.

Estudillo, Jonna P., Agnes R. Quisumbing, and Keijiro Otsuka, 'Gender Differences in Land Inheritance, Schooling and Lifetime Income: Evidence from the Rural Philippines', *Journal of Development Studies*, 2001, *37(4)*, 23–48.

Eswaran, Mukesh and Ashok Kotwal, 'A Theory of Contractual Structure in Agriculture', *Amer. Econ. Rev.*, 1985, *75(3)*, 352–67.

—— and ——, 'Access to Capital and Agrarian Production Organization', *Economic Journal*, 1986, *96(382)*, 482–98.

Evans-Pritchard, E.E., *The Nuer*, Oxford: Clarendon Press, 1940.

Fafchamps, Marcel, *Labor Use and Productivity and Technological Change in African Smallholder Agriculture: A Case Study of Sudan*, Addis Ababa: Jobs and Skills Programme for Africa, International Labor Organization, 1985.

——, *Labor Use and Productivity and Technological Change in African Smallholder Agriculture: Synthesis Report*, Addis Ababa: Jobs and Skills Programme for Africa, International Labor Organization, 1986.

——, 'Cash Crop Production, Food Price Volatility and Rural Market Integration in the Third World', *Amer. J. Agric. Econ.*, 1992a, *74(1)*, 90–9.

——, 'Solidarity Networks in Pre-Industrial Societies: Rational Peasants with a Moral Economy', *Econ. Devel. Cult. Change*, 1992b, *41(1)*, 147–74.

——, 'Sequential Labor Decisions Under Uncertainty: An Estimable Household Model of West-African Farmers', *Econometrica*, 1993, *61(5)*, 1173–97.

——, 'Industrial Structure and Microenterprises in Africa', *J. Developing Areas*, 1994, *29(1)*, 1–30.

——, 'The Enforcement of Commercial Contracts in Ghana', *World Development*, 1996a, *24(3)*, 427–48.

——, 'Sovereign Debt, Structural Adjustment, and Conditionality', *J. Dev. Econ.*, 1996b, *50*, 313–35.

——, 'Trade Credit in Zimbabwean Manufacturing', *World Development*, 1997, *25(3)*, 795–815.

——, 'The Tragedy of the Commons, Cycles and Sustainability', *Journal of African Economies*, 1998, *7(3)*, 384–423.

——, 'Risk Sharing and Quasi-Credit', *Journal of International Trade and Economic Development*, 1999a, *8(3)*, 257–78.

——, *Rural Poverty, Risk, and Development*, Rome: FAO, 1999b. Economic and Social Development Paper No. 144.

——, 'Ethnicity and Credit in African Manufacturing', *Journal of Development Economics*, 2000, *61(1)*, 205–35.

——, 'Intrahousehold Access to Land and Sources of Inefficiency: Theory and Concepts', in *Access to Land, Rural Poverty, and Public Action*, Alain de Janvry, Gustavo Gordillo, Jean-Philippe Platteau, and Elisabeth Sadoulet (eds), Oxford and New York: Oxford University Press, 2001. UNU/WIDER Studies in Development Economics.

——, 'Spontaneous Market Emergence', *Topics in Theoretical Economics*, 2002, *2(1), Article 2*. Berkeley Electronic Press at www.bepress.com,.

——, 'Inequality and Risk', in *Insurance against Poverty*, Stefan Dercon (ed.), Helsinki: WIDER, 2003a. (forthcoming).

——, *Market Institutions in Africa*, Cambridge, MA.: MIT Press, 2003b (forthcoming).

—— and Sarah Gavian, 'The Spatial Integration of Livestock Markets in Niger', *Journal of African Economies*, 1996, *5(3)*, 366–405.

—— and ——, 'The Determinants of Livestock Prices in Niger', *Journal of African Economies*, *6(2)*, 1997.

—— and Flore Gubert, 'Contingent Loan Repayment in the Philippines', 2002. (mimeograph)

—— and Brigit Helms, 'Local Demand, Investment Multipliers, and Industrialization: Theory and Application to the Guatemalan Highlands', *J. Devel. Econ.*, 1996, *49*, 61–92.

—— and Susan Lund, 'Risk Sharing Networks in Rural Philippines', *Journal of Development Economics*, 2003 (forthcoming).

—— and Bart Minten, 'Relationships and Traders in Madagascar', *Journal of Development Studies*, 1999, *35(6)*, 1–35.

—— and ——, 'Returns to Social Network Capital Among Traders', *Oxford Economic Papers*, 2002, *54*, 173–206.

—— and John Pender, 'Precautionary Saving, Credit Constraints, and Irreversible Investment: Theory and Evidence from Semi-Arid India', *J. Business and Economic Statistics*, 1997, *15(2)*, 180–94.

—— and Agnes R. Quisumbing, 'Human Capital, Productivity, and Labor Allocation in Rural Pakistan', *Journal of Human Resources*, 1999, *34(2)*, 369–406.

—— and ——, 'Social Roles, Human Capital, and the Intrahousehold Division of Labor: Evidence from Pakistan', *Oxford Economic Papers*, 2003, *55(1)*, 36–80.

——, Tyler Biggs, Jonathan Conning, and Pradeep Srivastava, *Enterprise Finance in Kenya*, Washington, DC: Regional Program on Enterprise Development, Africa Region, The World Bank, 1994.

——, Jan Willem Gunning, and Remco Oostendorp, 'Inventory and Risk in African Manufacturing', *Economic Journal*, 2000, *110(466)*, 861–93.

——, John Pender, and Elizabeth Robinson, *Enterprise Finance in Zimbabwe*, Washington, DC: Regional Program for Enterprise Development, Africa Division, The World Bank, 1995.

——, Christopher Udry, and Katherine Czukas, 'Drought and Saving in West Africa: Are Livestock a Buffer Stock?', *Journal of Development Economics*, 1998, *55(2)*, 273–305.

Farrell, J. and E. Maskin, 'Renegotiation in Repeated Games', *Games and Economic Behavior*, 1989, *1*, 327–60.

Feder, G., 'Farm Size, Risk Aversion and the Adoption of New Technologies Under Uncertainty', *Oxford Economic Papers*, 1980, *32(2)*, 263–83.

——, 'The Relation Between Farm Size and Farm Productivity', *Journal of Development Economics*, 1985, *18(2–3)*, 297–314.

—— and Tongroj Onchan, 'Land Ownership, Security and Farm Investment in Thailand', *Amer. J. Agr. Econ.*, 1987, *69*, 311–20.

——, R. Just, and D. Zilberman, 'Adoption of Agricultural Innovations in Developing Countries: A Survey', *Economic Development and Cultural Change, 33(2): 255–98, 1985.

Feeny, David, 'The Moral or the Rational Peasant? Competing Hypotheses of Collective Action', *J. Asian Stud.*, 1983, *42(4)*, 769–89.

Feinerman, Eli and Edward J. Seiler, 'Private Transfers with Incomplete Information: A Contribution to the Altruism-Exchange Motivation for Transfers Debate', *Journal of Population Economics*, 2002, *15*, 715–36.

Fogel, Robert William, *The Conquest of High Mortality and Hunger in Europe and America: Timing and Mechanisms*, Cambridge, MA: National Bureau of Economic Research, 1990.

Foster, Andrew D., 'Altruism, Household Coresidence and Women's Health Investments in Rural Bangladesh', 2002. (mimeograph)

—— and Mark R. Rosenzweig, 'Information, Learning, and Wage Rates in Low-Income Rural Areas', *Journal of Human Resources*, 1993, *28(4)*, 759–90.

—— and ——, 'Learning by Doing and Learning from Others: Human Capital and Technical Change in Agriculture', *Journal of Political Economy*, 1995, *103(6)*, 1176–209.

—— and ——, 'Comparative Advantage, Information and the Allocation of Workers to Tasks: Evidence from an Agricultural Labor Market', *Rev. Econ. Studies*, 1996, *63(3)*, 347–74.

—— and ——, 'Financial Intermediation, Transfers, and Commitment: Do Banks Crowd Out Private Insurance Arrangements in Low-Income Rural Areas?', in *Sharing the Wealth: Demographic Changes and Economic Transfers Between Generations*, A. Mason and G. Tapinos (eds), Oxford: Oxford University Press, 2000.

—— and ——, 'Imperfect Commitment, Altruism and the Family: Evidence from Transfer Behavior in Low-Income Rural Areas', *Review of Economics and Statistics*, 2001, *83(3)*, 389–407.

Freeman, Scott, 'Equilibrium Income Inequality Among Identical Agents', *Journal of Political Economy*, 1996, *104(5)*, 1047–64.

Fudenberg, Drew and E. Maskin, 'The Folk Theorem with Incomplete Public Information', *Econometrica*, 1994, *62(5)*, 997–1039.

——, D. Levine, and E. Maskin, 'The Folk Theorem with Unobserved Action', 1988.

Galor, Oded and Harl E. Ryder, 'Existence, Uniqueness, and Stability of Equilibrium in an Overlapping-Generations Model with Productive Capital', *J. Econ. Theory*, 1989, *49(2)*, 360–75.

Galor, Oded and Joseph Zeira, 'Income Distribution and Macroeconomics', *Review of Economic Studies*, 1993, *60*, 35–52.

—— and Marcel Fafchamps, 'Land Tenure and Allocative Efficiency in Niger', *American Journal of Agricultural Economics*, 1996, *78*, 460–71.

Gavian, Sarah and Amare Teklu, 'Land Tenure and Farming Practices: The Case of Tiyo Woreda, Arsi, Ethiopia', Addis Ababa: International Livestock Research Institute, 1996. Paper presented to the Annual Conference, Agricultural Economics Society of Ethiopia.

Geertz, Clifford, *Peddlers and Princes: Social Change and Economic Modernization in Two Indonesian Towns*, Chicago: University of Chicago Press, 1963.

——, Hildred Geertz, and Lawrence Rosen, *Meaning and Order in Moroccan Society*, Cambridge: Cambridge University Press, 1979.

Genicot, Garance, 'Bonded Labor and Serfdom: A Paradox of Voluntary Choice', *Journal of Development Economics*, 2002, *67(1)*, 101–27.

—— and Debraj Ray, 'Endogenous Group Formation in Risk-Sharing Arrangements', 2000. (mimeograph)

Gertler, Paul and Jonathan Gruber, 'Insuring Consumption Against Illness', *American Economic Review*, 2002, *92(1)*, 51–76.

—— and Roland Strum, 'Private Health Insurance and Public Expenditures in Jamaica', *Journal of Econometrics*, 1997, *77(1)*, 237–57.

——, Luis Locay, and Warren Sanderson, 'Are User Fees Regressive? The

Welfare Implications of Health Care Financing Proposals in Peru', *Journal of Econometrics*, 1987, *36(1/2)*, 67–88.

Giles, John T., 'Household Risk-Coping and the Opening of Labor Markets in Rural China', 1999. (mimeograph)

Gluckman, Max, *Custom and Conflict in Africa*, Oxford: Basil Blackwell, 1955.

Goldstein, Markus, Alain de Janvry, and Elisabeth Sadoulet, 'Is a Friend in Need a Friend Indeed? Inclusion and Exclusion in Mutual Insurance Networks in Southern Ghana', Technical Report, WIDER Discussion Paper No. 2002/25, Helsinki, 2002.

Gonzalez-Vega, Claudio, 'Credit Rationing Behavior of Agricultural Lenders: The Iron Law of Interest Rate Restrictions', in *Undermining Rural Development With Cheap Credit*, D.W. Adams, D.H. Graham, and J.D. Von Pischke, Boulder, CO: Westview Press, 1984.

Granovetter, Mark S., *Getting a Job: A Study of Contacts and Carreers*, second edition, Chicago: University of Chicago Press, 1995.

Greenough, Paul R., *Prosperity and Misery in Modern Bengal*, New York: Oxford University Press, 1982.

Greif, Avner, 'Contract Enforceability and Economic Institutions in Early Trade: The Maghribi Traders' Coalition', *Amer. Econ. Rev.*, 1993, *83(3)*, 525–48.

——, 'Cultural Beliefs and the Organization of Society: A Historical and Theoretical Reflection on Collectivist and Individualist Societies', *J. Polit. Econ.*, 1994, *102(5)*, 912–50.

Griliches, Ziv, 'Productivity Puzzles and R and D: Another Non-Explanation', *J. Econ. Perspectives*, 1988, *2(4)*, 9–21.

Grootaert, C. and Ravi Kanbur, 'Child Labour: An Economic Perspective', *International Labour Review*, 1995, *134(2)*, 187–203.

Grossman, Herschel I. and John B. Van Huyck, 'Sovereign Debt as a Contingent Claim: Excusable Default, Repudiation, and Reputation', *Amer. Econ. Review*, 1988, *78(5)*, 1088–97.

Hall, Robert E., 'Stochastic Implications of the Life Cycle-Permanent Income Hypothesis: Theory and Evidence', *J. Polit. Econ.*, 1978, *86(6)*, 461–81.

Hart, Keith, 'Kinship, Contract, and Trust: the Economic Organization of Migrants in an African City Slum', in *Trust: Making and Breaking Cooperative Relations*, D. Gambetta (ed.), New York: Basil Blackwell, 1988.

Hart, O. and B. Holmstrom, 'The Theory of Contracts', in *Advances in Economic Theory*, Truman F. Bewley (ed.), Cambridge: Cambridge University Press, 1987.

Hayashi, Fumio, 'Is the Japanese Extended Family Altruistically Linked? A Test Based on Engel Curves', *J. Polit. Econ.*, 1995, *103(3)*, 661–74.

———, Joseph Altonji, and Laurence Kotlikoff, 'Risk-Sharing, Altruism, and the Factor Structure of Consumption', Working Paper 3834, Evanston, ILL: National Bureau of Economic Research, 1991.

———, ———, and ———, 'Risk-Sharing Between and Within Families', *Econometrica*, 1996, *64(2)*, 261–94.

Heaton, John and Deborah Lucas, 'Portfolio Choice in the Presence of Background Risk', *Economic Journal*, 2000, *110(460)*, 1–26.

Herskovits, Melville J., *Economic Anthropology*, Knopf, New York, 1952.

Hildenbrand, Werner, *Core and Equilibria of a Large Economy*, Princeton, NJ: Princeton University Press, 1974.

Hoff, Karla, 'The Emergence of Organization in Informal Insurance', 1996. (mimeograph)

———, Avishay Braverman, and Joseph E. Stiglitz, *The Economics of Rural Organization: Theory, Practice, and Policy*, New York: Published for the World Bank by Oxford University Press, 1993.

Holmstrom, B., 'Moral Hazard in Teams', *Bell J. of Econ.*, 1982, *13*, 324–40.

Holmberg, Allan C., *Nomads of the Long Bow*, Garden City, NY: Natural History Press, 1969.

Hoogeveen, Hans, *Risk and Insurance in Rural Zimbabwe*, Amsterdam: Tinbergen Institute Research Series, Free University, 2001. (PhD thesis)

Hopkins, A.G., *An Economic History of West Africa*, London: Longman Group Ltd, 1973.

Horioka, Charles Y. and Wako Watanabe, 'Why Do People Save? A Micro-Analysis of Motives for Household Saving in Japan', *Economic Journal*, 1997, *107(442)*, 537–52.

Huysentruyt, Marieke, Christopher B. Barrett, and John G. McPeak, 'Social Identity and Manipulative Interhousehold Transfers among East African Pastoralists', 2002. (mimeograph)

ILO, *Emploi d'Abord au Bénin*, Addis Ababa: JASPA, International Labour Organization, 1984.

Imai, Katsushi, 'How Well Do Households Cope with Risk through Savings and Portfolio Adjustment? Evidence from Rural India', 2000a. (mimeograph)

———, 'Is Livestock Important for Risk Behaviour and Activity Choice of Rural Households? Evidence from Kenya', 2000b. (mimeograph)

———, 'Poverty Dynamics and Poverty Alleviation — The Case of the Employment Guarantee Scheme in Rural India', 2000c. (mimeograph)

———, 'Risk Benefits of Public and Market Employment in Rural India: How Do Households Respond to Anticipated and Unanticipated Shocks?', 2000d. (mimeograph)

Iqbal, Farrukh, 'The Demand and Supply of Funds Among Agricultural

Households in India', in *Agricultural Household Models*, I. Singh, L. Squire and J. Strauss (eds), Washington, DC: The World Bank, 1986.

Itoh, Hideshi, 'Incentives to Help in Multi-Agent Situations', *Econometrica*, 1991, *59(3)*, 611–36.

Jacoby, Hanan G. and Emmanuel Skoufias, 'Risk, Financial Markets, and Human Capital in a Developing Country', *Review of Economic Studies*, 1997, *64(3)*, 311–45.

——, Rinku Murgai, and Saeed Ur Rehman, 'Monopoly Power and Distribution in Fragmented Markets: The Case of Groundwater', 2002. (mimeograph)

Jaeger, William K., *Agricultural Mechanization: The Economics of Animal Draft Power in West Africa*, New York: Westview, 1986.

Jolliffe, Dean, 'The Impact of Education in Rural Ghana: Examining Productivity and Labor Allocation Effects', 1996. (mimeograph)

Jones, Christine W., 'Intra-Household Bargaining in Response to the Introduction of New Crops: A Case Study from North Cameroon', in *Understanding Africa's Rural Households and Farming Systems*, Joyce L. Moock (ed.), Boulder, CO and London: Westview Press, 1986.

Jones, William O., *Manioc in Africa*, Stanford, CA: Stanford University Press, 1959.

Kahn, James A., 'Inventories and the Volatility of Production', *American Economic Review*, 1987, *77(4)*, 667–79.

Kali, Raja, 'Endogenous Business Networks', *Journal of Law and Economic Organization*, 1999, *15(3)*, 615–36.

Kamanou, Gisele and Jonathan Morduch, 'Measuring Vulnerability to Poverty', Technical Report, WIDER Discussion Paper No. 2002/58, Helsinki, 2002.

Kang, Sung Jin and Yasuyuki Sawada, 'Household Coping Strategies and the Financial Crisis in Korea', 2002. (mimeograph)

Kargbo, Alimani, *Labor Use and Productivity and Technological Change in African Smallholder Agriculture: A Case Study of The Gambia*, Addis Ababa: ILO/JASPA, 1985.

Keyes, Charles F., 'Peasant Strategies in Asian Societies: Moral and Rational Economic Approaches – A Symposium: Introduction', *J. Asian Stud.*, 1983, *42(4)*, 753–68.

Kimball, Miles S., 'Farmers' Cooperatives as Behavior Toward Risk', *Amer. Econ. Rev.*, 1988, *78(1)*, 224–32.

——, 'Precautionary Savings in the Small and in the Large', *Econometrica*, 1990, *58(1)*, 53–73.

Kletzer, Kenneth M., 'Asymmetries of Information and LDC Borrowing with Sovereign Risk', *Econ. J.*, 1984, *94*, 287–307.

Kochar, Anjini, 'Smoothing Consumption by Smoothing Income: Hoursof-Work Responses to Idiosyncratic Agricultural Shocks in Rural India', *Review of Economics and Statistics*, 1999, *81(1)*, 50–61.

Kocherlakota, Narayana R., 'Implications of Efficient Risk Sharing Without Commitment', *Rev. Econ. Stud.*, 1996, *63(4)*, 595–609.

Krane, Spencer D., 'The Distinction Between Inventory Holding and Stockout Costs: Implications for Target Inventories, Asymmetric Adjustment, and the Effect of Aggregation on Production Smoothing', *International Economic Review*, 1994, *35(1)*, 117–36.

Kranton, Rachel E., 'The Formation of Cooperative Relationships', *Journal of Law, Economics, and Organizations*, 1996, *12(1)*, 214–33.

Kranton, Rachel and Deborah Minehart, 'Competition for Goods in Buyer-Seller Networks', *Review of Economic Design*, 2000, *5(3)*, 301–31.

—— and ——, 'A Theory of Buyer-Seller Networks', *American Economic Review*, 2001, *91(3)*, 485–508.

Kreps, David M., *A Course in Microeconomic Theory*, Princeton, NJ: Princeton University Press, 1990.

Kreps, D., Paul Milgrom, John Roberts, and Robert Wilson, 'Rational Cooperation in the Finitely Repeated Prisoner's Dilemma', *Journal of Economic Theory*, 1982, *27*, 245–52.

Krugman, Paul R., 'Financing vs. Forgiving a Debt Overhang', *J. Devel. Econ.*, 1988, *29*, 253–68.

Kurosaki, Takashi, 'Production Risk and Advantages of Mixed Farming in the Pakistan Punjab', *Developing Economies*, 1997, *35(1)*, 28–47.

——, 'Consumption Smoothing and the Structure of Risk and Time Preferences: Theory and Evidence from Village India', *Hitotsubashi Journal of Economics*, 2001a, *42(2)*, 103–17.

——, 'Consumption Vulnerability and Dynamic Poverty in the North-West Frontier Province, Pakistan', 2001b. (mimeograph)

—— and Marcel Fafchamps, 'Insurance Market Efficiency and Crop Choices in Pakistan', *Journal of Development Economics*, 2002, *67*, 419–53.

Kyle, Steven C. and Jeffrey D. Sachs, 'Developing Country Debt and the Market Value of Large Commercial Banks', Technical Report, National Bureau of Economic Research Working Paper No. 1470, 1984.

La Ferrara, Eliana, 'Descent Rules and Inter Vivos Transfers', 2002. (mimeograph)

Laferrere, A., 'Intergenerational Transmission Models: A Survey', in *The Economics of Reciprocity, Giving and Altruism*, L.A. Gerard-Varet, S.C. Kolm, and J.M. Ythier (eds), London: Macmillan Press, 2000.

Lee, Ronald D., 'Population Dynamics of Humans and Other Animals', *Demography*, 1987, *24(4)*, 443–65.

Leonard, Kenneth L., 'Institutional Structure of Health Care in Rural

Cameroon: Structural Estimation of Production in Teams with Unobservable Effort', Technical Report, Columbia University, Department of Economics Discussion Paper Series: 9798/16, New York, 1998.

Lewis, W. Arthur, 'Economic Development with Unlimited Supplies of Labour', *The Manchester School*, 1954, *XXII(2)*, 139–91.

Ligon, Ethan, 'Risk Sharing and Information in Village Economies', *Review of Economic Studies*, 1998, *65(4)*, 847–64.

——, 'Targeting and Informal Insurance Risk', Technical Report, WIDER Discussion Paper No. 2002/08, Helsinki, 2002.

——, Jonathan P. Thomas, and Tim Worrall, 'Mutual Insurance, Individual Savings, and Limited Commitment', *Review of Economic Dynamics*, 2000, *3(2)*, 216–46.

——, ——, and ——, 'Informal Insurance Arrangements in Village Economies', *Review of Economic Studies*, 2001, *69(1)*, 209–44.

Lim, Youngjae and Robert M. Townsend, 'General Equilibrium Models of Financial Systems: Theory and Measurement in Village Economies', *Review of Economic Dynamics*, 1998, *1(1)*, 58–118.

Livingstone, Ian, *Pastoralism: Practice, Process and Policy*, Rome: FAO, 1984.

Lockheed, Marlaine E., Dean T. Jamison, and Lawrence J. Lau, 'Farmer Education and Farm Efficiency: A Survey', *Economic Development and Cultural Change*, 1980, *29(1)*, 37–76.

Lorenz, Edward H., 'Neither Friends nor Strangers: Informal Networks of Subcontracting in French Industry', in *Trust: Making and Breaking Cooperative Relations*, D. Gambetta (ed.), New York: Basil Blackwell, 1988.

Lovejoy, Paul E., 'Pastoralism in Africa', *Peasant Studies*, 1979, *8(2)*, 73–85.

Lucas, Robert E., 'Asset Prices in an Exchange Economy', *Econometrica*, 1978, *46*, 1426–46.

——, 'On Efficiency and Distribution', *Econ. J.*, 1992, *102*, 233–47.

Lucas, Robert E.B. and Oded Stark, 'Motivations to Remit: Evidence from Botswana', *J. Polit. Econ.*, 1985, *93(5)*, 901–18.

Lundberg, Mattias, Mead Over, and Phare Mujinja, 'Sources of Financial Assistance for Households Suffering an Adult Death in Kagera, Tanzania', *South African Journal of Economics*, 2000, *68(5)*, 947–84.

Lybbert, Travis J., Christopher B. Barrett, Solomon Desta, and D. Layne Coppock, *Pastoral Risk and Wealth-Differentiated Herd Accumulation Patterns in Southern Ethiopia*, Ithaca, NY: Cornell University Press, 2000.

Mace, Barbara J., 'Full Insurance in the Presence of Aggregate Uncertainty', *J. Polit. Econ.*, 1991, *99(5)*, 928–56.

Mair, Lucy, *Primitive Government*, Bloomington, IN: Indiana University Press, 1962.

Mankiw, N.G., D. Romer, and D.N. Weil, 'A Contribution to the Empirics of Economic Growth', *Quarterly J. Econ.*, 1992, *CVII*, 407–37.

Maoz, Yishay D. and Omer Moav, 'Intergenerational Mobility and the Process of Development', *Economic Journal*, 1999, *109*, 677–97.

Matlon, Peter J., *Income Generation in Three Villages of Northern Nigeria*, Ithaca, NY: Cornell University, 1977. Unpublished PhD thesis.

——, *The ICRISAT Burkina-Faso Farm Level Studies: Survey Methods and Data Files*, Economic Group, VLS and Miscellaneous Paper Series, ICRISAT, 1988.

—— and Marcel Fafchamps, *Crop Budgets in Three Agro-Climatic Zones of Burkina Faso*, Hyderabad: ICRISAT Progress Report, 1989.

—— and Helga Vierich, *Annual Report of ICRISAT/Upper Volta Economics Program*, Ouagadougou: ICRISAT, 1982.

McKinnon, Ronald I., *Money and Capital in Economic Development*, Washington DC: The Brookings Institution, 1973.

McPeak, John G., 'Confronting the Risk of Asset Loss: Livestock Exchange in Northern Kenya', 2002. (mimeograph)

Meillassoux, Claude, *The Development of Indigenous Trade and Markets in West Africa*, Oxford: Oxford University Press, 1971.

Melmed-Sanjak, Jolyne S. and Michael R. Carter, 'The Economic Viability and Stability of Capitalised Family Farming: An Analysis of Agricultural Decollectivisation in Peru', *Journal of Development Studies*, 1991, *27(2)*, 190–210.

Minten, Bart, *Price Transmission and Transaction Cost in a Liberalized Food Marketing System: The Case of Zaire*, Ithaca, NY: Department of Agricultural Economics, Cornell University, 1995. Unpublished PhD thesis.

Mitchell, J. Clyde, *Social Networks in Urban Situations: Analyses of Personal Relationships in Central African Towns*, Manchester: Manchester University Press, 1969.

Moerman, D., *Agricultural Change and Peasant Choice in a Thai Village*, Berkeley, CA: University of California Press, 1968.

Monod, Theodore, 'Introduction', in *Pastoralism in Tropical Africa*, Theodore Monod (ed.), London: Oxford University Press, 1975.

Montgomery, James D., 'Social Networks and Labor-Market Outcomes: Toward an Economic Analysis', *Amer. Econ. Rev.*, 1991, *81(5)*, 1408–18.

——, 'Revisiting Tally's Corner: Mainstream Norms, Cognitive Dissonance, and Underclass Behavior', 1993. (mimeograph)

Mood, Alexander, Franklin Graybill, and Duane Boes, *Introduction to the Theory of Statistics*, New York: McGraw-Hill, 1974.

Mookherjee, Dilip and Debraj Ray, *Persistent Inequality*, Boston, MA:

Boston University, Institute for Economic Development Discussion Paper No. 108, 2000.

Morduch, Jonathan, 'Risk, Production and Savings: Theory and Evidence from Indian Households', 1990. (mimeograph)

——, 'Income Smoothing and Consumption Smoothing', *J. Econ. Perspectives*, 1995, *9(3)*, 103–14.

——, 'Between Market and State: Can Informal Insurance Patch the Safety Net?', *World Bank Research Observer*, 1999, *14(2)*, 187–207.

——, 'Consumption Smoothing Across Space: Testing Theories of Risk-Sharing in the ICRISAT Study Region of South India', Technical Report, WIDER Discussion Paper No. 2002/55, Helsinki, 2002.

—— and Terry Sicular, 'Risk and Insurance in Transition: Perspectives from Zouping County, China', 1999. (mimeograph)

Morris, Michael L. and Mark D. Newman, 'Official and Parallel Cereals Markets in Senegal: Empirical Evidence', *World Development*, 1989, *17, No.12*, 1895–1906.

Murphy, Kevin M., Andrei Shleifer, and Robert W. Vishny, 'Industrialization and the Big Push', *J. Polit. Econ.*, 1989, *97(5)*, 1003–26.

Nelson, R.R., 'A Theory of the Low-Level Equilibrium Trap in Underdeveloped Economies', *Amer. Econ. Review*, 1956, *46*, 894–908.

Newbery, David and Joseph Stiglitz, *The Theory of Commodity Price Stabilization: A Study in the Economics of Risk*, Oxford: Oxford University Press, 1981.

Norhona, R., *A Review of the Literature on Land Tenure Systems in sub-Saharan Africa*, Washington, DC: Research Unit of the Agriculture and Rural Development Department, World Bank Report ARU 43, 1985.

Norman, David W., 'Farming Systems Research to Improve the Livelihood of Small Farmers', *American Journal of Agricultural Economics*, 1978, *60(5)*, 813–18.

Nugent, Jeffrey B., 'The Old-Age Security Motive for Fertility', *Population and Development Review*, 1985, *11(1)*, 75–97.

——, 'Old Age Security and the Defense of Social Norms', *J. Cross-Cultural Gerontology*, 1990, *5*, 243–54.

—— and Nicolas Sanchez, 'The Efficiency of the Mesta: A Parable', *Explorations in Economic History*, 1989, *26*, 261–84.

—— and ——, 'Tribes, Chiefs, and Transhumance: A Comparative Institutional Analysis', *Economic Development and Cultural Change*, 1993, *42(1)*, 87–113.

Nurkse, Ragnar, *Problems of Capital Formation in Underdeveloped Countries*, New York: Oxford University Press, 1953.

Nwuke, Kasirim, 'Credit Transactions and Consumption Smoothing: Evidence from Rural Gambia', 1998. (mimeograph)

Oba, Gufu and Walter J. Lusigi, *An Overview of Drought Strategies and Land Use in African Pastoral Systems*, Vol. 23a, Overseas Development Institute, 1987.

Odegi-Awuondo, Casper, *Life in the Balance: Ecological Sociology of Turkana Nomads*, Nairobi: ACTS Press, 1990.

Pandey, Priyanka, 'Illness, Income and Poverty in a Developing Country', 2001. (mimeograph)

Park, Albert, 'Risk and Household Grain Management in Developing Countries', 2000. (mimeograph)

Paxson, Christina H., 'Using Weather Variability to Estimate the Response of Savings to Transitory Income in Thailand', *Amer. Econ. Rev.*, 1992, *82(1)*, 15–33.

——, 'Consumption and Income Seasonality in Thailand', *J. Polit. Econ.*, 1993, *101(1)*, 39–72.

Payne, Philip and Michael Lipton, 'How Third World Rural Households Adapt to Dietary Energy Stress: The Evidence and the Issues', *Food Policy Review*, 1994, *134*. International Food Policy Research Institute.

Pearce, D., 'Renegotiation-Proof Equilibria: Collective Rationality and Intertemporal Cooperation', 1987. (mimeograph)

Pender, John L., *Credit Rationing and Farmers' Irrigation Investments in South India: Theory and Evidence*, Stanford: Food Research Institute, Stanford University, 1992. Unpublished PhD thesis.

——, 'Discount Rates and Credit Markets: Theory and Evidence from Rural India', *Journal of Development Economics*, 1996, *50(2)*, 257–96.

Pender, John L. and Marcel Fafchamps, 'Land Lease Markets and Agricultural Efficiency: Theory and Evidence from Ethiopia', 2002. (mimeograph)

Phillips, Joseph M., 'A Comment on Farmer Education and Farm Efficiency: A Survey', *Econ. Development and Cult. Change*, 1987, *35(3)*, 637–44.

Piketty, Thomas, 'The Dynamics of the Wealth Distribution and the Interest Rate with Credit Rationing', *Review of Economic Studies*, 1997, *64(2)*, 173–89.

Pinckney, Thomas C. and Peter K. Kimuyu, 'Land Tenure Reform in East Africa: Good, Bad, or Unimportant?', *Journal of African Economies*, 1994, *3(1)*, 1–28.

Pingali, Prabhu L., Yves Bigot, and Hans P. Binswanger, *Agricultural Mechanization and the Evolution of Farming Systems in sub-Saharan Africa*, Baltimore, MD: Johns Hopkins University Press, 1987.

Piore, Michael J. and Charles F. Sabel, *The Second Industrial Divide: Possibilities for Prosperity*, New York: Basic Books, 1984.

Pitt, Mark M. and Shahidur R. Khandker, *Household and Intrahousehold*

Impact of the Grameen Bank and Similar Targeted Credit Programs in Bangladesh, Washington, DC: Discussion Paper, No. 320, The World Bank, 1996.

Platteau, Jean-Philippe, 'Traditional Systems of Social Security and Hunger Insurance: Past Achievements and Modern Challenges', in *Social Security in Developing Countries*, E. Ahmad, J. Dreze, J. Hills, and A. Sen (eds), Oxford: Clarendon Press, 1991.

——, 'Formalization and Privatization of Land Rights in Sub-Saharan Africa: A Critique of Current Orthodoxies and Structural Adjustment Programmes', in *The Development Economics Research Programme*, Vol. 34, London: London School of Economics, 1992.

——, 'Behind the Market Stage Where Real Societies Exist: Part I – The Role of Public and Private Order Institutions', *J. Development Studies*, 1994a, *30(3)*, 533–77.

——, 'Behind the Market Stage Where Real Societies Exist: Part II – The Role of Moral Norms', *J. Development Studies*, 1994b, *30(4)*, 753–815.

——, 'A Framework for the Analysis of Evolving Patron-Client Ties in Agrarian Economies', *World Development*, 1995a, *23(5)*, 767–86.

——, 'An Indian Model of Aristocratic Patronage', *Oxford Econ. Papers*, 1995b, *47(4)*, 636–62.

——, *Reforming Land Rights in Sub-Saharan Africa: Issues of Efficiency and Equity*, Geneva: United Nations Research Institute for Social Development, 1995c. Discussion Paper No. 60.

——, 'Traditional Sharing Norms as an Obstacle to Economic Growth in Tribal Societies', Technical Report, CRED, Facultés Universitaires Notre-Dame de la Paix, Namur, Belgium, 1996. Cahiers No. 173.

——, 'Allocating and Enforcing Property Rights in Land: Informal versus Formal Mechanisms in Sub-Saharan Africa', *Nordic Journal of Political Economy*, 2000a, *26(1)*, 55–81.

——, *Institutions, Social Norms, and Economic Development*, Amsterdam: Harwood Academic Publishers, 2000b.

—— and Anita Abraham, 'An Inquiry into Quasi-Credit Contracts: The Role of Reciprocal Credit and Interlinked Deals in Small-scale Fishing Communities', *J. Dev. Stud.*, 1987, *23(4)*, 461–90.

—— and Jean-Marie Baland, 'Income-Sharing Through Work-Spreading Arrangements: An Economic Analysis With Special Reference to Small-Scale Fishing', Cahiers de la Faculté des Sciences Economiques et Sociales de Namur, Facultés Universitaires Notre-Dame de la Paix, Namur, Belgium, 1989.

—— and Yujiro Hayami, *Resource Endowments and Agricultural Development: Africa vs. Asia*, Namur: University of Namur and Aoyama

Gakuin University, Tokyo, 1996. Paper presented at the IEA Round Table Conference.

——, Jose Murickan, and Etienne Delbar, *Technology, Credit and Indebtedness in Marine Fishing*, Delhi: Hindustan Publishing Corporation, 1985.

Poewe, Karla, *Religion, Kinship, and Economy in Luapula, Zambia*, Lewistone, NY: The Edwin Mellen Press, 1989.

Polanyi, Karl, *The Great Transformation*, New York: Holt, Rinehart, and Winston, 1944.

Popkin, Samuel L., *The Rational Peasant: The Political Economy of Rural Society in Vietnam*, Berkeley, CA: University of California Press, 1979.

Posner, Richard A., 'A Theory of Primitive Society, with Special Reference to Law', *J. of Law and Economics*, 1980, *XXIII*, 1–53.

Pratt, J., 'Risk Aversion in the Small and in the Large', *Econometrica*, 1964, *32*, 122–36.

Prescott, Edward C. and Rajnish Mehra, 'Recursive Competitive Equilibrium: The Case of Homogenous Households', *Econometrica*, 1980, *48(6)*, 1365–79.

Prudencio, Yves Coffi, *A Village Study of Soil Fertility Management and Food Crop Production in Upper Volta – Technical and Economic Analysis*, PhD thesis, University of Arizona, 1983.

——, *Soil and Crop Management in Selected Farming Systems of Burkina Faso*, Ouagadougou: OAU/STRC/SAFGRAD, 1987.

Putnam, Robert D., Robert Leonardi, and Raffaella Y. Nanetti, *Making Democracy Work: Civic Institutions in Modern Italy*, Princeton, NJ: Princeton University Press, 1993.

Raub, Werner and Jeroen Weesie, 'Reputation and Efficiency in Social Interactions: An Example of Network Effects', *Amer. J. Sociology*, 1990, *96(3)*, 626–54.

Raut, L.K. and L.H. Tran, 'Reciprocity with Two-Sided Altruism in Intergenerational Transfers: Evidence from Indonesian Family Life Survey Data', in *The Economics of Reciprocity, Giving and Altruism*, L.A. Gerard-Varet, S.C. Kolm, and J.M. Ythier (eds), London: Macmillan Press, 2000.

Ravallion, Martin, 'Testing Market Integration', *Amer. J. Agric. Econ.*, 1986, *68(1)*, 102–9.

—— and Lorraine Dearden, 'Social Security in a Moral Economy: An Empirical Analysis for Java', *Rev. Econ. and Stat.*, 1988, *70*, 36–44.

Reardon, Thomas, 'Using Evidence of Household Income Diversification to Inform Study of the Rural Nonfarm Labor Market in Africa', *World Development*, 1997, *25(5)*, 735–47.

—— and Peter Matlon, 'Seasonal Food Insecurity and Vulnerability in

Drought Affected Regions of Burkina Faso', in *Seasonal Variability in Third World Agriculture*, David Sahn (ed.), Johns Hopkins University Press, Baltimore, 1989.

——, Christopher Delgado, and Peter Matlon, 'Determinants and Effects of Income Diversification Amongst Farm Households in Burkina Faso', *J. Devel. Studies*, 1992, *28(2)*, 264–96.

——, Peter Matlon, and Christopher Delgado, 'Coping With Household Level Food Insecurity in Drought-Affected Areas of Burkina Faso', *World Development*, 1988, *16, No. 9*, 1065–74.

République du Mali, *Programme de Recherche Socio-Economique Appliquée dans la Zone de Production Cotonnière – Region Sikasso*, Bamako: Comité National de la Recherche Agronomique, 1979.

Roberts, Richard L., *Two Worlds of Cotton: Colonialism and the Regional Economy in the French Soudan, 1800–1946*, Stanford, CA: Stanford University Press, 1996.

Romani, Mattia, 'Love Thy Neighbour? Evidence from Ethnic Discrimination in Information Sharing within Villages in Cote d'Ivoire', *Journal of African Economies*, 2003, *11*, (forthcoming).

Rosenzweig, Mark R., 'Risk, Implicit Contracts and the Family in Rural Areas of Low-Income Countries', *Econ. J.*, 1988a, *98*, 1148–1170.

——, 'Risk, Private Information, and the Family', *American Econ. Review*, 1988b, *78 (2)*, 245–250.

—— and Hans P. Binswanger, 'Wealth, Weather Risk and the Composition and Profitability of Agricultural Investments', *Econ. J.*, 1993, *103*, 56–78.

—— and Oded Stark, 'Consumption Smoothing, Migration, and Marriage: Evidence from Rural India', *J. Polit. Econ.*, 1989, *97(4)*, 905–26.

—— and Kenneth I. Wolpin, 'Specific Experience, Household Structure, and Intergenerational Transfers: Farm Family Land and Labor Arrangements in Developing Countries', *Quarterly J. Econ.*, 1985, *100, Supplement*, 961–87.

—— and ——, 'Credit Market Constraints, Consumption Smoothing, and the Accumulation of Durable Production Assets in Low-Income Countries: Investments in Bullocks in India', *J. Polit. Econ.*, 1993, *101(2)*, 223–44.

Roumasset, J.A., *Rice and Risk: Decision Making Among Low-Income Farmers*, Amsterdam: North Holland, 1976.

Roumasset, James A., Jean-Marc Boussard, and Inderjit Singh, *Risk, Uncertainty, and Agricultural Development*, New York: Agricultural Development Council, 1979.

Sadoulet, Elisabeth, Seiichi Fukui, and Alain de Janvry, 'Efficient Share Tenancy Contracts under Risk: The Case of Two Rice-Growing Villages in Thailand', *Journal of Development Economics*, 1994, *45(2)*, 225–43.

Sahlins, Marshall, *Stone Age Economics*, Chicago: Aldine-Atherton, Inc., 1972.

Salanié, Bernard, *The Economics of Contracts: A Primer*, Cambridge, MA.: MIT Press, 1997.

Saloner, Garth, 'Old Boy Networks as Screening Mechanisms', *J. Labor Econ.*, 1985, *3(3)*, 255–67.

Samson, B., *The Economics of Insurgency in the Mekong Delta of Vietnam*, Cambridge, MA: MIT Press, 1970.

Sandford, Stephen, *Management of Pastoral Development in the Third World*, New York: John Wiley and Sons, 1983.

Sandmo, Agnar, 'On the Theory of the Competitive Firm Under Price Uncertainty', *Amer. Econ. Rev.*, 1971, *61(1)*, 65–73.

Sargent, M., J. Lichte, P. Matlon, and R. Bloom, 'An Assessment of Animal Traction in Francophone West-Africa', African Rural Economy Working Paper No. 34, Michigan State University, 1981.

Sargent, Thomas, *Dynamic Macroeconomic Theory*, Cambridge, MA.: Harvard University Press, 1987.

——, I. Ibrango, A. Nougtara, M. Borchert, M. Hien, J. Benzler, E. Koob, and H.J. Diesfeld, 'The Economic Costs of Illness for Rural Households in Burkina Faso', *Trop. Med. Parasitol.*, 1995, *46*, 54–60.

——, A. Nougtara, M. Hien, and J. Diesfeld, 'Seasonal Variations of Household Costs of Illness in Burkina Faso', *Soc. Sci. Med.*, 1996a, *43(3)*, 281–90.

Sauerborn, Rainer, A. Adams, and M. Hien, 'Household Strategies to Cope with the Economic Costs of Illness', *Soc. Sci. Med.*, 1996b, *43(3)*, 291–301.

Sawada, Yasuyuki, 'Human Capital Investments in Pakistan: Implications of Micro Evidence from Rural Households', *Pakistan Development Review*, 1997, *36(4)*, 695–710.

——, 'Income Risks, Gender, and Human Capital Investment in a Developing Country', 2002. (mimeograph)

Schaffner, Julie A., 'Attached Farm Labor, Limited Horizons, and Servility', *Journal of Development Economics*, 1995, *47(2)*, 241–70.

Schultz, Theodore W., 'Investment in Human Capital', *Amer. Econ. Rev.*, 1961, *LI(1)*, 1–17.

Scott, James C., *The Moral Economy of Peasants: Rebellion and Subsistence in South-East Asia*, New Haven, CT: Yale University Press, 1976.

Sen, Amartya, *Poverty and Famines*, Oxford: Clarendon Press, 1981.

Shaban, R.A., 'Testing Between Competing Models of Sharecropping', *Journal of Political Economy*, 1987, *95*, 893–920.

Shahabuddin, Quazi, Stuart Mestelman, and David Feeny, 'Peasant Behaviour Towards Risk and Socio-Economic and Structural

Characteristics of Farm Households in Bangladesh', *Oxford Economic Papers*, 1986, *38*, 122–30.

Shaw, Edward Stone, *Financial Deepening in Economic Development*, New York: Oxford University Press, 1973.

Shillington, Kevin, *History of Africa*, New York: St. Martin's Press, 1989.

Shively, Gerald E., 'Food Price Variability and Economic Reform: An ARCH Approach for Ghana', *American Journal of Agricultural Economics*, 1996, *78(1)*, 126–36.

Singh, I., L. Squire, and J. Strauss, *Agricultural Household Models: Extensions, Applications and Policy*, Washington, DC: World Bank, 1986.

Singh, Nirvikar, 'Theories of Sharecropping', in *The Economic Theory of Agrarian Institutions*, P. Bardhan (ed.), Oxford: Clarendon Press, 1989.

Skees, Jerry, Panos Varangis, Donald Larson, and Paul Siegel, 'Can Financial Markets be Tapped to Help Poor People Cope with Weather Risk?', Technical Report, WIDER Discussion Paper No. 2002/23, Helsinki, 2002.

Smith, Susan E., 'The Environmental Adaptation of Nomads in the West African Sahel: A Key to Understanding Prehistoric Pastoralists', in *Pastoralism in Tropical Africa*, Theodore Monod (ed.), London: 1975.

Sow, F., 'L'Economie du Poisson sur la Petite Cote (Senegal): Le Role des Femmes', in *Etudes Scientifiques*, Université de Dakar, 1986.

Spagnolo, Giancarlo, 'Social Relations and Cooperation in Organizations', *Journal of Economic Behavior and Organization*, 1999, *38(1)*, 1–25.

Srinivasan, T.N., 'On Choice Among Creditors and Bonded Labour Contracts', in 'The Economic Theory of Agrarian Institutions', Pranab Bardhan (ed.), Oxford: Clarendon Press, 1989.

Staatz, John M., *The Economics of Cattle and Meat Marketing in the Ivory Coast*, University of Michigan, 1979. Paper in the Livestock Production and Marketing in the Entente States of West Africa series.

Stark, Oded, *Altruism and Beyond*, Cambridge: Cambridge University Press, 1995.

—— and I. Falk, 'Transfers, Empathy Formation, and Reverse Transfers', in *The Economics of Reciprocity, Giving and Altruism*, L.A. Gerard-Varet, S.C. Kolm, and J.M. Ythier (eds), London: Macmillan Press, 2000.

—— and Robert E. Lucas, 'Migration, Remittances, and the Family', *Economic Development and Cultural Change*, 1988, *36, No.3*, 465–81.

Steel, William F., Ernest Aryeetey, Hemamala Hettige, and Machiko Nissanke, 'Informal Financial Markets Under Liberalization in Four African Countries', *World Development*, 1997, *25(5)*, 817–30.

Stiglitz, Joseph, 'Distribution of Income and Wealth Among Individuals', *Econometrica*, 1969, *37*, 382–97.

Stiglitz, Joseph E., 'Incentives and Risk Sharing in Sharecropping', *Rev. Econ. Stud.*, 1974, *41(2)*, 219–55.

—— and A.M. Weiss, 'Credit Rationing in Markets With Imperfect Information', *Amer. Econ. Rev.*, 1981, *71(3)*, 393–410.

Strauss, John et al., 'Gender and Life-Cycle Differentials in the Patterns and Determinants of Adult Health', *Journal of Human Resources*, 1993, *28(4)*, 791–837.

Takasaki, Yoshito, Bradford L. Barham, and Oliver T. Coomes, 'Are Endowments Fate in Biodiverse Environments? Dynamic Portfolio Analysis of Wealth and Livelihood among Amazonian Peasants', 2000. (mimeograph)

Thomas, Duncan, John Strauss, and Maria-Helena Henriques, 'Child Survival, Height for Age and Household Characteristics in Brazil', *Journal of Development Economics*, 1990, *33(2)*, 197–234.

Timmer, C. Peter, *Getting Prices Right: The Scope and Limits of Agricultural Price Policy*, Ithaca, NY: Cornell University Press, 1986.

Townsend, Robert M., 'Information Constrained Insurance: The Revelation Principle Extended', *J. Monetary Econ.*, 1988a, *21*, 411–50.

——, 'Models as Economies', *Econ. J.*, 1988b, *98*, 1–24.

——, 'Currency and Credit in a Private Information Economy', *J. Polit. Econ.*, 1989, *97(6)*, 1321–44.

——, 'Financial Systems in Northern Thai Villages', 1993. (mimeograph)

——, 'Risk and Insurance in Village India', *Econometrica*, 1994, *62(3)*, 539–91.

——, 'Consumption Insurance: An Evaluation of Risk-Bearing Systems in Low-Income Countries', *J. Econ. Perspectives*, 1995a, *9(3)*, 83–102.

——, 'Financial Systems in Northern Thai Villages', *Quarterly Journal of Economics*, 1995b, *110(4)*, 1011–46.

Tsiang, S.C., 'The Precautionary Demand for Money: An Inventory Theoretical Analysis', *Journal of Political Economy*, 1969, *77(1)*, 99–117.

Turnovsky, Stephen J., Haim Shalit, and Andrew Schmitz, 'Consumer's Surplus, Price Instability, and Consumer Welfare', *Econometrica*, 1980, *48(1)*, 135–52.

Udry, Christopher, 'Credit Markets in Northern Nigeria: Credit as Insurance in a Rural Economy', *World Bank Econ. Rev.*, 1990, *4(3)*, 251–69.

——, 'A Competitive Analysis of Rural Credit: State-Contingent Loans in Northern Nigeria', 1992. (mimeograph)

——, 'Risk and Insurance in a Rural Credit Market: An Empirical Investigation in Northern Nigeria', *Rev. Econ. Stud.*, 1994, *61(3)*, 495–526.

——, 'Gender, Agricultural Production and the Theory of the Household', *Journal of Political Economy*, 1996, *104(5)*, 1010–46.

van den Brink, Rogier and Jean-Paul Chavas, 'The Microeconomics of an Indigenous African Institution: The Rotating Savings and Credit Association', *Economic Development and Cultural Change*, 1997, *45(4)*, 745–72.

von Braun, Joachim and Patrick J.R. Webb, 'The Impact of New Crop Technology on the Agricultural Division of Labor in a West African Setting', *Economic Development and Cultural Change*, 1989, *37, No.3*, 513–34.

Wahba, Jackline, 'The Influence of Market Wages and Parental History on Child Labor and Schooling in Egypt', 2002. (mimeograph)

Walker, Thomas S. and J.G. Ryan, *Village and Household Economics in India's Semi-Arid Tropics*, Baltimore, MD: Johns Hopkins University Press, 1990.

Watts, Michael, *Silent Violence*, Berkeley, CA: University of California Press, 1983.

Wilson, Chris, 'On the Scale of Global Demographic Convergence 1950–2000', *Population and Development Review*, 2001, *27(1)*, 155–71.

—— and Pauline Airey, 'How Can a Homeostatic Perspective Enhance Demographic Transition Theory?', *Population Studies*, 1999, *53(2)*, 117–28.

Woodhouse, Philip and Ibrahima Ndiaye, 'Structural Adjustment and Irrigated Food Farming in Africa: The "Disengagement" of the state in the Senegal River Valley', DPP WP no.20, The Open University, June 1990.

World Bank, *Accelerated Development in sub-Saharan Africa: An Agenda for Action*, Washington, DC: The World Bank, 1981.

——, *Poverty and Hunger: Issues and Options for Food Security in Developing Countries*, Washington, DC: World Bank, 1986.

——, *Sub-Saharan Africa: From Crisis to Sustainable Growth*, Washington, DC: The World Bank, 1989.

——, *The East Asian Miracle: Economic Growth and Public Policy*, New York: Oxford University Press, 1993.

——, *World Development Report 2000/2001: Attacking Poverty*, New York: Published for the World Bank by Oxford University Press, 2000.

Yang, Dennis T., 'Education and Off-Farm Work', *Economic Development and Cultural Change*, 1997, *45 (3)*, 613–32.

Zame, William R., 'Efficiency and the Role of Default When Security Markets are Incomplete', *Amer. Econ. Rev.*, 1993, *83(5)*, 1142–64.

Zeldes, Stephen P., 'Consumption and Liquidity Constraints: An Empirical Investigation', *J. Polit. Econ.*, 1989a, *97(2)*, 305–43.

——, 'Optimal Consumption With Stochastic Income: Deviations from Certainty Equivalence', *Quarterly J. Econ.*, 1989b, *104(2)*, 275–98.

Zhang, Xiaobo and Ravi Kanbur, 'What Difference Do Polarisation Measures Make? An Application to China', *Journal of Development Studies*, 2001, *37(3)*, 85–98.

Zimmerman, Frederick J., 'Structural Evolution under Imperfect Markets in Developing Country Agriculture: A Dynamic Programming Simulation', 1993. (mimeograph)

Index

Abreu, D. 72
agriculture
    commercial crops, *vs.* subsistence
        farming 162–76, 199–200
    contract farming 157–8
    crop choices, and consumption
        preferences 164–7
    diversification 15–16, 20–21, 59,
        158–9, 160, 199
    market integration 10, 167–76, 200,
        209
    marketing boards 157
    policy recommendations 208–9, 211
    sharecropping 48, 102, 157
    specialization 15, 58, 158–9
    technological innovation/production
        choices 152–61, 175–6, 198–9
    see also livestock
aid 54, 206–7, 210–11
AIDS 207, 211
Albarran, P. 55, 73
altruism 74
animals
    disease 14
    risks from 8–9, 14–15, 207–8
    traction 160–61
    see also livestock
assets
    distribution following household
        dissolution 42
    markets 60, 64, 129, 143–4, 197
    and property rights 60–62
    saving and liquidating 21–32, 59–64,
        107
    see also inequality, modelling
Atanasio, O. 55, 73
autocorrelated risk 6

bankruptcy 141, 155, 156–7
Barrett, C.B. 15, 19
Binder, M. 151
Binswanger, H.P. 29

Bissuel, B. 138
Blundell, R. 31
borrowing *see* credit; credit
    constraints; debt peonage; debt
    trap; loans
Browning, M. 41
Bulow, J. 139, 142
business risk 9–10

Cabrales, A. 45
Carroll, C.D. 121
Carter, M.R. 22, 126
charity 69
child labour 23, 208
children 148
    and household formation 41
    nutrition/mortality 56, 146–7
    obligations to 70, 71
    school 56–7, 148, 150–51, 205, 208
coalitions 85–90
Coate, S. 72, 73, 76
collective risk, definition 6–7
common property resources 43–4, 46,
    129
compensation 79–80
consumption 7
    and credit constraints 30–31
    as indicator of income/wealth 98
    reduction of, to keep assets 25–6
    smoothing, use of term 13
contingent credit 46–47
contract farming 157–8
contracts
    debt 141
    enforcement of 94–5
    hedging 54–5
    indenture 144
    and risk sharing 48
contractual compliance/risk 9–10, 29
coping strategies 12–13, 196, 204–5
    assets, saving and liquidating 21–32,
        59–64, 107

coping strategies (*continued*)
 households, allocation of resources
  within 55–7, 204
 limits of 58–64, 108
 shocks, reducing exposure to 13–21
 see also risk sharing; risk sharing,
  difficulties/limits of
Cox, D. 44, 104
credit
 access to 209
 contingent 46–7
 formal 94–5
 and production choices 155–8
 quasi-credit 90–94
 see also debt peonage; loans
credit constraints
 and consumption 30–31
 and investment 176, 177, 179, 183–4,
  185–7, 200
crops 211
 commercial, *vs.* subsistence farming
  162–76, 199–200
 and consumption preferences
  164–7
 diversification 15–16, 20–21, 59,
  158–9
 flexibility 20–21, 59
 and market integration 167–76, 200
 specialization 15, 58, 158–9
 and technological innovation 158–9,
  175–6, 198–9

Deaton, A. 30, 31, 180
debt *see* credit; credit constraints; loans
debt peonage 25, 49–51, 62, 139,
  140–43
debt trap 138–43
deforestation 14
Dekker, M. 21
Dercon, S. 16, 41, 103
disease 8, 11, 14, 149, 207, 211
diversification, as risk reduction
  strategy 15–18, 20–21, 59, 158–9,
  160, 199
Dixit, A. 178, 180
Dreze, J.H. 183
Durlauf, S.N. 109

Edmonds, E.V. 151
education 56–7, 148, 150–51, 205, 208

effort, and incentive problems 98–101,
  188
Ellsworth, L. 69
employment 9, 21–22
 see also labour
environment, selecting and modifying
  14–15, 202–3, 206
environmental hazards 8–9, 14–15,
  207–8
ethics, functions of 108
Evans-Pritchard, E.E. 98
exploitation 82, 83–4, 208

Fafchamps, M. 19, 36, 189, 192
 debt 25, 143
 flexibility 59, 178
 gifts 44
 interlinking 48
 investment 59, 60, 184, 185
 labour 68
 livestock 26, 28, 64
 markets 10, 18
 networks 103
 savings 63
 stocks 29
 weeding 20
family values 70–71, 197
fertility 146–8
fines 78, 79–80
flexibility, and risk reduction 19–21,
  59, 178
food markets 18, 162, 167
 integration 167–76, 200, 209
food security *see* self-sufficiency
food transfers 103
Foster, A.D. 43, 55
frequency, risks 5–6

Gavian, S. 10, 26, 64
Genicot, G. 104
Gertler, P. 36
gifts 44–5, 69, 75–7, 93
Giles, J.T. 21–22
Goldstein, M. 41
government, policy interventions
  206–9
greed 98
growth 145, 201
 and education 150
 and health/nutrition 149–50

and networks 194–5
and patronage 193–5
and population growth 147–8
Gruber, J. 36
Gubert, F. 25, 143

Hall, R.E. 27
Hayami, Y. 188, 189
health 149–50
    disease 8, 11, 14, 149, 207, 211
    hazards 8–9, 14–15, 207–8
    services 11, 52–4, 207
    see also mortality; nutrition
Heaton, J. 29
hedging contracts 54–5
Hoff, K. 85
Hoogeveen, H. 21
households 203–4
    allocation of resources within 55–7,
        204
    family values/obligations within
        70–71
    and risk sharing 41–3

idiosyncratic risk, definition 6–7
Imai, K. 21
incentive problems *see* information
    asymmetries
income
    observability of 96–8
    pooling 99–100
    risk, definition 7
    smoothing, use of term 13
    see also inequality, modelling
inequality 106–7, 197–8, 204
    and growth 145
    and patronage 82–4, 134–6, 191
inequality, modelling 109–11, 143–5
    assets, assumption of no marketable
        113–16
    assumptions, basic 111–13
    debt trap 138–43
    imperfect commitment 133–6
    poverty trap 136–7
    wealth accumulation, with no risk
        sharing 116
        assets in fixed supply 124–9
        bounded accumulation, with
            unproductive assets 120–24
        unbounded accumulation 116–20

wealth accumulation, with risk
    sharing 129–33
inflation 63, 207, 211–12
information asymmetries 48, 104
    effort, observability of 98–101
    ex ante solidarity 101–3
    income/wealth, observability of
        96–8
    and networks 104, 105–6
information dissemination 161
innovation *see* technological
    innovation
insurance 34–5, 45–7, 84–5
    gifts and transfers as 44–5
    health services 52–4
    and inequality 130–33, 134–5, 142,
        144–5, 198
    social 68–69, 114–15
    see also risk sharing; risk sharing,
        difficulties/limits of; saving,
        precautionary
intensity, risks 5–6
interest rates
    'excessive' 51, 62, 140
    quasi-credit 93
    savings 63, 177
interlinking 47–9
international community/aid 54,
    210–12
investment 59–60, 93, 176–8, 205,
    209
    irreversible 177, 178, 179–82,
        184–7
    and patronage 193–5, 202
    and precautionary saving 176–87,
        190, 200–201
    reversible 177, 182–4
    and risk sharing 189–90, 201
    well construction, as example
        184–7

Jacoby, H.G. 56, 151

Kamanou, G. 8
Kang, S.J. 26, 31, 44
Kimball, M.S. 29, 72, 73, 76, 120, 183
Kochar, A. 21
Kocherlakota, N.R. 133, 134
Krishnan, P. 16, 41
Kurosaki, T. 15, 16, 19, 36, 43, 151

labour
    assistance 68, 102
    bonding 23–5, 60–62, 129, 140
    child 23, 208
    migration 52
    and social insurance 68
land
    borrowing 102
    distribution 22–3, 26, 128
    sales 22–3, 26, 60, 62
Lechene, V. 41
life risk, summary of types 5–8
Ligon, E. 8, 73, 133–4
Lim, Y. 26, 28, 32
livestock
    as buffer stock 28
    diversification 16
    and inequality 129
    liquidation, in response to shocks 26
    markets 10, 37–8, 64
    pastoralism 58–9, 129
    specialization 58–9
loans 25, 30–31, 207
    consumption *vs.* investment 93
    contracts 141
    formal 94–5
    informal 90–94, 103, 143
    see also credit; credit constraints;
        debt peonage; debt trap
Lucas, D. 29
Lund, S. 28, 44, 103
Lundberg, M. 44
Lybbert, T.J. 9, 26, 45, 129

markets 60, 64, 129
    assets 64, 129, 143–4, 197
    contingent credit 46–7
    efficiency of 37–8
    food 18, 162, 167
    integration of 10, 167–76, 200, 209
marriage 41, 70, 103
Matlon, P.J. 19, 68
McKinnon, R.I. 186
men, and nutrition 56
migration 52, 160, 202–3, 206–7
Minten, B. 189, 192
Mookherjee, D. 109
Morduch, J. 5, 8, 13, 31, 36, 43, 184
mortality 147, 149, 150
    children 56, 146–7

selective, and extreme deprivation
    55–6

networks 103–6, 107, 142–3, 194–5,
    204
non-stationary risk, definition 6
Nugent, J.B. 44
nutrition 11, 56, 146, 149–50, 208
    women 56, 204, 208
Nwuke, K. 51

old age
    and solidarity obligations 67
    support in 67, 146–7, 148, 205

Pandey, P. 149
parenthood obligations 70, 71
Park, A. 32
pastoralism 58–9, 129
patronage 49, 82–5, 89, 111, 192–5,
    201–2
    debt peonage 25, 49–51, 62, 139,
        140–43
    and inequality 82–4, 134–6, 191
    labour bonding 23–5, 60–62, 129,
        140
Paxson, C.H. 28
Pender, J. 59, 60, 183, 184, 185, 186
pensions 52
Platteau, J-P. 85, 142, 188, 189
Poewe, K. 69, 98
policy interventions, government
    206–9
Posner, R.A. 79–80
poverty trap 136–8
    and credit constraints 185–7
power
    centres of 85–6
    and coalitions 85–90
    individual wealth accumulation
        81–2, 189, 190–93
    and risk sharing 80–90, 204
    see also inequality, modelling;
        patronage
prices/price elasticity of demand, and
    market integration 167–75
primary products, dependence on 9
production choices, and risk aversion
    152–8, 175–6
property rights 60–62

punishments, for cooperation failure 65–6, 77–80, 97, 98, 101, 106

Ravallion, M. 72, 73, 76
Ray, D. 104, 109
Reardon, T. 16, 54
redistribution 80, 114–15, 144, 193–4, 201–2, 205–6
  and health costs 53–4
  and self-interest 75–6
relief organizations 54, 210–11
religion 69
'risk management', use of term 12
risk sharing 32–6
  explicit 38–40
  extra-village 51–5
  gifts and transfers 43–5, 55, 75–7, 93
  households and groups 41–3, 203–4
  implicit 37–8
  insurance, explicit 45–7
  interlinking and patronage 47–51
  norms of 188–9
  and redistribution 115
  and risk taking 188–95, 201
  see also inequality, modelling; patronage
risk sharing, difficulties/limits of 106–8
  coalitions 85–90
  commitment failure 65–80, 133–6, 197
  credit 90–95
  exclusion/renegotiation 77–80
  family values 70–71, 197
  gifts 75–7, 93
  informal risk sharing arrangements (IRSAs) 71–4
  information asymmetries 48, 96–103, 104, 105–6
  mutual insurance, with limited commitment 65–8, 74
  networks 103–6, 107, 142–3
  patron-client relationships 82–5
  power issues 80–90, 204
  saving, precautionary 190, 204–5
  social insurance 68–9, 114–15
  wealth accumulation, individual 81–2, 188–9, 190–91, 201–2
risk taking, and risk sharing 188–95, 201

ritual risk 7–8
Rogoff, K. 139, 142
Rosenzweig, M.R. 26, 29, 52, 55, 103, 178
rotating and savings associations (ROSCAs) 63–4

Sandmo, A. 152, 153–6, 198, 200
Sauerborn, R. 11, 149
saving, precautionary 27–9, 30–32, 60
  difficulties of 62–4
  institutions/mechanisms 63–4, 203, 207
  and investment 176–87, 190, 200–201
  and risk sharing 190, 204–5
  see also inequality, modelling; wealth
Sawada, Y. 26, 31, 44, 56, 151
school 56–57, 148, 150–51, 205, 208
Scott, J.C. 100, 108
self-sufficiency 18–19
  and consumption preferences 164–7
  and food markets 18, 162, 167
  and market integration 167–76, 200
  vs. commercial crops 162–76, 199–200
Sen, A. 9, 21, 75–6, 106
settlement, patterns of 14, 202–3, 206
sharecropping 48, 102, 157
sharing of risks *see* risk sharing; risk sharing, difficulties/limits of
shocks 6–7, 12–13, 196, 198
  assets, saving and liquidating as response to 21–32, 59–62, 107
  reducing exposure to 13–21
  see also coping strategies
Sicular, T. 43
Skoufias, E. 151
'smoothing', use of term 13
social insurance 68–69, 114–15
social mobility, and risk sharing 132
social programmes 10–11, 114–15, 208
solidarity mechanisms *see* risk sharing; risk sharing, difficulties/limits of
specialization, as risk reduction strategy 15, 16–17, 58–9, 158–9
Stark, O. 52, 103
stocks 29
stunting 149

subsistence, model of guaranteed
    100–101
subsistence farming *see* self-sufficiency

taxation 68, 69
technological innovation 151–2, 198–9,
    205
    diversification/specialization 158–9,
    199
    production choices, and risk 152–8,
    175–76
    technological uncertainty and
    learning 160–61
Townsend, R.M. 26, 28, 32, 36, 93
transfers 44–5, 52, 54, 55, 103

Udry, C. 51, 89, 143
utility risk, definition 7

wages, and labour bonding 24–5
war 210–11

wealth
    accumulation, individual 81–2, 98,
    188–9, 190–95, 201–2
    distribution 38
    and growth 145
    observability of 96–7, 98
    trap 136, 137
    see also inequality, modelling;
    patronage; saving, precautionary
weeding 20
Weerdt, J. de 103, 105
Wolpin, K.I. 26, 178
women 71
    and nutrition 56, 204, 208
    role of 41, 42
Woodruff, C. 151

Zame, W.R. 95
Zeldes, S.P. 30, 121
Zimmerman, F.J. 22, 26, 126, 128